W9-CBX-228

STEALING MYSPACE

STEALING MYSPACE

THE BATTLE TO CONTROL

THE MOST POPULAR

WEBSITE IN AMERICA

JULIA ANGWIN

DISCARDED

RANDOM HOUSE 🏠 NEW YORK

Copyright © 2009 by Julia Angwin

All rights reserved.

Published in the United States by Random House,
an imprint of The Random House Publishing Group,
a division of Random House, Inc., New York.

RANDOM HOUSE and colophon are registered
trademarks of Random House, Inc.

LIBRARY OF CONGRESS CATALOGING-IN-PUBLICATION DATA
Angwin, Julia.
Stealing MySpace : the battle to control the most
popular website in America /
Julia Angwin.
p.   cm.
Includes bibliographical references and index.
ISBN 978-1-4000-6694-0 (alk. paper)
1. MySpace (Firm)   2. Internet industry—United States.   I. Title.
HD9696.8.U64M973 2009
338.7'610067—dc22
2008023504

Printed in the United States of America on acid-free paper.

www.atrandom.com

2 4 6 8 9 7 5 3 1

FIRST EDITION

Book design by Debbie Glasserman

Contents

Author's Note

This narrative is based on hundreds of interviews conducted during 2007 and 2008. I have tried to reconstruct the key moments in MySpace's history, relying on the accounts of many sources. Because reconstructed dialogue tends to approximate the truth, I have noted where there are significant discrepancies in the memories of the participants.

Many of the people I interviewed did not want to be quoted. I have identified these sources in the endnotes with the phrase "a person familiar with the situation." In many cases, I was able to confirm these anonymous accounts with several confidential sources. To protect my sources, however, I have not listed how many people confirmed each incident.

The book also relies heavily on documents, including the following: financial reports filed by MySpace's parent company Intermix at the Securities and Exchange Commission; internal e-mails and documents obtained by the New York Attorney General during its investigation of Intermix; private e-mails between Intermix executives that were viewed by the author; and internal Intermix documents that were viewed by the author. In the event that a document contradicted the memories of a source, I usually chose to rely on the documentary evidence.

The founders of MySpace did not participate in this book. Over the course of a year of reporting and writing, I met repeatedly with various representatives of MySpace and its parent company News Corp. I kept them apprised of my progress through meetings and letters. They never said "no" to cooperation but continued to delay making a decision. Finally, the book was complete, and they had effectively made their decision: They had never said "no" to cooperation, but they had never cooperated. Therefore, this book is an unauthorized, but well-documented, account.

STEALING MYSPACE

Chapter 1

STEALING MYSPACE

Richard Rosenblatt's heart was pounding with nervous anticipation as he climbed a private staircase on the Fox Studios lot in Los Angeles.

It was the warm afternoon of July 12, 2005. On the Fox lot, the low buildings of the Fox TV and movie soundstages and offices were dwarfed by the high-rise jungle known as Century City. With his deep tan, athletic figure, and casual attire, Rosenblatt looked like he might be on the lot for an audition. But Rosenblatt was there to sell News Corporation chairman Rupert Murdoch on his version of the digital future.

Rosenblatt had arrived early for his meeting. Murdoch's office was in a modern glass-and-steel office building that, to many visitors, looked woefully out of place next to the graceful 1930s building that housed the historic 20th Century Fox movie production offices. As he waited in the ground-floor cafeteria, with sunlight streaming in through the sliding glass doors, Rosenblatt tapped out an e-mail on his BlackBerry to a friend: "At murdochs' . . . going in soon. Friggen nervous."

Finally an aide came to usher him up the back stairs that led from the cafeteria to Murdoch's office on the fifth floor. Ross Levinsohn, Murdoch's genial head of Internet strategy, was waiting for Rosenblatt outside Murdoch's office. Levinsohn put his hand on Rosenblatt's arm. "If you want to sell your company to us, now is the time to do it," Levinsohn said.

As soon as Rosenblatt stepped into Murdoch's spacious neutral-toned office suite, he wondered whether he should have worn a suit after all. Against the advice of his colleagues, Rosenblatt had decided to wear his usual business uniform of cargo pants, Vans sneakers, and a light blue short-sleeve button-down shirt. Murdoch, with his receding gray hair and rimless glasses, was waiting in a crisp suit.

Rosenblatt took a seat offered to him on the beige leather couch, introduced himself, and, in his high-pitched voice, launched into a ten-minute recital of all the reasons why Murdoch should buy his Internet company, Intermix Media.

On its own, Intermix was not much of a prize. It owned a bunch of websites offering games like bingo and animated fart jokes that users could e-mail to one another. It was barely profitable. It had been sued by New York attorney general Eliot Spitzer for distributing spyware inside screen savers, screen cursors, and games.

But Intermix also owned a majority stake in a fast-growing website—MySpace.com—which had attracted an impressive 17.7 million visitors the prior month. A consummate salesman, Rosenblatt focused his comments on the potential of adding MySpace's broad audience to complement Rupert Murdoch's already enviable empire of top-flight media companies.

"Mr. Murdoch, MySpace is the perfect media company," Rosenblatt said. "Unlike traditional media companies, MySpace generates free content, through its users; generates free traffic, by its users inviting their friends; and all you have to do is sell the ads!"

Gesturing at the four clocks on the wall showing the time in Los Angeles, London, Sydney, and Hong Kong, Rosenblatt said, "You have built the most incredible global media company. You have dominated in every area of media, from newspapers to television to film. But on the Internet, you are irrelevant.

"This deal will not only make you relevant, it will immediately make you as big a player as AOL or Yahoo online," Rosenblatt said. "If you do this deal, I predict you will be on the cover of *Wired* magazine twelve months from now."

Murdoch said softly in his thick Australian accent, "I heard you've been asking for twelve dollars a share. That's a significant premium." Intermix's stock was trading that day at $9.96 a share.

"Rich, you've got a reputation for selling when companies are at full value," Murdoch chided gently.

Rosenblatt took a deep breath but didn't back down. After all, he knew that Murdoch's archrival, Viacom, was interested in buying Intermix as well.

"With all due respect, the company is worth it," he told Murdoch. "The price is twelve dollars a share."

Murdoch stood up and said, "You got it. Can we get it done by Sunday?"

"I never go back on my word," Rosenblatt said, shaking Murdoch's hand. "Subject to my public company duties, I'll deliver you the company by Sunday." He was quickly ushered out of the room.

Rosenblatt was dazed; he couldn't believe that Murdoch had agreed to spend nearly $600 million in a twenty-minute meeting.

There was only one catch: MySpace didn't know it was about to be sold.

Chapter 2

CIRCLE OF FRIENDS

MySpace launched on August 15, 2003, on a blazing hot, overcast Friday afternoon in Los Angeles. MySpace cofounder Chris DeWolfe sat inside his windowless cubbyhole of an office in a building near the Los Angeles International Airport. While the tech guys downstairs were finalizing the computer code for the MySpace website and scanning for bugs in the system, DeWolfe was distracted. He was struggling with pesky issues about spyware—software that surreptitiously monitors Web surfers' movements and bombards them with related ads.

Spyware was substantial business for DeWolfe, who ran a division of an Internet company called eUniverse. When the U.S. invaded Iraq earlier in the year, for instance, DeWolfe's division had begun offering free "patriotic" cursors that turned a user's mouse pointer into an American flag. Many people who downloaded the cursors did not realize that they were also installing a hidden software program that displayed pop-up ads whenever they surfed the Web. Now DeWolfe was struggling to sell those pop-up ads to advertisers.

Advertisers liked the spyware pop-ups because they could target their ads to a user's specific behavior. For instance, a mortgage advertiser could display pop-up ads to people visiting real estate websites. But he was worried that the targeting technology appeared to be broken. At 3:58 p.m., he laid out the issues in an e-mail to his boss, Brad Greenspan, the chief executive of eUniverse. "Targeting is not working, and targeted advertisers are dropping out," DeWolfe wrote, amid a long list of issues with the pop-up advertising program. "Seems like issues have been brought up pretty continuously over the last three to four weeks that haven't really gotten addressed."

In fact, targeted pop-up ads were not the only thing broken at eUniverse. The struggling dot-com survivor was running out of money and had been kicked off the Nasdaq stock exchange because of an accounting restatement. DeWolfe's division of eUniverse—a unit called ResponseBase—had been hit especially hard. ResponseBase's e-mail marketing efforts were increasingly being blocked by software that scanned for "spam"—the industry term for pernicious junk e-mails touting pornography and sexual aids. And ResponseBase's online sales of items such as miniscooters and remote-control cars were plummeting amid high return rates. Now eUniverse wanted to shut down Response-Base and fold it into another division—a move that DeWolfe was fighting.

With all of his division's efforts falling apart, DeWolfe might have easily given up. But that wasn't his nature. A tall, rugged-looking blond with the laconic laid-back demeanor of a California surfer, DeWolfe was a tenacious optimist. Where others might see a hopeless situation, he refused to consider the downside.

Part of his attitude came from his experience sending out thousands of e-mails at a time. Only a tiny percentage of any given batch will succeed at generating a response. But in the world of e-mail marketing, a small response rate is not a reason to give up—it's just another reason to continue to experiment until you find a message that works.

DeWolfe took the same approach to business. Just because his previous efforts had failed didn't mean that his next effort wasn't about to light the world on fire. So once he finished dealing with the spyware issues, DeWolfe turned his attention to his next big gamble: a new website called MySpace, a replica of a trendy website called Friendster.

His team had thrown together its copycat site in just a few months. There was no reason to believe that MySpace would be able to stand out in the crowded field of Friendster rip-off sites. Still, if it worked, DeWolfe's twenty-five-person Internet division would be saved. If it flopped, he would lose control of his fiefdom at eUniverse.

At 5:37 p.m., DeWolfe sent another e-mail to his boss: "We launched

MySpace," he wrote. "It's sort of buggy, but the best way to find bugs is to let people use it and get feedback."

Thus was born the most popular website in the United States.

This is not how Google and Yahoo were born. The first generation of Internet behemoths was founded in the late 1990s by engineers, computer scientists, and people with advanced training who bragged about their knowledge of databases and algorithms. These first-generation websites took years to develop. They required massive computer resources and huge teams of computer programmers.

But by the summer of 2003, technology had become easier to tame. Computer prices had fallen dramatically. Computer processing power had increased. Some forms of computer programming had become simple enough that even high school students could build expert-looking webpages. High-speed Internet connections were finally becoming pervasive throughout the United States.

The time was ripe for a new kind of Internet giant to emerge—one where human creativity was at the center of the experience, not technology. In other words, a Hollywood-style media company—one where crazy creative people run the show, and nobody really knows what makes a hit or a flop. The story of MySpace is a story of the first Hollywood Internet company, a company that is a breed apart from its Silicon Valley brethren.

MySpace founders Chris DeWolfe and Tom Anderson were cubicle-dwelling marketing executives with no technical prowess or revolutionary ideas. They were employees of a shady Los Angeles Internet company called eUniverse (later renamed Intermix) that sold wrinkle cream and ink cartridges on the Internet from a bland office park near the Los Angeles airport. Before starting MySpace, DeWolfe specialized in sending spam e-mails, and Anderson ran a pornography website. When they started MySpace, they copied, rather than invented, many features from competing sites.

Just as MySpace was becoming popular, Intermix surreptitiously sold itself to Rupert Murdoch's News Corp. DeWolfe and Anderson watched as their site was subsumed by a media conglomerate, and they lost control of key decisions. Yet the sale turned out to be a blessing in disguise:

News Corp. provided the tools MySpace needed to become the most popular website in the United States.

In July 2008 Web surfers viewed 41.4 billion pages on MySpace, making it the most trafficked, in terms of page views, website in the United States by a wide margin. (Yahoo was number two, with about 10 billion fewer page views.) That meant that visitors to MySpace viewed more pages—and spent more time—than on any other site in the United States. Yahoo and Google still attracted more visitors per month than MySpace, but their visitors didn't stay as long or look at as many pages as MySpace visitors.

And despite spawning hundreds of imitators, MySpace is still by far the market leader in social networking. In July 2008 it attracted seventy-five million visitors, nearly twice the monthly visitors of its nearest rival, Facebook.

MySpace's unlikely success is a testament to the tenacity of its founders, who maintained a simple vision for their website. They wanted it to be a place where people could express themselves freely. They succeeded.

Log on to MySpace, and you'll discover a dazzling virtual locker room. Every member has a page to decorate any way that he or she likes, often with blinking wallpaper, blaring music, streaming videos, and oversized photographs. Nearly every element of a MySpace page can be customized, with few restrictions. Users can pretend to be anyone or anything they like on MySpace—from their favorite actor to their favorite pet. They can "befriend" their favorite rock stars or cars, nearly all of which have MySpace profiles. They can join groups devoted to every topic under the sun—from a "hookup club" to a group for volunteer firefighters.

The wild and unfettered atmosphere of MySpace has led critics to claim that the site is a dangerous haven for sexual predators, drug dealers, porn stars, and other unsavory characters. But that's not the whole story. MySpace has also proven to be an effective organizing tool for presidential candidates, a fund-raising tool for nonprofits, and a marketing tool for consumer brands. Individuals have used MySpace to meet their spouses, connect with long-lost relatives, and send baby photos to loved ones in the military overseas. More than anything, MySpace is a powerful vehicle for individual self-expression. It's a place where people can write their own narratives.

The story of Ashley Dupré is illustrative. Dupré was a prostitute whose rendezvous with New York governor Eliot Spitzer ended his career. When the story broke in March 2008, people flocked to her MySpace page to find out details about her life. What they found surprised them: Dupré was also an amateur singer, with several of her own songs on her website. Within a day, her songs had become hugely popular on the Internet. Without MySpace, Dupré would have been known to the public solely as the prostitute portrayed in the court filings and mainstream media. But MySpace empowered her to shape her image in popular culture.

The one story that has not been bared on MySpace is the story of the site itself. What follows is the narrative of MySpace—a story of betrayal, intrigue, and lucky breaks starring a cast of Los Angeles media executives ranging from media moguls Rupert Murdoch and Sumner Redstone to the hard-partying founders of MySpace.

MySpace was created by Chris DeWolfe and a circle of his friends. DeWolfe was not a tech wizard. He was not a man interested in optimizing computer performance. Instead DeWolfe's talent was in identifying gifted workers and optimizing their performance. "I like being around creative people, funny people, crazy people," he once said. By the time DeWolfe and his loyal team founded MySpace, they had worked together at two other Internet startups. Most of them still work at MySpace today.

Born in December 1965, DeWolfe grew up in Portland, Oregon. He was the younger son of two academics who hoped that he would follow in their footsteps. His father, Fred DeWolfe, was a historian who specialized in Portland architecture and contributed to five books on Portland history. His mother, Brigitte, taught German at a local college. The DeWolfe family lived in a relatively small house in the upscale southwest section of Portland. DeWolfe and his older brother, Andrew, attended the city's best public schools.

At Lincoln High School, DeWolfe was a jock; his family and friends called him by his nickname, "Beezer." He was president of his junior class, played varsity basketball and tennis, and went to the state doubles tennis championships with his brother. "He was kind of a cool man on campus," said classmate Josh Lowthian. "He was a really good basketball player, but a nice guy too."

DeWolfe valued loyalty highly. This was illustrated by his allegiance to a high school classmate. Andrew Wiederhorn was a close friend of DeWolfe's, and they had been classmates since kindergarten. Wiederhorn was entrepreneurial, often wearing suits to school and starting a Jet Ski business on the Willamette River. Later in life, Wiederhorn spent a year in prison after pleading guilty to two felonies related to a financial scandal. During most of Wiederhorn's incarceration, DeWolfe remained on the board of Wiederhorn's company, Wilshire Financial Services Group, and supported its controversial decision to keep paying Wiederhorn's salary while he was in jail.[1]

DeWolfe graduated high school in 1984 and moved to Seattle to attend the University of Washington. In college he was an enthusiastic member of the Beta Theta Pi fraternity. He received a degree in finance in 1988 and then drifted around the San Francisco Bay Area for several years. His family urged him to develop a five-year plan; it was not forthcoming. Finally DeWolfe applied for the MBA program at the University of Southern California (USC), graduating in 1997. "Business school was my opportunity to think for two years," DeWolfe said later.

At USC he fell in love with marketing and was entranced by the Internet. In 1997, for a class called "The Impact of Technology on Media and Entertainment," he wrote a business plan for a community website that he called Sitegeist. He got an A-minus on the paper. Much later, DeWolfe would retain his professor Paul Bricault, a William Morris Agency senior vice president, to promote MySpace.

DeWolfe also fell in love with a fellow business school student, Lorraine Hitselberger, whom he eventually married. She was an attractive brunette with ambitions to join the media business. After graduation in 1997, the couple moved into a condominium in Pasadena. DeWolfe's childhood friend Wiederhorn hired him to run the credit card division at the First Bank of Beverly Hills. Back in 1987, when he was just twenty-one, Wiederhorn had founded Wilshire Financial Services Group as a way to buy up troubled loans and enforce repayment. By the time he

---

[1] Wiederhorn's financial empire filed for Chapter 11 bankruptcy protection in 1999. In June 2004 Wiederhorn pled guilty to paying a gratuity to a pension fund adviser and filing a false tax return, and served an eighteen-month prison term.

was thirty-two, Wiederhorn employed seven hundred people and controlled $3.5 billion in assets, including the First Bank of Beverly Hills.

Although DeWolfe boosted revenue at the Beverly Hills bank's credit card division, the suburban commute and the banking life were ultimately too dull for him; he wanted in on the Internet revolution. It was 1999. The Internet was booming.

DeWolfe joined the dot-com industry through another friend, Josh Berman, whom he met at USC business school. Berman, a cheerful, dark-haired Los Angeles native with a quick smile, had been working as an accountant at PricewaterhouseCoopers. In 1999 Berman agreed to help put together a business plan for a dot-com company called XDrive. Founded by two brothers, Brett and Steven O'Brien, XDrive aimed to provide free Internet storage space for consumers to store their backup computer files.

From five o'clock to eight o'clock each morning, Berman sat at Starbucks writing the business plan for XDrive. Once the O'Briens launched XDrive, Berman quit his day job to work full-time as XDrive's deal maker. Soon after joining, Berman recruited DeWolfe to join XDrive as head of marketing.

XDrive's service was quite valuable at a time when computer storage was expensive. Like many dot-com companies, XDrive offered its services for free and hoped to make money by selling advertising. To fund its growth, XDrive raised a huge amount of money—about $110 million— from Goldman Sachs, AOL, and others. At its peak, XDrive's ranks swelled to about three hundred people and it burned through about $4 million a month.

DeWolfe oversaw more than eighty people in the consumer marketing group at XDrive. In addition to marketing XDrive's services, DeWolfe's team developed an e-newsletter called *IntelligentX* that offered news about technology and aimed to make money by selling advertising.

For a while, XDrive was a great place to work. The offices were in one of Santa Monica's fanciest buildings—the Water Garden—inhabited by big media giants such as Viacom. XDrive had rented so much space that employees rode scooters to get around the office. A free catered lunch was provided every day.

...

MySpace cofounder Tom Anderson first heard of XDrive in 2000 after graduating from the University of California, Los Angeles (UCLA) with a master's in film studies. He was walking through his neighborhood in the outer reaches of Santa Monica, near Interstate 405, when he saw a flyer promising $20 to anyone who answered the ad.

Anderson, dark haired and intense, was thirty years old and deeply in debt; a struggling musician trying to raise money for a trip to Singapore. Hoping for some quick cash, he answered the ad. The next week, Anderson showed up for what turned out to be a focus group interview for XDrive. The interviewer was so impressed with his intelligence that she hired him as a copywriter. Anderson planned to work there for just a few weeks to save up enough money for his trip.

XDrive was Anderson's first corporate job. A high school dropout and former hacker, he had spent most of his twenties studying and playing in rock bands. He didn't like how his father, a San Diego entrepreneur, had "one crazy idea after another"; Anderson planned to be a lifelong student.

An extremely private and self-described antisocial person, Anderson has sought to keep details of his childhood from public view. In fact, he has little to hide—he was a precocious kid whose rebelliousness paved the way for his success at MySpace.

Born on November 8, 1970, Anderson grew up in Escondido, a sleepy farm town about a half hour's drive north of San Diego. By the time he was a young teenager, Anderson was fascinated by the nascent world of computers and online bulletin board systems. At the time, many hobbyists ran online bulletin boards where users could post notices for one another. To connect, people had to dial a phone number and use relatively slow computer modems.

Anderson befriended a well-known local computer hacker, Bill Landreth, known as "the Cracker," through one of these boards. In 1983 sixteen-year-old Landreth had been indicted for computer fraud after he hacked into the GTE Telemail system, an early e-mail network based in Vienna, Virginia. Although Landreth didn't steal any money or secrets— in fact, all he did was peek at some innocuous e-mails—he had the bad luck to be caught during a time of heightened concern about computer security.

In 1983 the United States was in the midst of a personal computer revolution. Apple Computer had just gone public, and its shares were soaring. IBM had just launched a rival personal computer that used a newfangled operating system developed by a startup called Microsoft. Microsoft was racing to build a graphical interface that would make IBM's computers as intuitive as Apple's.

The media was portraying this new world as extremely dangerous. The movie *War Games* had just been released; in it, a young computer hacker nearly starts World War III. A group of Milwaukee hackers who called themselves the "414s" graced the cover of *Newsweek* that September. They had broken into several large computer systems, including one at the Memorial Sloan-Kettering Cancer Center. That fall lawmakers in Congress introduced several bills aimed at combating computer hacking.

In this context, Landreth's minor crime became a media sensation. But his sentence was relatively light: He was convicted of wire fraud in 1984, ordered to pay a fine of $87, and was placed on three years' probation. Landreth also won a $25,000 advance to write a book about his life as a hacker called *Out of the Inner Circle: A Hacker's Guide to Computer Security,* for Microsoft Press. To Anderson, Landreth was a role model. "I looked up to him a lot," Anderson recalled later. "He knew everything." Although only fourteen, Anderson often tagged along with Landreth and his college-age friends and joined them in hacking exploits. In October 1985 Anderson's computer equipment was confiscated by the FBI as part of a sweep of alleged computer hackers, but Anderson was not arrested.

Landreth's book agent, Bill Gladstone, recalls Landreth's showing up at his office with an entourage: a girlfriend, a friend with a car, and Tom Anderson. Although Anderson was the youngest of the group, Gladstone recalls that he was neatly dressed, intelligent, and mature for his age. Anderson was quite unlike the disorganized, shy Landreth. "Tom seemed the most normal" of Landreth's crowd, Gladstone recalled. "Bill and his other friend seemed to be much geekier and more limited in their future options."

In September 1986 Landreth and Anderson decided to try to make a movie about their hacking exploits. Since Anderson's computer had been confiscated by the FBI, Landreth brought his computer to Anderson's house. "He started to write the proposal for it on the computer, and I went to take a shower," Anderson said. "When I came out, he was gone. The proposal was in midsentence." Landreth had vanished.

At first Anderson wasn't concerned. Landreth would often vanish for a few days or weeks. But after Landreth's friends found a letter hinting at suicide, their concerns grew. The Cracker's disappearance ignited a flurry of news coverage. "We used to joke about what you could learn about life, especially since if you don't believe in a God, then there's not much point to life," Anderson told reporters. Almost a year later, Landreth was found wandering dirty and barefoot in a small town in Oregon and was arrested for violating his probation.

When Landreth returned to San Diego to serve the rest of his probation, he lived on the streets. Anderson kept in touch with him and let Landreth keep a computer at Anderson's home. But Anderson soon realized that his famous friend had serious issues. "Before, he was just real smart, even though his ideas were a bit strange. But he was just Bill," Anderson told a reporter. "Now I think something is wrong . . . He said he wanted to live on the streets because he wanted to experience being in a minority."

Around the same time, Anderson dropped out of high school. His hair was long, and he was playing in a heavy metal band called Top Hatt. Anderson kept in touch with some of Landreth's friends, including Steve Burnap, the friend who drove Landreth to his appointments with Gladstone.

In May 1987 Burnap and Anderson got arrested together. Late one night Burnap, Anderson, and a friend of Anderson's sneaked into the University of California, San Diego's underground maintenance tunnels. Underneath the campus, they could walk between buildings and watch the elevators from below. But when they tried to pick the lock on an underground door, they triggered a silent alarm. "All of a sudden there were cops pointing guns at us," Burnap said. "It was the campus police."

Burnap, Anderson, and Anderson's friend were handcuffed and hauled down to the police station. Anderson didn't take it seriously and began teasing the cop with fanciful stories about how he didn't need to attend school. "I'm going to be so rich," Anderson said. "You're a cop; how much do you make? I'm going to make millions." The cop seemed to think Anderson was talking about drug dealing, and lectured him about reforming his life.

Burnap was amused by Anderson's performance. "Watching him, it was hard to know how much he believed of what he was saying." Still, the police let Anderson, then seventeen, off without any penalty. Bur-

nap, because he was twenty, got a ticket for contributing to the delin-
quency of a minor.

Burnap, a student at UC San Diego, tried unsuccessfully to persuade
Anderson that a college degree was worth pursuing. "He was convinced
that he didn't have to go to college to be successful," Burnap said. "He
said, 'No, no, that's a waste of time.' "

Instead of finishing high school, Anderson wrote a book. In those
days, technical publishers were desperate for how-to computer manuals.
Landreth's book agent, Gladstone, got Anderson a contract—with an advance of about $5,000—to write a technical book about a type of soft-
ware that allowed personal computers to communicate with other
computers or with online services such CompuServe. "Because Tom was
so young, I checked with his parents before representing Tom," Gladstone recalled. *Using Crosstalk Mk.4* by Tom Anderson was published in
1989 by the publisher Scott Foresman.

Eventually Anderson changed his mind about attending college. In
1994 he enrolled at the highly competitive University of California at
Berkeley. He double majored in English and rhetoric and edited a poetry
and fiction journal.

Anderson continued to dabble in technology. He wrote video game
reviews for the website GameRevolution.com and engaged in lengthy
debates about various video games on the Usenet Internet bulletin board
system—a slightly more grown-up version of the online bulletin boards
that he frequented in high school. Sometimes Anderson used his real
name on Usenet. Sometimes he used his middle name, Tom Everett. And
sometimes he used the name of a friend, Melissa Loeffler. In one late-
night Usenet debate about the pros and cons of the baseball video game
High Heat, Anderson weighed in with a quote from Nietzsche:

"I believe it was Nietzsche that said, 'There are no facts, only interpre-
tations.' In this case, that statement makes a lot of sense—all of us have
a different understanding of what 'manage' means in terms of baseball."
The next poster wrote: "Tom's quoting Nietzsche, and that's a pretty
good sign that it's time to let this one rest."

After graduation in 1988, Anderson moved to San Francisco and
started playing in a rock back called Swank. He wanted to go to Asia. His
following post about Japan demonstrates the self-deprecating humor
that became his trademark on MySpace. "I'm currently living in San

Francisco and am about to head to Tokyo in the next week or two. I'm a singer with a sort of obnoxious twang (John Lennon meets Johnny Rotten), I can play guitar, write music, and have a lot of stage experience. If it matters, I'm white (no blonde hair sorry!). I will be living in Tokyo, so I'd like to join or form a band there. I like many kinds of music and would consider all types of situations."

In January 1999 Anderson switched his sights to Taiwan. "Can anyone tell me about Mucha or Panchiao?" he posted on soc.culture.taiwan. "I've been offered a job teaching and can choose either location. I know nothing about them, but want to be close to Taipei."

A few people responded that Mucha was a more interesting place to live, and Anderson pressed for more information. "I'm a night person and usually go to bed around 4:00 a.m. and wake up at 12:00 noon. Is there much to do at night in Mucha?" Anderson wrote.

Assured that there was nightlife in Mucha, Anderson posted about his other pretrip anxieties: "I'm a little worried about learning to drive a motorcylce [sic]. I'm used to living in neighborhoods where I can get everything I need within walking distance (Berkeley and San Francisco). Thanks for the advice, though! What times does public transport stop running?" he wrote. "It costs to use the phone in Taiwan even for local calls? Oh no! Looks like my Internet obsession is going to have to come to an end!" And a few days later: "Here's my problem: I don't own a laptop, so I want to bring my desktop computer with me to my new home in Taiwan . . . How should I pack it for a safe ride from S.F. to L.A. to Taipei?"

Anderson did eventually move to Taiwan. But he quickly returned, in the fall of 1999, to attend UCLA's graduate film studies program. His Usenet postings now began to focus on Asian films. "Does anyone know where you can buy/rent Taiwanese films with English subtitles?" Anderson posted on soc.culture.taiwan in October 1999. "Specifically, I'm looking for the works of Hou Hsiao-Hsien," the acclaimed Taiwanese film director.

After graduating from the two-year film program in one year, Anderson also began showing an interest in pornography. In July 2000 he posted in rec.arts.movies.erotica to see if anyone could help him identify the origin of some online pictures of a Vietnamese porn star named LeAnna Scott. At that time, Anderson was also apparently operating an

Asian porn site called TeamAsian.com. A colleague recalls Anderson describing the site as a porn affiliate site—meaning that it simply provided links to other porn sites, earning referral fees. In August 2000 Anderson posted twice on Usenet's alt.sex.women promoting TeamAsian.com as "free" and having "some exclusive pics." News Corp. later found evidence that Anderson had received a substantial amount of money from the site.

That summer Anderson was hired as a copywriter at XDrive. After one week of work, he decided that corporate culture didn't fit with his late-night lifestyle. "I'm quitting," Anderson told DeWolfe. "My boss is telling me I have to come in to work by ten in the morning." Despite Anderson's eclectic background and lack of business credentials, DeWolfe was impressed by him. "Tom was so obviously full of smart ideas, I wanted to work more closely with him," he told a reporter later. So DeWolfe gave Anderson permission to set his own hours and job description. "You can work from home," DeWolfe said. He told Anderson that his job was simply to "go figure out how to make money."

Soon, however, both Anderson and DeWolfe would be laid off from XDrive.

When Karl Klessig arrived at XDrive in February 2001, he was shocked at the wild spending on facilities, employees, and infrastructure that was going on at the company. A turnaround specialist, Klessig had been brought in by XDrive's new chief executive to help rein in costs.

The dot-com bubble had burst, and advertisers were fleeing the Internet. Very few people had signed up for XDrive's premium $4.95-a-month storage service. The stock market had turned sour on Internet companies. XDrive was trying to reposition itself as a paid storage provider for big telecommunications companies.

But with no revenue coming in, Klessig was charged with cutting costs. And DeWolfe's eighty-seven-person marketing department was a juicy target. "It was the largest marketing division I've ever had in my life," said Klessig, who had founded three technology companies and consulted for many others.

More to the point, DeWolfe's group was not focused on marketing XDrive's free or paid products. Instead the marketing staff was spending much of its time writing the e-newsletters called *IntelligentX* that were e-mailed to more than 6.5 million subscribers. The ultimate goal was to sell ads in the newsletters, but so far the newsletters hadn't attracted much revenue.

DeWolfe was a passionate defender of the business. But he couldn't win over Klessig. "I wish I could understand what you are doing so I could decide if it was a good business," Klessig told DeWolfe at their first meeting. In March XDrive laid off DeWolfe and the entire marketing division, including Anderson.

The layoffs didn't save XDrive. One year later, still hemorrhaging cash, XDrive filed for bankruptcy. By that time, DeWolfe, Berman, and Anderson had started a new Internet company called ResponseBase. It was doing so well that it placed a bid to buy XDrive. Although Response-Base's bid wasn't successful, it was a sign of more ambitious things to come.

Chapter 3

RISING FROM THE ASHES

When Chris DeWolfe and Tom Anderson were laid off from XDrive in March 2001, the job market was terrible. All across the nation, Internet companies' losses were mounting, and they were shedding employees. In 1999 and 2000, enthusiastic investors had poured billions of dollars into Internet startups without much thought to how the companies would make money. By mid-2000, however, investors began to realize that few of these companies were going to turn a profit anytime soon—and the mania for Internet stocks fizzled. By March 2001, the Nasdaq composite index—where many Internet and technology companies were listed—had fallen 60 percent from its peak in March 2000.

Without financial backing and without profits, Internet companies were slashing staff. In January 2001 alone, thirteen thousand people were laid off from dot-coms—with big cuts in the Los Angeles market at places like eToys and the Walt Disney Company's Web portal Go.com.

In this dismal environment, DeWolfe made the surprising decision to start an Internet company. He had no prospect of getting any financing from venture capitalists or other institutional backers. He had no hopes of getting any office space from landlords who had been burned by their previous dot-com tenants.

But in typical DeWolfe fashion, he had no doubts.

...

One thing DeWolfe did have was friends—lots of them. Finding employees for his startup was no problem; the town was littered with laid-off dot-commers. DeWolfe's startup team included former XDrive colleagues Tom Anderson, Josh Berman, and Aber Whitcomb. Whitcomb was an XDrive developer whom the others called the "chief nerd."

With a team in place, DeWolfe's next task was to get some office space. He called up another friend, Matt Coffin, who was running a startup called LowerMyBills.com.

"We've just left XDrive," DeWolfe told Coffin. "I hear you've got a lot of office space."

A consummate wheeler-dealer, Coffin saw the dot-com bust as an opportunity to upgrade his startup's quarters. Even though LowerMyBills was struggling to raise money, it needed to get out of its cramped, unheated, unairconditioned North Hollywood office.

Coffin had just cut a deal to pay only $100,000 for a year's lease in spacious Westwood offices that were being vacated by the struggling CareerPath.com, which had been paying nearly $1 million a year for the space. To pay for the lease, Coffin sold all the furniture that CareerPath left behind, making back about half his money. Then he agreed to sublet to DeWolfe to bring in some additional cash.

Finally, DeWolfe needed cash to finance his startup. He turned to his friend from high school, Andrew Wiederhorn, who was now running a small real estate investment fund in Portland, Fog Cutter Capital Group. Government regulators were investigating aspects of the bankruptcy of Wiederhorn's Wilshire Financial Services Group. Despite his own troubles and the industry's malaise, Wiederhorn had confidence in DeWolfe. "His business plan was conservative," Wiederhorn said.

Wiederhorn and a partner invested $300,000 in DeWolfe's company directly and through an investment vehicle, TTMM L.P. For their investment, Wiederhorn and TTMM received a gigantic 50 percent stake in DeWolfe's startup—a steep price for DeWolfe to pay. But in the spring of 2001, it was the only money DeWolfe was going to get.

In this financially strapped environment, DeWolfe's startup had to be profitable right away. That meant he couldn't launch a typical Hollywood Internet venture, creating costly entertainment such as videos or comedy and hoping that viewers and advertisers would show up. Instead DeWolfe aimed for the underbelly of the Internet: e-mail marketing, where it was still possible to make money.

In mid-2001 sending out e-mails was one of the few areas of the Internet that advertisers hadn't fled. During the dot-com bust, advertisers were turned off by the high prices of Internet ads and the fact that less than 1 percent of viewers were clicking on their Web advertising banners. But e-mail solicitations were cheap to send out and were still attracting astounding response rates of 5 percent to 15 percent.

At this time, the line between spam and legitimate e-mails was still blurry. There were more than thirty-five different state laws regulating e-mail marketing, and no federal standard. Some states simply required advertisements to be labeled in the subject line; others required the marketer to get explicit permission from the recipient to receive e-mails. E-mail marketers had to tread delicately. On one extreme were marketers such as Amazon.com, which legitimately sent out millions of e-mails to customers who had requested them and immediately honored requests to be removed from the list. On the other extreme were off-shore spammers who used stolen e-mail lists and sent millions of unsolicited e-mails touting Viagra and other products. In between the two extremes were tons of marketers for hire whose tactics varied greatly.

DeWolfe joined the in-between group.

One of his first e-mail consulting clients was a website called MySpace.com, an XDrive competitor that offered free online storage. MySpace had 7.5 million users and offered slightly more storage space—300 Mb (megabits)—than XDrive, which offered 100 Mb.

The MySpace contract didn't last long. On Sunday evening, June 3, at about eight o'clock, the MySpace website went dark. The company had run out of money, and an attempt to save itself through a merger had failed. During the liquidation process, DeWolfe bought the domain name MySpace.com from his former client for $5,000. He wasn't sure what he would do with it.

In his typically self-confident way, DeWolfe issued a press release announcing the formation of his new company, ResponseBase, on June 20, 2001, before it had really gotten off the ground. DeWolfe promised that it would replicate the success of the *IntelligentX* newsletters that he had developed at XDrive.

"Our mission is to share our Internet marketing experience and knowledge with both offline and online companies," he said in the press release. "During flat or low-growth economic times, direct marketing methods have proven to be the most efficient method of deploying marketing dollars."

One of ResponseBase's first clients was the company it was subleasing from, LowerMyBills, a free online service that allowed consumers to shop for cheap loans, mortgages, and debt consolidation services. It was well known for its aggressive pop-up ad campaigns in which consumers surfing the Web were bombarded with ads that popped up on their desktop in a separate Internet browser window. ResponseBase wrote and mailed a newsletter called *Cost Cutter* to LowerMyBills customers. The author was Tom Anderson, whose picture featured prominently on the newsletter.

Within thirty days, ResponseBase had turned a profit. Its clients included some of the remaining dot-coms in Los Angeles: Business.com, a business portal, and a video chat-room service called Paltalk. At the same time, ResponseBase branched out into a shadier business: sending out e-mails touting its own products. Without a customer list of its own, ResponseBase apparently gathered e-mails from XDrive's database, which the ResponseBase founders had copied when they left XDrive.

In June ResponseBase launched a website, StraightTonic.com, which promised to provide entrepreneurs with newsletters that would feature "distilled information delivered directly to your in-box." Within a few weeks, StraightTonic started showing up on spam complaint message boards on the Internet. In July a user identifiying himself as Michael Cheves posted that he had received an unsolicited e-mail from Straight-Tonic. "It claims I had registered for something called 'XDrive' and had agreed to receive sendings like he was sending me. Of course I knew this was untrue," Mr. Cheves wrote to the board. In August a user named "Russ3llr" posted a complaint on another message board about receiving unsolicited e-mail from Tom Anderson at StraightTonic.com.

"It seems like shitty Tom is collecting IP numbers to track visitors to his site; check out http://www.responsebase.com/privacy_policy.htm," wrote another bulletin board user, Wolfgang Moser, after receiving an e-mail from Tom Anderson at ed@straighttonic.com.

One month after the terrorist attacks of September 11, 2001, the lease ran out on the Westwood offices of LowerMyBills. DeWolfe and Matt Coffin decided that they liked working together, so they looked jointly for a new location. They found some space at another dying dot-com, eCompanies, run by their friend Jake Winebaum. The company had been set up during the dot-com heyday as an "incubator" that would provide free office space to startups in exchange for equity. But the incubator business had failed, and now Winebaum was using an entire floor to host his one remaining startup, Business.com.

On October 26 LowerMyBills and ResponseBase moved into Business.com's offices in Santa Monica. The office was cramped, but the location at the corner of Colorado Avenue and Cloverfield Boulevard was perfect. All of Los Angeles's top media companies, from Sony to Viacom, had offices within a few blocks. The pink-brick building with green glass windows was framed with palm trees and waterfalls, and had several restaurants, plus a Starbucks at street level.

The three companies divided the floor into three sections: the smallest for ResponseBase's team of twenty-five and the larger two sections for the employees of LowerMyBills and Business.com. During that jittery time after the World Trade Center attacks, the building received several bomb threats. Coffin and DeWolfe joked about which of their companies the terrorists were after: LowerMyBills, which was infamous on the Internet for its ubiquitous pop-up ads, or ResponseBase, which was sending out millions of unsolicited e-mails.

By February 2002 ResponseBase had expanded into selling electronic books that consumers could download onto their computers. ResponseBase had noticed that its e-mail advertising clients were successfully selling electronic books, so it began offering e-books of its own. ResponseBase's books had names like *How to Grow Taller* and *How to Date Pretty Girls*. They cost about $19.99 per book.

The marketing for the e-books was tabloidesque: "If you've always wanted to be taller but assumed you were at the mercy of your genetics, we have some exciting, even astonishing, news for you. *You can grow taller!* Whether you are age five or fifty, our safe, unique, and scientifically proven method can help you reach your *true* growth potential!" Users would pay by credit card and download the book to their computer, where they could read it online or print it out.

Selling e-books transformed ResponseBase from an e-mail marketing company into an e-commerce company. Suddenly it needed systems to track credit card transactions and to track commissions owed to marketers that promoted the books. In February ResponseBase advertised on Craigslist for a developer who knew the program ColdFusion. The company hired Gabe Harriman, a fresh-faced, sandy-haired young programmer who had previously built e-commerce platforms.

In one month Harriman built an e-commerce system that allowed ResponseBase's fifteen customer service representatives to manage more than one hundred products and the websites that promoted them. Soon ResponseBase's e-commerce websites were booming. In April Response-Base attracted 2.3 million visitors to PayMe2Shop.com—a website selling a $19.99 e-book that supposedly revealed how users could earn up to $100 to $400 a week as paid shoppers.

That same month, nine hundred thousand people visited Response-Base's CoolOnline Products.com website, which touted $29.99 software that let you spy on others who use the same computer. "Ever wonder where your kids or spouse visit when they are on the Internet?" asked the webpage promoting CyberDetective software. "We can show you that as well by logging everywhere the places they visit in a *secret* file only *you* can see."

Anderson was the personal face of ResponseBase. Somewhat naively, given the shady nature of the business, he often put his real name on outbound e-mails and personally responded to the people who asked to be removed from the e-mailing list. The phone number that was listed as a way to opt out of ResponseBase mailings often went directly to Anderson's desk.

In October 2001 Anderson even registered ResponseBase's Cool-SpyProducts.com domain name to his home address at 11970 Walnut Lane, Apartment 202, Los Angeles. CoolSpyProducts.com sold software

that allegedly allowed remote monitoring of a computer, according to
the e-mails sent out promoting it:

"See Everything That Happens on Anyone's Computer! Remotely Install &
Completely Undetectable!"

In March 2002 Anderson registered the domain name StationsNet-
work.com to ResponseBase's office address using another pseudonym he
often used online: Tom Hogan at sfbaseball@hotmail.com. Response-
Base appears to have used StationsNetwork.com as a landing page for
some of the e-mails it sent on behalf of clients. In May and June, ResponseBase sent e-mails with subject lines such as: "Try AOL 1,000
Hours FREE for 45 Days Today," "Mortgage Search Certificate Exclusively for You," "Get Paid to Shop! Get Paid to Eat Out," "Special Offers
on BellSouth(R) FastAccess(R) DSL," and "Attract More Women with
My Unique Reverse Approach!" These e-mails directed respondents to
StationsNetwork.com, according to postings on spam-tracking bulletin
boards.

Anderson occasionally signed e-mail solicitations as well, such as this
one, which popped up in June 2002:

From: Tom Anderson
To: Jeremy Wilker
How to Hypnotize
The Secrets of Hypnosis Revealed!
This powerful new electronic book will teach you all you need to know about
the secret art of Hypnosis!
No Experience necessary!

And another one from Anderson appeared on a spam-tracking bulletin board in April 2003:

From: Tom Anderson
Get Paid for Your Opinions!
Find out how your ideas and insight can work for you!
Start Earning Today!
Click Here!

By the spring of 2002, ResponseBase had grown to about twenty-five employees—predominantly men in their twenties. Some were already friends: Anderson recruited his college roommate Kyle Brinkman, and DeWolfe brought over his friend Colin Digiaro, with whom he had worked at First Bank of Beverly Hills. Others became friends after joining: Jason Feffer sent out his résumé blindly and aced his interview. His background of working at other local Internet companies inspired confidence in the close-knit group. "It was a big issue with them trusting me," he said.

It was a young, hip environment where colleagues often worked late and would order dinner or go out for drinks after work. Some staffers were also roommates: Anderson and Brinkman shared an apartment in eastern Santa Monica. Aber Whitcomb and Gabe Harriman, the programmer hired to build the e-commerce system, lived in an apartment near Venice Beach, where they hosted a lot of parties.

Anderson didn't quite fit into the hypersocial environment at Response-Base. He worked around the clock and didn't drink, smoke, or do drugs. He was more retro than trendy: In Los Angeles, where your car defines your personality, he drove a 1984 Jaguar. He was antisocial and avoided confrontation—so if he disagreed with someone, he preferred to ignore them. "If I sent him an e-mail or instant message [with an unwanted suggestion], he wouldn't respond," Feffer said. "He didn't want to explain why he had to say no. If I pestered him and followed up, he would explain, and he often had a very good reason."

Anderson's lack of finesse caused a small incident to develop into a major rift at ResponseBase. It started on April 1, 2002, when Anderson went out for a late afterwork dinner with one of the few women in the office—an attractive Asian-American in the finance department. Over dinner the woman told Anderson that she didn't want to date anyone she worked with. Even so, she and Anderson became increasingly friendly, sending instant messages throughout the workday.

One afternoon the young woman told Anderson that she was going out to a bar for a friend's birthday party that evening. Anderson asked her to call him when she left the party, just to make sure she got home safely. When the young woman called him from her cell phone, Anderson asked her to come over to his apartment and hang out. She refused. A few days later, Anderson sent an e-mail to the young woman apologizing for his behavior. But relations between the two became awkward. Finally, after a month of strained silence between them, Anderson invited her to join him at the Starbucks downstairs one afternoon.

Over coffee Anderson again apologized for his behavior, and the two discussed how they could reduce the tension. The woman explained that she had been keeping her distance because she didn't want Anderson to get the wrong idea. Anderson asked her to keep their conversation private, and the two returned to the office.

But in such a small office, everyone had noticed that they were gone. As soon as the woman sat down at her desk, a colleague instant-messaged to find out where she'd been. "I went to Starbucks with Tom. He gave me a headache," she replied.

Anderson somehow realized that the woman was chatting about him online, and he became enraged. He marched over to her desk and demanded that she come to the conference room. "I thought I told you not to say anything," he said.

"I didn't," she said. "This is ridiculous. We haven't even dated. You're making things worse."

Outraged by Anderson's scolding, the woman complained to DeWolfe and Berman. From that day forward, Anderson began working from home most of the time. Anderson would not work from the office consistently again until the woman left the company about a year later.

Anderson's reaction to the awkward situation was extreme, but it highlighted the shyness that would eventually lead him to create a new avenue for online communication.

Anderson eventually found a way to get even farther away from the office. Following his interest in Asia, Anderson convinced DeWolfe to let him go to China to find a factory willing to manufacture goods that ResponseBase could then sell through its e-mail newsletters and websites.

DeWolfe sent him off to China with carte blanche to negotiate a manufacturing deal. Amazingly, he returned two weeks later with a batch of miniature cars that ResponseBase could sell online.

Anderson began making regular trips to China to manufacture everything from scooters to spy cameras you could slip in your shoe. "We had a hard time getting him to come back," Feffer said. "He loved it so much. He had so much creative control."

By the fall, ResponseBase was on a roll. Its scooters and remote-control cars were selling fast. ResponseBase's monthly revenues soared to more than $1 million in October, up from around $600,000 in August and September. News of ResponseBase's success traveled quickly among the small network of Los Angeles Internet entrepreneurs. Soon a suitor came knocking on the door. A company called eUniverse wanted to buy ResponseBase.

Chapter 4

THE TRAILER PARK
OF THE INTERNET

The tightly knit Los Angeles Internet community looked down its nose at eUniverse. Unlike the glamorous Hollywood-backed online entertainment ventures that sprouted during the dot-com boom, eUniverse was known as a copycat company, specializing in building cheap imitation websites that piggybacked off other people's good ideas. "EUniverse was really the trailer park of the Internet," said Matt Coffin, founder of LowerMyBills.com.

But in many ways, eUniverse was the perfect partner for Response-Base. Both companies had histories of operating on the fringes of the Internet economy.

Twenty-six-year-old Brad Greenspan founded eUniverse in 1999, near the height of the bubble, along with cofounders Joe Abrams, a seasoned Silicon Valley entrepreneur, and Brett Brewer, Greenspan's college friend.[1]

Greenspan and Brewer became friends when they were Sigma Nu fraternity brothers at the University of California, Los Angeles. The two were from very different backgrounds but shared an entrepreneurial spirit and a love of finance. Greenspan, a hyperactive fast-talker with piercing green eyes, grew up in privileged Atherton, an expensive enclave

---

[1] Greenspan and Brewer have since had a falling out. Greenspan now says Brewer does not deserve the title of cofounder and regrets that he previously allowed Brewer to describe himself as such.

near San Francisco, and went to an exclusive private high school where he dabbled in computers at an early age. Greenspan played varsity soccer and was a starter on the football team in high school. Smart and argumentative, he also had a streak of rage in him that his friends attributed to his parents' acrimonious divorce when he was young. "He would declare war on people," said one high school friend.

Brewer, one year older than Greenspan, was tall, gangly, gregarious, and easygoing. He grew up in Turlock, a farming community in California's Central Valley, and attended public high school. He was always interested in business; in fourth grade he bought up all the designer pencils in town and sold them to his classmates at a 300 percent markup. Still, Brewer struggled in school because he was a slow reader. "My SATs, I got a 1,090," he said. "I got 700 on math and 390 on verbal, and I took it twice—and I even went to those SAT prep classes. I would be that guy who would have to study for hours because I'm just not a fast reader, but I never looked at it as a disadvantage, because I just knew I had to work harder."

In college the two fraternity brothers spent hours together at the Coffee Bean & Tea Leaf café, drinking blended ice coffees, poring over financial newspapers, and strategizing over stock option trades. They weren't very successful—they traded through a friend's E*Trade account—and lost hundreds of dollars. But they loved the chase. Brewer made endless calls to a stockbroker he had met on a ski trip who was their only access to real-time stock quotes. "Hey, it's Brett and the gang," Brewer would say. "I know we've called you five times today, but could you just check one more quote?"

After graduating in 1997, Brewer and Greenspan moved into a rented house in Manhattan Beach along with three other former Sigma Nus. The three all worked at big investment banks or media companies, making upward of $80,000 a year—the standard path for fraternity brothers. But neither Greenspan nor Brewer wanted to join a big firm. Brewer began selling and leasing office space for the commercial real estate brokerage CB Richard Ellis, making just $17,000 a year plus commissions. And Greenspan set up his own company called Palisades Capital.

Greenspan's work was audacious and grueling. Every day he scoured newspapers, press releases, and regulatory filings to see if he could identify companies that might need to raise money. Then he cold-called those companies until one seemed interested in Greenspan's pitch to raise money for the company. Once he found a prospect, Greenspan called investors to see if any wanted to invest. If he brokered a successful match, he got paid a commission on the financing. Sometimes he would make $5,000 or $10,000 a pop; often he had long dry spells. Brewer also tried to broker similar deals on the side while he was working in commercial real estate.

Greenspan and Brewer were often broke. Greenspan's mother had agreed to pay his rent for a year after graduation—despite opposition from Greenspan's father—so Greenspan was able to pay $865 a month for the master bedroom suite in the Manhattan Beach rental. Brewer paid $365 a month for his bedroom, which was literally a converted closet that just fit a queen bed. Brewer drove a tiny two-seat Toyota coupe that the Sigma Nus called the "Pocket Rocket." Greenspan drove a used blue Acura Integra, which he had bought for $2,500 and was always breaking down. The guys called it "Blue Magic."

One of their roommates, who worked at Morgan Stanley, would take Brewer and Greenspan out to dinner whenever he got a $25 dinner voucher for working late. The three friends would meet at Islands, a festive burger joint in Manhattan Beach. Using the voucher, Brewer and Greenspan could each get a burger plus a salad or a Coke—but not both. It was a depressing choice. After about a year of this life, despite making nearly $35,000, including commissions, Brewer recalled, "I wasn't that far from throwing in the towel."

But in 1997 Greenspan had a breakthrough. He lined up a $45 million financing deal for Hayes Microcomputers, which earned him a fee of $1.2 million. The huge windfall justified Greenspan's unconventional work. The first thing he did was to buy a black Mercedes convertible and drive it up to the house of a childhood friend who didn't believe he had a real job. Greenspan's roommates called the car "Black Magic." Inspired by Greenspan's success, Brewer began devoting more time to pursuing similar deals.

The two friends rented office space next door to each other near the Los Angeles airport to work on their respective deal-making operations. As the stock market heated up, Greenspan decided that he wanted to start a public company. But he wasn't sure what the company should do. His thoughts naturally turned to what he knew best: matchmaking. One afternoon in early 1998, Greenspan came into Brewer's office and said, "Brett, listen to this: There are all these sites that have lots of traffic but no way to make money off them. And there are all these commerce sites that need audiences." Greenspan decided to make a match between the two kinds of websites.

Greenspan turned for advice to Joe Abrams, a Silicon Valley executive he had met while fund-raising for a website called Shopping.com. Abrams had cofounded a company, Software Toolworks, in the eighties that developed, published, and sold the wildly popular Mavis Beacon Teaches Typing software. Abrams was part of the management team that sold the company for $462 million in 1994. Since then, he had acted as an adviser to many technology startups.

"I'd like to do exactly what you did at Software Toolworks," Greenspan told Abrams on the phone. "I'd like to take that model and duplicate it on the Internet."

Abrams was impressed and agreed to meet Greenspan. But when the two met at a Korean barbecue restaurant in the Stonestown Galleria in San Francisco, Abrams was surprised by the youthful-looking Greenspan, then twenty-five years old. "I had no idea how old he was until I met him," Abrams said.

Still, he decided to take a chance on the scrappy young entrepreneur. The time was right for Internet startups. Silicon Valley was in the grip of Internet fever in the wake of Netscape Communication's stellar public offering. In August 1995, Netscape planned to sell its shares to the public at $28 per share; the shares reached $75 on the first day of trading. In this heady environment, Greenspan's idea of connecting commerce and entertainment resonated with Abrams. So the two shook hands and agreed to start the company together. Greenspan would put in all the money—and own 90 percent of the company—and Abrams would contribute his expertise in exchange for a 10 percent stake.

Greenspan and Abrams found a struggling Internet site that was selling CDs online—CD Universe—and a popular gaming website called Case's Ladder. Both agreed to sell. The idea was that Case's Ladder could finally make some money by persuading the game fans on its site to buy CDs at CD Universe, while CD Universe could stem its losses by cheaply tapping a new group of customers. They decided to name the new company Entertainment Universe—or eUniverse for short.

After lining up the potential acquisitions, Greenspan and Abrams started calling investors, hoping to persuade them to fund the purchase of the two websites. Eventually they found Emanuel Gerard, cofounder and chairman at a respected New York firm, Gerard Klauer Mattison. Mattison loved to buy his music CDs on CD Universe's website and agreed to put in $250,000. Greenspan then tapped another relationship he had developed during his freelance fund-raising days, with a Lehman Brothers banker named Steve Weinstein. Weinstein persuaded Lehman Brothers to be the lead investor in a $6.6 million fund-raising round for eUniverse.

Meanwhile, Brewer quit his job at the commercial real estate brokerage in December 1998 to focus on launching eUniverse. Working unpaid for the promise of a small stake in eUniverse, he searched for a shell public company that eUniverse could use to get publicly listed quickly. EUniverse planned to bypass the traditional method of an initial public offering in favor of a cheap and fast method of going public known as a "reverse merger," in which a publicly traded company whose business is defunct trades its stock for shares in a growing private business. That allows the private business to go public without paying the banking fees associated with an IPO and without having to create the track record of profitability required by the big institutional investors that back IPOs.

Eventually eUniverse agreed to buy the shares of the defunct Motorcycle Centers of America. With the newly acquired stock, it bought CD Universe for $1.9 million in cash and $7.3 million worth of stock. A few months later, eUniverse bought Case's Ladder for stock valued at $7 million. The newly created firm went public on April 14, 1999.

Greenspan, then twenty-six, was suddenly chairman of a publicly traded company with fifty-one employees. Brewer, twenty-seven, was vice president of e-commerce; he moved back East to manage the CD Universe operation from its headquarters in an industrial office park in Wallingford, Connecticut. Greenspan continued to work from home in Los Angeles, and engineered a series of small acquisitions of game-related websites. Abrams served in an advisory role, helping eUniverse to acquire new companies.

But within six months, eUniverse was struggling: CD Universe was losing $400,000 a month and was competing with giants like Amazon .com that were spending huge amounts of money on marketing. And the strategy of tapping video game fans on Case's Ladder to buy CDs wasn't working; the young male gaming audience didn't have credit cards and wasn't interested in buying CDs online. By the middle of 2000, Greenspan admitted defeat; he and Brewer negotiated to sell CD Universe back to its founder, who had been working for eUniverse, for $1 million—a fraction of what eUniverse had paid for it.

Brewer moved back to Los Angeles with about ten executives he had recruited in Connecticut. Many of eUniverse's employees slept and worked in a six-bedroom house that Brewer rented in Beverly Hills. Greenspan continued to work from home—he had moved to Hollywood—scouring the Web to see what was hot and firing off e-mails to his employees at all hours of the night. "I have a certain style of research that I can do, and I can't do it in the office, where people come in and interrupt me a lot," Greenspan said. "My therapist calls it ADHD," or attention deficit/hyperactivity disorder. Sitting at home surfing the Web and devouring analyst reports, Greenspan was good at spotting new trends on the Web.

Greenspan's idea was to retool eUniverse around a new demographic: older women. He was excited about a website he had bought called FunOne.com, which offered greeting cards and short animations, and attracted women aged thirty-four to fifty-four. Unlike young male video gamers, these older women were much more likely to click on advertising banners and purchase items online. EUniverse couldn't attract upscale advertisers to sites like FunOne, but it had great success selling spots to credit card companies—which paid a finder's fee of as much as $40 for each customer who filled out an application.

Even so, eUniverse couldn't avoid the fact that the rest of the Internet industry was imploding. By March 31, 2001, eUniverse was in dire straits: It had $218,000 in cash and $13.4 million in debt.

"All right, everybody, put on your hard hats; we're going in," Brett Brewer said. It was late in 2000, and he was showing off eUniverse to a contingent of visiting executives from Sony Corp., which he hoped would invest.

Brewer was standing in front of eUniverse's "offices"—the six-bedroom house on Palm Drive, in a residential neighborhood of Beverly

Hills. The front door was locked, so he was taking them in the side door by the kitchen.

Brewer opened the door. A cat, surprised by the intruders, jumped onto a stack of empty pizza boxes and knocked them onto the kitchen floor. The Sony executives' eyes widened.

Sony, the Japanese electronics giant, had expanded into Hollywood and gotten burned on the Internet. It was looking to unwind its portfolio of Internet investments. One of Sony's biggest Internet properties was an e-mail newsletter called *InfoBeat*. Sony purchased the newsletter when it had fewer than two million subscribers, and expanded its reach to nine million subscribers—in part by paying commissions to third parties that generated new subscribers. EUniverse was a top marketer of *InfoBeat*, generating more than one million subscribers through promotions on its greeting card websites. As a result, Sony executives thought that eUniverse would be a natural fit to buy *InfoBeat*.

When the contingent arrived at eUniverse's house in Beverly Hills, they were shocked. It was like a fraternity house. The day-to-day business was being managed by twenty-year-old Adam Goldenberg, who had dropped out of high school at age eighteen when eUniverse bought his company, Gamer's Alliance. Another seventeen-year-old high school dropout was sleeping in his cubicle on an air mattress because there were no bedrooms. No maid service in Los Angeles would agree to clean the house because it was so filthy.

Still, Sony wanted to unload *InfoBeat*, and eUniverse was the only taker. The only problem was that eUniverse had no cash. So Sony made a compromise: It agreed to sell *InfoBeat* to eUniverse for $9.94 million in eUniverse stock and at the same time invest $5 million cash in eUniverse. Considering the risk of accepting eUniverse stock as payment, it was almost as if Sony were paying eUniverse to take a money-losing business off its hands.

In May 2000 eUniverse moved into its first real office space, a sublease from a law office on Wilshire Boulevard, just east of Beverly Hills. It was finally becoming a real company. Now eUniverse had to figure out how to make money.

At this time, the only Web companies making consistent profits were commerce engines such as eBay and subscription-based services such as AOL. Companies that relied solely on advertising, such as Yahoo, were struggling to break even as advertisers debated whether online advertising really worked. So eUniverse decided to diversify into subscriptions and commerce.

Under Greenspan, eUniverse was an acquisition machine, constantly buying up companies to help it expand. He had a knack for convincing innovative websites to sell to eUniverse for small amounts of cash upfront. In the second half of 2001, for instance, eUniverse bought Funbug.com, expage.com, FitnessHeaven.com, Hobbyrat.com, eMusic Games.com, and SportsTriviaClub.com—all for little or no cash up front.

In June 2001 eUniverse launched CupidJunction, a dating website. Within two months, CupidJunction had attracted 450,000 paying subscribers. Soon after, the company relaunched FitnessHeaven.com, which sold fitness products and services, and AllYouCanInk.com, which sold ink-jet cartridges.

In addition, eUniverse began expanding into e-mail marketing, where advertisers were still spending money. In July eUniverse bought the *IntelligentX* newsletter, which DeWolfe had created, from XDrive for a few hundred thousand dollars. By then, however, DeWolfe had left XDrive to start his own company.

The diversification strategy worked. In the last three months of 2001, eUniverse had its first profitable quarter ever—it made $2 million net income on $10.1 million in revenues. One-third of the revenue was coming from products and services such as ink-jet cartridges.

At the same time, the rest of the industry was falling apart. In the summer of 2001, two of the best-known entertainment websites in Los Angeles folded: a well-funded animation website called Icebox.com and an animation site, Romp.com, headed by the son of Walt Disney chief Michael Eisner.

In early 2002 eUniverse chief financial officer Joe Varraveto recommended that Greenspan take a look at a startup that seemed to be doing well, called ResponseBase. Varraveto had worked with DeWolfe's wife, Lori, at a previous startup called ememories.com and was impressed by what he heard about ResponseBase. The young company's e-mail marketing and e-book sales didn't excite Varraveto, but he liked that ResponseBase was profitable and, most important, headed by responsible adults.

Although ResponseBase executives were only in their thirties, Varraveto believed that they would provide some management depth among eUniverse's cadre of twentysomething executives. "We needed to build a bench of deeper talent in case anything happened," said Varraveto, who was in his forties and was one of the oldest executives at eUniverse.

When Greenspan got in touch with DeWolfe, he was impressed that ResponseBase managed more than thirty million e-mail accounts and was consistently profitable. ResponseBase had a roster of high-end e-mail marketing clients such as Hewlett-Packard and British Telecom. "Our e-mail marketing group didn't cater to the high-end brands, and that's what ResponseBase brought to the table," said Dan Mosher, an eUniverse board member who was Greenspan's best friend in high school.

In his usual fashion, Greenspan offered to buy ResponseBase with eUniverse stock. But ResponseBase refused. "We valued the [eUniverse] stock at zero," said ResponseBase cofounder Josh Berman. Finally, on September 4, 2002, eUniverse agreed to pay $3.3 million in cash for ResponseBase as well as up to $3 million in bonuses to ResponseBase's top executives if they met certain performance goals over the next two years.

It was an unusually expensive price for eUniverse, reflecting Greenspan's high hopes for ResponseBase.

Chapter 5

STRUGGLING TO SURVIVE

Chris DeWolfe pulled up to the Belmont nightclub in West Hollywood in the back of a rented white Hummer limousine. His entire thirty-person ResponseBase team piled out onto the sidewalk. They were fashionably late to the eUniverse 2002 Christmas party—and they wanted to make a grand entrance.

Wearing an extravagant thigh-length leather jacket with a sheepskin lining and his trademark pointy-toed boots, DeWolfe led his staff into the restaurant. The young, predominantly male ResponseBase employees, all dressed to the nines, followed behind in a line. The entire eUniverse staff stopped to stare at the posse of hipsters. It even seemed like the music stopped for a minute.

"Chris, you're just like Hansel from *Zoolander*," eUniverse president Brett Brewer said in admiration. In the film, the screen often froze for a second when the character Hansel, played by actor Owen Wilson, entered a room.

The ResponseBase crew was indeed the cooler crowd. While eUniverse was populated by geeky technology types, many of whom hailed from the Midwest, ResponseBase was a group of young marketing executives with Santa Monica offices and Hollywood aspirations.

And ResponseBase wasn't just flash. The September acquisition of ResponseBase had helped propel eUniverse to its best quarter ever. In the last three months of 2002, eUniverse would report net income of $3.26

million on sales of $25.8 million[1]—an increase in profits of 60 percent from the previous year. The increase was due in large part to eUniverse's increased focus on e-commerce, including ResponseBase's brisk sales of $24.99 mini remote-control cars during Christmas. During the month of December alone, ResponseBase raked in $2.5 million in sales.

EUniverse was flying high. It had survived the dot-com bust—and was even making money. In April *Business Week* had profiled eUniverse as one of the few advertising-supported websites to turn a profit. And eUniverse stock had recently traded as high as $7 a share. For the first time, eUniverse had rented an entire restaurant for its holiday party instead of just gathering in a corner of a bar somewhere. There was an open bar, and the drinks were flowing.

At the end of the night, eUniverse human resources director Barbara Saunders, a sixty-year-old who served as mother hen to the young eUniverse staffers, stood by the door of the club holding a paper bag filled with cash. She checked to see if the departing revelers were sober enough to drive. If not, she gave them a wad of cash to pay for a taxi. This was a tradition. At most eUniverse parties, she doled out hundreds of dollars on taxi fare. That night, she handed out a record amount— nearly $2,000.

ResponseBase stayed in its Santa Monica offices for the first six months after being acquired by eUniverse. At first the separation was mutually agreeable: EUniverse didn't have room for ResponseBase, and Response-Base didn't want to leave its trendy Santa Monica digs. By late spring, however, ResponseBase grumpily succumbed to its new owner's request and moved into eUniverse's offices near the airport. EUniverse was located on the third floor of a nondescript office building across the street from the Promenade at Howard Hughes Center, a working-class shopping mall that looms over the I-405 freeway. The office was an open plan with a vast sea of cubicles surrounding a center core of interior conference rooms.

DeWolfe and Josh Berman were given a cubbyhole office with linoleum floors that was really a converted storage closet. Some of the ResponseBase staff sat in cubicles outside DeWolfe and Berman's office, while others sat downstairs on the first floor in an overflow office.

---

[1] EUniverse later had to restate this quarter and recorded a loss.

DeWolfe and Berman were miserable in their unglamorous new setting. "They weren't so nice to us," recalled Berman. But the two had an incentive to stay. They wanted to profit from their "earnout"—which meant that they and the other owners of ResponseBase shared a portion of ResponseBase's profits for the first year after the acquisition and a bonus for hitting certain targets.

By March 31, 2003, ResponseBase had accrued $1.3 million in its earnout. According to the terms of its contract, this implied that ResponseBase had net income of $3 million for the six-month period ending March 31. No wonder the ResponseBase staffers felt cocky. "We make as much money as all of them," they told themselves.

But eUniverse didn't have the cash to pay ResponseBase its earnout.

"Brad, why hasn't our rent been paid?" asked Jeremy Rusnak of Case's Ladder.

In January 2003 eUniverse chief executive Brad Greenspan was getting a lot of questions like that from his executives. The company had always run with barely enough cash in the bank, but this time the cash crunch seemed to be worse. Now the credit card companies were holding back a higher portion of eUniverse's sales for anticipated returns than eUniverse thought was necessary. It was strange that eUniverse appeared to be broke, considering it just had its best, most profitable quarter ever.

Greenspan hired a consultant to investigate the cash situation. The consultant recommended that eUniverse improve its accounting systems and hire a new controller. While looking for a new controller, Brett Brewer hired a consultant who specialized in accounting software, Michael Mincieli, through one of his friends at the Young Presidents' Organization. Over the next few months, Mincieli would find a host of problems in eUniverse's accounting systems.

Meanwhile, ResponseBase's e-mail marketing business was struggling. In early 2003 the dot-com boom was over, and the next Internet boom had not yet begun. During this in-between period, only the big three companies—AOL, MSN, and Yahoo (DeWolfe called them "the untouchable triumvirate")—were thriving. (Google had not yet taken off.)

Antispam sentiment was growing, and it was getting harder and harder to send out e-newsletters—ResponseBase's core business. The Federal Trade Commission had launched an antispam effort in February 2002, and New York attorney general Eliot Spitzer had started prosecuting spammers in May. Microsoft, AOL, and other Internet service providers were getting increasingly sophisticated at blocking mass e-mails. "It was a daily battle," said Dan Mosher. "AOL, Yahoo, or Hotmail would put in a new rule that would block us. Then we'd have to figure out some way to get our e-mails delivered." As a result, ResponseBase's clients were reducing their e-mail marketing budgets.

At the same time, ResponseBase started getting an influx of returns after its big Christmas selling season. The company didn't have a place to store the returned items, so the $99 kids' electric scooters and $24.99 remote-control rechargeable minicars started to pile up in the hallways.

ResponseBase dropped the price of its mini remote-control motorcycle from $24.99 to $19.95 and began offering its mini spy cameras for less than $100. Still, sales slowed dramatically, falling from $2.5 million in December to $1.8 million in January. By February the unit's monthly revenue had fallen even further, to $1.4 million.

Customers seemed to be catching on to the shady nature of ResponseBase's products. Consumer bulletin boards were filled with complaints about its $29.99 e-booklet *GetPaid4Opinions.com,* which purported to list places that might pay customers for participating in surveys. "I did this, and it is a scam," wrote one poster on the "Make Money Fast Hall of Humiliation" Internet bulletin board in March 2003. "It is only a list of companies that *may* pay you for taking their surveys, but none of them even do that."

Similarly, Donna, from Tempe, Arizona, wrote to the RipoffReport.com that she had paid for but never received a $19.95 e-book, *AuctionSources Exposed,* that claimed to help users "Make Loads of Cash on eBay." She had been unable to get a refund. "The phone number they provide always answers with a recording," she wrote.

Desperate for a new approach, ResponseBase experimented with setting up a kiosk on the Santa Monica pedestrian promenade to sell ResponseBase's spy cameras. ResponseBase hoped that it could roll out kiosks across the country if the concept worked. But the concept flopped.

Soon the complaints about ResponseBase's products and services started trickling out into the mainstream media as well. Cary A. Jones, a resident of Ocean City, Maryland, was intrigued by an ad on Cool

OnlineProducts.com for a program that claimed it would double the speed of his computer. When he clicked on DoublePCSpeed.com, he saw even more promises: "I don't care what your technical ability is, you can easily get 100 percent more speed and efficiency out of your system," the site claimed.

The offer appeared risk free, since it was fully refundable. "If you don't like the package for any reason—even because you don't like the font size I use—you can return it for an immediate 100 percent refund of your purchase price," the website promised. So Jones paid $40 to download the program onto his computer.

At the time, faster computer speed was elusive. Most Americans in early 2003 were spending more and more time on the Internet, but they weren't willing to pay the $60 a month for high-speed Internet access from home. Only 13 percent of U.S. households were using broadband. So a market had sprung up for ways to boost surfing speed by compressing graphics and storing data in central locations so that it could be quickly recalled.

But DoublePCSpeed was not using those tried-and-true tactics for boosting speed. Having downloaded the program, Jones realized that DoublePCSpeed had sold him a set of instructions on how to tweak the Windows operating system to enhance performance. Most infuriatingly, the enhancements actually slowed down his computer.

Outraged, Jones tried to get his money back. After weeks of getting no response from DoublePCSpeed or CoolOnlineProducts, he wrote to the influential computer magazine *PC World* for help. Grace Aquino, a reporter at *PC World,* took up the challenge and sent several e-mails to customer service at DoublePCSpeed and CoolOnlineProducts—since no phone numbers were listed on the websites. Finally, after receiving several automated responses, Aquino received a note from a customer service representative promising to give Jones a refund.

On February 1 *PC World* published an article detailing Jones's travails and warning customers away from purchasing products from sites like CoolOnlineProducts that don't provide valid phone numbers and a postal address. She apparently hadn't discovered that CoolOnline Products was run by ResponseBase.

...

On March 20 the United States invaded Iraq. On April 9 the U.S. Marines rode into one of Baghdad's central squares, hitched an armored personnel carrier to a chain, and helped pull down a statue of Saddam Hussein that had loomed over the square. The image resonated around the world as a symbol of the U.S. victory in Iraq.

Two days later, U.S. Army brigadier general Vincent Brooks of the U.S. Central Command held up a pack of playing cards at a press conference in Doha, Qatar. The cards displayed the faces of fifty-five of Iraq's most wanted deposed leaders. Brooks said the military had produced two hundred decks of the cards to distribute to soldiers as they hunted for the Iraqis.

But the military hadn't anticipated the American public's demand for the cards. The Pentagon was deluged with calls from people wanting to buy them. Unable to meet the demand, the U.S. Central Command posted images of the cards on its website for anybody to download for free. Soon copies of the playing cards were circulating like wild on the Internet. None of the decks for sale online was the real thing, but many tried to pass themselves off as the Pentagon's own cards.

ResponseBase didn't pretend that it had the authentic Pentagon decks, but it did try to distinguish its cards from the rest of the pack. On April 17 ResponseBase's CoolOnlineProducts website offered packs of "Iraq's 55 Most Wanted" with the following promise: "Don't be fooled by the many cheap imitations now floating about the Internet. These are *not* simply paper copies, shabbily cut, and passed off as the 'real thing.' Rather, these are an authentic replication of the actual cards issued to our troops, professionally printed on playing card stock with a laminated finish."

"Where's the quarterly report?" for the three months ending March 30, Greenspan asked his chief financial officer, Joe Varraveto, in April.

"There are a few items totaling fifty thousand dollars that we may not have a clean cut-off on," Varraveto responded. He and Mincieli were investigating whether those items should have been accounted for in the previous quarter ending December 31.

Late one night, at nine o'clock, Brewer wandered over to Mincieli's desk. "How's it looking?" he asked.

"I don't know if the numbers are right or wrong," Mincieli replied. "But what I do know is this accounting team doesn't know if the numbers are right or wrong."

Brewer's heart sank. EUniverse had been poised to report its best year ever for the year ending March 30. "Stay here," he said. "I'll go call Brad and the other guys."

Greenspan was outraged. When he was told that a restatement was needed, he exploded. "Wait a second, I just said we had the greatest quarter ever, and you guys are now telling me that I can't rely on our financials for the last couple weeks and months?!"

Eventually eUniverse sorted out the problem: The finance team's numbers didn't match the operations department's numbers. The finance guys were booking returned merchandise using one method of accounting, and the operations guys were using another method. So the amount of returns in each set of books didn't match—the result being that eUniverse had understated the amount of returns it was getting.

The company had two e-commerce divisions: ResponseBase, which sold novelty items like scooters and Iraqi trading cards; and Performance Marketing Group, which sold ink-jet cartridges and other products. It wasn't clear which of the two divisions shouldered more of the blame for the high return rate, but Greenspan decided that the two should merge to streamline operations. By this point, ResponseBase's business had basically collapsed. The unit's monthly revenues in May sank to $450,000, down from the peak of $2.5 million in December.

DeWolfe vehemently disagreed with the idea of merging ResponseBase into eUniverse. He argued that ResponseBase needed to stay independent to accrue the rest of its earnout, since it would be difficult to keep track of the division's profits in a merged entity. Instead DeWolfe proposed that eUniverse "roll up" its advertising sales force under his top advertising executive, Colin Digiaro. DeWolfe e-mailed Greenspan about his desire to combine business units at eUniverse so that the ResponseBase's "high end" sales representatives could sell more than just e-mail.

But DeWolfe's idea remained on the back burner as eUniverse grappled with its mounting problems.

On May 6 eUniverse announced publicly that it had discovered accounting issues and would have to restate its results. The Nasdaq immediately halted trading on the stock at $3.62 a share, down from a high of

$7.30 just a few months earlier. The Securities and Exchange Commission (SEC) began an investigation. Eight separate shareholder lawsuits were filed against eUniverse.

During the summer, the investigation dragged on. Armies of accountants and auditors combed through the company's books. The board's audit committee hired its own lawyers to protect itself. Sony was disillusioned with its investment and wanted out. And to top it all off, with no access to financial markets, eUniverse was running out of money.

The stress of it changed Greenspan. Before the restatement, he was content to work from home and let Brewer run the day-to-day operations. But after the accounting investigation commenced, Greenspan began taking a more active role. Inevitably, he started noticing a lot of things he didn't like. His friends were running the company sloppily, he thought; it was time to bring in professional managers.

Meanwhile, Greenspan thought the company could create value by spinning off its gaming division into a separately traded public company. He threw himself into the plans for a new company called GameUniverse that would encompass all of eUniverse's gaming assets. Separately, Brewer started pursuing Ronco Corporation, a company run by inventor Ron Popeil, who hawked his products such as the Veg-O-Matic on television infomercials. Brewer thought that the acquisition of Ronco could boost eUniverse's e-commerce business.

Brewer and Greenspan remained friends, but as their paths diverged, there were new strains in their relationship.

Bob Sullivan, a reporter for MSNBC.com, was appalled when he stumbled onto the ResponseBase website MyFreeCursors.com. "Show your support for our troops by downloading our free cursors!" it promised. But the downloadable cursors—which turned users' mouse pointers into American flags—were loaded with spying software.

The software, called KeenValue, tracked users' behavior as they surfed the Internet, as well as the software on their computer, their first and last name, their country, and their zip code. While users were surfing the Web, KeenValue would display pop-up ads. Users were informed about KeenValue through a tiny "Privacy" link at the bottom of the website.

The story was right up Sullivan's alley. As a reporter who specialized in covering the seamy side of the Internet, he was getting a lot of e-mails from readers complaining about a kind of spyware called "adware" that secretly downloaded onto their computer and then placed pop-up ads as they were surfing. The patriotic cursors seemed like a particularly good example of that type of bad behavior, since they were cynically capitalizing on good old-fashioned American patriotism.

On May 20 Sullivan wrote a column on MSNBC.com titled "Patriotism? No, Just More Pop-ups. EUniverse Adware Comes Cloaked in Old Glory." The story named ResponseBase as the creator of the pop-ups.

It also quoted an eUniverse representative defending the practice. "EUniverse is not in the spyware business," said spokesman Todd Smith. "Unlike spyware, our KeenValue product does not track the user's key stroke or gather any personal or confidential information that the user does not voluntarily provide to us."

In fact, eUniverse's distinction between adware and spyware was hollow. By almost any definition, ResponseBase was trafficking in spyware.

Internally, the MSNBC inquiry caused an uproar. Greenspan, always sensitive to press coverage, asked DeWolfe to review the privacy policies on his websites to make sure that they complied with industry standards. Greenspan proposed that ResponseBase curtail some of KeenValue's more obnoxious features. "Can we reduce what Keen is keeping/tracking from users at the present time so that we can become user-friendly application?" Greenspan wrote in an e-mail to DeWolfe. But KeenValue's features were never substantially changed.

In June Greenspan finally found an investor interested in eUniverse: VantagePoint Venture Partners, a Silicon Valley venture capital group that was just dipping its toe back into the Internet.

VantagePoint managing director David Carlick, an avuncular white-haired former advertising executive, had taken time off after many of his investments collapsed during the dot-com bust of 2000 and 2001. In the spring of 2003, he rejoined VantagePoint to scope out some new Internet properties.

Carlick heard of eUniverse through a friend at an advertising company called Zedo. When Carlick went to visit eUniverse in Los Angeles in April 2003, he was impressed. "They had traffic. They had grown by acquisition," he said. "We were looking for something to be the basis of a roll-up." ("Roll-up" is a term venture capitalists use to describe acquiring several small companies and combining them into a bigger company for synergy and economies of scale.)

He wasn't put off by eUniverse's unsavory reputation. As a former advertising executive, Carlick felt that "marketing has always been kind of on the scary edge of ethical." And he was impressed by eUniverse's creativity; its vast array of websites was constantly being updated with new jokes and new offers. He likened eUniverse's creativity to the culture of TV scriptwriters. "Every day you have to write a new monologue," he said. "Silicon Valley doesn't work that way."

After Carlick's visit, Carlick wanted to loan eUniverse $2 million to help it get back on its feet while VantagePoint considered investing an additional $10 million. But Carlick felt that Greenspan wasn't a good choice to stay on as CEO. After all, the accounting mess had happened on his watch. Greenspan was clearly a strategic visionary, but his style wasn't hands-on enough for a company of eUniverse's size.

Greenspan agreed that he would step aside if VantagePoint invested. "I'll be chairman, and we'll find a CEO," Greenspan said.

In June, Bob Sullivan, the MSNBC.com reporter who had written about the adware contained in ResponseBase's patriotic cursors, got a phone call from a friend at the New York State Consumer Protection Board. "You should check out these free car sites," said Jon Sorenson.

When he began investigating, Sullivan found that dozens of sites had sprung up on the Internet offering "free cars" for fees ranging from $10 to $50. But consumers who applied for the free cars received only a list of websites where they could apply to drive cars wrapped in advertising. The services actually offering advertising-laden cars didn't charge an application fee. "These people have created a real headache for us," the operator of one free car service told Sullivan.

Sullivan found that the culprit from his cursor column—ResponseBase—was behind many of the free car sites. ResponseBase operated three of them: GetPaidDriving.com, AllFreeCars.com, and AllFreeCars.net. These sites were being advertised with spam e-mails, with promises such as "Get paid *real money* to drive your car" and "Free new cars for the taking!"

On June 20 MSNBC published Sullivan's column titled " 'Free Car' Spam a Growing Problem; Protection Agency: Consumers Pay $10 to $50 and Get Nothing in Return." In the article, eUniverse defended the free car websites. "Basically, this fee is to cover our expenses for maintaining the site and updating the database on a regular basis," eUniverse spokesman Todd Smith told Sullivan.

Internally, however, eUniverse was not satisfied with ResponseBase. By the end of the summer, its revenues had shrunk to $300,000 a month—mostly from sales of pop-up ads in existing cursors and screen savers. Greenspan wanted to shut down ResponseBase. But DeWolfe and his team were still holding out for their earnout payment, and arguing about how much they were owed.

Finally eUniverse president Brett Brewer suggested a compromise: "Instead of going back and forth about how many returns [ResponseBase was responsible for], let's come up with a new idea." Brewer's proposal accommodated DeWolfe's desire to keep ResponseBase as a separate division. But it also forced ResponseBase to come up with a better business model.

DeWolfe and Berman began brainstorming ideas in their tiny conference room. They considered launching a dating service or a reunion website. The one consistent theme was that the new venture would be "as far away from direct e-commerce marketing as possible," Brewer recalled.

Chapter 6

THE FAKESTER REVOLUTION

During the summer of 2003, Silicon Valley was buzzing about a new startup called Friendster.com. Friendster had raised more than $1 million in its second round of financing and had turned down Google's offer to buy it for $30 million. Silicon Valley hadn't seen numbers like this for two years, and neither had Chris DeWolfe.

DeWolfe saw the Friendster valuation as a sign that the market for Internet investments was finally reviving. In an e-mail to his boss, Brad Greenspan, DeWolfe described the appeal of Friendster.

"Friendster is truly a revolution," DeWolfe wrote. "Over 1.5 million active users without a penny spent on advertising. *Active* is an important distinction. One is hard pressed to find a user on Friendster who has not been on the site within twenty-four hours. No wonder the site is painfully slow."

Friendster was indeed revolutionary. Jonathan Abrams, a former programmer at Netscape, founded Friendster to improve upon traditional online dating sites such as the Jewish dating service JDate.com. "With JDate, a guy is almost bound to be twenty pounds heavier or twenty years older than he is in his photo," Abrams told a reporter. "We're trying to make the process more accountable. People will put a more accurate picture of themselves on Friendster because you know your friends will see it."

Working out of his apartment in Sunnyvale, California, Abrams created a private version of Friendster in June 2002 that was accessible only to his friends. It was immediately popular. Users set up their own profiles, with a photo and description of their interests. Then they invited their friends to join. Launched to the public in March 2003, Friendster shot up to one million members by the end of the year.

The idea of setting up an online identity was not new. Since the beginning of the digital age, people have found ways to establish their identity online. In the early days of electronic bulletin board systems, users identified themselves by aliases, known as "handles." On the WELL (Whole Earth 'Lectronic Link), founded in 1985, readers and writers of the *Whole Earth Catalog* created "pseuds"—or pseudonyms, that identified their postings. With the advent of the Web, users could set up more elaborate online identities. On GeoCities, founded in 1994, users could set up a free webpage describing themselves through photos and text, and by affiliating themselves with groups of like-minded people. Dozens of similar sites followed with different slants on identity. Xanga and Blogger, both founded in 1999, focused on blogging—online diaries. And dating sites such as Match.com, founded in 1995, allowed people to present themselves to potential mates.

Friendster's innovation was to add a feature linking people's online personas together. Each Friendster profile contained pictures not only of the member but of the member's friends. Clicking on the friend's picture would take you to the friend's profile page. While it seems like a small thing, this was a huge innovation. Suddenly all these stand-alone Web identities could be placed in an understandable context—the context of their friends. After all, Abrams argued, that's how humans judge each other in real life. Why not online?

Linking profiles by friendship also provided Friendster members with a built-in audience. At the time, it wasn't that difficult to build a stand-alone website, but it's always been difficult to lure visitors to a website. On Friendster, users had an instant audience of their friends.

By allowing members to link their identities, Friendster was inadvertently building a more powerful network. An oft-cited axiom on the Internet is Metcalfe's Law, which holds that the value of a network grows faster than the number of its users. Friendster had stumbled onto a corollary called Reed's Law, which holds that networks that contain subgroups are even more valuable than those without subgroups. The reasoning is that subgroups encourage more communication among users, thus increasing the time and attention people pay to the network as a whole.

Friendster could be viewed as a network of groups—each group being composed of a community of friends. As such, the site became extremely valuable to its users.

Friendster was not the first to link online identities by friendship. In 1996 twenty-eight-year-old New York entrepreneur Andrew Weinreich created SixDegrees.com, a website devoted to the idea that everyone in the world is connected through six degrees of separation. At the site's New York City launch party in 1997, Weinreich presciently declared that SixDegrees would revolutionize human networks. "Today networking is the same as it was ten years ago, twenty years ago, two hundred years ago," he said. "But with the click of a button, we're going to change that forever. It no longer makes sense for your Rolodex to live on your computer. We'll place your Rolodex in a central location. If everyone uploads their Rolodex, you should be able to traverse the world."

On SixDegrees, users could identify their friends (one degree of separation), their friends' friends (two degrees of separation), and so on. Their friends didn't have to join to be identified. SixDegrees grew to be quite popular, amassing about 3.5 million members at its peak. In 1999 Weinreich sold SixDegrees for $125 million to YouthStream Media Networks, but the unprofitable site was shut down about a year later.

In 1999 Portland programmer Brad Fitzpatrick revived the idea of online friendship when he created LiveJournal.com. Although Live-Journal was aimed primarily at blogging, users could also list their friends on their pages. Friends could gain privileged access to their friends' blogs, giving the blog authors a sense of privacy and intimacy with their readers. Unlike SixDegrees, LiveJournal did not focus on re-creating off-line friendships; people could befriend anyone whose blog they liked to read.

By the time Friendster launched in 2003, digital photography had entered the mainstream, allowing users to easily post photos of themselves on their profile pages. This simple change made a huge difference to online social networks. "We were able to see early on that most social networks are used mostly for dating, and what's most important in dating is pictures," said Weinreich. But SixDegrees was too early for the digital photography revolution. "We had board meetings where we would discuss how to get people to send in their pictures and scan them in. The real difference in 2002 was that by then people had digital cameras."

Friendster put friendship at the front and center of its business model. Since it was designed as a dating tool, the site made friends introducing their friends to one another its defining activity. Suddenly the idea of "friending" online leapt to the forefront. Friendster users prided themselves on how many friends they had amassed and how many comments their friends left on their page. (Once two people were friends, they could leave public or private messages on each other's profile.) Friendster users began obsessively checking their profiles to see if anyone had left a comment or requested friendship.

In this age of e-mail ubiquity, it seems strange that a somewhat outdated method of communication—leaving messages on someone's webpage—would prove so popular. But, in fact, the posting of comments on people's webpages filled a need for public, asynchronous communication—that is, messages that didn't need to be responded to immediately and could be viewed by the public.

In the early days, most communication on the Internet was private, asynchronous communication, or e-mail. The ability to reply to e-mails at your own leisure, instead of responding immediately to phone calls, was incredibly popular. People finally felt free to be masters of their own time.

Of course, the Internet evolved to offer synchronous, or real-time, communication. The private form of synchronous communication is instant messaging, where two people chat in real time on the Internet. The public form is chat rooms, where many users post comments in a chat room instantaneously for anyone to see. Both forms of real-time communication proved extremely popular, driving the growth of companies like America Online.

Public, asynchronous communication also developed in the form of bulletin boards and communities like the WELL, where people posted their thoughts publicly, and others responded publicly. These forums, once again, allowed people to control their time, by responding when it was convenient for them. But it also added a performance aspect to the act of communication; a posting on a bulletin board was a necessarily public act. Many people were attracted to the idea of developing a public persona as a way to seek attention or to connect with other like-minded people.

Friendster improved on bulletin boards by offering a more visual environment and more rewards for postings. A bulletin board posting was usually some text posted in a rather techie environment, and there were few ways to compare which posters were getting more positive feedback for their postings. By comparison, a posting on Friendster was on a user's own page. It included a photo of the commenter and immediately increased the status of the person being commented upon. Checking out a person's friends and the kinds of comments they posted became an integral part of evaluating a prospective friend on Friendster. Thus Friendster stumbled onto an improved form of Internet communication that proved to be wildly popular.

But Friendster made a big mistake: It discouraged members from pretending to be someone they weren't. That meant no "Fakesters"—people pretending to be Homer Simpson or God or Harvard University or some other entity that clearly was not a real individual. It also meant no "Fraudsters"—people pretending to be someone else, such as Britney Spears or their cousin Billy. "The whole point of Friendster is that you're connected to somebody through mutual friends, not by virtue of the fact that you both like Reese's Peanut Butter Cups," Abrams told a local newspaper.

But the "No Fakester" approach violated one of the Internet's central tenets—anonymity—best embodied by the *New Yorker* cartoon showing a dog in front of a computer screen with the caption "On the Internet, nobody knows you're a dog." To many, the power of anonymity is not a luxury but a political necessity, the essence of freedom. By gathering online anonymously, people are free to find others who share their political views or their sexual orientation without fear of repercussions.

As a result, Friendster's negative approach to Fakesters and Fraudsters rubbed many of Friendster's young, hip San Francisco users the wrong way. One Fakester—who named himself Roy Batty after a character in the movie *Blade Runner*—organized a group that fought for the rights of Fakesters. Calling themselves the "Borg Collective" after a mythical group of cyborgs that appeared on the *Star Trek* TV shows, the group created dozens of fake Abrams profiles and littered them throughout Friendster's site. They decried the "Fakester Genocide" and vowed to start a "Fakester Revolution." They wrote a revolutionary document, the "Fakester Manifesto," based on the Declaration of Independence.

The first declaration was as follows:

"Identity is provisional. Who we are is whom we choose to be at any given moment, depending on personality, whim, temperament, or subjective need. No other person or organization can abridge that right, as shape-shifting is inherent to human consciousness, and allows us to thrive and survive under greatly differing circumstances by becoming different people as need or desire arises. By assuming the mantle of the Other, it allows us, paradoxically, to complete ourselves. Every day is Halloween."

In the Fakester revolution, Tom Anderson saw an opportunity. He thought that Friendster was wrong to delete the Fakesters. Anderson wanted to create a site where users could create any identity they liked.

Anderson was fed up with eUniverse. He wanted to retire. He hadn't made that much money on the sale of ResponseBase, but it was enough for him. He had a roommate, a used Jaguar, and was taking regular trips to Asia. He didn't need much money to support his lifestyle.

But he was also intrigued by Friendster. To him it was reminiscent of GeoCities—an Internet sensation from the late nineties, where users set up their own home pages. GeoCities marked the first time that anyone could build a website. Anderson thought that Friendster was fun to play around on. But it was also frustrating. The site was slow and restrictive. Anderson sensed an opportunity to compete.

On one of his rare visits to eUniverse, Anderson barged into DeWolfe's office. "Dude, we've got to talk. I've been thinking about Friendster."

Anderson suggested that ResponseBase could build an improved version of Friendster by adding features such as blogging and classifieds. "The idea was that if it was a cool thing to do online, you should be able to do it" on the new website, Anderson said later.

At first, DeWolfe was skeptical. "I kind of blew it off because he has a lot of wacky ideas," DeWolfe later said.

But the next day, DeWolfe received three friend requests from Friendster and another networking site, LinkedIn—and started reconsidering Anderson's proposal. "It seemed like an amazing kind of marketing where you didn't have to pay for acquiring customers," he reflected.

ResponseBase's number two executive, Josh Berman, was doubtful. There was no real business model. Friendster was losing money. But DeWolfe decided to take a chance on Anderson's idea. After all, what did he have to lose? ResponseBase was sinking, and its parent company was faring no better.

"I bet the farm on it," DeWolfe later said.

In fact, DeWolfe did not bet the farm. Betting the farm, for most Internet entrepreneurs, means starting an independent business in a garage somewhere. At this point, DeWolfe and his team could have quit eUniverse and started a Friendster competitor on their own. The Internet market was reviving, and with their track record at ResponseBase, they probably could have rounded up some investors. That would have allowed them to be true entrepreneurs—owners of their idea instead of employees with an idea.

But doing so would have entailed giving up their promised earnout of hundreds of thousands of dollars. It might have meant investing some of their own money into the venture as well. And it certainly meant placing a risky bet that social networking would prove as popular with advertisers as it had with consumers.

Unlike most Silicon Valley entrepreneurs who quit their jobs when they get a startup idea, DeWolfe and Company weren't willing to take that risk. They decided to launch the site within the confines of eUniverse. The parent company would fund the initial startup costs, pay their salaries, and absorb the losses until it broke even.

The decision was a trade-off. If the concept failed, DeWolfe and his team would get paid regardless. If it succeeded, however, eUniverse would be the major beneficiary of their hard work.

Ever the savvy marketer, DeWolfe pitched the idea of building a Friendster competitor to eUniverse's twenty-three-year-old CEO, Brad Greenspan, as a way to unify eUniverse's diverse businesses under one portal, "allowing access to everything that eUniverse has to offer,"

DeWolfe wrote in an e-mail to Greenspan. "The simplest way to get the jump on Friendster is to leverage the user base of eUniverse's multiple properties."

DeWolfe and Berman also asked for input on the name. They considered YoPeeps.com and Comingle.com before finally settling on MySpace—the name that DeWolfe had bought from a consulting client two years earlier. Brett Brewer initially wasn't thrilled by the name. "It sounded like kind of a funny name," he said.

Greenspan was enthusiastic about the project and the name. He had discovered an old high school acquaintance through Friendster and thought it was an intriguing service. In July Greenspan asked an associate to check out if Friendster was interested in selling or partnering, but the answer was no. He also thought that MySpace could be a good fit with the online gaming spin-off he was trying to assemble. "Maybe we spin MySpace into GameUniverse and add a real sexiness to the spinoff," Greenspan wrote in an e-mail to the head of eUniverse's gaming division.

Like all eUniverse projects, MySpace started on a shoestring budget. It was initially a sideline business; during the summer of 2003, most employees at ResponseBase continued selling pop-up ads, while Anderson's roommate Kyle Brinkman managed the creation of MySpace.

ResponseBase employee Duc Chau, who had been running the company's e-mail system, built the MySpace website using the programming language Perl, running on an Apache server. Meanwhile, ResponseBase's e-commerce programmer, Gabe Harriman, built the MySpace database, which would store the data for each member. They scrounged up some used equipment from eUniverse and some machines purchased on eBay.

Finally, on August 15, they were ready to launch their bare-bones site. Like Friendster, MySpace allotted each user a profile page with pictures and interests and links to friends. It also had a mishmash of features, including horoscopes, games, and blogging, then called journals. "We didn't know what it was going to be about," said MySpace staffer Jason Feffer.

"When we flipped the switch, everybody raced to sign up for the first account," Chau recalled. Harriman was the fastest—he got the first account. "I was slow, so I got the second account," Chau said.

Chief technology officer Aber Whitcomb got the third account, followed by Feffer and Brinkman. Anderson, despite being the inspiration for the site, didn't sign up until September 2.

"It was me who said, 'Let's do this,' but then I actually dropped out of the picture for about a month while a team of two worked on it," Anderson recalled. "Once we had something tangible to look at, I stepped back in, and it became a full-time job."

Chapter 7

BUILDING MYSPACE

MySpace was founded just as the United States was getting wired for high-speed Internet connections—known as broadband. In 2003 the percent of Americans with broadband at home shot up to 25 percent from 15 percent.

Broadband provided dramatically faster surfing speeds, but even more important for MySpace, it provided faster "upload" speeds. On a dial-up Internet connection, it might take two to three minutes to upload a 2-megapixel photo to the Internet. On a broadband connection, it usually took less than thirty seconds; and, depending on the type of connection, it could be as little as five seconds.

That simple fact changed the nature of the Internet dramatically. Before broadband, most Web surfers were seeking information or buying products. Their main activity was receiving or downloading information. Their main uploading activity was sending simple text-based files such as e-mail or instant messages.

Broadband made consumers' relationship with the Internet more interactive. Suddenly Web surfers could upload pictures or music files to the Internet to share with their friends. As with most computer technologies, the early adopters of broadband were older, affluent men. But in 2003 a new class of early adopters was also emerging: teenage girls. In their quest to keep in touch with their friends around the clock, teenage girls were among the first groups to begin actively blogging and posting photos online. They wanted more from the Internet than just techie features—they wanted to express themselves to their friends.

Inadvertently, MySpace stumbled onto a killer application for this cohort of tech-savvy teenage girls by allowing them to customize their profiles with colorful wallpaper and backgrounds.

It happened one month after MySpace launched, when its lead developer, Duc Chau, quit. His expertise was in e-mail systems, and he didn't feel technically challenged by the work at MySpace. So he left for a job at an e-mail marketing company. Soon after leaving, Chau bought the domain name MySpaceSucks.com and began hosting a bulletin board for users to complain about MySpace. (Chau says the site was meant to be funny. Since then, he has taken it down.)

Without Chau, MySpace was at a loss. No one else at the company knew the Perl programming language that he had used to build the site. That meant that MySpace could not update the site and keep it running. So DeWolfe paid Gabe Harriman $2,000 to work nights and weekends rebuilding the website in ColdFusion, a programming language that eUniverse was already using for the rest of its websites. Greenspan also hired a former eUniverse employee, Toan Nguyen, as a contract programmer to help.

While rebuilding the site, Harriman and Nguyen made a mistake. Normally, websites that accept contributions from users—such as text entries or photographs—block users from inserting Web markup language, such as HTML, into those submissions. Web markup language is the computer code that controls what appears on a webpage, such as the colors or fonts or background images. But Nguyen forgot to block Web markup language in user submissions.

His mistake allowed users to build colorful backgrounds and wallpaper and load them onto their MySpace pages. Suddenly teenage girls could decorate their MySpace page with hearts and glitter and smiley faces the same way that they were decorating their lockers and book bags. At first MySpace didn't realize what had happened. Kyle Brinkman, the product manager, noticed that one of the profile pages looked strange.

"Hey, there's a problem; somebody hacked into our site," he told Nguyen, pointing out some profiles that included color and background graphics. Nguyen investigated and realized that people were inserting Web markup language into their profiles. The customized pages were slower to load. Nguyen and Brinkman considered fixing the omission because it was "making some pages look ugly and exposing security holes," said Jason Feffer. But ultimately MySpace decided that "users come first, and this is what they want," according to Feffer.

The ability to cut and paste features directly onto MySpace pages appealed to a generation of teenagers who were used to downloading music from the Internet and "mashing up" songs together to create remixes. By the end of 2004, more than half the nation's teenagers—sometimes dubbed the Remix Generation—had created some kind of online content, such as a blog or a webpage. One in five of them had found content online and remixed it into their own artistic creation.

As a result, teenagers' relationship with media was changing dramatically. Historically, the media model had been "There are senders and receivers, and nothing in between," said Aram Sinnreich, founder of Radar Research, a company that studies this generational switch. The new model is "a much more nuanced world where it's not so easy to say who is a producer and who is a consumer," he said.

One casualty of this new world was copyright protections. The majority of teens surveyed in 2004 said that it was "unrealistic" to expect people not to illegally download and share music files. MySpace users also showed no qualms about placing copyrighted music or text on their profiles.

But at the same time, a newfound creativity was blossoming online, as teenagers trolled the Web searching for elements of self-expression to place on their MySpace pages.

Central to MySpace's freewheeling ethos was the decision to allow Fakesters. From the beginning, MySpace differentiated itself from Friendster by welcoming all users and allowing them to be whoever they wanted to be.

"People kept telling us, 'You have to have a closed network,' " Tom Anderson recalled. " 'People will want to talk only to friends they already know.' We just didn't believe it. We never wanted to limit people from talking to each other."

MySpace did not even seek to verify the e-mail addresses of people who registered on the site—a standard practice on the Internet. Most websites send an e-mail to the address used to sign up for an account and will register the account only if that e-mail address is valid (meaning it doesn't bounce back) and the user confirms receipt of the e-mail.

As a result, the process of "friending" on MySpace took on a different tone than on Friendster. On both sites, friending is a formal process. To become someone's friend on MySpace, you must click on the "Add to Friends" button on their profile. That person then receives an e-mail in his MySpace in-box asking him to approve the connection. If he says yes, he is added to your friends list, and you are added to his.

On Friendster, because people used their real identities, they tended to friend people they knew in real life. On MySpace, where fake identities flourished, friending did not imply that the two people knew each other. Social networking researcher Danah Boyd surveyed MySpace users about why they approved friendship requests and got this illustrative list of reasons:

Actual friends.
Acquaintances, family members, colleagues.
It would be socially inappropriate to say no, because you know them.
Having lots of friends makes you look popular.
It's a way of indicating that you are a fan (of that person, band, product, and so on).
Your list of friends reveals who you are.
Their profile is cool, so being friends makes you look cool.
It's the only way to see a private profile.
Being friends lets you see someone's bulletins and his friends-only blog posts.
You want friends to see your bulletins, private profile, private blog.
You can use your friends list to find someone later.
It's easier to say yes than no.

Time magazine columnist Joel Stein neatly summed up the process of friending on social networks as follows: "In the pre-internet days, neither of us would have even thought of calling each other friends. We'd have called ourselves friends of friends who met once and yet, for some reason, kept sending each other grammatically challenged, inappropriately flirty letters with photos of ourselves attached. Police might have gotten involved."

Venture capitalist Jeremy Liew says that MySpace can be thought of as a game where the winner is the one with the most friends. Like most video games, he says, MySpace also has "levels." Novices start with a rudimentary profile. Then they realize they have to take actions—such as requesting friends or leaving comments on others' pages—to get to the next level. "People are competing," Liew said. "They're trying to win and doing things to try to make them win."

It is this gamelike aspect of MySpace that has made it so addictive for many users.

The most important friends on a MySpace page are the top eight friends whose pictures automatically show up on the bottom right of a profile page. Those friends are assumed to have the closest relationship to the MySpace member on whose page they appear.

In the beginning, MySpace members didn't have much control over their top eight. The top eight were simply the first eight people that the MySpace member friended. The top eight friends were sorted according to when they joined MySpace—so a friend who joined in August would appear before a friend who joined in September. MySpace later changed it so that users could customize their top eight.

Because of this ranking system, early users of MySpace, such as programmer Chau, became minicelebrities—because their pictures were displayed on so many members' top eight.

For features beyond the core concept of friending, MySpace was an aggregator, not an innovator. Every night Anderson would scour the Internet looking for interesting websites, and then ask the MySpace developers to copy the features on those sites.

"We would fast and furiously build something and throw it out there," recalls Peter Amiri, who was director of technical operations at MySpace. "That was the name of the game during those first six months. Not all of it was done through good programming methodologies, not all of it was QA'd [quality assured], but there was always something new being added to the site."

Some websites—such as HotOrNot.com and Xanga—objected to MySpace's blatant rip-offs. Founded in 2000 by two Silicon Valley graduate students, HotOrNot was an Internet sensation. The concept was simple: women and men submitted their pictures to HotOrNot, and users ranked each photo on a scale of 1 through 10. Borrowing a good idea, MySpace launched a section called "Hot or Not," where users could rank other people's photos. HotOrNot cofounder James Hong called up DeWolfe and asked him to rename the section. DeWolfe agreed, and the section became known as "Hot or Cold." It was later changed to "Ranking" and eventually dropped.

MySpace also borrowed some features from Xanga, a popular blogging site. Founded in 1998 as a site for users to exchange book and music reviews, it was focused on blogging. Xanga users had their own blogs and could post comments on one another's blogs. To compliment a blog, a Xanga user would give it "Props." And groups of bloggers could join together in a "blogring."

In November Xanga sent a letter threatening to sue MySpace. It alleged that MySpace had infringed on Xanga's intellectual property by using the terms *props* and *blogring*. Eventually MySpace agreed to pay Xanga $40,000, to refrain from using the trademarked names, and to change its site design to avoid any similarity to Xanga.

At first MySpace tried to market itself through banner ads across the Internet. But they were a "miserable failure," according to Anderson. Users would click on the ad, but once they arrived at MySpace, they saw that no one else was there and left.

MySpace quickly started focusing on recruiting new members through word of mouth. Anderson, drawing on his history of sending mass e-mails, personally sent e-mails to five hundred of his friends on Friendster, inviting them to join MySpace.

Brett Brewer, president of eUniverse, sent an e-mail to all two hundred fifty of his employees, asking them to create their own MySpace page and promising to give a $1,000 cash prize to the person who established the largest personal network of friends. The company also sent out e-mails to some of the customers from its other divisions, such as the dating site CupidJunction, asking them to join MySpace. "MySpace.com is a fun new way to meet people," the e-mail said. "YOU CAN CONTACT ANYONE FREE OF CHARGE."

Tila Tequila was one of the most popular people on Friendster, but her account kept getting deleted. "I was getting too many friend requests, and the pictures were too hot," Tequila said.

Tequila, a Vietnamese model whose real last name is Nguyen, had created an online sensation by posting pictures of herself scantily clad in provocative poses. Her Friendster profile had attracted tens of thousands of friends. But each time she got deleted from Friendster, she lost her list of friends.

Rebuilding a network of friends on Friendster was not easy. First Tequila had to locate all her friends' profiles. Then she had to send individual "Add Friend" requests to each one. To prevent spam, Friendster frowned on sending too many friend requests at a time, so she had to send them in small batches. Friendster also prevented people from requesting friendship from people who were separated by more than four degrees, so Tequila could contact only people who were friends of her friends' friends. Finally, after that arduous process, Tequila's contacts had to agree that they were her friends. Once both parties approved the friendship, then Tequila's friends would be displayed on her list of friends.

The fifth time that Tequila's profile was deleted, she was fed up. Anderson had repeatedly been sending her e-mail invitations to join MySpace. Until now, she had rebuffed him, since all the cool people were on Friendster. But the prospect of starting from scratch again on Friendster was daunting. So Tequila joined MySpace.

At first it was lonely. "No one was really on there; everyone was on Friendster," Tequila recalled. But she soon changed that. Feeling vindictive, Tequila e-mailed all forty thousand of her Friendster friends and asked them to join MySpace.

Soon she had plenty of friends.

On Friday, September 26, 2003, one month after launching the site, MySpace had its biggest day ever, attracting six thousand new users. The previous record was Wednesday of that week, when four thousand new users signed up. DeWolfe and Anderson were thrilled.

"MySpace huge 2 days," DeWolfe crowed in an e-mail to his boss, Greenspan. "I know these numbers may still seem small, but momentum is huge, and it's only been just over a month." MySpace rose from the thirty thousandth most popular site on the Internet to the three thousandth most popular site.

The next day, Anderson, a baseball fan, flew to San Francisco to watch the Los Angeles Dodgers play the San Francisco Giants. Before he left, Anderson posted a "Pre-Dodgers Update" on MySpace:

Many new users, glad to see you here! Bad news: You still can't delete your trash. Good news: Do you really care? We'll have this in soon. We promise. Bulletin deletes will be there soon as well.

MySpace is going to Dodgers-Giants series and will NOT be working this weekend. So no new updates until Monday.

As he watched the Giants win, Anderson realized that the number of people in the ballpark—filled to capacity with about forty-one thousand fans—was about the same as the number of people who had signed up for MySpace so far. It seemed like MySpace was off to an impressive start.

By October MySpace had attracted one hundred thousand users and finally got noticed in the press—sort of. Influential blogger Jason Calacanis wrote an item titled "Another Day, Another Friendster Knockoff: MySpace Works the 'Free' Angle."

Calacanis noted that MySpace was touting itself as a free service but was hedging its bets by saying, "In the future, MySpace may add paid premium services." "Anyone know who is behind this site?" he asked.

The next day, a reader tipped Calacanis that MySpace was owned by eUniverse. But when Calacanis called eUniverse for a comment, the public relations person didn't call him back. "Perhaps they're embarrassed by the fact that they literally photocopied the Friendster.com site?" Calacanis speculated on his blog.

Neither Friendster nor MySpace anticipated the technical burden of running a social networking website. Unlike many websites that display static information, social networking pages are always changing.

Users were constantly updating their profile pages with new photos, adding new friends, and posting comments on their friends' pages. That meant that each time a user clicked on a profile, the website had to dynamically update all of the links contained on that page. Two of the most difficult tasks were calculating the number of friends in a person's network and calculating the degrees of separation between two members, both of which required massive amounts of memory and computing power.

With such a large user base, Friendster struggled to keep up. Often its servers would slow to a crawl and then crash completely. In October

2003 Friendster obtained $13 million in funding—at an astounding $53 million valuation—from some of Silicon Valley's top venture capitalists. Their plan was to bring Friendster up to speed.

Friendster, founded by engineers, wanted to be on the cutting edge of technology as it improved its service. It used its cash infusion to buy expensive equipment and hire top-flight engineers from the best Silicon Valley companies. Friendster hired two engineers who had written textbooks on Apache Tomcat, the kind of computer server that the company was using. Friendster also installed a $3 million storage network that had been implemented only one or two times before. The network proved to be buggy, so Friendster hired a new head of engineering, who ordered the fifteen-person engineering team to rewrite the software code underlying the entire Friendster website—a huge undertaking that stalled Friendster's development for nearly a year.

Meanwhile, MySpace, founded by a cash-strapped dot-com and run by marketers, had no appetite for expensive technology or programmers. Initially the site was powered by just two Dell computers, each with 4 gigabytes of memory, running a single database. Within one month of launch, MySpace needed more equipment. On September 24 MySpace requested that eUniverse purchase two more Dell servers, two Cisco switches, and a Dell PowerVault storage service for a total of $33,000. EUniverse leased the equipment through 0 percent no-cash-down leases.

MySpace developers quickly realized that the biggest drain on computer resources was the calculation of the degrees of separation between two members. Rather than throw resources at it, as Friendster was doing, MySpace decided to scrap the degrees of separation.

"Within a week (or maybe even less time, hard to remember), we realized that this network concept was really hard to scale," Anderson wrote later on his blog. "The site was slowing down trying to process this relationship each time you viewed a profile . . . To keep the site running fast, I decided to just get rid of the networking code and let everyone view everyone else. It took all of about five minutes for me to realize that users preferred this greatly—you guys are very vocal! Within minutes I got tons of comments and e-mails supporting the change. It turned out that very few people were interested in 'degrees' of friendship or the concept of a network."

Instead of calculating degrees of friendship, MySpace decided to simply make Tom everybody's first friend. "I made myself the first friend so that people could see each other on the site—when you signed up, everyone was connected through me," Anderson wrote on his blog. "If a user wanted to only see a network of people they actually knew, they could just remove me as a friend."

However, Anderson was not entirely honest with his MySpace friends. On his MySpace profile, he shaved a few years off his age—claiming to be born on October 13, 1975, instead of his actual birth date, November 8, 1970. Presumably, Anderson, then thirty-two, thought that pretending to be twenty-seven would more closely align himself with MySpace's youthful audience.

As a result of such quick fixes, MySpace's cobbled-together technology held up better than Friendster's expensive, overengineered technology. Soon Friendster's pages were taking twenty seconds to load, while MySpace pages were only taking two to three seconds.

Chapter 8

THE BOARDROOM COUP

By October 2003, eUniverse had $1.9 million in the bank and was losing $300,000 a month. The consultants who had helped with the restatement were owed payments that would likely total about $1 million over the next few months. Over the summer, eUniverse founder and chief executive Brad Greenspan had lined up a financing deal with VantagePoint Venture Partners, but the Silicon Valley firm's promised investment of an additional $10 million had not yet materialized.

Still, Greenspan saw the light at the end of the tunnel. In late August eUniverse had finally issued its restated results of the nine months ending December 31, 2002. The new results slashed revenue by $5.9 million and cut net income by $6.1 million for the nine-month period. Even so, eUniverse managed to eke out its second straight year of profitability—making just $553,000 on sales of $65.7 million at year-end.[1]

Most important, the company's stock had started trading again. Sure, it was only on the extremely unglamorous over-the-counter market, known as the "pink sheets," but it still gave the company some liquidity. By October eUniverse shares had climbed above $2 a share.

Greenspan started feeling that maybe he didn't have to accept VantagePoint's terms. After all, VantagePoint wanted to invest at a valuation of only $1.33 a share. VantagePoint also wanted to replace Greenspan as

---

[1] EUniverse's fiscal year-end was March 31, 2003.

CEO with a Silicon Valley Internet ad executive named George Garrick. Greenspan didn't like the fact that Garrick planned to continue living in the San Francisco Bay Area and commute down to Los Angeles four days a week. "George isn't an operator," Greenspan told VantagePoint. "I want a CEO with more experience."

Greenspan decided that he wanted a better financial backer than VantagePoint. However, the terms of his deal with VantagePoint prevented him from raising more than $2.5 million without triggering a repayment of VantagePoint's $2 million loan to eUniverse.

Soon Greenspan found an investment bank willing to raise $2.5 million for him: a San Francisco boutique called ThinkEquity Partners.

Meanwhile at MySpace, Chris DeWolfe was growing increasingly irritated with eUniverse. During the restatement, DeWolfe and his team had been patiently awaiting their earnout—the portion of profits that they were entitled to under the ResponseBase acquisition agreement.

DeWolfe believed that ResponseBase was owed about $500,000 by the end of October. But Greenspan kept stalling him, saying that the company didn't have any money to pay. Instead Greenspan proposed that in lieu of a cash payment, eUniverse could set up MySpace as a separate business unit with its own profit-sharing arrangement. Greenspan proposed that MySpace could get 10 percent of MySpace's after-tax profits for three years. This wasn't likely to be a very lucrative deal, since MySpace didn't have any prospect of reaching profitability anytime soon.

As eUniverse struggled to get back on its feet, it needed an experienced chief financial officer to get it back on track. On October 6 Tom Flahie was appointed chief financial officer. Flahie was a hardheaded businessman who had helped take the nutrition company Balance Bar public and sell it to Kraft Foods.

When he arrived at eUniverse, he was appalled at the organizational structure. There were dozens of business units, some with overlapping responsibilities. And he was totally opposed to the idea of setting up a new business unit for MySpace.

"We're not forming one more new entity!" Flahie told Brett Brewer. "This company already has too many."

On October 9 VantagePoint sent a letter asking for an extension of its exclusive negotiating period with eUniverse. The venture capitalists wanted to extend the deadline to October 17 so they could hammer out the last few details.

But Greenspan had other ideas. ThinkEquity was willing to raise $2.5 million at $1.85 a share. VantagePoint was offering to invest $8 million at $1.33 a share. From Greenspan's point of view, ThinkEquity was offering a better deal. Not only was it a higher price, but raising less money meant that he didn't have to shrink his ownership stake as much. As the biggest individual shareholder in eUniverse, with a 21.31 percent stake, Greenspan felt that the company could raise money again in a few months when it needed to, and probably at an even better valuation.

ThinkEquity also was willing to invest in common stock, while VantagePoint wanted preferred stock. Preferred stock owners generally have more rights than common stock owners. In this case, VantagePoint's preferred stock would have a guaranteed dividend, a guaranteed amount of board representation, and would provide VantagePoint with the right to block eUniverse from doing other financing or corporate deals unless two-thirds of the board overrode VantagePoint. Greenspan hated the idea that VantagePoint would have so much power over his company.

Of course, there was also the fact that ThinkEquity wasn't demanding his resignation as chief executive.

DeWolfe was on his way to the Direct Marketing Association conference in Orlando, Florida. But before he left, he dashed off a note to Greenspan saying that he thought his team should get 100 percent of the MySpace assets in return for forgiving the $500,000 owed to ResponseBase. "Although MySpace revenue model is unproven, we are excited about the project," he wrote to Greenspan on October 12.

In return, DeWolfe offered to hand over ResponseBase's future products—and its contracts in China—to eUniverse's other e-commerce division. In particular, DeWolfe was excited about XoomDigital—a tiny wireless video camera that could be used for spying.

XoomDigital competed with the X-10, a tiny "security" camera, which had flooded the Internet with pop-up advertisements featuring pictures of seductive women, implying that customers could use the tiny camera to spy on women. The X-10's pop-up ads had become a huge nuisance on the Internet. Even as its business was shutting down, ResponseBase was flooding the Internet with e-mails promoting XoomDigital as an alternative wireless video camera that was "smaller than the X-10."

"We have quite a bit planned for XoomDigital we could hand over, to make it compete with X-10," DeWolfe wrote.

DeWolfe suggested that the trade-off could be a "tenable solution that could be a win-win for everyone."

EUniverse didn't agree.

On October 16 Greenspan presented the idea of his alternative investment to the board. Desperate for cash, the members agreed to pursue both sets of financings simultaneously. "Because of the company's cash position, the company should consummate the transaction able to close in the shortest time frame," the board declared.

But some board members were starting to suspect that eUniverse's motives and Greenspan's motives were not aligned. The company needed a huge chunk of cash as soon as possible, but Greenspan seemed to be seeking a deal that would primarily preserve his own equity.

Amid all the chaos over financing, Greenspan was also trying to change the makeup of the board. On October 17 he proposed a new slate for the coming year, which would remove the chairman of the audit committee, Larry Moreau.

Greenspan had just appointed Moreau to the board in May. But in July the *Los Angeles Business Journal* wrote an article pointing out that Moreau had a spotty track record in his previous stints as chief financial officer.

But Greenspan's timing was awkward. The SEC investigation of eUniverse's restatement wasn't complete. The board wasn't ready to throw out the head of the audit committee in the midst of an investigation.

The board conference call was heated. Greenspan nominated a new slate of directors that he said would "upgrade the quality of the board." But others on the board opposed him. When Greenspan's motion failed, he became irate and threatened to resign.[2]

Finally the VantagePoint deal was nearing completion. The lawyers had hammered out most of the points. VantagePoint managing director David Carlick flew to Los Angeles on Tuesday, October 22, to finalize the deal. When Carlick arrived at eUniverse's offices, Greenspan was sit-

---

[2] Greenspan denies threatening to resign. The board minutes say that he did.

ting in his chair, one leg crossed, and his foot was vibrating. He was angry. "We have other financing," Greenspan told Carlick. "You took too long."

"The people at VantagePoint are not going to be happy about this at all," Carlick replied.

Greenspan explained that he had rounded up $2.5 million at $1.85 a share. "You can invest on the same terms as the new offering," Greenspan proposed.

Carlick wasn't interested. "We will consider legal options," he replied.

Greenspan became enraged. "Get out of my office!" he said, pointing his finger at Carlick. "I'm not going to do your deal."

Carlick slunk out of the office, wondering how he had so misjudged Greenspan. But Greenspan's action wasn't totally out of the blue. Carlick had been hearing from other board members that they were growing frustrated with Greenspan. In fact, Carlick had agreed to attend a secret meeting with some eUniverse board members to discuss Greenspan's erratic behavior.

Carlick walked downstairs to the outdoor parking structure behind eUniverse's office building to wait for Larry Moreau to pick him up. Moreau did not want to be seen at eUniverse, so Carlick hid behind the elevator bank until Moreau arrived in his Acura Infiniti Q45.

The two drove off to the Del Ray Yacht Club, where they met eUniverse director Jeff Edell for a clandestine rendezvous. It wasn't totally kosher for Carlick to be negotiating his financing deal directly with the board of directors instead of with the chief executive. But Moreau had called the three together to discuss their options in the face of Greenspan's opposition.

Edell, a nephew of the syndicated radio show host Dr. Dean Edell, had just joined the eUniverse board two weeks earlier. He and Brewer were colleagues in the Young Presidents' Organization. For three years the two had been part of a group of company presidents who met monthly for confidential discussions. After the restatement, Brewer had recruited Edell to join the board and help clean up the company.

Once he arrived at eUniverse, Edell was shocked by Greenspan's behavior. Within a week, he had gotten into a shouting match with the chief executive. Greenspan had apologized. "I pledge to try not to get so hot around the collar and will work on not losing my cool," Greenspan wrote in an e-mail to Edell two days before the yacht club meeting. But Edell wasn't convinced that Greenspan was going to change, and he worried that the CEO was putting his own interests ahead of the company's.

Over lunch, Edell laid out the concessions he wanted from Vantage-Point.

"If you change those things in your deal by Monday, the board will have no choice but to vote on it," Edell said to Carlick.

That night Carlick and Brett Brewer had dinner together at Vito, an upscale Italian restaurant in Santa Monica.

Carlick was horrified at Greenspan's behavior in the office and asked Brewer if this type of conduct was typical.

Unfortunately, such violent mood swings were part of Greenspan's character, Brewer said. Carlick said that VantagePoint would not wire money until it had an agreement with eUniverse, and that agreement had to include a commitment from Greenspan to hire a new CEO.

Brewer himself was starting to have his doubts about Greenspan. Over the next two days, as Greenspan continued to insist that VantagePoint had to go, Brewer realized that he would have to choose between his friend and the company.

Brewer discussed the problem with eUniverse's top executives: Chris Lipp, the general counsel; Flahie, the chief financial officer; and Adam Goldenberg, the chief operating officer. They all believed that eUniverse desperately needed VantagePoint's investment in order to survive. The decision to back VantagePoint was hardest for Goldenberg, who considered Greenspan his best friend and mentor. "At that point, I would have made him best man at my wedding," Goldenberg recalled. But ultimately Goldenberg agreed with his colleagues that eUniverse needed the VantagePoint investment.

Together the eUniverse executives decided to do what they could to keep the VantagePoint deal alive.

By Friday, October 23, Greenspan had $2.3 million in escrow from ThinkEquity and was set to close the financing on Monday. He knew that the company would need more money soon, but he hoped that with a cash infusion, eUniverse could get back on its feet and raise another round on even better terms.

On Sunday Greenspan was feeling bullish enough to fly to San Francisco for the day to negotiate an improved compensation package for himself with eUniverse board member Dan Mosher. The two childhood friends sat together drinking beers at a bar in Noe Valley, watching a Dallas Cowboys football game and debating whether Greenspan really deserved the increased compensation he was seeking.

Greenspan thought he had pulled off a victory—he had raised money for eUniverse and negotiated a new deal for himself that included two years of severance. He couldn't have been more wrong.

On Monday, October 27, a carefully orchestrated coup at eUniverse was set in motion.

At nine in the morning, Brewer, Lipp, and Flahie walked into Greenspan's office and said they planned to resign if he didn't close the VantagePoint deal. Greenspan said he didn't care—he could run the place without them.

At ten o'clock, Greenspan started the board conference call and launched into a discussion of the ThinkEquity financing without mentioning the management resignations.

Board member Jeff Edell said, "Wait a minute, Brad. Isn't there something you need to tell us? Tom Flahie is my friend, and I know that he just submitted his resignation. I think that's a material event."

Greenspan realized that they must all be in it together.

He admitted that eUniverse's top four officers had threatened to quit if he remained as CEO. But he said he was confident that he could find replacements for them all. Then, sensing that Edell was part of the conspiracy, Greenspan asked Edell to resign.

Edell listened to Greenspan's tirade and quietly sent a text message to Carlick at VantagePoint: "You need to send your proposal to the board in the next hour."

Carlick was pacing in his office in San Bruno, California. He needed one of the fund's two directors to sign the eUniverse financing term sheet before he could send it over. One was on vacation, and he had finally rounded up the other. But now the director was peppering Carlick with questions about all the details of the term sheet. Meanwhile, Carlick was getting pelted with messages from the eUniverse board, who were anxious for a commitment they could consider. Finally Carlick lost his patience. "Look, this thing has been agreed to six ways from Sunday! There's a boardroom vote going on—you've got to sign!"

The director signed.

Lipp acted surprised when the VantagePoint e-mail arrived in the middle of the board meeting. "I've just received the proposal from VantagePoint," he told the board.

Greenspan was stunned. He was alone in his office on a speakerphone. He realized it had all been well thought out. "This is fraud," Greenspan protested. "Either close my deal, or you will defraud the common stock investors."

But the board ignored his protests. Edell asked another board member, Dan Mosher, to call VantagePoint to discuss the deal terms.

Brewer, Lipp, and Flahie reiterated that they would resign if Greenspan refused to close the VantagePoint deal. Flahie explained that the company was in a cash emergency. The $2.5 million that Greenspan wanted to raise from ThinkEquity would only be a "temporary and inadequate solution to the company's liquidity crisis," he told the board.

Greenspan argued that eUniverse was endangering the company by *not* accepting the money that he had already raised. He said the uncertainty was causing the company's stock to decline. The board should accept the $2.5 million "to avoid a further drop in share price."

Greenspan added that he would resign if the board approved the VantagePoint deal. "You are trying to become CEO of this company," he accused Edell.

That night Greenspan went home and signed all the documents approving the $2.5 million ThinkEquity financing. He knew the board wouldn't be happy, but he told himself that the members had authorized him to close whichever deal he could finish first.

The next day, the directors were shocked when they learned that Greenspan had signed the financing deal without their approval. They began discussing how to remove him as CEO. They agreed to work out a lucrative severance package and consulting deal for Greenspan if he agreed not to sue the company.

That night Greenspan took his top executives, Brewer, Lipp, Flahie, and Goldenberg, to dinner at the shopping mall across the street from eUniverse's office. It still hadn't sunk in that they had all turned against him. He tried to persuade them to join him in opposing the VantagePoint deal. He was alternately contrite and threatening. But his friends were not persuaded.

Late that night, October 28, Edell sent a note to the board recounting the dinner. "Tonight he played all the cards. Emotion, kindness, insults, and threats. We must stick together and *not* allow any new tactic or game to deter us. VantagePoint is ready to sign tomorrow . . ."

MySpace was still seeking its $500,000 earnout. The morning after Greenspan took his colleagues out to dinner, MySpace's Josh Berman sent an e-mail to eUniverse's controller claiming that his revised calculations showed that ResponseBase was owed an additional $47,000 on top of the previous calculations.

Flahie was outraged. The more he looked at it, the more it seemed that ResponseBase was owed nothing. After all, its division had caused a restatement and was losing money. In the six months ending in September, ResponseBase had the second-highest revenue of any division of eUniverse, with sales of $5.4 million, but it was unprofitable, losing $50,000. ResponseBase also had a relatively large staff of thirty-six employees (out of a total of two hundred seventy at eUniverse) who were now spending all their time on a tiny, unprofitable website called MySpace. Flahie suggested that MySpace's assets should be divided into thirds—eUniverse would keep two-thirds, and MySpace would keep one-third. It was an unorthodox approach because it made it difficult for either party to sell assets. After all, how do you sell one-third of a computer server? But Flahie was stubborn. It was his way or the highway.

The next morning, October 30, Greenspan resigned as chief executive. The next day, Friday, eUniverse finalized the VantagePoint agreement, selling VantagePoint 5.3 million shares of preferred stock for $8 million—a valuation of $1.50 a share.

For a few days, it seemed like everybody could be happy. The board offered Greenspan a package to stay on as chief strategic officer. VantagePoint was able to invest and begin a search for a new CEO. The company had enough money to get back on its feet. And, maybe, everyone could stay friends.

But everything fell apart on Wednesday night. Greenspan was having dinner with Goldenberg and Brewer at his favorite sushi joint, Tengu, in Westwood Village, to discuss the terms of his exit.

"You lost me millions of dollars of options," Greenspan said. "How are you going to make it up to me?"

Goldenberg was incensed. "Are you fucking joking?" he said. "We busted our butts for years to make this company work." To Goldenberg, it was ludicrous for Greenspan to be quibbling about his stock options, when Greenspan still owned a massive stake in eUniverse. After all, if eUniverse survived its financial crisis, Greenspan would get the biggest payday of anybody. "To hell with this," Goldenberg muttered, and stormed out of the restaurant, knocking over a chair as he left.

Greenspan then turned to Brewer and started in with the same complaints. But Brewer had also had enough of Greenspan. "Forget it," he said.

Greenspan stormed out of the restaurant as well.

Brewer was left alone at the table, eating his edamame. Through the restaurant window, he watched Greenspan waiting for his car to arrive from the valet. It was the end of their friendship.

Greenspan turned down eUniverse's exit package, which would have required him to give up his rights to sue eUniverse. On December 11 Greenspan quit the board and filed a lawsuit alleging that the directors breached their fiduciary duty in accepting the VantagePoint financing and changing the composition of the board to entrench themselves. In court, most of Greenspan's claims were dismissed, but one survived. It emerged that eUniverse had placed two current directors in the seats that were designated for Sony's appointees without seeking approval from Sony. But when eUniverse belatedly won Sony's approval for the move, Greenspan dropped his final legal claim.

Still, he wasn't done fighting. In the new year, Greenspan launched an aggressive proxy contest against eUniverse, running his own slate of directors against eUniverse's four nominees. Greenspan and Brewer, former roommates, friends, and colleagues, were now on opposing sides. The two separately crisscrossed the country, meeting with eUniverse's investors to try to persuade them to vote for their candidates.

It was an exhausting and vitriolic battle. Greenspan argued that eUniverse's preferred shareholders—VantagePoint and Sony—had effectively seized control of the company from the common stockholders by stacking the board with their representatives. Greenspan also warned that eUniverse had violated the rules of the Nasdaq stock exchange, on which eUniverse was hoping to get relisted once it got back on its feet.

Greenspan proved to be right on that point: Nasdaq did not approve eUniverse's listing, and the company ultimately ended up on the American Stock Exchange.

For his part, Brewer argued to investors that their only hope of recouping their investment in eUniverse was to stick with the current management. After all, it was under Greenspan's watch that the accounting restatement had happened, and it had become clear that Greenspan wasn't able to lead the company out of its troubles. In a January 7, 2004, mailing to shareholders, eUniverse declared: "Greenspan wanted to protect his job, not your investment."

Many investors were justifiably confused. It could be argued that VantagePoint had capitalized on the fact that the company was crippled financially and managerially in order to gain advantageous financial terms for itself. But Greenspan had also proven himself incapable of leading eUniverse back to financial health, spending time apportioning blame rather than positioning the company for the future.

Chapter 9

THE FIX-IT-LATER PHILOSOPHY

On November 4, 2003, Tom Anderson was exhausted. It was six in the morning, and he had been up all night trying to fix the MySpace website, which had crashed.

Anderson had just returned from a trip to China. EUniverse was in the process of shutting down ResponseBase's operations in China and the United States while ramping up MySpace. In the meantime, Anderson was working both jobs.

Before departing, he had warned MySpace's several thousand members that he would be gone and that the site might be unattended for a while.

"Hey folks. I'm going to Hong Kong, leaving 2:00 am on Tuesday morning," Anderson wrote on his MySpace blog on October 20. "So, I'll be offline for 15 hours while I travel. Might not get online until later that night, so it could be a whole 24 hours. Unbelievable. Hehe."

When Anderson returned to Los Angeles on Halloween, he immediately started adding new features to the site, such as a classifieds section and more places where the "online now" status could be seen. As usual, the features were rushed out without much testing, and the site soon crashed. MySpace put up a game of Pac-Man for users to play while waiting for the site to restart.

At six in the morning, after a night of fruitless troubleshooting, Anderson posted an update on his blog:

Starting around 6:00pm last night there were some major probs with MySpace. Sorry for those who could not login. Tried to put up a game of Pacman for you to play while I was waiting. I actually got distracted/hooked and played it for 9 minutes. Reminds me of when I used to play Pacman for 3 hours after school on one quarter.

But, in any case, even the Pacman wasn't working for most people. Will give you an update when I wake up in a few hours. And we'll try to get some game working, so you can play whenever the site is being updated.

MySpace's philosophy was "Get it out fast, fix it later," according to chief technologist Aber Whitcomb. That philosophy was the antithesis of the Silicon Valley point of view, which values getting the technology right. In Silicon Valley, startups often work for months in "'stealth mode" secretly developing features and programs and hoping that nobody gets wind of their idea. MySpace took the opposite approach, throwing a totally unworkable website online and trying to fix problems on the fly—all while constantly adding new features that crashed the site.

MySpace's philosophy meant that users dictated the site's focus. If a feature didn't prove popular, MySpace didn't waste time perfecting it. In the early days, the site offered a grab bag of features ranging from games, to HotOrNot-type picture ratings, to Evite-style invitations, but only a few survived.

Still, MySpace's approach was not easy for its developers. Peter Amiri, who was hired in October to manage a team of developers, was constantly trying to find more time for the developers to test new features before the code was "pushed out." "When I joined, the way we pushed out code was that somebody would walk through the developers' area and ask for code that they thought was ready for release," he said. "We would push it out, and then the site would go down for four hours."

After numerous debates, Amiri finally got Anderson and Aber Whitcomb to agree that new features would go live on the site only on Tuesdays and Thursdays, so that the developers would have time to test the new features before they were released. But two days later, on a Wednesday, Anderson called Amiri and asked if he could "push code out this morning"—violating the agreement they had just struck.

Amiri argued with Anderson for forty-five minutes before finally relenting. "Fine, send me the code, and I'll see what I can do," he said.

"Okay, I'll get the developer to build it and send it over," Anderson replied.

Amiri was amazed. *We just spent forty-five minutes arguing about code you haven't built yet?* he thought.

But that was the environment MySpace operated in—everything had to be done yesterday. Quality was secondary to speed. The quest for speed was driven in large part by Tom Anderson's passion. In a blog posting, on Thursday, October 16, at 3:31 a.m., Anderson revealed the toll that his frenzied pace was taking on him: "Not sure how long I can keep going sleeping two to four hours a night. This has been quite an experience."

MySpace users were surprisingly tolerant of the site's quirks, in part because Anderson's humorous and self-deprecating blog postings and news updates created a sense of intimacy between them.

A typical notice from Anderson appeared on October 10, 2003: "Hey Folks—The site was a little slow from 1:00pm–5:00pm today; we were installing a new image server. WHY?? Seems you all like to upload lots of pics and we ran out of space!"

Anderson highlighted that intimacy by hosting parties for MySpace members to meet one another—and to meet him. The first party was organized by MySpace member Gary Sato, a Los Angeles club promoter who hosted parties every Tuesday night at Barfly, a trendy nightclub on the Sunset Strip in Hollywood. On November 11, Veterans Day, Sato invited the MySpace crowd to Barfly.

"YES, I will actually be OFFLINE!" Anderson wrote on his blog. "If the system goes down while we're at the party, then deal with it. You lose cause you didn't come to the party :) ! The first fifty guests will receive a MySpace T-shirt."

By the end of the night, the club, which could hold six hundred people, was packed. But the attendees were predominantly male. One woman who attended the party left soon after arriving because "it was all dudes."

Still, parties were a cheap way to market MySpace and stir enthusiasm among the members, so Anderson began flying around the country, hosting a series of ad hoc MySpace parties—including one on December

5 in New York and another on January 12 in Miami. "I'm going to Miami this weekend and want to have a MySpace party on MONDAY. This Monday," Anderson wrote on his blog on a Tuesday.

"So, Floridians, please discuss amongst yourselves how we should do this, and where . . . can you guys figure it out? I don't got time to plan this thing! Haha Sorta last minute, but go here to vote it's now between Purdy & Marlin . . . OK and start finding some fake IDs for the Under 21. we can pool together something right?"

On New Year's Eve 2003, MySpace got a safety wake-up call. At 11:57 p.m. that night, a twenty-seven-year-old Miami nightclub worker named RJ Lockwood called 911 from his cell phone. There was no sound on the line, and because it was a cell phone, police could not trace the location.

Four days later, RJ's roommates came home and found him dead on the floor of their loft apartment in Overtown, a drug-infested Miami neighborhood. RJ had been shot in the chest and was still holding his phone. Nothing had been stolen from the apartment. His friends immediately suspected that his death might have had something to do with a relationship he had struck up with a girl named Kaytlynn, whom he met on MySpace. Katylynn had a boyfriend, but after a whirlwind six-week cyber-courtship with RJ, she had promised that she would break up with her boyfriend and get together with him on January 1.

By the time MySpace heard about the murder, it was too late for the police to gather much information. MySpace hadn't captured any information from RJ or Katylynn's pages at the time of the crime, allowing for the possibility that the suspects could have deleted incriminating comments or e-mails from RJ's or Katylynn's profiles. RJ's murder remains unsolved today.

It was the first murder to be connected with MySpace. MySpace staffer Jason Feffer realized that the website needed someone who could help police capture information from MySpace pages soon after a crime. Feffer, whose father was a Los Angeles Superior Court judge, volunteered to set up a system of storing files and a twenty-four-hour hotline phone number that police could call for assistance. Soon Feffer became known internally as head of MySpace's "Fef.B.I." division.

...

By the end of 2003, the eUniverse board had to decide what to do about the earnout money it allegedly owed to its now-defunct ResponseBase division. Chris DeWolfe and Josh Berman argued that they were owed about $400,000. EUniverse disputed the figure and, according to Chairman of the Board Jeff Edell, "couldn't afford it" anyway.

On December 17, the two sides agreed to a compromise: ResponseBase would trade its earnout for a one-third stake in MySpace. The one-third stake would primarily be owned by DeWolfe and Anderson, with smaller stakes shared among MySpace's Berman, Whitcomb, Colin Digiaro, and Kyle Brinkman. "We thought we made a great deal because we didn't think they had anything," Edell said.

Still, the board was divided about the prospect of funding MySpace's future losses. MySpace was entering a crowded field. Dozens of social networks such as Tribe.net and Ryze were attracting much more buzz than MySpace. And none of the new social networks was making money.

Board member Andrew Sheehan, a managing director at Vantage-Point Venture Partners, proposed a compromise. "Can't we do this with little or no capital?" he asked. EUniverse and MySpace agreed to jointly create a budget for MySpace, with initial funding of $50,000. Once MySpace became profitable, it would receive quarterly distributions of one-third of the division's profits. The agreement also gave MySpace a "put" option, which required eUniverse to purchase the one-third stake in MySpace in the event that eUniverse received a bona fide offer for the eUniverse business.

With such tight purse strings at eUniverse, MySpace was constantly battling to get more computer equipment. The site's requests for new servers would often take months to get fulfilled. In the meantime, its staff would sometimes steal servers that were being delivered to other divisions of eUniverse. "The other divisions got pissed," said eUniverse chief technology officer Jeff Rajewski. One division had to wait two months for its servers because every time the division ordered them, MySpace grabbed them first.

Finally, in January 2004, as MySpace was nearing its millionth member, the site got its first batch of ten brand-new large-scale computer servers. "We were so proud of taking ten servers, imaging them, and installing them in two days' time," MySpace developer Amiri said. "Prior to that, we were running off of used IBM boxes that had been salvaged from the ResponseBase era."

With no marketing budget, MySpace had to use guerrilla marketing to attract users. In the evenings, DeWolfe and Anderson prowled the Viper Room in Hollywood, the celebrated nightclub founded by actor Johnny Depp and best known for the fact that actor River Phoenix died of a drug overdose on the sidewalk outside the club in 1993. Even with its credentials among celebrities and gossip columnists, the Viper Room's cover charge was low, there was no dress code, and nobodies could gain entrance if they were willing to wait in line. The place was crawling with wannabe actors, screenwriters, models, and musicians. At least once a week, after work, the two would go to a show at the Viper Room and try to recruit musicians to use MySpace as a marketing tool.

They had a compelling sales pitch. With the music industry in a slump, which it blamed on Internet piracy, many big acts, such as Madonna and Britney Spears, were starting to use the big portals—AOL, MSN, and Yahoo—as promotional vehicles by offering online listeners the first chance to hear their songs. The results were striking: In October 2003 AOL attracted more than three million listeners to Spears's debut of "Me Against the Music." But smaller bands couldn't get onto the AOL lineup any easier than they could get a recording contract, and their other online options were limited. The website mp3.com, which had provided independent musicians with a place to stream their music, had been shut down in late 2003 after being sued by record labels for copyright infringement.

MySpace offered musicians what amounted to free online marketing. Even penniless, unknown bands could set up a profile on MySpace for free and then could connect with fans through the website immediately.

Based just on word of mouth, DeWolfe and Anderson recruited more than five thousand acts to set up profiles on MySpace by March. In a press release announcing the milestone, Anderson crowed, "MySpace is fast becoming what mp3.com should have been: a place for fans to find music."

In March, MySpace hired Gabe Harriman to build a music player. One of MySpace's original developers, Harriman had left soon after My-

Space launched to set up his own consulting business. Anderson wanted Harriman to build something similar to the player on a website called PureVolume. A lot of local bands were loading their music onto Pure-Volume and letting listeners stream the music using Flash technology.

Harriman worked on the player for three months, but in the middle of June, he took his planned vacation to Mexico's Cabo San Lucas for a week. That proved to be too much of a delay for the fast-moving MySpace team. While Harriman was gone, MySpace decided to bring the project in-house and asked Harriman to give up his copyright to the work he had done.

Harriman was furious at his old colleagues. "They left me hanging out to dry," he said. He hired a lawyer and eventually won a small monetary settlement in exchange for giving up his rights to the code. (After the dispute, MySpace terminated Harriman's status as the first MySpace account.) Finally, in July, MySpace launched its music player and asked all the bands on the site to register themselves as a "band" in order to use it. Bands also got to rename their MySpace pages with real names, such as the group Weezer's myspace.com/weezer, instead of the previous user ID number. Eventually everyone on MySpace was given that opportunity.

One of the early bands on MySpace was a group of four guys from New Jersey called the Billionaire Boys Club. The independent band had been promoting itself on Friendster but switched to MySpace in December 2003.

"Friendster is so two months ago," bassist Leigh Nelson wrote on the band's Web journal on December 11, 2003. "We've had a profile there for a few months, and though it's still a cool site, we've found the latest and greatest: MySpace." Nelson was impressed with MySpace's music ranking system, in which members could vote to determine the top songs on the site.

In April Anderson invited the Billionaire Boys Club to play at MySpace's New York party at the Plaid nightclub—singer/actress Courtney Love had just been arrested there the previous week.

"We hung around after the show," drummer Matt Lewis recounted on the band's website, "and Tom from MySpace (who happens to be the nicest guy ever) hooked us up with some of those overpriced bottles of vodka that come with O.J. and cranberry juice for mixing."

"We danced all night . . . and usually we are not ones to dance," added

Nelson, in a posting on the band's MySpace blog. "It's 6:28 a.m. eastern time, daylight savings time is in effect, and it's finally time to call it a night."

Another surefire way to attract viewers, as any marketer knows, is to feature scantily clad attractive girls. This was particularly true for MySpace, which, like its rival Friendster, was aimed at introducing people who might want to date one another. Most dating sites at the time, such as eUniverse's CupidJunction, failed because they attracted too many men and too few women. So attracting women—and, hopefully, attractive women—to MySpace was a priority.

At one of MySpace's parties in Los Angeles in May, Anderson met someone who could guarantee a steady stream of attractive women to MySpace events: Ted Skillet, whose roommate was Michael Vincent, a budding Hollywood photographer. Vincent specialized in what he describes as "shooting booty." His erotic photos of practically naked women were shot in the style of the popular men's magazine *Maxim,* which carved out a middle ground between pornographic magazines and traditional men's magazines like *GQ. Maxim* simply proclaimed itself a promoter of "Hot Girls, Sex, Sports, Technology, and Stupid Jokes." Soon dozens of *Maxim* imitators crowded the field. Vincent's new breed of photography fit right into the new, flesh-baring milieu of popular culture.

For years Vincent and Skillet had been promoting Vincent's photography at nightclub events. Vincent would waive his usual $500 fee and shoot photographs of all the attractive girls that showed up at the club. Aspiring models would flock to the club, hoping to be discovered by a famous photographer. Club owners would pay Vincent a fee of $5,000 to $10,000 for bringing in a glamorous crowd. "I'm like a mini Hugh Hefner in the fact that I control massive amounts of women," Vincent claimed.

Together Anderson, Vincent, and Skillet decided to use similar nightclub events to promote MySpace. In June 2004 they embarked on a seventeen-city tour with nightclub parties for MySpace, starting in Los Angeles and then heading across the country to stops including Florida, Texas, and Chicago. Anderson promoted the parties through banner advertisements on MySpace. Skillet hired the DJs and the clubs, and Vincent brought the girls. MySpace was still a small social network, so the parties helped create a feeling of membership in an exclusive club. "We helped create a cool buzz about MySpace," Vincent said.

Men showed up at the parties to gawk at the models. Even more enticing was the possibility of becoming "friends" with the women they admired. Eventually the pictures of aspiring models on MySpace became so risqué that the site had to start using image review software. Feffer's staffers began viewing the pictures being uploaded to the site to make sure they weren't pornographic. Still, a lot of images slipped through the cracks.

If you knew what keywords to search under, "ninety-nine percent of the time, you could get a nude image," recalled MySpace developer Amiri.

Rumors were flying that Friendster was about to release a paid subscription service. So in April, MySpace developed its own competing paid service: Members who paid a monthly fee would be allowed access to special features such as extra photo storage. The service was ready to roll out—but didn't. MySpace was waiting for Friendster to make the first move.

But in April Friendster fired its founding chief executive, Jonathan Abrams, and hired a new chief executive, Tim Koogle, the former president and CEO of Yahoo. Koogle was a big believer in online advertising and decided to abandon Friendster's plans for a premium service in favor of an entirely advertising-supported business model. MySpace also put the idea of charging fees on the back burner.

With its renewed commitment to online advertising, MySpace also realized that it had to open up its website to the outside world. Prior to April, only MySpace members could view the profiles of other MySpace members. As a result, the metric that was most closely watched at MySpace was the number of daily sign-ups. "If we had five thousand sign-ups, it was a good day, ten thousand was a great day, and one thousand was a bad day," Amiri said.

But if advertising was going to be the company's revenue source, MySpace needed viewers more than it needed members. So in April, My-

Space dropped the membership requirement and allowed anybody to view member profiles. Sign-ups initially plummeted from ten thousand a day to a few thousand a day as lurkers realized they didn't need to join MySpace to check out the pages of MySpace members. But the number of pages viewed by each MySpace visitor soared. By July MySpace visitors were viewing more than twice as many pages per visit (690,000) as they had in May (269,000).

Voyeurism had suddenly become the hallmark of MySpace.

Chapter 10

OPERATION SHOW TIME

By January 2004 eUniverse president Brett Brewer was exhausted. He had been on the road for forty straight days, fighting a grueling proxy battle against ousted eUniverse chief executive Brad Greenspan. Brewer had been in Maine on the coldest day of the year. He had run into Greenspan in the lobby of a hotel in Delaware. He had been deposed by Greenspan's lawyers. All the while, Brewer was trying to run the company, search for a CEO, and convince eUniverse's investors to vote against Greenspan's proposed slate of directors at the upcoming annual meeting. Driving west on Interstate 10, on his way to his Pacific Palisades home to pick up some clothes for another three-day trip, Brewer thought to himself, *I just can't do this alone anymore.*

His mind turned to his neighbor, Richard Rosenblatt. Brewer first met Rosenblatt through Greenspan. Later, when Brewer moved into Rosenblatt's neighborhood, he kept up the acquaintance with Rosenblatt, playing tennis occasionally and chatting about business. Rosenblatt wasn't the perfect choice for eUniverse—the company needed an operations guy who could make the trains run on time, and Rosenblatt was more of a marketing guy. But Brewer suddenly wanted Rosenblatt for another reason: "I just wanted his positive energy."

Rosenblatt, then thirty-four, was an enthusiastic personality. He sent his friends e-mails saying "luv ya" and "friends for life," and, like a true salesman, sold himself as much as he sold his businesses. He made his first million dollars as a senior in college at the University of California,

Los Angeles. While selling ads for a weekly newspaper near campus, Rosenblatt realized that some out-of-town advertisers were paying too much for their classified ads. They didn't know the market, so they were paying the price on the newspaper's published rate card. Rosenblatt knew that nobody really paid those rates—most advertisers negotiated lower rates. So in 1991 he and his girlfriend Lisa started brokering ads for out-of-town advertisers in all the local community newspapers in Los Angeles. Rosenblatt's firm, R&R Advertising, took a 15 percent commission. In its peak year, the business earned about $1 million.

After college, Rosenblatt went straight to law school at the University of Southern California. By his final year, he was spending more time on the pay phone negotiating advertising deals than in the classroom. Still, he graduated with honors, and went to work at a big law firm. But Rosenblatt soon discovered that corporate life at a big law firm was not for him.

Rosenblatt was intrigued by what his father was telling him about the World Wide Web. It was the early days of the Internet—at that time, new software called Mosaic had just come out that let people access the Web easily. Most people outside of academia and the defense industry were still unaware of the Internet, but Rosenblatt's father had been using it for years. In 1994 Rosenblatt's father quit his job as a vice president at the defense contractor Titan Corporation to start a Web development company.

Rosenblatt was quickly sold on the idea that the Web was a great untapped marketing opportunity. After working six months at the law firm, he quit and began trying to persuade his advertising clients to build websites. Some agreed, although many had no idea what they were buying. To help explain the Web to his clients, Rosenblatt teamed up with a company in Utah to form what became iMall, which allowed businesses to set up their own storefronts in a virtual mall. Together they developed a $2,995 training course for business owners to build their own Internet destinations. The price included two websites built by Rosenblatt and his father's company, which iMall acquired for $160,000 in stock.

In 1995 the Internet landscape changed dramatically with the initial public offering of Netscape Communications. A few months later, in January 1996, iMall capitalized on the stock market's subsequent frenzy for all things Internet by going public. The stock opened at $18 and within a few months had soared as high as $112.

By 1997, however, iMall shares had sunk to $9, and the company was close to declaring bankruptcy. The training course business had never been profitable, and the e-commerce business was still too tiny to amount to anything. In July Rosenblatt took over as CEO and immediately set about raising money to keep iMall afloat. Just as he got the company back on its feet, the seminar business came under fire from regulators. In May of 1998 the Federal Trade Commission teamed up with twenty-five state regulatory agencies to launch "Operation Show Time," a coordinated attack on deceptive practices in the seminar business. One of the first targets of Operation Show Time was iMall, which received a cease and desist order from the Maryland Securities Division.

Government regulators were concerned about iMall's promotional claims that people who had attended its Internet seminars were earning as much as $11,000 a month from their websites—a claim the FTC said was untrue.

Rosenblatt quickly shut down the seminar business, slashing the company's revenues from $20 million to $500,000, and started marketing the company as a one-stop shop for businesses to build a website. In 1999 iMall agreed to pay a $750,000 fine to the Federal Trade Commission. As the newly installed CEO, Rosenblatt avoided prosecution. But his partners, Mark Comer and Craig Pickering, agreed to pay a combined $3.25 million fine and were barred for life from selling or promoting any Internet-related business opportunities.

Despite the battle with the regulators, two months later, in July 1999, Rosenblatt still managed to turn around and sell iMall for $425 million in stock to Excite@Home—one of the hottest Internet properties in Silicon Valley. Excite@Home was the result of a merger between the Web portal Excite and a broadband provider called @Home. During the heady days of 1999 and 2000, Excite@Home had some of the hippest offices in Silicon Valley—with a fire-engine-red slide between floors—and a market valuation of $35 billion.

Rosenblatt sold iMall just as the dot-com market was bursting. By the time the iMall acquisition closed in October, Excite@Home shares had fallen so low that the deal was worth only $347 million. Still, Rosenblatt's 16.3 percent stake was worth about $56 million; he celebrated by buying himself a Ferrari.

Once Rosenblatt was known as the turnaround artist from iMall, other ailing dot-coms sought his expertise. Commonwealth Associates, which had backed iMall, presented Rosenblatt with a difficult but irresistibly high-profile opportunity: rescuing the ailing website Drkoop.com. The site, founded by former U.S. surgeon general C. Everett Koop, was one of the most spectacular boom-and-bust stories of the dot-com bubble.

Founded in 1999, Drkoop.com had a successful initial public offering and then went on a spending spree—agreeing to pay $89 million over four years for prominent placement on America Online—and was basically out of money in less than a year. Based in Austin, Texas, it was grossly overstaffed, with two hundred employees, a full-time masseuse, catered meals, and expensive furniture. Rosenblatt saw an opportunity to cut costs and turn it around.

In August 2000 Rosenblatt and Commonwealth raised $27 million for Drkoop days before it filed for bankruptcy. Commonwealth asked Rosenblatt to act as interim CEO. He quickly fired half the staff, streamlined operations, and began refocusing the business on selling brand-name health products rather than selling advertising. But he couldn't move fast enough. The Internet advertising markets shrank faster than he could get his nutritional supplements business and at-home intravenous care services effectively to market. In December 2001 Drkoop.com filed for bankruptcy protection.

Rosenblatt was depressed by his first experience with failure. "It hit me hard. I wasn't sure I wanted to do another public company again," he said. Instead he retreated into a totally different venture: he started a website called Superdudes.net—which let people transform pictures of themselves into virtual versions of superheroes—and invested in a San Diego nightclub.

Still, when Brewer called about eUniverse, Rosenblatt was excited. "Ohmigod, this would be so fun to do together," he said.

The day after Brewer called Rosenblatt, Tom Flahie, eUniverse's hard-headed chief financial officer, walked into Brewer's office and shivered. Brewer, perennially hot, kept the thermostat in his office at 63 degrees, and Flahie was always freezing in his office.

Flahie had done his due diligence on Rosenblatt, and he didn't like what he found. Drkoop.com had gone bust during Rosenblatt's tenure. "I went back and looked at iMall, and it never had any profits," Flahie said. "I'm not sure he's a skilled operator." In fact, Flahie understated the case: IMall incurred nearly $20 million in losses in its short three-year existence as an independent company.

"I don't disagree with you," Brewer responded. "But we can solve that by bringing in a strong chief operating officer. With Rich, the main attraction is we need his positive energy."

The board of directors was equally dubious. They wanted an operations specialist who could roll up his sleeves and fix the nitty-gritty aspects of the business.

Rosenblatt's fate was still unresolved when, on January 29, he slipped into eUniverse's annual meeting and found a seat next to VantagePoint managing director David Carlick in the windowless conference room.

The meeting promised to be the climax to the six-month proxy contest waged between Greenspan and eUniverse's management. The battle of words had reached a frenzied pitch. Just before the meeting, Greenspan issued his fifteenth letter to shareholders titled, "Just Who Are Brett Brewer and Chris Lipp?" In a two-page list of claims against his old friends, peppered with sections in capital letters, he stated, "Brett Brewer was *not* responsible for any major business development deal during his tenure at the company," and "Chris Lipp is the lawyer who remained silent when a demand letter was served on the full board on October 27 threatening litigation from VantagePoint if VantagePoint's financing terms were not accepted."

EUniverse responded with its own sixth and final letter, filled with bold-faced all-capital-letter claims of its own. "Don't be fooled by Mr. Greenspan's empty rhetoric. Protect your investment," the letter exhorted. In a section titled, "Greenspan's Sour Grapes," eUniverse pointed out that Greenspan had already dropped many of the claims from his separate lawsuit against the company. "Ask yourself, how are Mr. Greenspan's threats in your best interest?" eUniverse put to its shareholders.

The meeting was anticlimactic. Greenspan didn't show up, and eUniverse won the vote by a landslide. EUniverse's slate of directors garnered about 18.4 million votes, while Greenspan's slate generated about 8.4 million votes—mostly from Greenspan, who was still a big shareholder.

For Rosenblatt, the proxy contest was a sideshow. The annual meeting was his opportunity to woo Carlick in person. To get the CEO job, he knew he needed an ally on the board. So Rosenblatt had called Carlick directly and gotten a favorable response. During the one-hour phone conversation, Rosenblatt explained how he would fix the business: by streamlining eUniverse's diverse divisions, focusing on the most profitable ones, and reinvigorating the staff after its depressing fight with Greenspan. Carlick liked Rosenblatt's ideas and his enthusiasm.

At the annual meeting, Rosenblatt pressed his case again with Carlick and won him over.

"I fell in love with the guy," Carlick said. "He's a reality distortion field. You say to yourself, 'I don't know what he said, but I want to buy it.' " Carlick decided to push for Rosenblatt to get the job.

But the board members were not immediately sold on Rosenblatt. They were particularly worried about his attention to detail. To assure themselves, the board made Rosenblatt take the Myers-Briggs psychological test. Based on the philosophy of Swiss psychiatrist Carl Jung, the test categorizes people into sixteen different categories based on four attributes. Rosenblatt's test showed that he was an extrovert and a hard worker. The results assuaged the board's concerns. In February Rosenblatt was named CEO of eUniverse.

When Rosenblatt arrived at the company, eUniverse had been posting losses of about $3 million a quarter for the past year. As he made the rounds of each division, Rosenblatt met MySpace's Chris DeWolfe and Josh Berman, who were ensconced in a windowless converted closet.

"Hey, we've put up this site called MySpace.com," DeWolfe explained. "It's never got much attention, but we think it has a lot of potential."

As DeWolfe gave Rosenblatt a briefing on MySpace's growing popularity, Rosenblatt liked what he heard. MySpace reminded him of his former company iMall. In this case, it was individuals setting up their own personalized pages. Of course, it was losing money hand over fist, but Rosenblatt thought the site was worth the investment.

"You have my one hundred percent support," he told DeWolfe.

Over the next few months, Rosenblatt's faith in MySpace.com would be sorely tested.

Chapter 11

ARE WE MISSING
THE NEXT GOOGLE?

i

In March 2004 MySpace claimed to have surpassed Friendster as the largest social networking website in terms of the number of pages viewed by its members.

Chris DeWolfe trumpeted the achievement in MySpace's first-ever press release. "By allowing our users to dictate the features they want, we've been able to develop an offering that keeps them coming back," he wrote. The release obscured the fact that Friendster, with more than one million monthly unique visitors, still had more traffic than MySpace, with its 756,000 monthly visitors, according to the Web measurement service comScore Media Metrix. Monthly unique visitors, which measures the number of people who visit a website each month, is the benchmark for the Internet industry. But MySpace's fewer visitors were viewing more pages on each visit, indicating that they were more engaged by the website. Surpassing Friendster in page views highlighted an important point: MySpace was growing quickly, while Friendster was flat-lining.

MySpace posed a dilemma for newly appointed eUniverse chief executive Richard Rosenblatt. Although it had tripled in size between November and March, its revenues were paltry—just $135,000 for the month of March—and profits were nonexistent. Rosenblatt estimated that MySpace had lost $319,000 in its first six months of existence.

The problem was that many advertisers were skeptical that their ads would get noticed on MySpace's unruly homespun pages. MySpace members decorated their profile pages with a crazy quilt of blinking, flashing graphics, displayed photos of themselves in various states of undress, and left provocative comments on one another's pages. MySpace was only able to sell ads on those pages for the minuscule price of less than 20 cents per thousand viewers, while eUniverse's other websites charged $2 per thousand viewers.

During his state-of-the-company address to the eUniverse board on April 22, 2004, Rosenblatt proposed a twofold solution: Consider charging MySpace members fees for some services and expand social networking beyond teens and young adults to different content areas that would attract an older audience.

EUniverse had learned in the past that older women were much more likely than teenagers to click on advertisements. Rosenblatt envisioned a new social networking site called Grab.com, aimed at twenty-five- to fifty-five-year-old women that was focused on casual games and humor. He hoped Grab.com would attract a broader base of advertisers than MySpace could with its youthful audience.

Rosenblatt began spending one-third of his time overseeing the creation of Grab.com. He viewed it as a laboratory where he sought to prove that social networking could become an integral component of all websites. But MySpace viewed Grab.com as competition for scarce resources at eUniverse.

MySpace's ascent caught the eye of David Siminoff, a money manager who had just joined the board of a Los Angeles–based online dating company called MatchNet. Siminoff had heard about MySpace from a friend and thought the website might fit into MatchNet's portfolio of online dating sites, including AmericanSingles.com and Jdate.com, the leading Jewish online dating service.

Siminoff and the newly installed MatchNet chief executive, Todd Tappin, called and e-mailed Tom Anderson repeatedly, trying to set up a meeting, but they got no response from Anderson. So finally the Match-Net executives turned to MatchNet's founder, Joe Shapira, who was well known in the Los Angeles Internet community, to see if he got a better response. The strategy worked: Anderson responded to Shapira and set up a meeting.

Siminoff and Chris DeWolfe met in MatchNet's Beverly Hills offices. Siminoff was wearing a suit; DeWolfe, all black.

Siminoff, a classic rock fan, started off by jokingly complaining that old-style rock bands like Aerosmith weren't well represented on My-Space.

"You're a suit who is a wannabe rocker," DeWolfe teased.

The two hit it off and started discussing MySpace's situation. DeWolfe explained that MySpace was in a totally different business than its parent company, eUniverse, which was busy selling tooth whiteners and ink-jet cartridges.

"MySpace is not a direct marketing company," DeWolfe said. "We are trying to be a vehicle for self-expression of individuals. We have a different DNA and a different culture that needs to be set free . . .We need a suit who loves Aerosmith to bridge the gap."

Siminoff was impressed with DeWolfe but a bit wary. Friendster was still the hot social networking property. He thought that maybe Match-Net could combine the two companies and own the social networking space.

Still, MatchNet founder Shapira was enthusiastic to buy MySpace, especially since MatchNet was gearing up for an initial public offering later in the year. MySpace, with its fast user growth and different approach to dating, might be a good choice to round out MatchNet's portfolio. So a few weeks later, MatchNet's Siminoff and Tappin approached Rosen-blatt with an offer to buy MySpace for $40 million in cash. Under the terms of the agreement between MySpace and eUniverse, the MySpace founders would get $13.3 million for their one-third share of MySpace, and eUniverse would receive $26.7 million for its two-thirds stake.

It was an incredibly tempting offer that would have "ensured the business forever," said eUniverse president Brett Brewer.

EUniverse was in terrible shape. In the year ending March 31, 2004, revenues fell 13 percent to $57.3 million from $65.7 million a year earlier, and the company racked up $13.5 million in losses for the year.

Much of the loss was attributed to the shutdown of ResponseBase, which had generated $7 million in product sales in the twelve months ending March 31, 2003—sales that evaporated amid a flurry of returns during the following year. The costs associated with closing down

ResponseBase also added $1.2 million to eUniverse's losses. The company's stock price was in the dumps. In March eUniverse's shares were trading at $2.75 at their peak.

To signal a break with the past, Rosenblatt decided to rename the company Intermix Media. As he sorted through the businesses at Intermix, Rosenblatt discovered that one of the most profitable business units was called Alena, which sold a wrinkle-reducing cream called Hydroderm and a diet pill called Dream Shape online and through television infomercials. Hydroderm alone brought in $6.9 million in revenues for the year, or 12 percent of the company's total sales, while Dream Shape generated $4.4 million in sales, or 8 percent of the total sales.

Alena's success was due in large part to its aggressive marketing tactics. Alena blanketed the Web with ads for the wrinkle cream, promoting it as "Better than Botox" and offering customers a free trial. But the free trial *wasn't* free: Customers were charged a shipping and handling fee of $5.95 and were automatically enrolled for monthly shipments of $49.95 bottles of wrinkle cream. Customers often failed to cancel before the first shipment arrived, and the Internet message boards were full of complaints from customers lamenting Hydroderm's tactics. The Los Angeles Better Business Bureau was deluged with hundreds of complaints about Hydroderm. After investigating the complaints, the bureau awarded Hydroderm an F—on a grading system of A to F—for promoting an "offer [that] is misleading and deceptive."

Alena's diet pill was also under fire from the U.S. Food and Drug Administration (FDA). On March 26 the FDA sent a letter to Intermix's website IncreaseYourHealth.com, demanding that the company stop promoting Dream Shape with claims such as: "Take 3 capsules before bedtime, watch the fat disappear!" "Increases Lean Muscle Mass," and "Decreases Fat." Joseph Baca, director of compliance for the FDA Center for Food Safety and Applied Nutrition, wrote, "We have reviewed these claims and have concluded that they are not supported by reliable scientific evidence. If you have scientific evidence which you believe substantiates that your claims for 'Dream Shape' are truthful and not misleading, please provide it to us within fifteen working days of receipt of this letter." In response, Intermix sent some clinical substantiation of the claims to the FDA and amended some of its promotional language for Dream Shape.

Despite its problems, Rosenblatt wasn't ready to forgo Alena's money-

making magic just yet. Instead he decided to transform Alena into a marketing engine that could eventually sell any type of product online.
Rosenblatt then reorganized the remaining Intermix divisions into
advertising-supported websites, including MySpace, which he called the
network division; and commerce-supported websites, including Alena,
which he called product marketing.

Rosenblatt also sold several unprofitable businesses, including a mul-
tilevel marketing company called 24 Hour Paycheck, which sold herbal
products, and an exercise product called Body Dome. He also began
looking for a buyer for SkillJam, a division that had been one of Brad
Greenspan's favorites. SkillJam offered skill-based online gambling, a
concept that exploited a loophole in the law against online gambling in
the United States by offering only skill-based games such as backgam-
mon, solitaire, and Scrabble. Skill games were legal, unlike games of
chance such as roulette and blackjack, but were a risky business, in
Rosenblatt's assessment.

In July Rosenblatt engaged in a rather dodgy transaction, in which
Intermix bought his former company Superdudes.com for $2 million in
cash and stock, thus enriching himself (he owned 25 percent of Superdudes) and the investors who had backed him. "We exchanged our ownership in Superdudes for Intermix," said Gerald Cramer, an investor who
had backed all of Rosenblatt's ventures, including Superdudes. "From
my perspective, it means he doesn't abandon his investors. He remembered the rest of us."

Rosenblatt defended the transaction as being essential to his plans
to build a new social-networking site, Grab.com. Superdudes' technology eventually became the guts of Grab.com, powering its avatars
and its points system. "It allowed us to demonstrate and prove that
social networking went beyond teens on MySpace," Rosenblatt later
said.

Persuaded by Rosenblatt's enthusiasm, the board of directors approved the deal, even though it had to waive its conflict-of-interest
prohibitions to allow the Superdudes transaction. Later, many of them
regretted the decision. "It was a bad deal," recalls Dan Mosher, Intermix
board member. "It was immaterial to the company, so we trusted the
management team, but we never got much value out of it."

...

Intermix board member Andrew Sheehan felt out of place as he stepped into Air Conditioned, a San Diego nightclub owned by Rosenblatt. With his balding pate, khakis, and button-down dress shirt, Sheehan was sure that he was the oldest and frumpiest guy in the room. But Sheehan, a managing partner at Intermix's biggest shareholder, VantagePoint Venture Partners, had promised Rosenblatt that he would stop by his club while in town for a meeting.

From the outside, the nightclub looked like a dive. Inside, however, it was a cool scene with padded leather walls, shag couches, young beautiful people, and live music. As soon as he entered, the manager walked up to him and said, "Hello, Mr. Sheehan."

"How did you know who I was?" Sheehan protested. But even as he said the words, he realized that the answer was obvious. Rosenblatt had called the manager and told him to look out for an old guy.

The manager offered Sheehan a soybean martini.

Sitting at the bar, Sheehan decided to conduct some market research. "Have you heard of MySpace?" he asked the bartender.

"Are you kidding?" the bartender replied. "I live my whole life on MySpace."

Surprised, Sheehan turned to the woman sitting next to him. The answer was the same. As the night wore on, he was amazed to hear that nearly everyone at the bar frequented MySpace. He was starting to think maybe it wasn't such a good idea to sell MySpace to MatchNet.

At the end of the evening, the manager waved the band over. Sheehan asked them how they promoted their act. The answer: MySpace.

That summer MySpace was quietly hitting its stride among musicians. The up-and-coming "emo" band Fall Out Boy had just joined MySpace and started amassing friends. Another emo sensation, My Chemical Romance, joined MySpace in May; in its first week in release, the group's album *Three Cheers for Sweet Revenge* hit number one on *Billboard*'s Top Heatseekers chart, which tracks up-and-coming artists.

The mainstream press hadn't yet picked up on MySpace's increasing popularity, but the hipsters inside the San Diego bar knew that MySpace was hot. By the end of the evening, Sheehan was convinced that MySpace was a hidden gem at Intermix. As he was leaving, Sheehan called Rosenblatt and told him that everyone at the bar was on MySpace, and it would be a mistake to sell it. "We've got to blow up the MatchNet deal," Sheehan said.

...

MatchNet's Todd Tappin walked into the Ivy, the celebrated, celebrity-studded West Hollywood restaurant, and slumped in his chair. Brewer eyed him nervously. Tappin's body language wasn't a good sign.

Brewer, Rosenblatt, DeWolfe, and Josh Berman had gathered to meet with Tappin to discuss the $40 million all-cash deal to buy MySpace. Business protocol dictated that they had to chat about other things first. Finally, halfway through dinner, Tappin came out with his news.

"I think we can still do the forty million dollars, but it will be primarily all stock," he blurted. As MatchNet prepared for its public offering, it had discovered that its cash reserves were plummeting, due in part to huge increases in marketing expenses.

But Intermix wasn't so interested in MatchNet's stock. The meal was uncomfortable. Tappin left early.

Rosenblatt, Brewer, DeWolfe, and Berman stayed at the restaurant for two more hours, drinking and talking. By the end of the evening, they had convinced themselves that they didn't want to sell MySpace anyway.

A few weeks later, Tappin quit MatchNet, and MatchNet withdrew its plans for an initial public offering.

Although the MatchNet-MySpace deal had gone south, MatchNet director David Siminoff was convinced that MySpace had a bright future. So when DeWolfe asked him to help MySpace find another outside investor, Siminoff agreed. Siminoff's first thought was Geoff Yang, a top-flight Silicon Valley venture capitalist at Redpoint Ventures. Yang had funded Siminoff's wife's company and was someone Siminoff trusted. Siminoff called up Yang and pitched him on MySpace.

"Are you guys interested in social networks?" Siminoff asked.

"We're really not," Yang replied. Yang had turned down several wannabe Friendster sites because they didn't have coherent plans to make money.

Siminoff persisted. "These guys really need some help," he said. "I told them that if there was one guy that could help them, it would be you."

Yang reluctantly agreed to meet with MySpace.

...

For his part, Rosenblatt still wasn't sure what Intermix should do with MySpace. At the company's August 31 board meeting, he presented the directors with a question, displayed on a light blue slide with green writing: "MySpace: Build or Sell?"

"Do we sell MySpace?" Rosenblatt asked the board. He put up another slide: "Pros: immediate cash and potentially monetize at the peak. Significant competition will enter the market unpredictable growth, and we may not have the resources or focus to be successful. Cons: Very compelling growth story seems to be more than a fad. Are we missing the next Google?"

At that point, MySpace had 3.3 million members and was displaying 85 million advertisements per day, but it was still losing money. In the first half of the year, MySpace lost $600,000. Rosenblatt estimated that it would cost another $2 million to $3 million to build MySpace before it could break even. Based on MatchNet's offer, Rosenblatt estimated that Intermix could sell MySpace for $50 million—which would net an astounding $23.5 million for Intermix.

Chris DeWolfe and Josh Berman presented the board with statistics about MySpace's growth. In the last two weeks of August, that growth had accelerated. The site was adding 23,000 new users per day. At peak hours, it had 90,000 users logged on simultaneously. The music initiative, launched in March, had been a huge success: So far 35,000 artists had uploaded music to the site. Most important, MySpace had finally surpassed Friendster. The two sites were neck and neck in May, in terms of unique visitors to their site—the metric that advertisers most valued. In June MySpace pulled ahead with 1.2 million visitors compared with 940,000 unique visitors to Friendster. The gap widened in July, with MySpace hitting 1.6 million and Friendster falling to 733,000.

But MySpace desperately needed more staff and more computers to keep up with its breakneck growth. MySpace employed thirty people. DeWolfe said that he needed to double the size of the staff in the next year. "There are fifteen to twenty features and improvements that we can't work on due to lack of technical resources," he told the board. DeWolfe also urgently needed a sales staff to beef up his meager advertising team and to lure big-name advertisers. Its biggest advertisers were a few movie studios and Garnier Fructis shampoo.

The directors were divided. MySpace's growth was impressive, but costly. Rosenblatt pointed out that MySpace was worthwhile because Wall Street investors pay for growth, and MySpace was growing like a weed. After some debate, the meeting ended without a vote on MySpace's future. But since there was no offer on the table, the decision was to keep MySpace for now. At the same time, the board hedged its bets, agreeing to spend $350,000 on the new site, Grab.com, and $200,000 on MySpace during the second quarter. Rosenblatt also proposed combining the technology staffs of MySpace and Grab.com into one staff that would support both websites, thus trimming MySpace's staff to fifteen.

It wasn't exactly a ringing endorsement.

Geoff Yang wasn't impressed. Chris DeWolfe and Josh Berman were in his Los Angeles office, right after Labor Day, describing their backgrounds—how they met in business school, worked together at XDrive, and founded ResponseBase. It wasn't a typical Silicon Valley startup résumé filled with risk-taking moves and innovative bets on technology. *It isn't obvious that these guys are the wild entrepreneur types,* Yang thought to himself.

Still, the investor asked the question that he always asks entrepreneurs: "Tell me what you want to be when you grow up."

"We want to be the MTV of the Internet," DeWolfe replied. "We want to serve this demographic of users and create a compelling user experience for them." That's why MySpace focused on music and communication tools, DeWolfe said. "This demographic really likes music and really likes to be in touch with their friends."

Wow, Yang thought. Most Silicon Valley social networking startups had described their business to him in terms of technology and features, but had only the vaguest idea how they would make money. Talking about demographics was one step closer to having a real path to profitability—because a demographic was something you could sell to advertisers.

This guy has espoused a vision I could actually buy into, Yang thought to himself. He agreed to meet with MySpace again and began researching the online potential of the MTV demographic.

...

In late October Rosenblatt was in his hotel room at the posh Ritz-Carlton, overlooking the Pacific Ocean in Half Moon Bay, California, attending an investment conference. He finally had some good news to report—Intermix was about to be listed on the American Stock Exchange, moving it off of the so-called pink sheets and giving the company some much-needed legitimacy. Intermix had also just quietly launched it social network for older women, Grab.com.

The phone rang. It was prominent Silicon Valley venture capitalist Bob Kagle, a general partner at Benchmark Capital, which was a backer of Friendster. He had been following MySpace's ascent.

After a few pleasantries, Kagle suggested merging Friendster and MySpace into one social networking site. "Let's use the MySpace technology and the Friendster brand," he suggested.

Rosenblatt was skeptical about the idea but knew that some of Intermix's directors would like to get rid of the money-losing MySpace. He agreed to meet with Kagle when he got back to Los Angeles.

The next week, Kagle flew down to Los Angeles on a private jet, bringing Intermix board member Andrew Sheehan along for the ride. Kagle introduced Rosenblatt and DeWolfe to Friendster's newly hired CEO, Scott Sassa, a former NBC executive who had overseen development of the hit TV dramas *The West Wing* and *Law & Order.* Sassa was new to the Internet business and wanted to increase the time users spent on Friendster by adding features such as news, horoscopes, and content from old-media companies. He was in the midst of a deal-making frenzy, trying to acquire features such as instant messaging and content from MTV that would bolster the site. Meanwhile, Sassa struggled unsuccessfully to recruit a new engineering team to replace the group that had launched the costly and misguided rewrite of the entire Friendster software code base.

DeWolfe wasn't impressed. Sassa didn't bring any technical expertise or fresh ideas that MySpace hadn't thought of already, and MySpace was widening its lead over Friendster every month. Still, DeWolfe was desperate to beef up his advertising sales force, and a combination with Friendster would give him a strong sales team.

For Rosenblatt, the sticking point was the structure of the deal.

Friendster was proposing to spin the combined companies off into a separate publicly traded company. But Rosenblatt didn't want to lose control of the fast-growing MySpace property—and a spin-off would likely require Intermix's ownership to dip below 50 percent.

The structure didn't seem fair, given that MySpace had finally overtaken Friendster. By October MySpace had rocketed to 3.4 million visitors, while Friendster was stagnant at about 945,000 monthly visitors.

Back in Silicon Valley, Sassa met with Intermix's venture capitalists to discuss the merger prospects. VantagePoint managing director David Carlick suggested that a merger should be split more like 20–80 or 10–90, given MySpace's success.

But Sassa was adamant: "The backers of Friendster would never take less than fifty percent," he said. So Intermix dropped the merger idea. Meanwhile, Friendster continued to lose ground.

By December Yang was ready to invest in MySpace. He had spent three months asking advertisers whether the MTV demographic was a valuable one to pursue, and the answer had been resoundingly positive.

Advertisers believed that it was important to reach teenagers when they were still forming their brand loyalties. But advertisers were finding it difficult to reach this elusive group online. With boys, advertisers could sell ads on video game websites. But girls were harder to find online. Making the task even more difficult, advertisers told Yang that "this demographic doesn't like to be shouted at." The youth wanted their advertising to be subtle and sophisticated.

His second concern was that MySpace might be too edgy for conservative advertisers. So Yang interviewed several MySpace advertisers who were pleased with the performance of their advertisements on MySpace. Advertisers were just dipping their toes into the water at MySpace. In the summer of 2004, the movie studio DreamWorks SKG built a profile for the fictional character Ron Burgundy from the comedy *Anchorman*. It attracted 3,615 friends and 571 comments. "It was a no-brainer for this film because it was very character driven," said a DreamWorks spokesman. "It's not going to work for every film."

In December 2004 Procter & Gamble experimented with promoting its Secret Sparkle deodorant on the MySpace profile of teen singer Hilary

Duff. The promotion was subtle, with just a few references to Secret Sparkle on Duff's page. But P&G was pleased with the results. "We wondered if the MySpace crowd would see us the way they do pop-up ads—as an annoying presence," said Michelle Vaeth, a P&G communications director. "But nearly two-thirds said they liked Secret Sparkle that much more after seeing us affiliated with Hilary Duff on MySpace."

Yang also worried about competition from well-funded media giants. He asked a friend, an executive at MTV, to take a look at MySpace and give his opinion. "It looks like it was done in a garage," his friend told Yang. "It's edgy and dirty—and it's exactly what this demographic will like." Yang asked if MTV could replicate such a site. His friend said no: "If MTV does it, it looks like 'the Man' did it."

Satisfied, Yang began negotiating with Intermix to buy a stake in MySpace. In the worst-case scenario, he told himself, MySpace's traffic alone would be worth something. In the best-case scenario, he projected that in a few years MySpace could be worth as much as iVillage.com, with its market valuation of about $430 million. Yang thought that would be a home run.

In his wildest dreams, Yang thought that MySpace could become a lifestyle portal, which he saw as a billion-dollar opportunity.

For DeWolfe, an investment from Yang would finally allow MySpace to break free from Intermix and become an independent company. He was frustrated with the constraints of working within Intermix, where MySpace was chronically underfunded, was forced to use Intermix's technology platform, and was crammed into Intermix's ever more crowded offices by the airport. DeWolfe wanted MySpace to be more like a Silicon Valley startup, with its own offices in hip Santa Monica, a high-octane venture capital backer, and a public offering in its future.

Rosenblatt had hoped that MySpace would be a team player and help Intermix expand social networking to its other properties such as Grab.com. But DeWolfe refused to play ball. "I want to be independent," DeWolfe told the board. "To get full value for MySpace, we need to be spun off as our own public company."

Rosenblatt would agree to a split-up only if Intermix could benefit from MySpace's future success.

Shelton State Libraries
Shelton State Community College

Chapter 12

TSUNAMI

i

When an earthquake in the Indian Ocean triggered a series of deadly tsunamis on December 26, 2004, News Corp. chairman Rupert Murdoch was relaxing at his 10,000-square-foot Federal-style beachfront mansion overlooking Long Island's Oyster Bay.

Murdoch, then seventy-three, was not very tech savvy. He didn't keep a computer on his office desk and had hired a computer expert to teach him how to use the Web just a few years earlier. Still, the mogul wanted to follow the storm's progress on the Internet. He asked Robert Thomson, then editor of the *Times* of London, to help him navigate the news online.

Like most people watching the devastating events that killed more than two hundred thousand people across the globe, Murdoch was amazed that some of the best footage of the massive waves was available online through amateur video—and not on television or in newspapers. What he saw persuaded him that he needed to make the Internet a higher priority at News Corp. His company had endured a lackluster year; the economy was soaring, but traditional media advertising was not.

"In a booming economy, we should have been up seven percent to eight percent, and we were pretty flat," he recalled. At the same time, in 2004, Internet advertising revenues had increased a remarkable 33 percent to $9.6 billion, according to PricewaterhouseCoopers. "That was a wakeup call," Murdoch said later.

So Murdoch called up one of his employees with Internet experience, Jeremy Philips. Prior to joining News Corp., the thirty-one-year-old had run several Internet properties in Australia, including one of Australia's largest Web portals. Murdoch reached Philips as he was vacationing in Australia, and asked him to organize a Web initiative for News Corp. when he returned to New York.

Murdoch's Internet awakening in 2004 was not his first Internet infatuation. The first time he got swept up in that frenzy, it was intertwined with a wrenching change in his personal life.

It was July 1998. Murdoch had gathered his top executives in Sun Valley, Idaho, for a retreat with their spouses. The lineup of speakers featured thought-provoking talks by Yahoo founder Jerry Yang, Russian tycoon Boris Berezovsky, and British politician Gordon Brown. But the most stirring speech may have come from Murdoch himself, when he stood on the stage and apologized for the disruption his divorce was causing the company.

Murdoch had been married to Anna for thirty years. They met when she was a teenage clerk at one of his first newspapers, the racy tabloid *Daily Mirror* in Sydney, Australia. While Murdoch raced around the globe assembling a larger and larger media portfolio, Anna raised their three children—Lachlan, Elisabeth, and James—and entertained a never-ending series of executives and politicians in a succession of homes in Australia, London, and finally New York. But Anna wasn't just a wife, she was a member of the board. She had an office and an assistant. And most of News Corp.'s top executives knew her personally.

At that time, Murdoch was in his late sixties, and his global media empire spanned 175 newspapers, the Fox Broadcasting Company, satellite television operators BSkyB in the UK and Star TV in Asia, as well as the publishing company HarperCollins. Anna thought it was time to slow down; she urged him to spend more time at their ranch in Carmel, California, and on their yacht. But Murdoch had no interest in slowing down—he liked to tell colleagues that he planned to invite them to his one hundredth birthday party. He was hoping to break into China, and he was hot on the trail of his next big acquisition: the satellite television operator DirecTV.

He started spending time with a young News Corp. employee, Wendi

Deng, who worked in News Corp.'s Hong Kong office and had served as Murdoch's interpreter in China. When Murdoch was apologizing for his divorce in Sun Valley, most of the executives didn't know that Deng was staying in his bungalow that week.

One year later, the two were married in a twilight ceremony on Murdoch's yacht, *Morning Glory*, in New York Harbor. He was sixty-eight, she was thirty—younger than his daughter, Elisabeth. It was seventeen days after his divorce was finalized. The marriage was a turning point for Murdoch, both personally and professionally. At home he turned in his London diet of bangers and mash for a Chinese diet of vegetables and fish, and began exercising religiously. At work he ordered all of the office decorations to be overseen by a wizened feng shui master, who stuck tiny elephants in the corners of conference rooms and slipped coins under the carpets.

On his honeymoon in Tuscany, Italy, Murdoch caught Internet fever. Until then he had been an Internet skeptic. Unlike other media moguls, like Time Warner's Jerry Levin, he had no interest in jumping into bed with a brash Internet startup like AOL. But by 1999 Yahoo's market value was twice News Corp.'s, despite having less than 3 percent of News Corp.'s revenues. Murdoch decided to jump in.

He summoned some of his top executives to Italy to plot Internet strategy and soon afterward gave his son James control of the company's new digital arm. During a frenzied year, Murdoch and his son invested more than $1 billion in Internet companies such as WebMD, Juno.com, TheStreet.com, and the original social networking website, SixDegrees.com.

By June 2000 the dot-com stock bubble had burst. Murdoch, facing significant losses on his investments, abruptly shut down News Corp.'s Internet division. He sent James off to run News Corp.'s satellite television operation in Asia while Murdoch focused on more pressing issues: moving his company's headquarters to New York from Australia and consolidating his control of the global satellite television industry.

Five years later, however, Murdoch had amassed a large satellite television portfolio, only to find that satellite was poorly positioned for the Internet era. While cable and phone companies were hooking consumers with high-speed Internet connections, satellite television operators did not have a comparable offer.

Murdoch, in his usual way, did not spend time regretting the past. Instead he simply moved forward toward his next admittedly vague goal: conquering the Internet. Taking a journalistic approach, Murdoch interviewed experts inside and outside of News Corp. to see what direction he should take. When Murdoch flew to Los Angeles for meetings after the New Year, he called up the most prominent Internet executive at Fox: Ross Levinsohn, who was in charge of the FoxSports.com website. Murdoch asked Levinsohn to meet him for lunch in the ground-floor cafeteria in twenty minutes.

Levinsohn had never met Murdoch before. A former college football player with blond hair and an engaging smile, Levinsohn joined News Corp. in 2000 after stints at the Web search engine AltaVista, the website CBS SportsLine, and the HBO Sports cable channel.

At FoxSports, Levinsohn had cut a deal with Microsoft Corporation to feature FoxSports content on MSN. The deal boosted FoxSports's traffic immensely but wasn't very profitable, since Microsoft got a big cut of the advertising revenue. Still, the MSN deal was considered a success at News Corp. because it had vaulted FoxSports.com from an also-ran site to one that was often tied with ESPN.com, the number one sports website.

Levinsohn, forty-one, was stunned to hear from the chairman directly. At first he thought it might be a friend playing a joke on him. But there was no mistaking the Australian accent and the commanding manner. When he put down the phone, he wished he hadn't worn jeans and a T-shirt to the office that day. He quickly put on a sports jacket that he had in his office on Sepulveda Boulevard and drove over to the Fox movie studio, where Murdoch's office was located.

When Levinsohn met Murdoch in the cafeteria, the two stood in line with their trays along with everybody else. They sat down at Murdoch's usual booth—the one right next to the door to the cafeteria. Settling onto the light wood bench, Murdoch asked Levinsohn, "Should I buy AskJeeves.com for two billion dollars?"

Levinsohn took a deep breath and replied, "I believe it would be a bad idea to enter the highly competitive search market."

Murdoch nodded and said he agreed. Levinsohn realized that he had just passed a test.

One month later, Levinsohn stood on the stage of a conference room at the W Hotel in New York, showcasing FoxSports.com to a highly skeptical audience. Murdoch had flown two hundred of News Corp.'s senior executives from around the world to New York for an Internet summit. He had even hired the high-profile management consulting group McKinsey & Company to help develop his Internet strategy. Usually Murdoch was not a big fan of consultants. But having assigned only one senior executive, Jeremy Philips, to work on the project full-time, Murdoch needed help. So he turned to McKinsey's top media consultant, Michael Wolf.

Orchestrating a companywide strategy was unusual at News Corp. Murdoch had always run his global empire as an assemblage of fiefdoms. Each division was judged simply on profits, forcing the divisions to compete with one another for resources. One result of Murdoch's relentless focus on the bottom line was that very few divisions had developed Internet strategies. After all, the divisions were reluctant to invest in a new initiative that was unlikely to produce profits anytime soon. To generate enthusiasm, Wolf and his team at McKinsey combed News Corp.'s global empire for examples of inspiring Internet success stories. They came up short. They found only three News Corp. divisions whose Internet operations were presentable, and of those, Levinsohn's Fox Sports.com was the only one with any pizzazz. Well funded by its partnership with Microsoft, FoxSports.com was up to date, with advanced features such as video clips.

Murdoch was impressed and asked Levinsohn to head up News Corp.'s Internet efforts—a huge elevation for Levinsohn. Picking such an unlikely candidate for an important job was a classic Murdoch maneuver. He could have recruited any number of high-profile Internet executives to blaze News Corp.'s path to the Internet. But choosing an outsider with a track record would have cramped his style. Murdoch wanted to dive into the Internet and master the space. He couldn't do that with a senior Internet executive second-guessing his decisions. But he could interfere as much as he liked with Levinsohn at the helm.

"Rupert really wanted to run it himself," said an executive close to the situation.

On April 13, in a groundbreaking speech at the American Society of Newspaper Editors, Murdoch lambasted the industry—including himself—for not innovating fast enough. Citing a Carnegie Corporation study that showed that 44 percent of young people checked Internet portals for their daily news versus a meager 19 percent who relied on newspapers, Murdoch called on the industry to respond. "In the face of this revolution, we've been slow to react," he said. "We've sat by and watched while our newspapers have gradually lost circulation . . . So unless we awaken to these changes, which are quite different to those of five or six years ago, we will, as an industry, be relegated to the status of also-rans."

News Corp. hadn't yet found an answer. Murdoch was honest about this. But he stressed that the Internet was now the media giant's top priority. "I do not underestimate the tests before us," he concluded. "It is a monumental, once-in-a-generation opportunity, but it is also an exciting one, because if we're successful, our industry has the potential to reshape itself and to be healthier than ever before."

The next day, McKinsey submitted its recommendations for News Corp.'s Internet strategy. The 109-page document suggested pursuing a three-part strategy. First: Build four Web portals in news, entertainment, sports, and finance, using News Corp.'s existing content. Second: Pursue high-risk, high-return Internet opportunities in China and India and in online gambling. Third: Avoid high-cost acquisitions in the United States.

MySpace was mentioned on pages 24 and 25 of the McKinsey report as one of several emerging Internet communities (including Pogo.com, Neopets, and Xanga) that were driving significant traffic online. In the report's conclusion, MySpace was mentioned as a possible "small acquisition"—along with the DrudgeReport and Xanga—that could help drive traffic to the portals News Corp. would create.

Murdoch didn't agree that News Corp. should build portals with its own content. "Rupert was very clear that existing content would not carry the day," said Michael Wolf of McKinsey. "When you looked at Yahoo, MSN, Google, and AOL, what was keeping people there were the applications, not the content."

In the end, Murdoch didn't follow any of McKinsey's advice. As usual, he followed his gut.

Before Levinsohn could take the helm of News Corp.'s Internet division, he had to submit his vision for the unit to the company's senior executives. The day before the presentation, Levinsohn gave Murdoch a preview of his recommendations. "It's great, it's terrific," Murdoch enthused. "If you don't screw it up tomorrow, you can go do it." Levinsohn barely slept that night.

The next morning, Levinsohn presented his hundred-page plan for News Corp. to Murdoch, Murdoch's son Lachlan, and several other high-ranking corporate executives. Levinsohn's strategy wasn't that different from the one that McKinsey had proposed, except that it was centralized under a single business unit. But Levinsohn's plan still envisioned four content portals containing 70 percent News Corp. content and 30 percent independent content.

To build these portals, Levinsohn proposed creating a five-hundred-person organization and embarking on an aggressive acquisition hunt. He highlighted more than a dozen possible acquisition candidates that could help bolster News Corp.'s four portals, including sports websites, film websites, and even an online advertising service provider. MySpace was not on the list.

Levinsohn's plan was ambitious. At one point during the presentation, an executive protested, "You can't do that!" Levinsohn felt a knot in his stomach as he waited for a rebuke. But Murdoch slapped his hand on the table and responded, "Of course we can."

Murdoch authorized Levinsohn to start a new division, and Levinsohn began drawing up a list of possible acquisitions. By June he'd compiled his list. The top three choices were: Intermix; the video game fan site IGN.com; and WeatherBug, a website that installed a weather icon on customers' computers.

Levinsohn presented his list to News Corp. president Peter Chernin and suggested that News Corp. should buy one of the three companies.

"Why don't we buy all three of them?" Chernin responded.

"Can we do that?"

"Sure," Chernin said.

Levinsohn was learning how quickly things could be set in motion at News Corp. once Murdoch had issued a decree.

Chapter 13

INDEPENDENCE

In the fall of 2004, Intermix chief executive Rich Rosenblatt stuck his head in Chris DeWolfe's tiny linoleum-floored office. "Chris, I want to make sure we put the Intermix logo on the sleeves of your T-shirts," he said.

DeWolfe leaned back in his chair. "I don't think we can do that," he said. He didn't believe that MySpace users would want their hip site to be associated with Intermix.

A skirmish was unfolding between Rosenblatt and DeWolfe about MySpace's role at Intermix. Rosenblatt wanted to promote MySpace's torrid growth to Intermix investors. DeWolfe wanted nothing to do with Intermix's tawdry businesses of pushing wrinkle creams and animated greeting cards. Rosenblatt wanted the Intermix logo on MySpace's T-shirts—DeWolfe did not. Rosenblatt wanted the Intermix logo on the back of MySpace business cards—DeWolfe did not. Rosenblatt treated MySpace like another Intermix division—DeWolfe chafed at the intrusions.

The MySpace T-shirts became an unlikely symbol of the friction between MySpace and Intermix. To DeWolfe the T-shirts were a cheap way to promote MySpace to its core audience. But DeWolfe's request for $5,000 to spend on T-shirts was turned down by Intermix's finance department.

DeWolfe didn't give up. He went to Intermix board member Andrew

Sheehan and begged for the $5,000. Sheehan was shocked that DeWolfe's request for T-shirt money had been turned down—after all, MySpace was Intermix's hottest property. He vowed to help MySpace break free from Intermix's fierce finance department.

"That was the tipping point for me," Sheehan later recalled. He became a supporter of DeWolfe's effort to spin off MySpace into an independent company.

On November 2, 2004, MySpace signed up its 5 millionth account—up from just 1 million on February 15. In that same period, monthly traffic to MySpace had increased to 3.5 million visitors, up from just 550,000 monthly visitors—meaning that the load on MySpace's computers had increased sevenfold in less than nine months. The good news was that MySpace finally turned a profit in the fall of 2004. In November advertisers paid, on average, 20 cents to reach one thousand viewers on MySpace, while the cost of displaying one thousand pages on MySpace was only about 7 cents per page. Even with other costs factored in, MySpace was finally breaking even consistently.

MySpace was becoming an underground sensation, fueled largely by its focus on independent musicians. Matt Friction, the lead guitarist for the Nashville pop rock band Pink Spiders, neatly summarized the site's appeal: "I would say MySpace is actually more effective than our real website, 'cause every kid in America is on that website with nothing to do, just looking around for bands and stuff," Friction told a Nashville journalist. "It's a cultural revolution that hasn't been picked up on by the mainstream media yet."

The bad news was that Intermix didn't have the money or the expertise to keep up with MySpace's rapid growth. A typical request from MySpace for new computers could take a month or two to get approved. "By the time we got the request up the ladder, we were in deep waters," said Peter Amiri, a MySpace technical manager. Once the request was approved, it would take another six to seven weeks for the equipment to arrive and be placed online. In the meantime, Amiri said, "the site was dying."

Every few months, DeWolfe and Josh Berman, head of operations at MySpace, would complain about the purchasing issues to Rosenblatt and Brett Brewer in what Brewer called "Come to Jesus" meetings. Invariably DeWolfe and Berman would claim that their purchasing requests were getting delayed. But when Brewer would check it out, he often found that MySpace had very recently turned in the disputed purchasing requests. In fact, MySpace's requests were getting turned around just as fast as any others at Intermix. The problem was that MySpace's needs were outstripping Intermix's ability to fulfill them.

By December Rosenblatt agreed with DeWolfe that MySpace needed an infusion of outside funding. But Rosenblatt wanted the deal to be done in a way that allowed Intermix to retain control of MySpace.

To keep its stake above 50 percent, Intermix agreed to sell only 25 percent of MySpace to Redpoint for $11.5 million—valuing MySpace at $46 million. That meant that after the transaction, Intermix would still own 53 percent of MySpace.

Intermix also crafted an unusual option that would let Intermix buy back its stake in MySpace if Intermix were sold. Normally, companies in Intermix's situation would create something called a "drag-along" rights agreement, which allows the parent company to force a subsidiary to be sold if there is an acquisition of the parent company. A drag-along agreement usually requires the subsidiary to accept the same price per share that the parent company receives.

In this case, Intermix created a different type of drag-along agreement for MySpace. Instead of agreeing to accept whatever price Intermix negotiated for itself, MySpace was guaranteed a fixed price of $125 million if Intermix were sold within twelve months of the closing of the Redpoint financing.

At the time, it seemed that DeWolfe had cut a clever deal— guaranteeing a hefty payout for MySpace even if Intermix were sold on the cheap. But the agreement also limited MySpace's upside: If Intermix managed to sell itself for an astronomical price, MySpace would not benefit from Intermix's success.

DeWolfe's strategy didn't acknowledge how closely MySpace's success was tied to the valuation of Intermix. As MySpace's popularity soared, so would Intermix's value to a potential buyer. By not tying MySpace's payout to Intermix's value, he substantially underestimated the financial ties between the two entities.

In fact, it can be argued that DeWolfe's decision to accept the fixed price of $125 million for MySpace was the biggest mistake of his career.

To be fair, DeWolfe did negotiate an "out" for MySpace: an unusual agreement that allowed MySpace to block Intermix from exercising its right to buy MySpace for $125 million.

Usually a subsidiary does not have the right to block its parent company from selling the subsidiary. But in this case, MySpace was given the right to prevent Intermix from exercising the option under two scenarios: if MySpace received an offer for itself that valued MySpace at more than $125 million or if MySpace filed for a public offering. In effect, MySpace could block Intermix from selling itself, because no buyer of Intermix would want to own just a portion of MySpace without the right to buy the rest of it. DeWolfe was betting that within a year, he would be able to take MySpace public or sell it for more than $125 million. At the time, with the Internet market heating up, it may not have seemed like a risky bet. But the downside was substantial: If DeWolfe couldn't take MySpace public or sell it, Intermix would control MySpace's fate.

For his part, Geoff Yang of Redpoint was reluctant to agree to the complex MySpace buyback option but felt he didn't have a choice. "I didn't want to risk losing the deal," Yang later said. "And I honestly thought nothing would happen in a year."

In anticipation of its independence, MySpace moved into new offices in Santa Monica in February 2005.

Located on the ground floor on a slightly seedy side street, just one block from Santa Monica's pedestrian shopping promenade, MySpace's new digs were not glamorous. The offices were strangely laid out, with most of the employees in a big, open, windowless interior, and managers' offices lining the windows facing the street. DeWolfe had a nice big office with a door to a small outside patio, but Josh Berman took an internal conference room to be closer to the staff. DeWolfe installed a big flat-panel monitor in the bullpen with live traffic statistics from MySpace so that staffers could always see what was happening on the site.

Despite the office's flaws, its location was great. Instead of going to lunch at the shopping mall across from the airport office park, employees could now choose from all the trendy juice joints and hamburger stands lining Santa Monica's main shopping district. And since the beach was just a few blocks away, some employees started storing their boogie boards, skateboards, and bicycles at their desks. The staff began frequenting the happy hours at various bars on the promenade, and occasionally the festivities would return to the office. "People would come in the next morning to look for their jackets, and someone would have used it as a pillow," recalled MySpace staffer Jason Feffer. "Employees sometimes came back to the office drunk. It was like a fraternity."

Meanwhile, executives at Viacom's MTV cable network had noticed that MySpace was increasingly popular among its audience of hipster teenage music lovers. Back in July 2004, when MySpace was a small site with just 1.6 million monthly visitors, MTV executive Nick Lehman noticed that one of the most popular areas of MySpace was a section devoted to the MTV show *Laguna Beach*. Intrigued, Lehman joined the site and began tracking MySpace's huge audience gains. "It's growing like a hockey stick," Lehman told his boss, Jason Hirschhorn.

At the time, Viacom was in the midst of trying to develop a digital strategy. In August 2004, Viacom copresidents Tom Freston, the legendary cofounder of MTV, and Les Moonves, former president of CBS, had convened a "digital show-and-tell" for all the Viacom divisions to present their proposals for an Internet strategy.

Among Viacom's many divisions, MTV may have had the most dire need for a digital strategy. Despite the fact that its audience was spending more and more time online, MTV had largely ignored the Internet ever since 2000, when it pulled the plug on the planned initial public offering of its MTV Interactive division, which was losing about $45 million a year.

At the Viacom show-and-tell confab, Hirschhorn presented MTV's acquisition wish list: He wanted to buy MySpace as well as the websites iFilm.com, IGN.com, and Atom Shockwave as part of a plan to spend $500 million on Internet acquisitions.

It wasn't until the November budget meetings that Hirschhorn got approval to pursue MySpace. By that time, MySpace had doubled in size to 3.5 million visitors, and Hirschhorn figured he could get MySpace for about $30 million to $40 million. Freston thought it was a good idea. "Go for it," he told Hirschhorn.

Finally, on December 4, Hirschhorn called Chris DeWolfe to introduce himself.

"Listen, we love what you're doing, and I want to come and meet you," Hirschhorn said.

Within a month, Hirschhorn and Lehman arrived at the MySpace offices to check out the company. The MTV executives loved the vibe of the place; it was just like MTV in its early days. Tom Anderson had a mattress in his office and often slept there so that he could work around the clock. DeWolfe and Berman were hipsters who knew how to have a good time. The vibe was antiauthoritarian, with MySpace executives making no secret of their disdain for their parent company, Intermix.

Over the next few months, dozens of MTV executives paraded through the MySpace offices, trying to get a handle on the rapidly growing business. MySpace was growing so fast that Hirschhorn had to keep revising how much Viacom might need to pay for it. Meanwhile, Viacom's corporate lawyers were fretting about whether MySpace could be sued for pirated music and other materials that users posted to its site.

Illegal use of copyrighted material was a growing problem on MySpace, due in part to the practice of remixing. To decorate their profiles, many MySpace users posted photos, music, and video clips that expressed their tastes. Often the video clips would contain a mixture of elements, such as a homemade video of a cat set to the music of the rapper Jay-Z. But very few remixers sought copyright permission for anything they did.

The Digital Millennium Copyright Act, passed in 1998, grants websites broad immunity from what their users post online. MySpace's main responsibility under the law was to take down copyright-infringing content once it was notified of the problem. But Viacom's lawyers were still worried that MySpace could be sued.

As Viacom considered its options, MySpace's venture capital backers discovered an intriguing competitor. One of Geoff Yang's partners at Redpoint mentioned that he was interested in a startup called Facebook. At first Yang wasn't interested. "I don't even know if I want one of these social networks, much less two of them," Yang told his partner.

But Yang changed his mind as MySpace's traffic started to soar. By February 2005 MySpace's traffic was increasing by about 6 percent a week, and the ratings firm Hitwise had just declared it the twelfth most visited website in the United States. In his twenty years as a venture capitalist, Yang had never seen a company grow so quickly. Yang started to think that doubling down on social networks wasn't such a bad idea. So he asked DeWolfe to go check out Facebook.

"Let's go buy it for five or ten million dollars," Yang told DeWolfe.

DeWolfe flew to Silicon Valley to visit Facebook founder Mark Zuckerberg. Zuckerberg, then twenty years old, had created Thefacebook .com in his dorm room at Harvard as an online equivalent of the printed facebook that Harvard distributed to freshmen, which included photos and biographical information about incoming freshmen. Within two weeks of the site's launch in February 2004, half of Harvard's student body had signed up. By May Facebook had expanded to other prestigious campuses such as Stanford and Yale universities. During the summer, Zuckerberg moved out to Silicon Valley to try to make it as an entrepreneur.

By the time DeWolfe arrived in the spring of 2005, Facebook was attracting more than one million monthly visitors from Ivy League colleges, and was growing at an even faster rate than MySpace. It had received $500,000 in seed money from one of the cofounders of PayPal, a Silicon Valley heavyweight. But it was still a tiny company: Zuckerberg and his few employees were writing their software code while sitting on rickety furniture in a sublet in Palo Alto, and the company hadn't yet closed on its first big round of venture capital financing.

Facebook had a very different philosophy than MySpace. Unlike MySpace, Facebook was a closed network. It allowed only members who had valid e-mail addresses from the universities that it represented. In contrast to MySpace's embrace of Fakesters, Facebook encouraged people to use their own names and to connect to people who they already knew in the real world. Zuckerberg liked to describe Facebook in mathematical terms: as a social graph on which people could map out their connections.

This was hardly a perfect match for MySpace, which described itself as a competitor to MTV. Not to mention the fact that Zuckerberg wanted $75 million for his site.

DeWolfe was stunned. MySpace was four times bigger than Facebook, and it was being valued by Redpoint at only $46 million. So DeWolfe and Yang dropped the idea of buying Facebook. "We went on our merry way," Yang said.

It wouldn't be the last time MySpace considered buying Facebook.

...

On February 11, 2005, MySpace won partial independence from Intermix. With the $125 million buyout provision in place, Intermix and
MySpace signed an agreement allowing MySpace to sell one-quarter of
itself to Redpoint Ventures. Under the agreement, Intermix would now
own 52 percent of the independent subsidiary MySpace Inc., Redpoint
would own 25 percent and the founders would own 19.9 percent. The
rest was reserved for employee stock options. As part of the transaction,
DeWolfe and the other MySpace founders sold about $3 million worth
of their stock to Redpoint, allowing them to cash out a bit.

In a separate transaction, Redpoint also reluctantly agreed to invest
$4 million in Intermix. "We looked at it as an entrance fee for investing
in MySpace," said Redpoint's Yang.

Independence from Intermix meant closer connections to Silicon
Valley. "We were a Los Angeles company on our own island," DeWolfe
said. "We didn't really have any connections in Silicon Valley."

MySpace couldn't afford to ignore Silicon Valley's technology expertise any longer. Intermix's chief technology officer, Jeff Rajewski, had
been helping MySpace when the companies were together. But now
DeWolfe wanted to hire a heavy-hitting chief technologist.

The technical challenges facing MySpace were enormous. In October, when MySpace had amassed three million accounts, the company
had faced a crucial decision known in the technology industry as "scale
up" or "scale out." For months MySpace had been scaling up—meaning
that it had been buying continuously larger and more powerful computers on which to store members' account information. But outages would
still occur—for instance, everything in a user's account would work except the blog. Finally Intermix board member David Carlick called his
friend, Silicon Valley technologist Peter Adams, to see if he could help
MySpace as a consultant. Adams, who had worked with Carlick at a previous venture, was the most accomplished Internet architect that Carlick
knew.

Adams recommended that MySpace scale out by partitioning its database, which essentially means cutting the database into smaller pieces
and spreading those pieces across multiple computers. Partitioning
sounds easier than it is because there's a risk of losing track of the data
during the partition. Doing a good job of partitioning includes solving

the difficult problems of distributed computing, which are usually tackled only by giant firms like Google and Amazon. "It was really tough medicine they had to hear," Adams recalled.

MySpace swallowed its medicine and partitioned the database—a process that took several months—onto several computers that each stored data for one million accounts. But the databases kept filling up faster and faster. For instance, the seventh database of one million accounts filled up in just seven days, due in large part to the efforts of a Florida band that successfully convinced legions of its fans to join MySpace. Whenever one of the member databases was overloaded, it would strain the computers that provided backup information for that database, and MySpace had to manually redistribute the load. "That became a full-time job for about two people," said Jim Benedetto, MySpace's vice president of technology. MySpace needed a long-term solution that could provide automatic load balancing among its storage computers.

MySpace was also struggling to keep its servers from melting down. MySpace, like most websites, leased space at a local data center. But by the fall of 2004, MySpace had crammed so many servers onto its leased racks that the computers were starting to overheat. "Our servers were melting," says Peter Amiri. "At some point, they were hot enough that you could fry an egg on top of the servers." So MySpace developed what it called the "four on, four off" model—with four servers on racks, then four empty spots in between, to allow for cooling. It was more expensive to lease empty racks, but at least the computers weren't melting down.

At the same time, MySpace was contemplating finally transitioning from ColdFusion, the programming language it had started with, to the more robust ASP.NET Microsoft programming language. ColdFusion was a programming language for quick and dirty websites, not for heavy-duty database applications. Intermix board member Andrew Sheehan, who had joined MySpace's fledgling board, helped MySpace get some discount software licenses from Microsoft. But MySpace needed someone to lead them through this next technology transition.

"We were going one hundred miles per hour and always on the edge of blowing up," said Redpoint's Geoff Yang. "I wanted to run at the edge of craziness but with a little more structure."

Yang thought he had found a perfect candidate in Ron Rose, the chief technology officer of Priceline.com. After all, Priceline was a huge database of constantly changing airline and hotel information—not unlike MySpace's huge database of constantly changing blogs, photos, and videos. And in its early days, Priceline had grown almost as quickly as MySpace, requiring a lot of tough technology decisions about how to increase capacity in a hurry. Rose was interested in the technical challenge but worried about working for a company that had no stock options of its own. At Priceline he had lucrative stock options in a publicly traded company. At MySpace he would have received Intermix stock options and the hope of receiving MySpace options if MySpace succeeded in going public. But after reviewing the relationship between Intermix and MySpace, Rose was worried that MySpace would get sold before it could pull off an IPO. He decided to remain with Priceline.

In the spring of 2005, the MSNBC reporter Bob Sullivan—who had written two articles critical of ResponseBase a year earlier—got a panicked call from his sister. She had just discovered that her thirteen-year-old daughter had listed all sorts of personal information about herself on her MySpace page.

Sullivan had never heard of MySpace, but it seemed like a good topic for his online column. So he called Parry Aftab, a lawyer specializing in cyber security and privacy, for advice. Aftab ran a foundation called WiredSafety, which advised parents and teens how to stay safe on the Internet. "Have you heard of MySpace?" Sullivan asked Aftab.

"Nobody goes there," Aftab responded. "It's for independent musicians. It's not really a very popular social networking site, but some of the kids are starting to go there because they can customize their profile."

For Aftab, blogs were the big thing on the Web. Most of the teens that she was advising were blogging on Xanga, which had an audience of 6.8 million at the time, or on LiveJournal.com, which had an audience of 9.6 million. MySpace had quietly amassed 13 million visitors but hadn't yet appeared on Aftab's radar screen.

Aftab told Sullivan that she didn't think blogs or MySpace-type sites were safe for kids. "There are underage kids on every social networking site on the Net," she said. "They are engaging in highly provocative conversations and doing things they would never do offline." Aftab's position was that kids shouldn't be providing any personal details online that could allow a stalker to track them down.

Sullivan's article "Kids, Blogs, and Too Much Information" appeared on MSNBC.com on April 29, 2005. It highlighted MySpace as one of many places where children were providing too much personal information online. It was the first mainstream media article highlighting safety issues at MySpace.

After the article appeared, Aftab called MySpace's general counsel, Matthew Polesetsky, to let him know that she thought that MySpace was breaking the law. Although MySpace members had to submit their age during the sign-up process, it was too easy to lie. If a child was rejected as too young (under sixteen), all he or she had to do was hit the "back" button on his or her Web browser and submit a new age. Aftab believed that this was a violation of the Children's Online Privacy Protection Act, enacted in 1998.

To Aftab's surprise, Polesetsky called back and asked her for help in fixing the site. Aftab demurred, saying that her nonprofit organization—staffed entirely by volunteers—provided assistance to individuals, not companies. But Polesetsky insisted that MySpace needed help. "We want to make sure everybody is safe, and we're willing to listen," he said.

Aftab hung up the phone feeling confused. She generally thought that sites like MySpace weren't safe for kids. But if such a site wanted to try to make itself safer, she felt obliged to help. After discussing it with her board, she agreed to work through her charity to advise MySpace.

Kids and the Internet have always had an uneasy relationship. Children are among the most active Web surfers and early adopters of new technology. But as long as children have been online, adults have worried about marketers and sexual predators having access to them.

Congress addressed the marketing issue when it passed the Children's Online Privacy Protection Act of 1998 requiring all websites to obtain parental consent before collecting personal information from children under thirteen. Since then, the FTC has taken action against several companies for violating the act—including levying a $1 million fine against the social network Xanga.com for allowing kids under thirteen to join its site without parental consent.

But the predator issue has proven harder to fix. Studies show that kids who engage in risky behaviors online—such as instant messaging about sex with strangers in a chat room—are more likely to be victim-ized offline. But most chat rooms remain unpoliced. It wasn't until 2005 that New York attorney general Eliot Spitzer forced Yahoo to shut down chat rooms with labels such as "girls 13 & up for much older men," "8–12 yo girls for older men," and "teen girls for older fat men." And Yahoo's cleanup was just a drop in the bucket; anyone who has ever visited a chat room can attest that sexual solicitation occurs on a regular basis.

However, adult sexual chatter is perfectly legal. On sites like MySpace, it's practically part of the culture. The problem is in sorting out the children from the adults. Without a verifiable form of identification for children—equivalent to a driver's license for adults—it's difficult for websites to verify the ages of their users. MySpace, like many websites, required members to enter their age when signing up but made no at-tempt to verify the truthfulness of the responses.

One of Aftab's first recommendations was for MySpace to lower its age limit even further: to fourteen years old from sixteen years old. One year earlier, MySpace safety czar Jason Feffer had convinced MySpace to lower its age limit to sixteen from eighteen in the hopes of convincing MySpace members to stop lying about their ages. But kids were still lying about their ages to join.

Aftab's view was that lowering the age limit would encourage more kids to be truthful about their ages, allowing MySpace to put build spe-cial privacy protections for younger users.

In the meantime, some high schools had started banning access to MySpace from their campuses. "Anytime a teen puts their own photo or biographical information on a website, it's something that parents at least need to know about," explained the principal of one Vermont high school that banned MySpace.

But MySpace's slightly dangerous image only fueled interest in the site. By April 2005 MySpace had amassed 13.5 million monthly visitors and finally landed on comScore Media Metrix's closely watched list of the top fifty Web properties in the United States. MySpace was number forty-four.

MySpace had been eking out a slim profit for six months. For the month of March, revenues totaled $1.69 million, while expenses were just $1.55 million. MySpace projected that within a year, its revenues would double to $2.6 million a month, while expenses would rise only to $1.8 million, giving it a healthy profit margin.

As a result, MySpace finally caught the attention of the mainstream press. On May 31, *BusinessWeek* profiled MySpace, describing it as "something akin to the hottest bar in town, teeming with musicians and models." DeWolfe was justifiably proud of MySpace's success.

"We're crushing it," he told the magazine.

Chapter 14

THE KING OF SPYWARE

In the fall of 2004, New York attorney general Eliot Spitzer was looking for a big spyware case. Spyware is software that secretly monitors the behavior of Web users. Spyware companies make money selling this valuable information about user behavior to advertisers.

Earlier in the year, Utah passed the nation's first antispyware law, and the Federal Trade Commission held an antispyware forum. The press was writing constantly about the menace of spyware. But no one had yet brought a really big case to court. Spitzer wanted to be first.

Spitzer was known for being first. In 1999 he was the first state attorney general to set up an Internet bureau. With about fifteen people, it was the smallest division of the attorney general's office, but it aimed to have maximum impact. The Internet division brought in one of the first high-profile spam cases—against the so-called Buffalo spammer—and forced Yahoo to clean up its chat rooms. In the fall of 2004, Spitzer's office was in the midst of an ambitious assault on Wall Street, winning more than $3.5 billion in settlements from mutual funds for improper trading practices. Now Spitzer was accusing the insurance industry of price-fixing. At the same time, he wanted to stage a landmark Internet spyware case.

Ken Dreifach, the chief of the New York attorney general's Internet bureau, initially considered targeting one of the top two spyware companies: Claria or WhenU. But as he looked at them more closely, it became clear that neither company would be an easy target. Claria had just settled a lawsuit brought by top newspaper publishers. And WhenU had just won an injunction against the state of Utah's antispyware law. As a result of bad publicity, Claria and WhenU "had both cleaned up their act," Dreifach said. "We realized that most of the egregious spyware activity out there was probably coming from companies that were a little bit below the radar."

So Dreifach assigned the task of finding a suitable target to the newest attorney in the office: Justin Brookman, a young, ambitious lawyer with tousled hair and heavy-framed glasses. Brookman set up three computers in a small interior conference room and christened the space "the Lab." Every day he and an investigator went through a painstaking process of looking for spyware. First they had to purge the computer clean—a process that took several hours. Then they visited websites offering free downloads of song lyrics, screen savers, cursors, and games like tic-tac-toe. After each download, they searched the computer for spyware. If they found evidence of spyware, they stored it.

"It was painstaking work that alternated between quite creative and arduously dull," Dreifach recalled.

Finally, after three months, Brookman found his target: Intermix. First of all, Intermix hadn't provided the proper disclosure of the spyware in its legal and privacy disclaimers. Second, Intermix was a public company, which meant that more information was publicly available about its revenues and, importantly, that a lawsuit against it would be sure to generate media attention. Third, Intermix distributed spyware both directly and through third-party distributors, which meant the case would set a precedent for both types of spyware distribution. Finally, Intermix had been blatantly stupid about its spyware practices—even defending ResponseBase's cursor spyware to an MSNBC.com reporter the previous year. In short, a prosecutor's dream.

Still, a spyware case would be a test. No one had yet applied the consumer deceptive practices statute to spyware. Creative legal theories were Spitzer's specialty; most of the time they worked, but sometimes they didn't.

By December 2004 Brookman had pretty much built a complete case against Intermix. One of his key examples was a screen saver called "Hot Jalapeno Dance," which his assistant had downloaded from an Intermix website called MyCoolScreen.com. The program was advertised as "Spyware-checked: Passed." But, in fact, the screen saver secretly installed several programs on the user's computer: a toolbar that appeared in the Web browser, a program called KeenValue that displayed pop-up ads as the user surfed the Web, and a program that prevented the user from accessing certain websites and instead directed the browser toward an Intermix website called Incredifind.

Brookman suspected that Intermix wasn't making much money from the KeenValue pop-up ads, but it was making a bundle from ad links on Incredifind. Web surfers would land on Incredifind, which displayed links to sites related to where they were trying to go. If the user clicked on a link, the website would pay Intermix a finder's fee for bringing in a new customer.

Brookman and Dreifach debated whether to notify Intermix of their investigation or to simply slap the company with a lawsuit. They thought they had enough evidence to sue Intermix, and in that situation, "there's considerable incentive to simply file a proceeding—because your leverage goes up," Dreifach said. "Because if you start out with a dialogue, it drags on, and then you settle for less." But they also wanted to obtain documents from Intermix about how much money it was making from downloads. So on December 3 Brookman sent a letter to Intermix general counsel Chris Lipp asking for documents relating to its download division.

To Intermix, the New York attorney general's request seemed like a routine inquiry about an unimportant, tiny division of the company. No one had really championed the software download business since Brad Greenspan's departure. Since then, the division had been mostly on autopilot. When Spitzer's request arrived, General Counsel Lipp forwarded the request to an outside attorney, Linda Goldstein at Manatt, Phelps & Phillips, which was already handling some of the company's regulatory compliance issues.

On December 23 Goldstein's associate sent Brookman a letter detailing the extent of Intermix's download business. Intermix claimed that it was already in the process of shutting down several of the download programs and that it had not received any complaints from New York State residents.

At the same time, Intermix sent all of its download partners a notice stating that it would terminate their relationship if they didn't agree to an amended agreement—requiring users to view and agree to the privacy policy before downloading the software.

Intermix also turned over to Spitzer's office boxes of documents containing e-mails from Greenspan from the early days of the spyware business. The boxes contained one smoking-gun e-mail: On October 31, 2002, Greenspan laid out his four-page business plan for the spyware business, called "Operation Super Trojan."

> Goal: get deeply integrated on the user desktop and in the browser. Make money.
>
> Rationale: guaranteed way to reach consumer. Hedge against e-mail weakness and our Web traffic.
>
> Early general thoughts: Each application should have separate installations so that a consumer that removes one application does not automatically remove other applications.
>
> Applications should not be made simple to uninstall.

Spitzer's office opened a separate investigation against Greenspan.

In February Intermix squeaked out its third consecutive profitable quarter since Richard Rosenblatt's arrival but warned Wall Street that it would lose money in the following quarter. In his first six months, Rosenblatt had been able to turn the business around by cutting back divisions and selling off the SkillJam unit. But now that the low-hanging fruit was gone, he had to face the fact that the Alena wrinkle cream business was really the only profit driver at Intermix.

Sales of the Alena division's wrinkle cream, cellulite cream, and weight-loss pills soared to $12.4 million in the quarter, up 32 percent from the prior year. The profit margins on Alena's business were as high as 33 percent. Rosenblatt had promised Wall Street he would expand Alena's division.

Rosenblatt tried to make Alena's business sound a bit more glamorous. "Alena utilizes a technology-driven marketing solution that serves, tests, monitors, and optimizes the sale of high-margin products directly to consumers," he told investors. "We believe that the success we've experienced with multiple products in the health and beauty category can be expanded greatly into other categories."

Until then Intermix had to be satisfied with eking out a quarterly net income of $38,000 from revenues of $20.3 million.

The correspondence between Spitzer's office and Intermix dragged on, just as Brookman and Dreifach had feared. Intermix took its time combing through its records to figure out how many New York consumers had downloaded the company's spyware. Intermix also stalled on delivering the revenue figures that Brookman and Dreifach needed to begin negotiating the fine.

At the same time, Intermix was quietly pressuring one of its download partners, a small outfit in upstate New York called Acez Software, not to give in to pressure from the attorney general. Acez was one of the primary distributors of one of Intermix's spyware programs—bundling the spyware with the free screen savers it offered on its website. Intermix shared the revenue it generated from the spyware programs with Acez; during the two-year relationship Acez had earned $173,810. But once Spitzer's office contacted Acez president Bryan Sambrook about the investigation, Sambrook told Intermix that he wanted to terminate the relationship.

Intermix's Todd Smith wrote to Sambrook, "I just hate for you to give up all the revenue when I don't think you have done anything wrong. I just don't want to send the wrong message to the AG office that you did something wrong by discontinuing." Even as the investigation continued into February, Smith was sending notes to Sambrook saying, "I just don't see how anyone did anything wrong."

Sambrook turned over his correspondence to the attorney general's office. It certainly didn't seem to jibe with Intermix's contention that it was changing its policies and shutting down much of its download operations. Dreifach and Brookman were growing frustrated.

The final straw came in mid-March. For seventeen days Intermix's outside attorney, Linda Goldstein, stopped returning calls and e-mails. Finally Brookman walked into Dreifach's office and said, "This is bizarre. What should we do?"

"Let's draft the papers," Dreifach responded.

Brookman began pulling together the case against Intermix. On April 5 he mailed a certified letter to Intermix titled "Notice of Proposed Litigation." It gave Intermix five business days to show "why such proceedings should not be instituted."

Suddenly Intermix had to take Spitzer seriously. Rosenblatt and Lipp called Ken Dreifach directly to plead their case. Dreifach was sympathetic to their deferential, cooperative tone. But Spitzer had already signed off on the decision to sue Intermix, and he wasn't one to change his mind easily.

Rosenblatt offered to fly to New York to persuade Spitzer in person. But Dreifach demurred. "It was too little too late," he recalled.

Late on Tuesday night, April 12, Intermix disclosed in a filing with the Securities and Exchange Commission that the New York attorney general's office might take action against it. The company's stock price plunged from $8 to $4 per share.

The press lauded Spitzer for making another bold move to clean up the business world. "Eliot Spitzer is turning up the heat on spyware," wrote *BusinessWeek*. Intermix became a whipping boy for antispyware sentiment. The penny-stock blog Stocklemon.com began digging into Intermix's business and writing incendiary reports about the legal complaints against Alena's wrinkle cream and the lack of revenues at MySpace.

The lawsuit dealt MySpace a crushing blow. AOL's Advertising.com subsidiary pulled its ads from all of Intermix's websites, citing its policy of not doing business with spyware companies. Chris DeWolfe was incensed; Advertising.com was MySpace's biggest source of revenue. He called AOL and begged them to consider MySpace a separate entity from Intermix; five days later he was able to get the ads restored. Still, DeWolfe estimated that MySpace lost several hundred thousand dollars in the interim.

Spitzer's suit also killed MySpace's talks with MTV. After the lawsuit was announced, Viacom's general counsel, Mike Fricklas, raised concerns about the legal issues involved in buying MySpace while it was under investigation. MTV executive Jason Hirschhorn argued that the investigation was a good time to buy because it depressed the price of MySpace. "To me, the obvious thing is that everybody will be backing away from Intermix during the investigation, so we should pounce and lock them up," he argued. Hirschhorn speculated that if in the worst-case scenario, Spitzer uncovered spyware at MySpace, Viacom could walk away from the deal before it closed, paying what is known as a "breakup fee" to cover Intermix's transaction costs. But Hirschhorn had no authority to buy MySpace without the support of Viacom's corporate deal makers. So the talks died.

Rosenblatt's advisers told him that it would take months, if not years, to settle with Spitzer, who was notoriously difficult to negotiate with. Rosenblatt decided his only option was to throw cash at the situation as fast as possible. It didn't matter that he didn't have much cash; he certainly wasn't going to have *any* if he didn't settle soon.

Rosenblatt knew it was important to settle with regulators as soon as possible. Back when he was running iMall, the company had been fined by the Federal Trade Commission just as he was trying to sell it. Rosenblatt learned that investors were willing to swallow a fine once they could quantify the size of it. Uncertainty about the size of a fine is what drives the stock price down. So Rosenblatt felt that getting a fast settlement was his best strategy for survival—no matter the price.

Two days later, on April 14, Intermix celebrated its six-year anniversary with a party at the movie theater in the shopping mall across the street. The company had hired a hypnotist to entrance various audience members.

While the hypnotist was working the crowd, Chris Lipp found Rosenblatt and Brett Brewer. "Spitzer has offered to settle the case for one and a half million dollars," the general counsel whispered. Rosenblatt and Brewer were shocked. Intermix's outside attorney had advised them that the fine would likely be around $200,000, since that was the amount of revenue Intermix had generated from downloads in New York. But Spitzer's office was looking beyond the state of New York. Intermix's global profits from downloads totaled $3.67 million. Spitzer wanted a piece of that too.

The next morning, Rosenblatt got a call from Intermix's outside attorney, Linda Goldstein.

"Are you sitting down?" she asked.

"No, I'm driving," Rosenblatt replied.

"Well, you better pull over," Goldstein advised.

Rosenblatt pulled his wife's Lexus sports utility vehicle over to the side of the road.

"Eliot Spitzer wants fifty million dollars," she said. Spitzer had read the Internet division's case against Intermix overnight and decided that it was too strong a case to settle for just $1.5 million. Dreifach had withdrawn the $1.5 million settlement offer early that morning.

Rosenblatt felt like he was going to have a heart attack. Intermix had only about $7.5 million in cash. There was no way the company could pay a $50 million fine. He started to think that the only way Intermix could get out of this situation was to raise money fast. His idea was that he could find a company to buy Intermix, take it private, and sell off pieces of the company for cash. The purchase price would be contingent on the size of the Spitzer settlement. Once the settlement was agreed upon, Intermix's buyer could simply deduct the settlement fine from the purchase price.

On April 29, one day after Spitzer filed his lawsuit against Intermix, Rosenblatt met with Los Angeles investment banker Michael Montgomery to discuss his options. Montgomery, a laid-back former Disney executive, specialized in Los Angeles's nascent Internet market and also knew his way around Hollywood. Montgomery had invited Brett Brewer to present at his investment bank's conference in March and was intrigued by MySpace's fast growth.

Montgomery advised Rosenblatt that the real value of Intermix was in its ownership of the MySpace option, but he thought it would be hard to find a buyer during the Spitzer investigation. Still, by the first week in May, Montgomery had rounded up an interested buyer: Livedoor, a Japanese Internet portal that was looking to expand into the United States. Rosenblatt met several times with Livedoor's executives but couldn't convince them to offer more than $6 per share for Intermix. He decided to hold out for a higher price. It was a prescient decision: Livedoor's top executives were later indicted in Tokyo for allegedly spreading false information about a takeover.

Around the same time, another prospective buyer also knocked on Intermix's door separately from Montgomery: AOL, the giant Internet service provider. AOL was trying to become a portal as its Internet access business declined, and it needed content to make its site competitive with Yahoo. AOL executive Jim Bankoff thought that MySpace would be a great way to attract people to AOL's music site and would be a natural fit with AOL's popular instant messaging software. But AOL was trying to win customers with its antispam and antispyware message. It couldn't afford to team up with a company being sued for spyware.

The May 4 MySpace board meeting was consumed in large part by a discussion of how the Spitzer lawsuit was hurting MySpace. DeWolfe presented a slide titled "Mix majority ownership of MySpace is causing immediate damage to value of MySpace," followed by fifteen bullet points explaining how MySpace had been harmed by the Spitzer lawsuit.

DeWolfe listed the damage: The Viacom-MTV deal was dead, AOL's Advertising.com division had shut off MySpace's ad revenues to the tune of $500,000 per month, several large ad agencies were considering pulling their business as well, and Google was refusing to work with MySpace.

DeWolfe was also worried about the impact on the MySpace brand, stating in one of his bullet points: "Some reporters are mentioning MySpace in the first or second sentence of their articles as being 'owned and operated' by Intermix, which implies involvement in AG action (*Wall Street Journal, Ad Week, Dow Jones Newswires, MarketWatch*, etc.)."

DeWolfe proposed that Intermix should drop below 50 percent ownership of MySpace, by selling some of its shares to Redpoint, to the MySpace founders, or to another investor. He put up another slide: "Mix will realize a higher return on their investment if they go below 50 percent now as the incremental value won't be drained out of the company from negative associations and innuendo."

Rosenblatt understood DeWolfe's frustration. But he had always intended for Intermix to own a majority stake in MySpace. Now that the rest of Intermix's businesses were under fire, keeping control of MySpace was more important than ever.

DeWolfe's outrage was somewhat disingenuous. Until 2004 he had been distributing spyware through downloadable cursors and selling spyware pop-up ads at his ResponseBase division. It wasn't until ResponseBase morphed into MySpace that he developed his newfound antipathy to spyware.

In fact, DeWolfe was lucky that Spitzer didn't go after him as well as Greenspan. When Intermix turned over documents to Spitzer, many of them were ResponseBase insertion orders for pop-up ads in the Keen-

Value spyware program. A typical ResponseBase insertion order dated July 29, 2003, documented ResponseBase's sale of ten thousand Keen-Value pop-up ads at 28 cents per click to an online e-mail marketing company called Digital Arrow. There were boxes full of similar documents at Spitzer's office.

But, luckily for DeWolfe, the investigators in Spitzer's office didn't pursue ResponseBase—most likely because it was defunct, and the KeenValue pop-up ads were no longer generating significant revenue for Intermix.

"So, are you here to learn about MySpace or to meet the king of spyware?" Rosenblatt joked.

The audience of several hundred money managers and Internet executives gasped. It was May 16, and Rosenblatt was speaking to the Silicon Valley elite at the Thomas Weisel Partners Internet Conference at the Four Seasons Hotel in San Francisco. This was not a crowd that approved of spyware companies.

"Well, let me tell you why you ought to be here," Rosenblatt continued, and began talking about the growth prospects at MySpace and Alena.

Shawn Colo, a private equity fund manager in the audience, was astonished at Rosenblatt's neat verbal pirouette. *He could easily have spent fifteen minutes talking about the Spitzer case,* Colo thought to himself.

Impressed, Colo introduced himself to Rosenblatt after the speech. Rosenblatt wasted no time pitching him on his latest plan: to take Intermix private. His objective was to sell off the Alena division, spin off MySpace as an initial public offering, and develop Intermix's websites, such as Grab.com, as a pure media company.

But Colo wasn't interested in financing a company that was being pursued by Eliot Spitzer. After all, if someone with deep pockets backed Intermix, it would just encourage Spitzer—and possibly other state attorney generals—to reach for a bigger fine.

"I don't think this makes sense," Colo told Rosenblatt.

Rosenblatt heard the same response from all the other private equity players he approached. No one wanted to pay more than $4 a share for Intermix, whose shares had just sunk to a low of $3.20 a week earlier.

...

Rosenblatt's spyware jokes might have soothed the San Francisco crowd, but they were driving DeWolfe crazy. He was trying to steer his high-growth startup toward an initial public offering. MySpace didn't need the taint of spyware on its journey to the public markets.

On May 17, one day after Rosenblatt's speech, DeWolfe sent an e-mail to the MySpace board members beseeching them again to separate Intermix from MySpace. In the e-mail, DeWolfe claimed that the "Intermix situation" was damaging the value of MySpace. MySpace had lost several hundred thousand dollars of advertising revenues when Advertising.com cut off the relationship due to Intermix's spyware. Google also didn't want to be associated with Intermix, and MySpace's discussions with Overture and Viacom were in a holding pattern.

To mitigate further damage, DeWolfe requested that Intermix no longer mention MySpace in press releases or sales and marketing materials. He also asked Intermix to ensure that MySpace was "carved out" of any consent decree with the attorney general. DeWolfe also suggested setting up a trigger that would force Intermix to drop its ownership of MySpace below 50 percent if there was another crisis. "We are concerned that the dust may not settle or that a new cloud of dust will appear with another problem from a different Intermix business unit," DeWolfe wrote.

Rosenblatt's reply the next morning was essentially a brush-off:

As you all know, I am doing all I can to mitigate any impact this may have on Intermix and MySpace. As I mentioned at dinner and at the meeting, dropping below 50 percent has tremendous implications. The entire board would have to meet, discuss, and receive outside opinions before we could make any decision.

MySpace is one of our most valuable assets, and anything we do that damages our ownership or control is clearly material and needs to be well thought out and studied. We are close to putting this behind us, and I hope everything will improve going forward.

All my best, RR

"You are going to put our company out of business," Rosenblatt told Dietrich Snell, one of Spitzer's top lieutenants.

Once Rosenblatt realized that Spitzer's Internet bureau was not calling the shots, he decided to go over its head and began negotiating with Snell. Rosenblatt offered to give Spitzer all the money Intermix had in the bank: $7.5 million.

But Rosenblatt didn't want to give it all away in one lump sum; he was hoping to spread out the payments over several years. Finally, in June, Intermix agreed to pay $7.5 million over three years to settle the case with Spitzer. It was one of the biggest fines that any Internet company had ever paid to Spitzer's office.

In October Brad Greenspan agreed to pay $750,000 in a separate settlement with Spitzer's office for his role in promoting spyware. Greenspan also donated $50,000 to the antispyware efforts at the Center for Democracy and Technology, a nonprofit institution promoting free expression, privacy, and open access on the Internet.

For MySpace, the Spitzer settlement cleared the way to restart sale talks with Viacom.

Chapter 15

SCHMUCK INSURANCE

D uring the summer of 2005, the value of MySpace was increasing by the day. Between January and March, MySpace's traffic doubled from 5.8 million unique visitors to 11.3 million. By May MySpace had grown another astounding 50 percent, attracting 15.6 million unique visitors.

At the same time, the Internet market was finally starting to heat up. In February, the website About.com with its twenty-two million monthly visitors sold to the *New York Times* for $410 million in cash. In April, the website Shopping.com with twenty-two million monthly visitors sold to eBay for $620 million in cash. And in June, the website Shopzilla with fourteen million monthly visitors sold to E. W. Scripps for $525 million in cash.

Intermix chief executive Richard Rosenblatt realized that the $125 million price tag for MySpace that Intermix had negotiated in February was a bargain-basement price. Based on the recent sales, MySpace could possibly fetch as much as $500 million.

But it would be tricky for Intermix to get the full value for its ownership of MySpace. Rosenblatt had to handle the situation carefully.

The relationship between Intermix and MySpace was complex.

In February, when MySpace obtained financing from Redpoint Ventures and set itself up as an independent subsidiary of Intermix, MySpace had agreed to a complicated ownership arrangement with Intermix. Under the terms of the option agreement, Intermix owned a controlling 53 percent of MySpace. More important, if Intermix received a bona fide offer for more than 50 percent of Intermix, it had the right to automatically purchase the 47 percent of MySpace it didn't already own for $69 million.

Intermix's right to buy back a portion of MySpace was a time-honored technique among companies that want to hedge against the future. Time Warner chief executive Richard Parsons employed a similar tactic when he sold off the Warner Music Group in 2003. At the time, the music industry was in a slump, so Parsons jettisoned the business. But Parsons also kept an option to buy back a piece of Warner Music just in case he had been wrong about the prospects for the music industry.

"I like to call it schmuck insurance," Parsons said at the time. "In case the music industry starts to go like gangbusters, we won't look like schmucks for selling."

The MySpace option was a type of schmuck insurance for Intermix, ensuring that if MySpace started to take off, Intermix would benefit from MySpace's success. But the MySpace option was to expire in February 2006. And Intermix could not exercise its option if MySpace had previously received a bona fide offer of more than $125 million or had filed a registration statement for an initial public offering.

The details of the schmuck insurance clause were not secret. They were detailed in Intermix's public filings with the Securities and Exchange Commission. That meant that Intermix was sitting on a time bomb. Anyone could jump in with a bid for MySpace and render Intermix's schmuck insurance ineffective.

On June 9 banker Michael Montgomery presented the situation to the Intermix board of directors.

Essentially it boiled down to this: MySpace was Intermix's most valuable asset. But to sell MySpace, Intermix had to sell itself. If MySpace was sold as a separate unit, it would trigger a huge capital gains tax bill for Intermix. But if Intermix sold itself outright, then Intermix's shareholders would each pay a much smaller tax on the sale of the shares they owned. Montgomery calculated that MySpace would have to sell for far more than $1 billion to be equivalent to a sale of Intermix for $600 million for Intermix shareholders.

Selling Intermix would not be easy either, because a buyer would want to be sure that it was getting full control of MySpace as part of the package. That could happen only if Intermix exercised its option to buy back the portion of MySpace it didn't already own.

Two things could prevent Intermix from exercising its option: an IPO for MySpace or MySpace cutting an agreement to sell itself for more than $125 million. With Viacom sniffing around MySpace, the latter option did not seem far-fetched. Montgomery advised the Intermix board to keep MySpace and Viacom in the dark about any Intermix sale talks. If Viacom told MySpace that Intermix was up for sale, MySpace could have rushed to sell itself to another bidder before Intermix could close the deal. "There's no way we can talk to Viacom, because they're already talking to MySpace," Montgomery advised the board. "The sale has to be very carefully done because of the dual option. If you do it wrong, you lose the value of the option."

It went against Rosenblatt's straightforward nature to take covert action. But as CEO of Intermix, Rosenblatt's duty was to provide the greatest returns to the Intermix shareholders, not the MySpace minority shareholders. Legally, in fact, he would be breaching his fiduciary duty to Intermix if he notified MySpace of sale talks. So he agreed to conduct a discreet sale and promised himself that he would alert MySpace as soon as possible.

Intermix had to tread delicately with its plans for a quiet auction. In 1986 the Delaware Chancery Court handed down a landmark opinion in *Revlon v. MacAndrews,* asserting that the directors of public companies have a duty to obtain the highest price when selling their company. In the *Revlon* case, the court ruled that the directors of Revlon had improperly ended an auction too early in order to secure a preferred bidder rather than the highest bidder. Since then, the *Revlon* case has set the standard for public company mergers and acquisitions, particularly for companies being sold for cash.

In the case of Intermix, two questions arose: What constitutes an auction? And is it possible to hold a quiet auction? In practice, if a company's bankers make inquiries to a list of qualified buyers, that generally qualifies as an auction. Montgomery determined that he could satisfy the auction requirement by discreetly contacting a few select companies.

Under Delaware corporate law, the directors of a majority shareholder have a duty to deal with a publicly traded subsidiary in "good faith." But there is no such requirement for a privately held subsidiary such as

MySpace. Therefore the Intermix directors were free to negotiate a sale behind MySpace's back. Montgomery advised the board that the best way for Intermix to get the best price for itself would be to exercise its MySpace option—and the only way Intermix could exercise the option would be to get a bona fide offer for Intermix.

Montgomery's view was that other bidders could always emerge after Intermix had bought out MySpace. "I wanted a binding offer that put the company in play because they could then exercise the option," he said later.

Montgomery already had in mind the idea of a buyer for Intermix: News Corp.

MySpace executives were starting to regret having issued the schmuck insurance option to Intermix. As MySpace's popularity soared, its executives were increasingly optimistic about their prospects for going public. Google had gone public the previous year at $85 a share, and by July 2005 it was trading at around $280 per share, making its founders billionaires. MySpace's founders, who collectively owned 19.9 percent of the company, could reasonably expect to become multimillionaires if it went public at a $500 million valuation.

But before it could win the confidence of Wall Street investors, MySpace had to address some issues. It had to recruit seasoned executives, prove its financial model was profitable, and make sure its technology was bulletproof. In the meantime, MySpace was hoping that Intermix wouldn't exercise its option to buy MySpace at a $125 million valuation. Although the founders would still get wealthy, it wouldn't be anywhere near as much money as they could earn if sold in the free market.

Josh Berman, MySpace's chief operating officer, asked Rosenblatt several times to rescind the option. But his proposal was naive. Legally, the option could expire before February 2006 only if MySpace were sold or went public.

Intermix had no intention of letting MySpace out of its obligation.

News Corp. didn't want to talk to Intermix until the Spitzer settlement was done. But once the tentative settlement was announced, Montgomery set up a matchmaking meeting between the two companies.

On June 23 Montgomery and Rosenblatt visited News Corp.'s newly anointed Internet strategist, Ross Levinsohn, and gave him an overview of Intermix's businesses. In a conference room on the Fox lot, Rosenblatt explained Intermix to Levinsohn's team, describing all the divisions, from MySpace to online pet food sales.

Initially Rosenblatt suggested that he wasn't looking to sell Intermix. "We'd consider working with Fox to do strategic fund-raising," Rosenblatt said.

But Levinsohn didn't buy it. "No," he replied, "we should just acquire you guys."

After the meeting, Rosenblatt was elated. He sent an e-mail to Intermix board member Andrew Sheehan reminding him of a promise to accelerate Rosenblatt's stock options if Rosenblatt managed to sell the company. Rosenblatt also joked that if he sold the company, Sheehan should be grateful to him. "Name ur next kid rich," Rosenblatt wrote.

At the five o'clock MySpace board meeting on June 30, Chris DeWolfe again proposed that Intermix should rescind the schmuck insurance clause and focus on spinning off MySpace into a multibillion-dollar public company.

"They believe that the option restricts their hiring of a world-class CTO and CFO," Rosenblatt wrote in an e-mail to News Corp.'s Levinsohn following the meeting. "Obviously we did not agree to the relinquishment of our options."

Josh Berman, always the hotheaded one, had asked Rosenblatt several times to cancel the option. At the meeting, he threatened to call Viacom and Yahoo and ask them to send offers to MySpace directly, which would cause the option to expire.

"Do whatever you need to do," Rosenblatt replied. He couldn't prevent MySpace from rounding up a competing offer, but he could try to dissuade them from doing so.

After the board meeting, Rosenblatt cornered DeWolfe privately and told him that News Corp. was already in talks with Intermix and wanted to meet with MySpace as well. "I also made him aware that we all needed to be open to ideas, because we *could* simply sell Intermix to some media company, and [MySpace] management would end up with an illiquid 47 percent of a major subsidiary, which is the worse-case scenario," Rosenblatt wrote in an e-mail following the meeting.

Rosenblatt's position was a bit of a bluff. Intermix would have a hard time selling itself if it didn't have full control of its major asset, MySpace. But the bluff worked. With the threat of an Intermix sale hanging over his head, DeWolfe agreed to meet with News Corp. "Chris very much appreciated that both Intermix and Fox wanted to meet with him and discuss his role and his team's comp [compensation] instead of just exercising the option," Rosenblatt wrote in the e-mail to Levinsohn.

"Chris and I continue to be on the same page, and our conversation was very constructive and positive," Rosenblatt continued. "In fact, I am quite relieved, and this should make us all determine if there is a deal or not much quicker."

Rosenblatt spent the Fourth of July weekend at his vacation home in Lake Arrowhead, a resort community nestled in the San Bernardino Mountains, east of Los Angeles. But Rosenblatt assured News Corp.'s Levinsohn that he would be reachable the whole time. "My kids are bringing friends, so I will be working most of the weekend guilt free, so feel free to call, e-mail, or come visit," he wrote to Levinsohn. "I get Internet connection from the boat!"

It wasn't Levinsohn who called over the weekend. It was Thomas Weisel of the well-known merchant bank Thomas Weisel Partners (TWP) in Silicon Valley. Rosenblatt was friendly with Weisel; he had given his "king of spyware" speech at Weisel's conference earlier in the year. Weisel's friend Michael Dolan had just been appointed chief financial officer of Viacom and wanted to renew discussions with MySpace. Dolan tapped Weisel to make the introduction to Rosenblatt.

"Viacom realizes Intermix controls MySpace and wants to talk to you," Weisel told Rosenblatt.

"Great, I'd love to meet Viacom," Rosenblatt said.

Montgomery, Rosenblatt's banker, was miffed to see another banker sniffing around the same prey. "My advise [sic], ignore him," Montgomery wrote to Rosenblatt. "Last thing you need is another person shpping [sic] you," he wrote, referring to Weisel.

But Rosenblatt ignored Montgomery's complaints. He was happy to have two bankers vying for his business. As the CEO of a public company, he knew that he had to run as open an auction as possible to maximize the value of Intermix shares. Intermix could only benefit from a fight between two media giants.

"The Game is on!" Rosenblatt e-mailed Levinsohn.

Chapter 16

THE GAME IS ON

On Tuesday, July 5, 2005, News Corp. chairman Rupert Murdoch's Gulfstream jet was one of the first to touch down in Sun Valley, Idaho, for the annual media mogul powerfest held by investment banker Herb Allen. Other attendees of the exclusive conference in the Sawtooth Mountains included Microsoft founder Bill Gates, legendary investor Warren Buffet, Apple founder Steve Jobs, and Disney chief executive Michael Eisner.

The mood among old-time moguls like Murdoch was gloomy. Every day as they ate lunch by the duck pond after a morning of presentations inside the chateaulike ski lodge, the conversation turned to the same topics: Box-office receipts from films were falling; DVD sales were slowing; big media stocks had been stagnant for three years; and, most galling, Google and Yahoo stocks were soaring.

Viacom chairman Sumner Redstone was so frustrated that he had decided to break up his company into two pieces. "The age of the conglomerate is over," Redstone told a gaggle of reporters who were lurking near the duck pond, hoping to glimpse the moguls.

Thursday morning, as the guests wandered into the ski lodge for a seven o'clock breakfast, they were greeted by the news that terrorists had bombed London's Underground. Sony chief executive Howard Stringer, whose family lived in London, appeared ashen. Murdoch, whose older children, James and Liz, both lived in London, spent most of the day on the phone with them and his newspaper editors in London who were covering the mayhem. News Corp. president Peter Chernin, for his part, was also worried, but about something else: He had heard that Viacom was courting Intermix.

"We want to buy three Internet companies: Intermix, WeatherBug, and IGN," Chernin told Murdoch.

"Great, go do it," his boss replied.

Chernin told Murdoch that they had to move particularly fast on Intermix. "We've only got a forty-eight- to seventy-two-hour head start on Viacom," he said.

Sumner Redstone and Rupert Murdoch are often seen as similar types of media moguls. After all, both men built their media empires from scratch, assembling disparate media assets through a series of bigger and bigger deals. Both men are in their twilight years, with much younger wives, but have refused to give up control of their companies. Both men own controlling stakes in their media empires and hope to pass on their empires to their families. And the two are immensely competitive with each other. Redstone once said, "I have always wanted to be number one in my job, and to be number one, you have to be ahead of Rupert Murdoch."

But the similarities end there. Redstone, a pugnacious redhead, is constantly firing the people who work for him; Murdoch has a loyal team that has been with him for decades. Redstone is at war with his children; Murdoch's children are devoted to him. Redstone rules his empire from afar, calling his lieutenants from his mansion in Beverly Hills; Murdoch divides his time between his New York and Los Angeles offices, while visiting his home base in Australia at least once a year. Redstone is cautious with his money, preferring not to spend too much on acquisitions; Murdoch has a habit of paying whatever it takes to get assets that he believes are of strategic importance. Redstone is obsessed with Viacom's stock price, spending much of his day on the phone with his stockbroker; Murdoch isn't focused solely on News Corp's share price, and, in fact, often does deals—such as his December 2007 purchase of the *Wall Street Journal*—that he knows will lower News Corp.'s share price in the near term.

During the summer of 2005, the two men were reacting very differently to the slump in their stock prices. Murdoch was hunting for Internet acquisitions that could position News Corp. for the digital future. Redstone was placing his bets on financial engineering: He planned to split Viacom into two separate companies—Viacom and CBS—in a move that he believed would boost the company's share price. Viacom would contain the fast-growing cable networks division, including MTV and Comedy Central, as well as the Paramount Pictures film studio. CBS would own the slow-growing broadcast television and radio assets, as well as the outdoor billboard business. The idea was that investors who wanted big dividends could invest in the mature assets at CBS, while those who wanted stock momentum could invest in the faster-growing assets at Viacom.

But the Viacom split-up was causing no end of management turmoil. The problem was that Redstone—then eighty-two years old—wanted to be CEO of both companies. His two deputies, Tom Freston of MTV and Leslie Moonves of CBS, had shared the title of copresident for a year, and now each wanted to run one of the two new companies. By the time of the summer meeting in Sun Valley, a few months prior to the split-up taking place, Redstone still hadn't agreed to hand over the CEO title to either man. That meant that the corporate executives who controlled deal making and legal strategy still reported to Redstone. So at the time that Intermix quietly put itself up for sale, Viacom's top executives were struggling for power instead of focusing on the future.

Back in Los Angeles, on the day of the London bombing, Richard Rosenblatt was making the same presentation to Viacom that he had made to News Corp. executive Ross Levinsohn a week earlier.

Rosenblatt didn't really trust Viacom. The company had approached Intermix late in the game after courting the MySpace executives for months. This troubled the Intermix chief executive, who worried that Viacom might make a bid for MySpace just to stop the sale to News Corp. Even so, Rosenblatt wouldn't mind a competing bid for Intermix if Viacom was willing to top News Corp.'s offer.

Rosenblatt's banker, Michael Montgomery, was also urging caution. Montgomery believed that it would be difficult to negotiate with Viacom without notifying MySpace, given the history the two had together. His view was that Intermix should delay bringing Viacom into the fold, in order to delay having to tell MySpace that Intermix was looking for a buyer.

"You need to dance with them . . . slow them down. I know you can do it," Montgomery wrote in an e-mail to Rosenblatt before the meeting.

Rosenblatt assured Montgomery that he was loyal to Levinsohn. "I love Ross, no question!" he replied.

The Viacom-Intermix meeting, as it turned out, was frustrating. MTV had nine executives present, and it wasn't clear how serious they were about a deal. Viacom chief operating officer Bob Bakish was there, and seemed enthusiastic. But Viacom's top decision makers, Chief Financial Officer Mike Dolan and General Counsel Mike Fricklas, were not there.

After the meeting, Joseph Ianniello, who had just been appointed head of Viacom's mergers and acquisitions team, fought with the bankers at Thomas Weisel Partners, which had set up the meeting.

"We typically use bigger firms that want the marketing benefits of saying they advised Viacom," Ianniello told Blake Warner of TWP. "But I'd be willing to pay you maybe a quarter million dollars if you get the deal done and up to another quarter million as a performance bonus at our sole discretion."

By Viacom's standards, Ianniello's offer was generous. Viacom usually didn't hire bankers when it made acquisitions, preferring to negotiate deals on its own. But by banking industry standards, Ianniello's offer was insultingly low. Bankers typically charge between 0.5 percent and 1 percent of the value of a transaction. With Intermix shares trading at about $8, any deal to buy Intermix would be worth at least $400 million. So Thomas Weisel Partners could expect to earn, at the bare minimum, $2 million in fees for such a deal.

Outraged, Warner refused to let his bank represent Viacom. "We're not in the business just for the marketing benefits of representing Viacom," he told Ianniello.

Thomas Weisel later said, "We gave them a golden opportunity to get in on the ground-floor bidding on one of the truly great properties in the Internet space, and, frankly, they let their arrogance get in the way of reasoning."

The MTV executives were shocked and disappointed that the folks in the corporate suite had alienated a banker who seemed to have a close relationship with Intermix. Viacom then scrambled to line up the services of well-known media banker Stuart Epstein at Morgan Stanley in New York. But Epstein was starting from scratch; he didn't know anything about Intermix, MySpace, or the schmuck insurance clause.

Meanwhile, Thomas Weisel turned around and called Rosenblatt. "Hey, Rich, let us represent you," he said.

Rosenblatt was surprised. "Aren't you retained by Viacom?" he asked.

"No, I would rather be retained by you," Weisel replied. "I always want to be retained by the seller, not the buyer." Like real estate agents, investment bankers work on commission and are paid their fee only upon a completed transaction. From Weisel's point of view, a commission was more likely if he represented the seller rather than one of many potential buyers. Rosenblatt agreed to retain TWP as well as Montgomery. After all, he reasoned, Montgomery was a small up-and-coming banker with just a few guys in a Santa Monica office. For a transaction of this size, it would be nice to have the added credibility of a well-known bank approving the deal.

Intermix board member Andrew Sheehan thought that having two bankers would complicate the deal. "Not sure it makes sense to have the two banks at cross purposes," he wrote in an e-mail to Rosenblatt on Friday, July 8.

Of course, Sheehan was right. Intermix's two sets of bankers began quarreling almost immediately. Montgomery was assigned to oversee the News Corp. negotiations, while Weisel would oversee the Viacom negotiations. But both bankers were worried that the other one would leak information.

"The last thing I wanted was another banker," Montgomery recalled. "I was concerned Weisel would tell Viacom how far along we were with News Corp."

Montgomery worried that Viacom would simply bid for MySpace in order to stop the Intermix–News Corp. talks. "It was very tricky game theory to decide whether Viacom would suicidally try to stop the deal," he said. "It could have been mutually assured destruction."

Meanwhile, the Thomas Weisel Partners team was shocked to learn that News Corp. had information about the mechanics of an Intermix convertible preferred security that had some special rights around transferability. "It would have required somebody with very unique and in-depth knowledge of that security" to learn that information, said Blake Warner. "We became paranoid that Montgomery was feeding informa-tion to Fox."

The paranoia about Thomas Weisel Partners spread to News Corp. as well. News Corp. deal maker Mike Lang declared in an e-mail to Mont-gomery that he only trusted "you and Richard"—not Thomas Weisel Partners and VantagePoint Ventures.

On the Tuesday after the Fourth of July weekend, News Corp.'s Ross Levinsohn spent the day at Intermix's offices. Intermix executives briefed him on all aspects of the business, from sales of wrinkle cream, to their online greeting card business—everything except MySpace.

Montgomery's banking team had surreptitiously prepared some esti-mates of MySpace's financial performance to present to News Corp. But they were careful not to ask MySpace for any documentation that would raise suspicions about sale talks. Montgomery banker James Min esti-mated that in the year ending December 31, 2005, MySpace's earnings before interest, taxes, depreciation, and amortization would be $9.8 mil-lion on revenues of $29.3 million. For the year 2006, he estimated that MySpace would earn $25.6 million on sales of $57.4 million. Although he was projecting a doubling of revenues and nearly a tripling of profits, his estimates ultimately proved to be far too conservative.

Levinsohn wasn't scheduled to meet Chris DeWolfe until Wednesday morning. From Intermix's point of view, the meeting between Levinsohn and DeWolfe had to be handled carefully. Rosenblatt was worried that if MySpace's executives and venture capital backers knew Intermix was going to be sold, they could round up a competing offer for MySpace. Any offer for MySpace that was over $125 million would freeze the negotiations between Intermix and News Corp. After an entire day at Intermix, Levinsohn and Rosenblatt went out to dinner to "discuss the best approach to Chris DeWolfe the following morning," according to Rosenblatt.

"Obviously this meeting is completely confidential, and no one but Chris knows about it at MS," Rosenblatt wrote in an e-mail to Levin-sohn while preparing for the meeting. "This will be a final check to make sure everyone is on the same 'vision' page and get a sense of whether Fox, MySpace, and Intermix can satisfy everyone's needs and create a true win-win-win. MySpace does not drive the decision, but their enthusiastic participation is important for all of us, and I have some ideas. Chris and I will speak more this morning and weekend."

Rosenblatt downplayed the significance of the meeting to DeWolfe, telling him it was exploratory. "We're thinking of doing something with Fox, an investment or more," Rosenblatt told DeWolfe.

DeWolfe had already sat through dozens of exploratory meetings with MTV, AOL, and others, which ultimately had led to nothing. There was no reason for him to view this meeting any differently.

Levinsohn and DeWolfe met at ten o'clock on July 6 in Michael Montgomery's Santa Monica office overlooking the Pacific Ocean. Levinsohn had wanted to meet with others at MySpace as well, but to keep things quiet, Montgomery insisted that he meet only with DeWolfe.

The meeting was meant to be a high-level discussion. There was no talk about price or deal terms, or even how far along the discussions were between Intermix and News Corp. But right away, the meeting got off to a rocky start.

Levinsohn pitched DeWolfe on how News Corp. could help MySpace reach the next level. DeWolfe sat quietly, but his eyes were growing wider with each suggestion by Levinsohn. Montgomery was horrified; Levinsohn's speech wasn't going over well at all.

Finally DeWolfe excused himself to go to the bathroom. Montgomery took the opportunity to advise Levinsohn to change his tactics. "If you really want to do this, you have to apologize to Chris," Montgomery urged.

When DeWolfe returned, Levinsohn backpedaled. "You know, I've been thinking," he said to DeWolfe. "What you guys are doing is incredible. We wouldn't change anything."

Montgomery heaved a sigh of relief. The meeting was back on track.

Afterward, Levinsohn and DeWolfe walked to a nearby Starbucks. Lifting his voice above the din of milk being steamed and lattes being ordered, DeWolfe told Levinsohn he was worried that the brand, personality, and culture of MySpace would be killed by big, conservative News Corp.

"Don't think of us as a big, stodgy media company," said Levinsohn.

News Corp. may be known for the conservative Fox News Channel, he explained, but it was also the home of the Fox broadcast network's *The Simpsons* and *24*—"edgy, risk-taking stuff."

DeWolfe nodded but didn't reply. He was going to keep his options open.

Still, Levinsohn viewed DeWolfe's lack of opposition as a good sign—and called Rosenblatt to report.

Rosenblatt immediately fired off an e-mail to the banker Montgomery with the subject line "Ross is fired up." Rosenblatt wrote, "DeWolfe is in." However, Rosenblatt's assessment was slightly overoptimistic. DeWolfe didn't really know what he was in for.

Later that night, Rosenblatt sent an e-mail to the Intermix board with an update on the News Corp. negotiations.

All,

On our last board meeting (10-K review), I mentioned we were in the early stages of negotiating a potential strategic deal with Fox. Those meetings have progressed and are looking promising. I met with the president of the new Fox Internet division last night for dinner, and he is very interested in making a bid in the next week or so . . .

The MySpace issue is a tricky one, and we are working through creative solutions. A requirement of any deal is that MS [MySpace] management is 100 percent on board—you can only imagine how complicated that is!

Best, Richard

On Friday, July 8, Intermix shares suddenly started soaring after one of the company's biggest critics suddenly recommended the stock. The penny-stock blog Stocklemon.com had been attacking Intermix in regular columns since April, claiming that Intermix's wrinkle cream business was based on defrauding consumers, that MySpace was an unprofitable den of iniquity, and that the company was disguising its thin profits with asset sales that boosted the bottom line. "Stocklemon believes that Intermix Media is the Paris Hilton of the Internet," wrote the site's author, Andrew Left, in a typical posting a month earlier.

But, strangely, after three months of barraging the company with negative press, and accumulating a "short position" in the stock—meaning that Left bought options that would increase in value if Intermix shares declined in value—the blogger had a change of heart. The Los Angeles–based Left attributed his reversal (the only one in Stocklemon's four-year history) to the sudden realization that MySpace was more than a flash in the pan. "One day I woke up, and there were fourteen or fifteen stories on MySpace in my Google alerts," he said. "Then I went to the Apple store in the mall and see three kids working on their MySpace accounts. I realized I was standing in front of a freight train . . . Whether it's a business or not, it's a phenomenon. And there's no reason to short a phenomenon."

The next morning, Left issued a positive report about Intermix. "We are sweetening our 'lemon' assessment about Intermix to 'potential lemonade,' " he wrote. "The magnetic attraction that MySpace has over the youth of America is so strong that even that most cynical short-seller cannot deny its reach." Left also dug up the details of Intermix's option to buy MySpace and concluded that "management has a strong incentive to sell MySpace before February 2006." He added that Intermix CEO Richard Rosenblatt has a "history of selling companies for big money."

Within two days, Intermix shares had soared to nearly $10, up from about $8. News Corp.'s Ross Levinsohn was furious; it seemed that someone at Intermix had tipped off the blogger to boost the price of the company. Suddenly Intermix's market value had shot up to nearly $441 million from about $350 million.

Rosenblatt was thrilled. Now he was more likely to reach his goal of selling Intermix for $12 per share, or $580 million.

Rupert Murdoch and Peter Chernin arrived back in Los Angeles from Sun Valley on Monday, July 11. Murdoch, always willing to pay for what he wanted, was undaunted by Intermix's increased stock price. For his part, Chernin was mulling tactics. Chernin knew that Viacom copresident Tom Freston was heading to Hawaii on vacation after Sun Valley, and Chernin wanted to get the deal done before Freston returned. Chernin also believed that Geoff Yang from Redpoint was going to be out of town for the weekend (which turned out to be incorrect), and thus would be less likely to hear about the deal and try to round up a competing bid for MySpace.

Chernin and Murdoch asked Rosenblatt to come into Murdoch's office on Tuesday afternoon to seal the deal.

On Tuesday morning Rosenblatt sent an e-mail to Levinsohn alerting him that MySpace's traffic had shot up again in June by 14 percent. "Left u a voicemail," Rosenblatt wrote. "Myspace hit 17.7 million uniques. Amazing, the rest of our network always drops 30-40% in the summer, and MySpace still grew big."

Meanwhile, Viacom sensed that things were heating up with Intermix. As Rosenblatt waited in the Fox cafeteria to meet with Murdoch, Viacom executive Van Toffler called to check in.

"Von [*sic*] just called w lots of luv," Rosenblatt typed on his Black-Berry to Intermix chief operating officer Sherman Atkinson. Atkinson replied, "Too funny. [MTV deal maker] Denmark [West] is very concerned they will get cut out of this deal due to the speed of the other partner."

Murdoch's intention was indeed to cut Viacom out. During his meeting with Rosenblatt on July 12, Murdoch issued what is known in the industry as an "exploding offer"—meaning that it would expire by the time the stock market opened on the following Monday morning. After that deadline expired, Murdoch wouldn't promise whether News Corp. would offer the same terms to Intermix.

Chapter 17

PROJECT IVORY

On Thursday, July 14, 2005, just two days after receiving the offer from Murdoch, Richard Rosenblatt was on the phone with Tom Freston, the copresident of Viacom. Freston was on vacation at the Four Seasons Resort in Maui, a lush enclave tucked above a private beach on the dry, sunny side of the Hawaiian island. Rosenblatt was in his banker's office in Los Angeles, overlooking the rather grittier beach in Santa Monica.

Rosenblatt was playing hardball. On the phone he told Freston that he was very close to getting a deal done with another company. "Things are moving really fast," Rosenblatt said. "We're going to do a deal by Sunday."

Freston, a seasoned business executive who built the MTV cable channel from scratch, was doubtful. He had heard that News Corp. was also looking at Intermix. But Freston and the other MTV executives believed they had a good strategy in place: The Viacom deal-making team was ensconced in a Los Angeles boardroom doing its final rounds of due diligence; Freston had approved Viacom to bid between $550 million and $810 million for Intermix, contingent on board approval; and Viacom was planning to send in its bid after the Viacom board meeting on Wednesday. Viacom was operating under the faulty assumption that sellers always have an incentive to wait for multiple bidders to show up, in order to drive a higher price. In this case, because of the schmuck insurance clause, Intermix had an incentive to take the first bid that arrived in order to prevent MySpace from selling itself separately.

Although the schmuck insurance clause was spelled out in Intermix's public filings, Freston and other top Viacom executives were unaware of its existence. As a result, Freston didn't take Rosenblatt's warning seriously.

"If it's moving that quickly, I'm not sure exactly what we can do about it," Freston said. He added that he would be in Los Angeles on Monday or Tuesday and would love to meet with Rosenblatt then.

Freston wasn't the only one who didn't believe that Rosenblatt could get the deal done by Sunday. "No one believed it except me and Murdoch," Rosenblatt recalled.

Rupert Murdoch had already made his bid. Now his team was just trying to make it airtight.

At six-thirty in the morning on Thursday, News Corp. negotiator Mike Lang laid out his concerns to Intermix's banker Michael Montgomery. "The one big issue that could kill this deal," Lang wrote, was if Intermix received a bid from News Corp., triggered the MySpace option, and then decided not to accept the bid from News Corp. by Sunday night. "We may walk on something like this," Lang wrote.

The issue was that under the terms of the MySpace option, Intermix had the right to buy out the rest of MySpace once it had a bona fide offer from News Corp. But Intermix wasn't required to accept News Corp.'s offer. So, theoretically, Intermix could use News Corp.'s offer as leverage to buy out the rest of MySpace, then turn around and sell itself to another bidder.

To prevent that from happening, News Corp. declined to send over a faxed preliminary offer until the deal was done. That put Intermix in a risky position for five days. Under the option, Intermix's negotiations with News Corp. would have to be halted if MySpace received its own bona fide offer during that time period. "All Viacom had to do was send an offer to MySpace for one hundred twenty-five million dollars, and we would have been frozen," Rosenblatt recalled.

But Rosenblatt agreed to take the risk in order to keep News Corp. happy.

"We are holding hands on this deal . . . both got our butts on the line," Rosenblatt wrote in an e-mail to News Corp.'s Ross Levinsohn. "Everyone is trusting us both."

News Corp. also wanted to make sure that Intermix's venture capital backer, VantagePoint Venture Partners, which controlled 23.4 percent of the Intermix shareholder votes, would vote in favor of the deal. On Thursday afternoon News Corp. president Peter Chernin invited VantagePoint partner Andrew Sheehan to come to his office in Los Angeles to discuss the pending deal.

Sheehan flew down to meet with Chernin, although he wasn't happy to leave his pregnant wife—who was due to give birth any day—at home in Marin County, north of San Francisco. Rosenblatt was at Viacom's offices making presentations about Intermix's business, but still he peppered Sheehan with e-mails about what kind of deal News Corp. was offering him.

"Chernin is a huge player. Make sure he knows I am the man. Got to get a good job, baby," Rosenblatt wrote in a joking e-mail to Sheehan a half hour before the meeting.

"What kind of deal do you want from Chernin?" Sheehan replied.

During the meeting, Sheehan suggested to Chernin that Rosenblatt would do a great job if he continued working at Fox. However, most of the meeting was not about Rosenblatt's future. Chernin wanted to discuss how VantagePoint was likely to vote on the deal. News Corp. was worried that MySpace would round up a competing offer for itself, thus halting the News Corp.–Intermix talks. Chernin wanted to lock up VantagePoint's vote in favor of the deal.

Sheehan couldn't give away VantagePoint's voting power with Viacom still looming on the horizon as potential higher bidder. Instead Sheehan promised to vote his shares in favor of the News Corp. deal—but with the caveat that if a better bid came along, the agreement was void. It wasn't a foolproof agreement, but it did make it harder for a competing bidder to cause trouble.

News Corp.'s Ross Levinsohn was anxious to seal the deal with Chris DeWolfe. On Wednesday, July 13, Levinsohn e-mailed Rosenblatt, "Am I meeting w/DeWolfe tomorrow?" Rosenblatt replied, "Yes. Chris will land in a couple of hrs."

But it wasn't until Friday morning that Rosenblatt stopped by DeWolfe's office in Santa Monica and told him that Intermix had re-

ceived an offer from News Corp. "I want to get you involved," Rosenblatt said.

DeWolfe took the news in his usual unflappable way. He didn't appear
to be upset or even shocked. Instead he calmly asked Rosenblatt what
would happen to him and his team.

"You need to work out your deal with Fox directly," Rosenblatt
replied.

So that afternoon, DeWolfe visited Murdoch and Chernin at their offices on the Fox lot. Rosenblatt was specifically not invited to attend. At
the meeting, Murdoch assured DeWolfe that he could keep running
MySpace. "We're not going to tell you how to run the site," Murdoch said.

"We'll be a better owner than Intermix," Chernin added.

But Murdoch and Chernin could not specifically address DeWolfe's
biggest concern: money. DeWolfe and the other founders would share
just $21.4 million generated by the sale of MySpace. DeWolfe would
also get another $1.5 million for his Intermix shares. That was a pittance,
considering that MySpace was the reason Intermix was being sold for
$580 million.

Murdoch and Chernin were willing to pay DeWolfe handsomely to
stay on board and run the site. But they couldn't put an actual dollar
amount on the table; if they did, it would have to be included in the
price of the deal. Wall Street was already going to be shocked at the size
of the deal, so News Corp. couldn't afford to add more millions to the
price tag.

Instead Murdoch and Chernin did a little dance with DeWolfe. Prior
to the meeting, DeWolfe had informed Michael Montgomery how
much he wanted to get paid, and Montgomery relayed the request to
News Corp. DeWolfe wanted $40 million after taxes for his top team.
That meant News Corp. would have to spend $75 million in cash.

Murdoch and Chernin told DeWolfe that the "retention bonus" that
he wanted for his team wouldn't be a problem. But they didn't name a
price or sign anything. DeWolfe had to take them at their word.

At any point during the next two days, DeWolfe could have called
Viacom and asked the company to place a bid for MySpace to stop the
Intermix–News Corp. deal, or he could have called his venture capital
backer Geoff Yang at Redpoint and asked him to round up a competing
offer. But he didn't.

A few weeks later, DeWolfe was rewarded for his discretion. Murdoch agreed to pay him $30 million in salary for the next two years. Tom Anderson also got $30 million for two years. The other MySpace founders, Josh Berman, Aber Whitcomb, Colin Digiaro, and Kyle Brinkman, shared another $15 million over two years.

On Saturday morning, Viacom's deal-making executives flew back to New York on the corporate jet. They had spent two days poring through Intermix's financial documents in a Los Angeles office and intended to finalize their bid over the weekend. Viacom planned to submit its bid after getting board approval on Wednesday.

Nobody at Intermix explicitly told Viacom that the deadline had moved. Instead Intermix executives mostly dodged calls from Viacom executives.

Stuart Epstein from Morgan Stanley called Andy Sheehan from VantagePoint on Friday afternoon. But Sheehan ducked the call and referred Epstein to Intermix's bankers. "Do not tell him anything about what I am doing or where I am," Sheehan e-mailed his assistant.

MTV Networks chief executive Judy McGrath got the same stonewall treatment when she called Rosenblatt on Friday. So she followed up with an e-mail to Rosenblatt at three in the afternoon.

"We are coming in with a bid early next week," McGrath wrote. "We really want to be with you on this and hope to get in the ring for it (just saw *Cinderella Man*). Tried to call you but didn't get through . . . Freston is with me on wanting to be in business with you. Speak to you soon."

Viacom was battling with one hand behind its back. Its corporate deal-making team and its just-hired banker were in the dark about how far along the Intermix talks with News Corp. were and the fact that Viacom could have blocked the deal by bidding directly for MySpace.

On Friday afternoon, anticipating the purchase of Intermix, News Corp. announced the formation of a new division called Fox Interactive Media. Headed by Ross Levinsohn, the unit would coordinate Internet activities for News Corp.'s U.S. television properties such as FoxNews.com, FoxSports.com, and Fox.com, as well as make acquisitions. "This is the first step toward creating a hub or portal," a News Corp. spokesman said.

The idea was that Levinsohn would build a team to sell advertising across all of Fox's properties—rather than those properties selling their own ads. Of course, not all the Fox properties were thrilled with the idea of integration. The Fox News Channel, for instance, was selling ads to an older and more conservative audience than the youth-oriented Fox broadcast network. But Murdoch had decreed integration, so everyone went along.

The timing of the announcement was awkward. Rosenblatt worried that it might spark some reporters to dig around to see what News Corp. was up to. "I hope this doesn't tip anyone's hand," he wrote in an e-mail to Levinsohn on Friday afternoon.

But luckily, no one, not even Viacom, noticed anything suspicious about the announcement.

At four o'clock, Rosenblatt arrived at News Corp.'s lawyers' offices on the twenty-eighth floor of the Ernst & Young building in downtown Los Angeles. He was wearing a baseball hat and a T-shirt to kick off "Project Ivory"—News Corp.'s code name for the acquisition. If Rosenblatt had known he was going to stay all weekend, he would have brought a toothbrush and a change of clothes.

Intermix's entire executive team was there, as was News Corp.'s team, representatives from Intermix's venture capitalists, VantagePoint, and dozens of lawyers and bankers from all sides. DeWolfe and Berman from MySpace showed up intermittently over the weekend as well. Each group was in its own glass-walled conference room.

The bankers from Thomas Weisel Partners did not show up. Instead they stayed at the offices where Viacom had been conducting due diligence and pretended that Viacom was still there—even though all the Viacom executives had returned to New York. The idea was to keep the pressure on News Corp. to close the deal. "We were trying to maintain the theatrics of it all," said banker Blake Warner. "It kept News Corp. going and kept them honest."

The tactic stressed out News Corp.'s negotiating team. At one point, Lang and Levinsohn called the TWP team and said, "We want you in our offices where we can see you." But Warner and his colleagues refused to come over for more than an hour at most. "They tried to trap us into a conference room, and we said, 'Look, we need to go,'" said Warner.

The negotiations were intense, as everyone raced to meet Murdoch's deadline of Monday morning. By Sunday everyone had been up for several nights in a row. Brett Brewer and Rosenblatt shared a hotel room across the street and took turns sleeping for a few hours at a time. Sheehan, the VantagePoint venture capitalist, got so exhausted that Rosenblatt ordered him to go across the street to the mall and buy new underwear and a chocolate milk shake. Those in the News Corp. conference room didn't fare any better: At one point, Fox negotiator Mike Lang told a joke, and an exhausted Fox Sports executive, Gary Ehrlich, laughed, stood up from the table, and promptly passed out.

Even Brewer, normally the most mild mannered of the Intermix executives, lost his temper during the ordeal. The lawyer for VantagePoint was arguing that VantagePoint's shares should be purchased by News Corp. first, prior to the sale of Intermix. Brewer erupted, "Who the fuck are you? I don't even know you. Get out of here!" and tossed the lawyer out of the conference room.

On Saturday afternoon Rosenblatt stormed out. News Corp. was insisting on canceling 50 percent of the stock options of Intermix employees. But Rosenblatt knew the rank-and-file members of Intermix were going to go ballistic. The whole reason these young staffers worked around the clock at a struggling Internet company for relatively low salaries was in the hopes of making big money on their stock. With the stock options canceled, Rosenblatt knew that he would have a rebellion on his hands.

Rosenblatt argued his point until he was blue in the face. But News Corp.'s team wouldn't budge. So Rosenblatt said, "I quit," and walked out of the office. Rosenblatt crossed the street and lay down on the concrete planters lining the steps of the shopping mall. Levinsohn and Brewer followed him. "Ross, I'm done," Rosenblatt said. "I will not sell this company if we can't take care of the employees."

In fact, Rosenblatt eventually caved in. News Corp. canceled 50 percent of the options held by Intermix employees. Those were replaced with options in Fox Interactive Media, but it was a far cry from the cash that most Intermix employees were hoping to receive.

All weekend, Intermix was worried that MySpace would round up a competing bid for itself, thus halting the News Corp.–Intermix negotiations under the terms of the complex relationship between the two companies.

Several times DeWolfe and Berman suggested that they might seek a bid for MySpace from Viacom or ask their venture capital backer Geoff Yang to round up an offer.

The bankers at Thomas Weisel Partners were extremely concerned that DeWolfe would call Viacom or other potential bidders. They tried to discourage a MySpace-only bid by claiming that only Intermix was for sale. "We are not offering the sale of MySpace alone," Blake Warner told Viacom. "The transaction being offered is for all of Intermix and with that comes the opportunity to own MySpace."

But the reality was murkier: If MySpace had received an offer, it would have been hard for Intermix to refuse to sell its stake. The board members of MySpace—even those from Intermix—had a duty to serve all MySpace shareholders. To vote against a MySpace sale could have exposed them to shareholder lawsuits.

DeWolfe understood the situation. He knew he could have crushed the News Corp. deal by calling Viacom or his venture capital backers. Instead he deliberately chose not to make any calls to round up a competing offer. It was a low-risk strategy: Murdoch's payout was surefire cash, while a higher bid for MySpace was not guaranteed.

Finally, on Sunday afternoon, Intermix reached out to Viacom. It was a delicate conversation: Intermix wanted to solicit a bid but not give away the exact deadline of when bids were due. Intermix still feared that Viacom would leap in with an offer for MySpace if it knew how close Intermix was to a deal with News Corp.

Intermix's banker Bob Kitts from TWP called Viacom's banker, Stuart Epstein, at Morgan Stanley and asked if Viacom could submit a bid by the end of the weekend. Epstein replied, "Viacom has a board meeting over the next few days, and we will discuss a possible bid at that meeting."

Accounts of the rest of this conversation differ. The bankers at Thomas Weisel Partners say they clearly indicated that submitting a bid later in the week might be too late. Epstein says he did not get that impression and was not told there was a firm deadline for the bid.

Epstein relayed the message to Viacom executives Bob Bakish and Mike Fricklas. "Intermix seems to be moving the goalposts, and Viacom may need to adapt to this new timeline," he said.

Collectively, Epstein, Bakish, and Fricklas decided to stick to their original plan of submitting a bid after the board meeting. They reasoned that Intermix had an incentive to wait for their bid and hadn't given them an explicit deadline. Nobody called Tom Freston or the other MTV executives to ask their opinions about submitting an earlier bid.

Finally Epstein called Kitts back and told him that Viacom would not be in a position to submit a bid by the end of the weekend.

The Intermix team was stunned. They were operating under the faulty assumption that Viacom had read the schmuck insurance clause and would understand the murkiness of the situation. "We were completely shocked that with this size deal we couldn't get [Viacom's] banker to fax anything," Rosenblatt said.

Still, to keep the possibility of a Viacom counterbid open, Intermix insisted on a relatively small $25 million breakup fee for the deal. That meant it would be relatively cheap for Intermix to throw out the News Corp. offer if Viacom offered a larger amount after the deal was announced.

At a quarter to four on Monday morning the Intermix board convened for a phone call to approve the News Corp. deal.

VantagePoint's David Carlick, wearing a T-shirt and pants that he usually wore to work in the garden, led the meeting by phone from a dark room in his Bay Area home. Carlick always started Intermix board meetings with a joke. This time, in acknowledgment of the early hour, he started with the shortest joke he knew: "An Irishman walks past a bar."

He paused. That was the end of the joke. Everyone laughed. What followed were bleary-eyed presentations from Intermix's lawyers and bankers, who had been up for two days straight. At last the Intermix board voted unanimously to approve the merger.

The board also unanimously approved the acceleration of Rosenblatt's stock options—to the tune of $23 million—as a reward for consummating the sale to News Corp. Rosenblatt's employment agreement required the company to vest only 50 percent of his stock options in the event of a sale, but the board decided that Rosenblatt deserved a richer package for turning around such a troubled company in such a short time for such a rich price. However, by cashing out his own options but allowing his employees' options to be canceled, Rosenblatt incurred the wrath of many Intermix employees.

...

A few hours later, in the wee hours of Monday morning, Intermix triggered its MySpace option. Under the schmuck insurance clause, Intermix had the right to buy out MySpace as soon as it had a bona fide offer. With a signed deal document in hand, Intermix's lawyers sent a letter to MySpace's lawyers stating that Intermix was purchasing the rest of MySpace effective immediately.

Geoff Yang of Redpoint was lying in his bed in Atherton, California, reading e-mails on his BlackBerry at five-thirty in the morning, when he saw an e-mail from MySpace's attorney informing him that Intermix had exercised its option to buy the rest of MySpace. "I cursed," he recalled.

Yang stormed downstairs to his home office and called Rosenblatt on his cell phone. "You've got to be kidding," he said.

"This came together really quickly," Rosenblatt explained. "We've got a great offer for the company."

Yang was furious. No one had told him a deal was coming. Although Chernin and others believed that Yang was out of town for the weekend, Yang had, in fact, been in town. But no one had called him.

Although Redpoint made about $65 million on its $15 million investment, Yang was disappointed. He believed that MySpace could have been a billion-dollar company if it had waited longer to sell or to go public.

Yang was correct. Within a few months, it was clear that MySpace was worth far more than the $125 million value assigned to it in the Intermix deal—and even far more that the $580 million that Intermix fetched.

But Yang was in an untenable position. Shareholders such as Redpoint, which own minority stakes in companies controlled by a majority shareholder, always face the risk that their interests will not be aligned with those of the larger owner. Eventually, Yang reconciled himself to Rosenblatt's decision. "Maybe I didn't do a good enough job impressing on him and Sheehan how much this thing could be worth," Yang later said. "And maybe I didn't do a good enough job telling Chris he was selling out way too cheap."

Early Monday morning, MTV Networks chief executive Judy McGrath and chief digital officer Jason Hirschhorn were sitting in a Viacom conference room reviewing the materials for the Intermix bid. A staffer walked in with the news that News Corp. had acquired Intermix for $580 million.

Hirschhorn was speechless. He had been chasing MySpace for an entire year and hadn't slept all weekend finalizing the bid. Hirschhorn had been working as head of digital strategy at Viacom's MTV division for six years, and the MySpace acquisition was supposed to be the culmination . of his efforts. He stormed out of Viacom's midtown office tower.

News Corp. announced the acquisition of Intermix on Monday morning. The press release described the deal as being worth $580 million— or $12 a share—a 20 percent premium over Intermix's trading price on Friday.

The press release didn't mention that News Corp. had agreed to "loan" Intermix $69 million to buy out the 47 percent of MySpace that Intermix didn't already own. Nor did it mention Rosenblatt's $23 million in accelerated stock options or the $75 million to be received by the MySpace founders over the next two years. Most of those numbers came out in subsequent disclosures with the Securities and Exchange Commission. In truth, News Corp. had agreed to pay nearly $750 million for Intermix.

The biggest financial winner in the deal was not Rosenblatt or the MySpace founders. It was ousted Intermix founder Brad Greenspan, whose 11 percent stake in Intermix was suddenly worth nearly $48 million.

Two days later, the dispirited MTV team appeared at Viacom's board meeting to plead for Redstone to approve a counterbid for Intermix. "There's still room to bid," Tom Freston said. "Our internal valuations are as high as $810 million."

Sumner Redstone's daughter, Shari, who ran the movie theater business, was surprised that Viacom had been outmaneuvered. "What took so long? We should have had this already," she said, adding that she supported a counterbid.

Board member Alan C. "Ace" Greenberg, a Wall Street legend, also supported the idea of a counterbid. "There's no harm in losing, but you gotta fight," he said. "At the worst, you make it more expensive for your competitor."

But Sumner Redstone disagreed. "Rupert is not afraid of overpaying," he said. "He doesn't care about the market, and he will outbid us."

Longtime Viacom board member Philippe Dauman concurred. With that the matter was dropped.

Viacom chief financial officer Mike Dolan tried to put a positive spin on the situation in the press. "Last year's MySpace was Friendster," he told the *Wall Street Journal*. "You have to be really careful, and you don't really want to plunk down blank checks, and new things are always coming down the pipe."

On Friday, July 22, Rosenblatt sent a thank-you e-mail to Murdoch:

"I want to thank you and Peter for moving so quickly and decisively in this Intermix transaction," he wrote. "We agreed to a certain price last Tuesday and promised to have the deal closed by that Sunday—the fact that we did is amazing . . .

"I remember telling you that this transaction took Newscorp from 0 to 60 mphs in one second. Well, from the calls I have received . . . Newscorp is being talked about in every circle, everywhere, as the new 'Big Dog' in town on the Internet."

Later in the fall, after the News Corp. deal to buy Intermix had been approved, banker Thomas Weisel flew Intermix's top executives—Rich Rosenblatt, Brett Brewer, Chris Lipp, and several others—and their wives on a private plane to a celebratory weekend in California's Napa Valley.

The MySpace executives were not invited. "They weren't our client," explained Blake Warner of Weisel. "Hopefully they were happy with the outcome they ultimately achieved. But you have to draw your advocacy lines pretty clearly."

The couples were greeted by limousines and whisked off to Meadowood, a 250-acre resort in the heart of wine country. Awaiting them in their suites were two iPod Nanos engraved, "Thanks for your effort with Intermix. April 14th, 1999–Oct 1st, 2005." Each morning a group of the Intermix executives would wake up early and take a twenty-five-mile bike ride with Weisel, an avid bicyclist. During the day, they toured the wineries by limousine and played golf on Meadowood's nine-hole golf course.

On Saturday night the entire Intermix board and Intermix's other banker, Michael Montgomery, were invited to a dinner at the Niebaum-Coppola Estate's private wine cellar. Each person took turns standing up to talk about what Intermix had meant to him.

Rosenblatt got all choked up recalling how much Intermix had changed since he took over one and a half years earlier. "Everybody had written us off for dead," he said. "Now we've created the biggest media company other than Google in the last decade."

Of course, the media company he was referring to was MySpace—which wasn't represented at the celebration.

Chapter 18

HOLDING A TIGER BY THE TAIL

i

Rupert Murdoch's right-hand man, Peter Chernin, was relaxing on Martha's Vineyard over Labor Day weekend in 2005, when he heard some disturbing news. His top deal maker, Mike Lang, called from vacation in Lake Tahoe, on the Nevada-California border, and said that Viacom was on the verge of closing a $550 million deal to buy IGN Entertainment. "We've got forty-eight hours" if we want to get it, Lang told Chernin.

IGN, a collection of primarily video game–related websites, was on Chernin's short list of Internet acquisitions, which had been approved by Rupert Murdoch. News Corp. had been in talks with IGN for months but was worried about the price being too high. Now, with a rival on the horizon, Chernin wanted to move fast.

On the Tuesday morning after the holiday weekend, he walked into Murdoch's New York office, and said, "I think IGN is going to get away." To Chernin, the issue was not price, it was the possibility of Viacom's catching up to News Corp. After the Intermix acquisition, News Corp.'s Fox Interactive had amassed about fifty million unique visitors per month, while Viacom was at about forty million. But if Viacom won IGN's twenty-eight million monthly visitors, it would suddenly be the leading media conglomerate on the Internet. "We have a choice of being in clear leadership or rough parity with Viacom," Chernin said. "I think it's worth doubling down."

Murdoch agreed with Chernin's logic. "Go get it," he told Chernin.

That morning, IGN's venture capital backer, Michael Kumin, flew to New York from Boston to try to seal a deal with News Corp. Kumin and IGN were frustrated with Viacom's deal-making team, which had spent the weekend haggling over minutiae in the proposed acquisition.

When Kumin landed in New York at one in the afternoon, he called Ross Levinsohn and said, "I have a bird in the hand; I need the deal done in twenty-four hours and at six hundred fifty million dollars."

"That's more than we think we can do," Levinsohn replied.

"That's the deal."

"Okay, we'll do it," Levinsohn replied. Kumin met with Murdoch and Chernin that afternoon and stayed up all night finalizing the details. By Wednesday afternoon News Corp. had signed a deal to acquire tiny, unprofitable IGN—with sales of just $42.9 million and losses of $14.2 million in 2004—for $650 million in cash. Once again, Viacom was stunned by the reversal.

When he got the news of having lost again to News Corp., Viacom copresident Tom Freston personally apologized to Viacom chief executive Sumner Redstone and explained the problem of having a deal-making team that didn't report to him. Redstone replied that Freston simply had to wait until Viacom completed its split-up, in January, to get control of the deal makers.

Meanwhile, Murdoch and Chernin were thrilled to have outmaneuvered Viacom again. But many on Wall Street were horrified. This was the third Internet acquisition announced by News Corp. in the space of six weeks. (In August News Corp.'s Internet unit had agreed to acquire Scout.com, a sports fan website, for $60 million.) Investors were starting to worry about how far Murdoch was going to go with his Internet spending spree.

Murdoch refused to put a limit on his spending. In August Murdoch's chief financial officer told investors that News Corp. might spend up to $2 billion on Internet acquisitions. But in September, after spending $1.4 billion, Murdoch said he wouldn't rule out exceeding the limit. "I don't want to be held [to $2 billion] hard and fast," Murdoch said at a conference. "You don't know what's around the corner."

The price of News Corp. shares started slipping.

On September 8, three days after announcing the acquisition of IGN,

Murdoch gathered the top executives from News Corp. and his three soon-to-be-acquired Internet properties at his ranch in Carmel for a three-day retreat to discuss Internet strategy. The lineup of speakers included the futurist George Gilder, venture capitalist Vinod Khosla, and technology blogger John Battelle.

The goal of the retreat was to figure out what to do with News Corp.'s newly acquired Internet assets.

Levinsohn's plan was to keep the structures of the acquired companies essentially intact, while adding a corporate layer that would handle legal and public relations, and, most important, sell advertising across all the properties. Unfortunately, this was somewhat emasculating to the acquired companies: Suddenly they were in charge of costs but had no control over their revenues.

The heads of Scout.com and IGN quickly recognized the situation and soon agreed to join Levinsohn's corporate team at Fox Interactive Media. Chris DeWolfe and Tom Anderson had no interest in joining the corporate team. Intermix chief executive Richard Rosenblatt would have liked to join Levinsohn's team as well but found he kept getting sidelined.

At the conference, Rosenblatt presented his vision of how Grab.com could be the centerpiece of Fox's social networking strategy. His idea was to build a feature called "Grab This," which would let Web surfers access News Corp.'s library of TV shows, movies, books, and other content. But News Corp.'s decentralized divisions weren't enthusiastic about making their valuable content available on the Internet for free, and the idea never went anywhere. (In 2008, however, News Corp. launched a website with essentially the same concept, called Hulu.com.)

Mark Jung, chief executive of IGN, offered the idea of combining IGN's audience of video game enthusiasts and MySpace's audience of teenagers for advertisers who wanted to reach youth online. But MySpace executives declined.

Over dinner one night, Ross Levinsohn, who was in charge of News Corp.'s Internet strategy, tried to lobby MySpace founders Chris DeWolfe, Tom Anderson, and Josh Berman to be more cooperative.

"Look, you're part of a bigger company now," Levinsohn said.

DeWolfe was unmoved. "We just want to be left alone," he told Levinsohn.

MySpace had fought for independence from Intermix and would now fight for independence from Fox Interactive.

Many rank-and-file Intermix employees were angry with Richard Rosenblatt when they learned that Intermix had agreed to accelerate $20 million worth of Rosenblatt's stock options but had canceled half the stock options of the rest of the Intermix employees. It didn't help that IGN negotiated a retention bonus pool of about $25 million for its employees as part of its News Corp. purchase price.

"Everyone thinks I sold them out," Rosenblatt lamented in an e-mail to Intermix board members. "I am sorry we did this deal. How do they not understand I had a preexisting deal and fought like hell for them? Should we even do this deal?"

News Corp. attempted to mollify Intermix employees by setting up what it called a long-term incentive plan. Murdoch came up with the idea after visiting eBay chief executive Meg Whitman and Google chief executive Eric Schmidt. Murdoch asked the Silicon Valley chiefs how Fox Interactive should structure itself to be competitive with other Internet companies. Whitman and Schmidt told Murdoch that the key to success was giving employees equity. So Murdoch decided to issue stock options to all the employees of Fox Interactive Media.

His new Internet division would include the three new properties as well as various News Corp. Internet properties such as FoxSports.com, Americanidol.com, Fox.com, and FoxNews.com. Since Fox Interactive Media was not a public company, News Corp. would determine the value of Fox Interactive as if it were a public company and then cash out employees' shares at that price once a year. It was a novel attempt to create a miniature Silicon Valley company within the confines of a huge media conglomerate.

The plan was immediately unpopular. Its first payout was two years away—too far in the future—and the formula for calculating the value of Fox Interactive Media was too abstract for many employees to consider it attractive. MySpace employees were particularly miffed: Collectively they got only about one-third of the shares of Fox Interactive Media despite generating the vast majority of the division's revenue.

Meanwhile, it was becoming clear that News Corp. wasn't interested in Intermix beyond MySpace. For months after the sale, few executives from News Corp. visited the Intermix offices near the airport. It was rumored that News Corp. was looking to sell the profitable wrinkle cream business. Although Intermix was helping to add blogs, games, and message boards to the *American Idol* website and some other News Corp. properties, the Intermix employees felt neglected.

In speeches, Murdoch spoke only about MySpace, not any of the other Intermix properties. At a Goldman Sachs conference on September 21, he even mistakenly attributed one of Intermix's successes to MySpace.

"The other day we launched a film called *Transporter 2,* a small, modest film for young men," Murdoch said. "We didn't spend much on traditional media advertising, but we went to MySpace and got ten million names and sent them an e-mail with a downloadable trailer. We got thirty to forty percent more money in the first weekend than we expected." In fact, it was Intermix properties such as Grab.com that had used their e-mail lists to promote *Transporter 2.* But the message from Murdoch was clear: MySpace was the crown jewel. Within a few months, most of the top employees from Intermix, including Brett Brewer and Adam Goldenberg, had quit.

Intermix employees weren't the only people unhappy with the buyout. Ousted Intermix chief executive Brad Greenspan was determined to stop the News Corp. acquisition of Intermix. As soon as Greenspan heard about the deal, he thought it was too cheap a price for the company he had founded. At 7:23 a.m. on July 18, the day the News Corp. deal was announced, Greenspan fired off an e-mail to DeWolfe:

> Are you in favor of this NewsCorp. deal?
> Seems ultra low price for Myspace . . .
> I can't believe you guys would like your option exercised . . .
> Brad

Greenspan believed that Intermix was worth more than $12 a share. After all, on its first day of trading as a public company in 1999, shares reached as high as $14. Greenspan's mother had bought shares at $14 that day. "I always wanted her to see a return on that," Greenspan said. The fact that his mother had died of cancer several years earlier made Greenspan's wish more poignant.

So Greenspan began laying plans to make a counterbid for Intermix.

In late July he described his idea to DeWolfe and Berman at Mood, a Hollywood nightclub. At that point, DeWolfe and Berman were still in shock that their site had been sold to News Corp. without their participation. They told Greenspan they had been forced to do the deal.

"If I find people to buy it and keep it public, are you on board?" Greenspan asked.

DeWolfe and Berman seemed interested.

Encouraged, Greenspan launched an aggressive campaign to buy Intermix. On September 23 he sent a letter to Intermix and issued a press release offering to top News Corp.'s $12-per-share bid for Intermix with a bid of $13.50 per share. However, Greenspan's offer was less than it seemed. Greenspan offered to buy only 50 percent of the company, and didn't identify how he would raise the $300 million needed to fund his offer. Greenspan pitched his offer as a way to free MySpace from the shackles of corporate ownership. He proposed to sell off Intermix's non-MySpace businesses and rename the remaining company MySpace.

But the MySpace founders never signed on to Greenspan's proposal. After the meeting at Mood, Greenspan never heard from DeWolfe and Berman again. And when he finally placed his counteroffer, they were conspicuously silent. Even Geoff Yang, MySpace's venture capital backer, who was opposed to the sale to News Corp., declined to support Greenspan's bid.

Not surprisingly, given the bad blood between Greenspan and his former company, Intermix's board of directors rejected the offer unanimously. "We found the proposal to be speculative and incomplete, creating obvious risks to our stockholders," Rosenblatt said in a press release.

Greenspan responded with a petition asking Intermix shareholders to vote against the sale to News Corp. But he couldn't muster enough support, and a few days later, the News Corp. deal was approved. Once again Greenspan took his fight for Intermix to court.

In October News Corp. began negotiating to lease a 165,000-square-foot building in Beverly Hills to house the seven hundred employees in its newly created Fox Interactive Media division. Anderson and DeWolfe were horrified. They loved their Santa Monica digs and wanted to stay

near the beaches, the bars, and the hipster scene. News Corp. had originally been negotiating a lease in Santa Monica's Water Garden office
complex, just down the street from ResponseBase's old offices. But the
Water Garden deal ultimately proved too expensive, so News Corp.
found the space in Beverly Hills.

Anderson told Chernin, over drinks at a Santa Monica hotel, that the
move would ruin MySpace's culture. The Beverly Hills office was indeed
in a slightly strange spot: on a residential street next to a Mercedes-Benz
dealership, with no restaurants or shops within walking distance. But
Chernin was unmoved by the MySpace founders' pleas, and the lease was
soon finalized.

At the opening-day party for the new offices, some of the more unruly
MySpace programmers threw balled-up wet paper towels down on
Chernin and Levinsohn from the catwalk above the courtyard. Several
people also jumped into the reflecting pool in the courtyard.

Levinsohn and his corporate executives were ensconced on the top
floor, while MySpace occupied the second floor. For the first few
months, there was no cafeteria, so News Corp. brought in boxed lunches
and Costco pizzas for the employees. It was a far cry from the Santa
Monica pedestrian shopping promenade that the MySpace employees
had frequented.

"We've gotten a dose of reality," DeWolfe told a reporter. "We don't
own the site anymore."

MySpace's lowly status at Fox Interactive was particularly provoking
in light of the website's wildly increasing popularity with consumers.

In October 2005 MySpace had a huge spike in traffic. After three
months of attracting about twenty-one million visitors per month, the
site suddenly lured twenty-four million visitors. The data also showed
that users were spending even more time on MySpace than on other
sites. For the first time, MySpace surpassed eBay, AOL, and Google in
terms of pages viewed.

But MySpace needed News Corp.'s help to keep up with the massive
growth. As it got bigger, MySpace became a juicier target for spammers,
hackers, and Internet deviants of all sorts. MySpace had always been particularly vulnerable to attacks because it allowed users to post Web code
directly onto their profile pages.

One of the first large-scale malicious hack attacks on MySpace had come in December 2003, before the site had even officially launched. A MySpace member placed some software code in the Web programming language called JavaScript on his profile. The code destroyed the profiles of people who visited his profile. MySpace lost half of its members' profiles in that attack—and subsequently banned JavaScript.

But MySpace's attackers kept finding creative new ways to bring down the service. In October and November 2004, a New York teenager named Anthony Greco wrote a computer program that created thousands of fraudulent MySpace accounts. MySpace members received more than 1.5 million spam instant messages for mortgage refinancing and pornography. After the attacks began, Greco contacted MySpace and threatened to show others how to "open a Pandora's box of spam" on MySpace unless MySpace paid him off.

MySpace executive Jason Feffer, with the assistance of a high-tech-crime law enforcement unit, pretended to be Tom Anderson and got on the phone to negotiate a "deal" with Greco. Feffer convinced the teenager that MySpace would pay him off if he came to a meeting in Los Angeles. When Greco stepped off the plane in Los Angeles, he was arrested by members of the U.S. Secret Service and the Los Angeles Police Department. Greco eventually pled guilty to a single count of threatening to damage the computer systems of MySpace with the intent to extort.

At midnight on October 4, 2005, nineteen-year-old Samy Kamkar slipped some software code into his MySpace profile that automatically made Samy the "friend" of anybody who viewed his page. The worm added the words "but most of all, Samy is my hero" to each new friend's profile and then infected anyone who viewed that profile as well. Soon the worm was spreading like wildfire throughout MySpace.

"It didn't take a rocket or computer scientist to figure out that it would be exponential; I just had no idea it would proliferate so quickly," Samy later wrote in an e-mail interview posted on a blog. "When I saw 200 friend requests after the first 8 hours, I was surprised. After 2,000 a few hours later, I was worried. Once it hit 200,000 in another few hours, I wasn't sure what to do but enjoy whatever freedom I had left, so I went to Chipotle and ordered myself a burrito. I went home, and it had hit one million."

After one million users were infected, MySpace's security team tracked

Kamkar down, shut down his profile, and handed him over to law enforcement officers. MySpace had to close the entire site for more than an hour while it removed the worm from member profiles. Kamkar eventually pled guilty to a felony count in Los Angeles Superior Court and was sentenced to three years of probation and ninety days of community service, and was banned from accessing the Internet for personal reasons for an unspecified period of time.

News Corp. was shocked to find how vulnerable MySpace was to such attacks. News Corp. had thought it was buying a technology company, but, in fact, MySpace was barely able to keep its site running. The fix-it-later approach had been a great advantage in its early days, but by late 2005, the website's mishmash of technology was strained to the breaking point.

Levinsohn found that managing the rapid growth at MySpace was overwhelming. He told colleagues it was like "holding a tiger by the tail."

Facebook was a much smaller website—with just ten million monthly visitors, compared with MySpace's twenty-four million—but it was growing quickly. In October, Facebook's traffic rose 10 percent as it increased photo capacity and began allowing high school students to join. Previously Facebook membership had been restricted to college students.

"How are you holding up with all the traffic?" Levinsohn asked the young Facebook founder, Mark Zuckerberg.

The two were sitting at the bar at the W Hotel in Los Angeles, waiting for MySpace chief executive Chris DeWolfe to arrive. Levinsohn had arranged the meeting because he was interested in buying Facebook.

"We're fine," Zuckerberg replied.

"Really?" Levinsohn asked. Considering all the problems MySpace was having, the answer seemed disingenuous.

"That's the difference between a Los Angeles company and a Silicon Valley company," Zuckerberg said. "We built this to last, and these guys [at MySpace] don't have a clue."

In fact, Facebook was facing its own technical challenges. Zuckerberg's brainchild had underestimated how quickly it would grow, and as it added more and more computer servers to its data center, its computers were overheating. "It was over one hundred ten degrees in some aisles," recalled Owen Van Natta, who was hired in late 2005 as chief operating officer. "I was, like, *Mayday*! We need to get on top of this!"

Still, Facebook's technical challenges were tiny compared to MySpace's issues. Facebook did not allow users to customize their pages or to insert Web code into their profiles, or even to join without a qualified e-mail address from a known institution. Zuckerberg had chosen to grow slower than MySpace, but more steadily.

Zuckerberg also was not going to sell his site cheaply. Already Yahoo was interested in buying a stake in Facebook at a $750 million valuation. But News Corp. wasn't willing to pay that much, particularly for a site with less than half the audience of MySpace.

Once again, the idea of combining MySpace and Facebook—first considered by venture capitalist Geoff Yang a year earlier—collapsed. Facebook would continue to cause trouble for MySpace in the future.

By November Peter Chernin wanted to speed up the integration at Fox Interactive Media. There was still no advertising sales force selling ads across News Corp.'s recently purchased websites. MySpace desperately needed to shore up its technology with disaster recovery plans and redundant systems. Meanwhile, Levinsohn was always out of the office scouting for acquisitions, and key decisions weren't getting made.

Chernin assigned his longtime friend and consultant Christos M. Cotsakos, the former chief executive of E*Trade, to come in and offer advice. Cotsakos interviewed all the managers of the companies that News Corp. had acquired and was blunt about their prospects at News Corp.

"Rich, it doesn't make sense for you to stay," Cotsakos told Rosenblatt, "and it doesn't make sense for Ross [Levinsohn] for you to stay."

Rosenblatt was stunned. "Am I getting fired?" he asked.

"No," Cotsakos replied. "It's just that your future lies in another way."

Rosenblatt was crushed. He had negotiated a deal to stay at News Corp., and he had hoped to help Levinsohn build Fox Interactive Media. For months Rosenblatt had been operating in a twilight zone, making suggestions to Levinsohn that went unheeded. It was time to cut the cord. Rosenblatt called Levinsohn and said he would leave and become a consultant to Fox Interactive. Levinsohn readily agreed.

...

By December 6 News Corp. shares had fallen 8.5 percent to $15.76, down from $17.22 before the Intermix sale was announced. Wall Street investors were mystified by News Corp.'s Internet strategy. Rupert Murdoch had talked publicly about creating a portal, but nothing had materialized yet. Ross Levinsohn decided to address the issues head-on in his first presentation to Wall Street.

At the UBS investment banking conference in New York, he put up a slide with a white background and three words: "Where's the portal?"

Then he put up another slide: "Why have 1 portal . . . when you can have 70 million portals?"

Each MySpace profile, Levinsohn explained, was its own miniature portal. MySpace members viewed the world through their profile and their friends' profiles, rather than through the filters of a traditional portal such as Yahoo.

Then he put up another slide: "How do you know MySpace is not a fad? Didn't you overpay?"

Levinsohn answered with another slide showing MySpace's hockey-stick-like growth. By November MySpace had attracted forty million registered users, with more than one hundred thousand new users signing up every day.

"If we keep pacing the way we're pacing, people will think we got a steal," Levinsohn said.

Chapter 19

A FINE LINE BETWEEN RISQUÉ
AND DIRTY

MySpace executive Jason Feffer was nervous. Rupert Murdoch was standing behind one of his employees as she screened photographs that had been posted on MySpace. The young woman was looking at one hundred thumbnail-sized photos on a single computer screen. Her job was to catch any nudity or obscenity, flag it, and move on to the next screenful of images.

She's going really fast, Feffer thought. *She must be nervous.*

She wasn't the only one who was nervous. Murdoch's first visit to MySpace's Santa Monica offices had been a surprise. Just before the chairman arrived with his entourage, Josh Berman asked Feffer to straighten up the office. Feffer raced around, cleaning up the men's bathroom and tearing down posters of Rupert Murdoch that were on the office walls. (Feffer had put up Murdoch's picture so that MySpace's customer service employees could identify all the fake Murdoch profiles that popped up after the deal was announced.) Now Feffer was standing behind the media mogul, hoping that the photo screener wouldn't miss anything.

"Stop," Murdoch said to the screener. "Back up."

Feffer's heart sank. The young woman backed up to the previous screen.

Murdoch leaned in and pointed to a picture of a shapely young woman in a bikini.

The screener started to defend herself. "She has clothing on," she sputtered. "That's not one to delete."

Murdoch laughed. "No, no," he said, "send that picture to this guy." He pointed to one of his aides.

Murdoch wasn't concerned about MySpace's reputation for hosting promiscuous pictures. After all, he was the newspaper publisher who introduced the topless "Page Three" girls in his London tabloid, the *Sun,* in 1970, boosting circulation by an estimated 40 percent. Murdoch's view of the content on MySpace was this: "There's a fine line between risqué and dirty." He believed that MySpace was walking that line appropriately, and that both users and the general public would think so too.

Big advertisers were less sanguine about the risqué nature of MySpace. When News Corp. bought MySpace, the website was taking in about $2 million a month in ad revenues—a pittance considering the size of its traffic. At the same time, AOL was making $109 million a month, and Google was making an astounding $520 million a month.

One big reason for the disparity: Despite Feffer's screening system, too many pornographic pictures were popping up on MySpace user profiles. Feffer's group didn't scan all pictures before they were uploaded onto MySpace's website. His staff looked at the pictures only after they were already online. The reason was that MySpace wanted to give members the instant gratification of seeing their photos pop up as soon as they were uploaded. That meant, however, that sometimes it could take a few days before MySpace screeners would catch a nude photo.

And many pictures were not being scanned by censors at all, because the photos were stored on third-party websites such as Photobucket and ImageShack. MySpace didn't have enough photo storage to allow members to store more than twelve photos each, so many MySpace users put additional pictures on other websites and linked those sites to their MySpace pages.

Many advertisers were put off by MySpace's user-created pages, which often contained partial nudity, obscenity, crude sexual jokes, and other objectionable content. When Ross Levinsohn went to New York to meet with the four biggest advertising agencies in the fall of 2005, he asked them how they felt about MySpace. All were hesitant about placing blue-chip advertising anywhere on MySpace other than the site's front page.

"I wouldn't be caught dead in that kind of environment," said David

Cohen, executive vice president for the influential advertising agency Universal McCann Interactive, speaking at a conference of advertisers in New York. "You only have to look around for five or ten minutes to find something offensive." Sir Martin Sorrell, the outspoken chief executive of leading advertising conglomerate WPP Group, went even further in a speech in London, speculating about Murdoch's state of mind in buying MySpace for such a lofty price. "Why is it that he is so preoccupied with this and willing, it appears, to make investments almost willy-nilly?" Sorrell asked. "I think I can use the word *panic*—that is probably overdoing it, but maybe I am not."

With big advertisers boycotting, MySpace sold most of its ads to third-party "remnant" advertising networks such as AOL's Advertising .com. These networks buy cheap ads across a large number of websites, and then sell the space to advertisers at a markup. But even under this third-party scenario, MySpace was not safe for advertisers. Amerisave Mortgage, for instance, bought ads on a network that promised to run ads on "loans and money and finance sites." But Amerisave discovered that one of its ads was adjacent to a photo of an erect penis on a MySpace profile page. "It's really alarming . . . I had no idea this could happen," said David Herpers, its chief marketing officer. Verizon Communications and Starwood Hotels & Resorts Worldwide also pulled ads from MySpace, after seeing them appear near pictures of scantily clad women.

Weight Watchers International pulled its ads from MySpace after its banners appeared on the porn star Tera Patrick's MySpace profile. And T-Mobile pulled its ads after finding them on porn star Jenna Jameson's MySpace page. A spokesperson for Weight Watchers blamed the problem on an advertising network. "We didn't honestly know that our ad was being run on that page in MySpace," she said.

MySpace was in a bind. It needed better screening methods to ensure that advertisers wouldn't find themselves next to objectionable content. But it didn't want the site to be so sanitary that users would complain of censorship. After all, some of MySpace's most popular members were scantily clad women.

On October 29 Christine "ForBiddeN" Dolce, a skinny platinum blonde with pneumatic breasts, stepped onto the stage at Dodger Stadium and pumped her fist in the air. She was wearing shredded jeans and a ripped white T-shirt that displayed her cleavage. The so-called Queen of MySpace was onstage at MySpace's two-year anniversary concert to introduce the band All-American Rejects—and she even brought her own film crew to record the moment.

Dolce embodied the self-made MySpace celebrity. In an age where the concept of celebrity was defined by negligible accomplishments, Dolce was among the first to turn her popularity on MySpace into a full-fledged career. A Southern California makeup artist who joined MySpace in September of 2003, Dolce created an online persona called ForBiddeN that was a cross between a porn star and a vampire. Dolce's profile was heavy on photos of her overly tanned breasts, hints of fake blood, and heavy black eye makeup. She was among the most popular people on MySpace in its early days.

In November 2004, having amassed about two thousand friends, Dolce signed on with a manager, Keith Ruby—whom she met on MySpace, of course. He helped her turn her sexy online persona into an actual business. Ruby recruited volunteers to help Dolce manually approve the five thousand friend requests she was getting every day. Next he began sorting through all the business overtures Dolce was receiving, such as offers to host parties at nightclubs for a fee. By the time of the MySpace concert, Dolce had amassed more than seven hundred thousand friends.

To some, Dolce was the Queen of MySpace, but others saw her as only a princess because rival MySpace pinup Tila Tequila had more friends. The diminutive Vietnamese model had amassed an even bigger following than Dolce. Fans of the two regularly debated whether Tequila or Dolce was more beautiful and talented.

As the competition escalated, Tequila posted a rap song on her profile called "Knock You Out"—a so-called dis rap against Dolce. ForBiddeN's friend, well-known MySpace drag queen Jeffree Star responded with a post belittling Tequila. Finally Tom Anderson had to break up the schoolyard fight between MySpace's best-known personalities. Anderson called Star and demanded that he take down the anti-Tequila post. Star took it down.

Despite such childish antics, Dolce and Tequila were businesswomen working to turn their MySpace celebrity into real money. Both women spent hours each day writing blog entries and sending e-mails to their fans. Unfortunately for them, the rules of MySpace prohibited Tequila and Dolce from hawking wares directly to their fans or from accepting advertising on their profile pages. "They're really sticky on allowing you to make money off your profile," said Dolce's manager, Ruby. MySpace's rules prevented Dolce from capturing thousands of dollars' worth of endorsement and sponsorship income, he said.

Still, Dolce managed to leverage her popularity on MySpace into a *Playboy* nude photo spread, a campaign for Zippo lighters, a modeling career, a fashion line, and a gig as a spokeswoman for Axe deodorant. Dolce also figured out how to skirt the rules on MySpace: She knew she couldn't promote a cologne called Pherlure there, so she got the fragrance renamed Forbidden Pherlure, so it could qualify as a personal project.

Meanwhile, Tequila had leveraged her nearly eight hundred thousand friends on MySpace into cover photos in *Maxim* and *Stuff*, a cameo appearance in the Adam Sandler movie *I Now Pronounce You Chuck & Larry*, an MTV reality show, *A Shot at Love with Tila Tequila*, and her own line of clothing.

Tequila was straightforward about the reason for her popularity. "There's a million hot naked chicks on the Internet," she told a reporter. "There's a difference between those girls and me: Those chicks don't talk back to you."

Anderson publicly defended the presence of porn stars on MySpace. He told the *New York Times* that Jenna Jameson's MySpace profile was legitimate because Jameson "is more than a porn star. She is an author and a celebrity and has been on *Oprah*." He added, "If we had a site that was 'My Name Is So-and-So, and This Is My Porn Site,' we would delete that."

But his public stance was slightly misleading. In fact, many porn stars who had *not* been on *Oprah* were making MySpace their online home. After all, the pornography industry had long been on the cutting edge of the Internet as an early adopter of live video, chat, and other interactive technologies.

Male porn star Christian, who declines to give his last name, estimated that 95 percent of porn industry professionals have MySpace pages that they check daily. Girls use them to chat with their fans and to promote their websites, he said. To keep from getting deleted by MySpace, porn stars had to make sure that their profiles didn't contain

MySpace cofounder Chris DeWolfe in a portrait published by his father in 1973, when he was about eight years old. *(Frederick DeWolfe/Portland West)*

DeWolfe was a varsity tennis player in high school. *(Lincoln High School)*

Chris "Beezer" DeWolfe's senior yearbook photo from Lincoln High School in Portland, Oregon.
(Lincoln High School)

Left: Tom Anderson's freshman yearbook photo at San Pasqual High School in Escondido, California, in 1985.

Right: By sophomore year, Anderson had grown his hair long and was hanging out with computer hackers.

(Both courtesy of The Right Studio)

Anderson recruited online pinup star Tila Tequila to leave Friendster and join MySpace. Tila Tequila is shown at the launch party for a company, Hoooka, about which she and Anderson had a falling out. *(Alexander Tamargo/ Getty Images)*

Brad Greenspan, the founder of eUniverse, bought DeWolfe's company hoping to break into e-mail marketing. *(Courtesy of Brad Greenspan)*

Brett Brewer, Brad Greenspan's friend and fraternity brother, at eUniverse's offices in June 2003, as the company was falling apart. *(Courtesy of David Carlick)*

Richard Rosenblatt with his champion at eUniverse, David Carlick, at the Ivy. *(Courtesy of David Carlick)*

Rosenblatt turned eUniverse around, renaming it Intermix and getting it listed on the American Stock Exchange. *(Alan Rosenberg)*

Right: Christine Dolce became a celebrity on MySpace by posting provocative photos, often taken by photographer Michael Vincent. *(Courtesy of Christine Dolce)*

Below: Tom Anderson, a former musician, promoted independent bands on MySpace, including the Billionaire Boys Club, at a New York MySpace party in April 2004. *(Courtesy of Billionaire Boys Club)*

A typical MySpace page contains graphics and features from across the Internet

1 The banner ad at the top of the MySpace page is the only part of the page that is not customizable.

2 MySpace navigation bar.

3 A relic of when MySpace used to calculate degrees of friendship between users. Now everyone is in everyone else's extended network.

4 Tiffany's blog or online diary

5 The glitter comes from a third-party called RockYou.

6 Becoming a top friend is highly competitive on MySpace.

7 Tom is everyone on MySpace's first friend.

8 Animated comments from GetMySpace Comments.com and YesComments.com.

9 A Barack Obama video from YouTube.

10 U2 is playing on the MySpace music player.

11 Tiffany's slide show is from Slide.com.

12 Tiffany's personal Information

Venture capitalist Geoff Yang gave MySpace its independence, only to see it sold out from underneath him.
(Redpoint Ventures)

Tom Anderson, Jim Heckman, and Josh Berman. Heckman crafted MySpace's $900 million deal with Google, causing friction with the MySpace founders.
(Courtesy of James Heckman)

Ross Levinsohn orchestrated News Corp.'s purchase of MySpace but was ultimately ousted over conflicts with the MySpace founders.
(Stephen Shugerman/Getty Images)

Chris DeWolfe in his Santa Monica office in February 2006. Soon afterward, News Corp. forced MySpace to Beverly Hills and political pressures forced DeWolfe to cut his hair to a more corporate length. *(Courtesy of Esther Dyson)*

Chris DeWolfe and Rupert Murdoch at the opening of MySpace's San Francisco offices in October 2007, which marked a turning point in MySpace's technical development. Soon after, DeWolfe regained full control of MySpace. *(Frank Micelotta/ Getty Images)*

nudity or links to pornography. But it wasn't hard to find a connection between a MySpace page and a nude website. Popular MySpace pinup girl Bobbi Billard, for instance, advised her MySpace viewers to visit her pay-per-view nude picture site by adding "a .com to the end of my name. Hint hint!"

MySpace had also become a fertile recruiting ground for new porn stars: Dana DeArmond, for instance, launched her career on MySpace. An early MySpace member, DeArmond styled her online image along the unconventional lines of SuicideGirls.com, a Portland, Oregon–based website that celebrated nude photos of women who often sported purple hair, tattoos, and non-enhanced breasts. This new style of pornography, sometimes called AltPorn, was considered an alternative to the tanned and enhanced blondes that populate mainstream pornography.

Although DeArmond's MySpace page didn't contain nude photos—that would have violated MySpace's rules—she displayed enough skin to attract a lot of friends and the attention of the AltPorn industry. For the first three years of her career, she got all of her work through agents who contacted her through MySpace and elsewhere online. Eventually she hired an agent. The porn industry also moved to capitalize on her three hundred thousand online fans by placing her in movies such as *Dana DeArmond Does the Internet* and *MyPlace 3: All-Star Edition*—a movie about men who hook up with the porn stars they befriend on MySpace.

"MySpace can make you famous," DeArmond said. "After my first movie, I went to porn parties, and people knew me not from the movie but from MySpace. I was like the Paris Hilton of porn, known for doing nothing. But I've made a lot of movies in the last couple years, so now I'm famous for that too."

Stories of girls being "discovered" by the porn industry on MySpace abound. According to male porn star Christian, all the porn talent agencies have staffers who search MySpace for prospects. "Before [MySpace], agents relied on people who worked in strip clubs to get new girls into the business," he said. "Now agents can hire someone to find those girls directly through MySpace."

To get advertisers on board, Levinsohn had to clean up MySpace's image. It was a difficult technical task, made trickier by the fact that MySpace didn't want to scare its users with strong-armed censorship techniques.

Feffer already had dozens of people looking at hundreds of images an hour and choosing which ones to delete. The rules were simple but hard to automate with computers: A bare bottom is not okay, but a bare bottom with a tiny thong passes muster; bare breasts are not okay, but bare breasts with the nipples covered with tape are acceptable.

A field of science called "computer vision" aims to teach computers how to make such distinctions. But so far it's been slow going. In the late 1990s, researchers David Forsyth and Margaret Fleck published a paper about a computer program that aimed to identify pornography through skin colors and body configurations. The program correctly identified only 43 percent of the nude pictures it viewed and misidentified 4 percent of the non-nudes. One of the misidentified pictures was a picture of an apple pie with a lattice crust; the computer identified the flesh-colored pieces of crust as limbs.

Since then, most computer vision programs take a different approach. They feed pornographic images into a computer and command it to find common characteristics of the photos. The computer can then rate each photo on a scale of how similar it is to the pornographic images. These systems are often better at finding nude pictures, but they frequently misidentify a lot of non-nude images as well, so human checkers still need to do a final check before images are deleted. Still, these systems allow the human checkers to prioritize their viewing so that they can first look through images that the computer has deemed likely to be inappropriate. So MySpace began testing an expensive computer system that could prioritize likely porn, while also beefing up its staff of human censors.

But that didn't solve the problem of photographs that were stored on sites other than MySpace. In December MySpace began pressuring third-party photo storage sites such as Photobucket to start scanning photographs as well. Photobucket, which had venture capital backing and was hoping for a public offering, couldn't afford to alienate MySpace. Starting in January Photobucket hired seven people to scan all the photographs being loaded onto its system.

Levinsohn thought it was risky to rely on third parties to censor photos for MySpace. He urged MySpace to buy a photo storage company of its own and stop relying on outside vendors. But Chris DeWolfe and Anderson opposed the idea; Anderson said he would rather build additional photo storage from scratch.

Eventually, MySpace pushed its crackdown on pornography too far. Worried that pornographic videos were slipping through the cracks through another third-party website, YouTube, MySpace shut down the links to YouTube a few days before Christmas. "There wasn't a way to catch people posting explicit clips," Levinsohn said.

YouTube was the video equivalent of Photobucket. Since MySpace didn't have the capacity to store videos, many MySpace users stored their online videos on YouTube and provided a link to the YouTube videos on their MySpace profiles. At the time, YouTube was just six months old and displaying three million videos per day.

Despite YouTube's relatively small audience, MySpace's crackdown sparked a huge backlash online. Bloggers railed against MySpace's unilateral move and blamed Rupert Murdoch's ownership for the "censorship."

"This is soooo like Fox and News Corp. to try and secretly seal our mouths with duct tape," one outraged user wrote to a blogging news website.

MySpace was shocked by the outcry. This was hardly the first time it had disabled a link due to security concerns. But MySpace was learning the hard way that bloggers and the mainstream media would be much less forgiving of a Murdoch-owned website than of a tiny Santa Monica startup.

When YouTube was shut down, DeWolfe was in Europe. After talking to YouTube about its porn screening procedures, DeWolfe quickly reversed the decision and turned the YouTube links back on. But the damage was done. Suddenly little-known YouTube was being hailed in the press as a scrappy underdog, and MySpace was being positioned as the big, bad media company bully.

Levinsohn distanced himself from MySpace's controversial decision. "We said when we bought MySpace that we weren't going to disrupt the flow of it, and I don't think we have," he said to a reporter. "We're not going to force something down the throats of that audience. And we know very quickly if there's something they don't want."

Meanwhile, Levinsohn was struggling to increase the prices MySpace could charge for ads. Prior to the News Corp. acquisition, MySpace had been selling ads for about 17 cents per thousand viewers.

Although many big advertisers preferred to place ads on MySpace's front page—where they would be sure not to appear on a porn star's profile—MySpace had not been charging higher prices for it. So Levinsohn decreed that MySpace had to stop selling the valuable front page through third-party ad networks. It was a risky decision.

At first MySpace took a hit: During the month after Levinsohn's decree, MySpace sold only four ads on the front page; the rest were in-house promotions. But eventually advertisers got the message, and MySpace was able to raise prices dramatically. Bolstered by the success, Levinsohn directed MySpace to start building more "safe areas" that advertisers could sponsor. Soon sections of MySpace featured topics ranging from books and movies to games, comedy, and horoscopes. Mainstream advertisers began signing on. PepsiCo's Aquafina bottled water sponsored the independent filmmaker section, while Pepsi's Sierra Mist lemon-lime soft drink sponsored the comedy section. "A key condition of working with MySpace was that they were working on safety issues," a Pepsi spokeswoman said.

At the same time, Levinsohn was trying to sell advertisers on the idea of buying across Fox Interactive Media's multiple Web properties. But it wasn't technically easy to mesh the different websites' advertising systems. MySpace's ad tracking system was crude, consisting of Excel spreadsheets and some three-ring binders. Meanwhile, Silicon Valley–based IGN was using a sophisticated Oracle database to track advertising and tie the results into its financial reports.

Even more daunting were the personnel and cultural challenges of integrating advertising across several News Corp. properties. Ad sales executives at the Fox News Channel, a conservative cable news network run by former Richard Nixon political operative Roger Ailes, were chafing at the Murdoch decree that they sell Web ads through the Fox Interactive Media division.

After taking control of Fox News, Levinsohn had beefed up the Fox News Web infrastructure and ad sales systems and added more sales representatives to the account. In the short term, the changes meant that costs rose faster than revenues—a significant problem in a company where each division head was rewarded based on divisional profits.

Fox News executives were upset that Levinsohn had hired a former CNN ad sales executive to run the ad sales group, because CNN was Fox News's chief rival. Fox News also doubted whether there was any natural advertising synergy between Fox News's audience of older men and MySpace's youth audience.

Finally, in December, Levinsohn met with Ailes to discuss the problems. Ailes complained that he didn't have enough control of the Fox News website. "Fine, you can have it back," Levinsohn replied. He had enough problems trying to get MySpace in order; the last thing Levinsohn needed was a headache from Fox News as well. In January Fox Interactive quietly shed its oversight of the Fox News website. In the New York offices, News Corp. built a wall to divide the Fox News ad sales staff from the Fox Interactive ad sales staffers on the other side of the floor.

Wall Street was in the dark about the technical problems at Fox Interactive. Still, investors remained doubtful of MySpace's ability to make money, and worried that Murdoch might throw more money into Internet investments. By December News Corp.'s stock price had fallen 15 percent to $15 per share, from about $17.50 when the MySpace deal had been first announced.

Murdoch, the eternal optimist, chalked it up to a general malaise among all the media conglomerates that was unfairly tainting News Corp. "It pains us, as it pains you," he told shareholders at News Corp.'s annual meeting in December. "We are living in—certainly as far as media goes—a bear market. You can't ignore that."

Even as Wall Street remained skeptical, MySpace was rapidly becoming a household name in the United States and the UK.

On Sunday, January 22, 2006, an obscure Yorkshire band called Arctic Monkeys released its debut album, *Whatever People Say I Am, That's What I'm Not.* It sold nearly five thousand copies an hour, quickly topped the charts in Britain, and became the fastest-selling British debut album in history.

The British press attributed Arctic Monkeys' success in large part to MySpace. The group had been quietly building a fan base on the site since 2004, when it released songs for free on its MySpace page. Fans swapped the songs and added new ones recorded at concerts. Through word of mouth online, Arctic Monkeys attracted enough attention to win a recording contract just before their single, "I Bet You Look Good on the Dancefloor," leapt to the top of the charts in October.

In February, an eleven-minute online movie about MySpace attracted more than six million viewings on YouTube and other sites. Created by a twenty-one-year-old Detroit resident named David Lehre, *MySpace: The Movie* parodied the culture of MySpace. One scene showed a teenager taking pictures of himself in his underwear for his MySpace page. Another scene showed a girl demanding her boyfriend's MySpace password so she can check whether he's been faithful. The final scene showed an actor pretending to be Tom Anderson being feted by MySpace users.

In this context, it was difficult to imagine the backlash that was just around the corner.

Chapter 20

"A PLACE FOR FIENDS"

Connecticut attorney general Richard Blumenthal was outraged by the stories he was hearing about MySpace. In February 2006 police in Middletown announced that they were investigating whether seven teenage girls had been sexually assaulted by men they'd met through MySpace. In January police in Bristol charged a twenty-one-year-old with second-degree sexual assault for allegedly having consensual sex in the back of his Camaro with a fourteen-year-old girl he met on MySpace. And in September police in nearby Port Washington, New York, arrested a thirty-seven-year-old who had allegedly spotted an attractive young woman's profile on MySpace, visited her workplace, lured her to a vacant parking lot, and sexually assaulted her.

Blumenthal, an aggressive prosecutor, had only vaguely heard of MySpace before these assaults came to his attention. He was more familiar with Facebook, since his oldest son had joined the collegiate website as a student at Harvard. Blumenthal's initial impression of Facebook was "Gee, that's pretty cool." He and his wife remembered how much harder it used to be to track down a girl to ask for a date before Facebook. "If you were lucky, you could find the phone number, and then if you were luckier still, the person answered the phone rather than a roommate," he said.

But when Blumenthal logged on to MySpace, he saw a much less innocent environment than Facebook's closed collegiate world. Children and adults could easily connect for sex by signing up to be "swingers." Pornography seemed to be rampant. Children were able to join sex-talk groups on the website. Predators and children were lying about their ages—and about everything else. MySpace wasn't making even the slightest effort to verify that people were the age they claimed.

Blumenthal was appalled. On February 2 he issued a press release announcing an investigation of MySpace "for allowing minors easy access to pornography and inappropriate material."

"This site is a parent's worst nightmare," he told reporters.

Blumenthal's assault was perfectly timed. Although the sexual assaults that he mentioned hardly constituted a national trend, they tapped into parents' growing concern about Internet-savvy teens. This generation was the first to grow up with the Internet fully enmeshed in their lives, and many kids were far more savvy about technology than their parents. While Mom and Dad were digesting prepackaged news and information on sites like Yahoo, the kids were building their own Web designs on MySpace.

Many parents found it difficult to police their kids' behavior in these new arenas. They didn't know what to do when their child complained that another child had written mean comments about them on their MySpace page, or if a fake MySpace page pretending to be by their child popped up online. Many schools were also struggling to police their students' Internet activities, whether on blogs, or instant messaging, or MySpace.

At the same time, a television news show had put online sexual predators on center stage. Since 2004, the evening newsmagazine *Dateline NBC* had been airing an occasional series called "To Catch a Predator"— in which men were lured to meet supposedly underage girls or boys through online chats with Internet decoys from a watchdog group called Perverted Justice. When the men arrived at the meeting place, they were filmed as they were arrested by the police. The show hadn't garnered much attention, however, until 2006—when suddenly its popularity soared amid parents' newfound concerns about sites like MySpace.

The episode of "To Catch a Predator" that aired the night after Blumenthal's announcement pulled the highest ratings of the year for *Dateline NBC.* In that episode, thirty-nine-year-old Scott Smith was arrested after setting up a meeting with what he thought was a thirteen-year-old girl he had met in a chat room. After his arrest, Smith chatted on camera with "To Catch a Predator" host Chris Hansen about MySpace.

"Do you check out the MySpace sites of young women?" Hansen asked.

"I just—whatever's in a chat room, and I go see their picture, whatever, and I click on it, and it goes to MySpace or something like that, yeah," Smith replied.

This exchange between Smith and Hansen—replayed frequently in future airings—helped plant the idea in the popular imagination that MySpace was a home for sexual predators.

The flurry of press that followed Blumenthal's announcement only served to cement that view. *NBC Nightly News* anchorman Brian Williams interviewed Facebook's chief privacy officer, Chris Kelly, about Internet safety. NBC's *Today* show interviewed Middletown police sergeant Bill McKenna about the investigation in Connecticut. The *CBS Evening News* reported on three girls, in Texas, New Jersey, and California, who had allegedly been assaulted by men they met on MySpace. Rita Cosby, an anchor on the MSNBC cable channel, interviewed a representative of Perverted Justice, who advised parents, "There's virtually no real reason that your kid should be on a social networking site."

The whole country seemed to be engulfed in what social networking researcher Danah Boyd called a "moral panic" over MySpace. "Welcome to a generational divide, where adults are unable to see the practices of their children on kids' terms," Boyd wrote on her blog.

It didn't help that amid the storm of criticism, MySpace declined to defend itself on camera.

In truth, sexual crimes against children had been declining in the United States since the early 1990s, according to the Crimes Against Children Research Center at the University of New Hampshire. Between 1992 and 2006, substantiated sexual abuse of children decreased by 53 percent. Researchers have not been able to isolate the exact reason for the dramatic decline, but suggest that it could be connected to the nation's overall drop in crime, increased policing, increasing wealth, and the increased numbers of sexual offenders who are in prison.

Direct sexual threats to children were also declining on the Internet.

During 1999 and 2000, 1 of 5 regular Internet users between the ages of ten and seventeen reported receiving an unwanted sexual solicitation. By 2005 only 1 out of 7 regular Internet users in the same age group reported receiving an unwanted sexual solicitation. Most children brushed off the solicitations, but a small portion of such solicitations were aggressive enough that they caused the recipient significant distress.

Of course, some children do respond to sexual solicitations on the Internet—with unfortunate results. In those cases, most of the victims are over the age of thirteen, and the vast majority of them know that they are meeting an adult for sex. Often contact is made in a chat room where the two talk explicitly about sex. Only 5 percent of sexual offenders in such situations concealed the fact that they were adults, and only 5 percent of the cases involved violence. The majority of the cases are acts of consensual sex that are, in fact, statutory rapes.

MySpace was blindsided by the public assault. Its public relations staff was used to promoting musical artists and touting new technology features, not defending itself against prosecutors on and off camera. It didn't have a chief privacy or security officer with hefty legal credentials it could trot out to the eager camera crews. It didn't have a lobbyist in Washington.

So News Corp.'s corporate staff took control. The day after the Connecticut attorney general's announcement, top News Corp. attorneys in New York called Blumenthal to arrange a meeting for the following Monday. Over the weekend, Chris DeWolfe cut his shaggy, long blond hair to a more businesslike length and flew to New York to join the News Corp. lawyers heading to Blumenthal's office in Hartford, Connecticut.

The executives settled into the attorney general's windowless interior office. Blumenthal, a tall, thin man with an angular face, sat across the coffee table from them in a red upholstered chair.

Blumenthal's staff wanted to start the meeting with a slide show of all the horrors they had encountered on MySpace. But the News Corp. attorney waved them off. "We don't need to see it; we're aware of the issues."

DeWolfe outlined all the steps that MySpace was taking to make the site safer. The site had a staff of eighty-five people screening photographs.

The site had links to safety tips from consultant Parry Aftab's nonprofit WiredSafety.org. MySpace had lowered the age limit to fourteen so that kids wouldn't have an incentive to lie about their age. And it had installed special protections so that adults couldn't search for kids younger than sixteen.

"We want MySpace to be the most open, well-lit site on the Internet," DeWolfe said. He invited Blumenthal to come visit its offices in Los Angeles and see all the steps the site was taking to improve safety.

"We're on a much shorter time frame," Blumenthal said. Every week, he said, new cases of girls being molested by men they met through MySpace were being reported. He wanted action now.

Blumenthal was particularly concerned about the category for swingers. When users registered for MySpace, they could choose a sexual orientation, including straight, bi, or swingers—a category that MySpace users had requested.

What about the pornography? Blumenthal asked.

DeWolfe agreed that it was a problem. "Unfortunately," he said, "MySpace is not responsible for many of these images because they are 'deep linked' and not hosted on the MySpace site."

The attorney general suggested raising the age limit to sixteen.

Once again, DeWolfe and the News Corp. team demurred. They believed that raising the age limit would be ineffective because it would essentially be unenforceable. MySpace did not believe it had a good way to verify the ages of its members.

Instead DeWolfe argued that MySpace would be safer by convincing kids to use their real ages, and by providing protections for younger users.

Blumenthal was not convinced by MySpace's argument that it was building a safe online playground. "It might be like some neighborhood playgrounds," he later recalled. "But it was not a safe place for everyone."

When DeWolfe got back to Santa Monica, his shorter haircut showed off more gray hair. His colleagues joked that he looked older and had "gone corporate" over the weekend. DeWolfe was destined to get grayer as the bad news continued to pile up.

On February 23 Stephen M. Letavec, a thirty-nine-year-old Pennsylvania resident, was arrested after traveling to Connecticut to engage in sexual activity with a fourteen-year-old girl he met on MySpace. When the two began communicating in March 2005, the girl told Letavec she was eighteen. But eventually, over the course of their nearly yearlong relationship, she told him her real age. During that time, they communicated almost daily on MySpace as well as on the phone. On August 13 he rode his motorcycle to Connecticut to meet her. He visited again in October and gave her gifts, including a black leather jacket, and visited again in January 2006. The two had sex on at least two of the visits. Letavec eventually pled guilty to using the Internet to persuade a minor to have sex and traveling interstate to have sex with a minor. He was sentenced to ten years in prison.

One day later, on February 24, Sonny I. Szeto, a twenty-two-year-old New York resident, was arrested after traveling to Connecticut to have sex with an eleven-year-old girl he met on MySpace the previous September. The two began talking on the phone and sending pictures of themselves to each other. Szeto eventually drove to Connecticut three times to visit the eleven-year-old, where he molested her in the family playroom while her parents were sleeping upstairs. Szeto pled guilty to using the Internet to persuade a minor to have sex and possessing child pornography. He was sentenced to fourteen years in prison.

Not all such crimes were legitimately linked with MySpace. On February 25 two teenage girls from Calabasas, California, disappeared from their homes. The girls' mothers claimed that their daughters had likely been lured away by men they met on MySpace. The story was all over television until the girls finally called home on March 1 and asked to be picked up in Carson, California. Detectives said that the two had run away voluntarily and that there was no link to MySpace.

Still, there were so many reports of crimes linked to MySpace that in February a blogger started a website called MyCrimeSpace: A Place for Fiends. It cataloged all the crimes connected with MySpace each day and boasted about three new entries per day.

MySpace debated several strategies for addressing the safety issue. Safety czar Jason Feffer argued that the site should highlight positive cases, such as when MySpace had helped police track down a missing girl based on where she had logged into her MySpace account. But that approach was a double-edged sword, since the media would then link stories of missing kids with MySpace.

Eventually MySpace decided to try to broaden the issue. After a month of silence about safety on MySpace, DeWolfe gave an interview to the press on March 6. "This isn't a MySpace issue," he told a reporter for the Associated Press. "It's an Internet issue."

DeWolfe said that parents should teach their children how to be safe on the Internet. "If you go to the mall and start talking to strange people, bad things can happen," he said. "You've got to take the same precaution on the Internet."

Not surprisingly, DeWolfe's decision to put the blame on parents didn't play well with concerned parents and lawmakers. Attorney General Blumenthal fired off a letter demanding MySpace make immediate changes in the site.

Behind the scenes, Jason Feffer's Fef.B.I. division had actually set up a rapid-response team following the RJ Lockwood murder in 2004. Feffer's staff manned a special phone number twenty-four hours a day that was available only to law enforcement officers. Feffer's group also helped investigators find information about victims and suspects on their MySpace pages, gave tours of MySpace to more than five hundred law enforcement officers, and aided twenty-four hundred police investigations.

Earlier in the year, MySpace had also retained Internet safety consultant Parry Aftab as an adviser on safety issues. Aftab wrote a guide for law enforcement officers describing what kind of information was available to them on MySpace. In October she and MySpace general counsel Matt Polesetsky flew to Boston to brief the Massachusetts attorney general about MySpace's approach to safety. "They were astounded at how law enforcement friendly" MySpace's policies were, Aftab recalled.

But MySpace's policies weren't as user-friendly for children, parents, and schools. MySpace had no phone number for parents and teachers to call, only an e-mail address. MySpace sent automated replies to the forty thousand to fifty thousand e-mails it received each day—many of them about mundane issues such as "How can I change my wallpaper?" In early 2005 Feffer's team had set up a program in Microsoft Outlook that would look for key words or phrases in an e-mail, such as "How do I delete a friend?" and send an automated reply tailored to that phrase. Certain keywords—such as *runaway* and *suicide*—were automatically forwarded to customer service agents for individualized replies.

Some of the most complex issues often fell through the cracks of the automated e-mail system. For instance, MySpace often received requests from parents to delete their child's MySpace profile. Feffer's group resisted such requests because they worried that the person demanding a profile deletion might not be a parent—it could be a kid playing a joke on a friend. So his group encouraged parents to get their kid's password and delete the account themselves. Of course, some parents are not able to convince their children to give up their password. Internet message boards were filled with complaints from parents about this policy, such as the following from Lynn from Colorado: "I am going crazy trying to get my son's account deleted."

"No one could respond to all the requests they were getting from parents," Aftab said. One of the thorniest problems on MySpace was cyberbullying, where bullies used the anonymity of MySpace to publicly taunt their prey. MySpace often found itself in the role of mediator, trying to decide when to delete fake or offensive profiles. The story of San Francisco radio personality Josh Kornbluth illustrates the difficulty of navigating MySpace's automated e-mail approach to such problems. One day Kornbluth discovered that someone had posted a fake profile pretending to be Kornbluth on MySpace. The fake profile was filled with disgusting pornographic materials. To delete the profile, Kornbluth had to prove to MySpace that he was the real Josh Kornbluth by sending a MySpace "salute": a picture of himself holding a sign that says "MySpace.com" and his e-mail address. However, the website didn't specify where Kornbluth should send the picture.

So Kornbluth wrote to MySpace's customer care e-mail address, asking what to do. Receiving no immediate reply, he started calling random phone numbers at MySpace to see if he could reach a customer service representative. Each time that he was transferred to the customer service department, he was greeted by a full voice-mail box or got no answer at all. Finally, at the end of the day, he received two e-mails from MySpace. One was an automatic reply asking him to send a salute. The second e-mail declared that the profile had been deleted. "I checked. The fake profile was, indeed, down," Kornbluth recalls. "That was Friday night. On Saturday afternoon [Kornbluth's boss] Michael Isip called me again. There was now *another* profile on MySpace, again purporting to be me and again containing disgusting materials."

Aftab had advised MySpace to drop the salute, which she said was "the stupidest thing I've ever heard of." But, she said, "Once News Corp. took it over, the willingness of MySpace to work closely with WiredSafety and adhere to its recommendations lessened." News Corp. also had a disincentive to take down profiles because it bragged about its huge number of profiles to Wall Street.

As a result, most MySpace users eventually learned to live with fake profiles of themselves, because it was too difficult to prevent new ones from popping up. Rupert Murdoch, for instance, tolerates dozens of fake profiles of himself on MySpace. On the other hand, MySpace once accidently deleted Microsoft chairman Bill Gates's real account—thinking it was a fake.

Meanwhile, MySpace quietly attempted to appease Richard Blumenthal with several changes to the site. It removed the swingers category as a browser function for users under eighteen, and it placed free software filters on the site that parents could download if they wanted to block access to MySpace from their computer. MySpace also designated certain groups, such as "Romance and Relationships," as adults only. It stepped up its efforts to remove profiles of children under the age of fourteen by scanning the site for terms often used by underage users. All of this was done without any formal announcement, so that MySpace could retain its rebellious, youthful image.

But on March 30 Ross Levinsohn blew MySpace's cover. At a Bank of America conference, he publicly announced that MySpace had deleted more than two hundred thousand underage, obscene, or pornographic profiles. Tom Anderson was livid. He believed that nothing would be more fatal to MySpace's appeal than to portray the site as a police state overseen by a giant corporation.

MySpace's concessions hadn't helped to win over Blumenthal, either. In the attorney general's view, MySpace hadn't addressed his biggest demands: raising the minimum age for membership to sixteen and verifying the ages of MySpace users. He believed that MySpace had merely gone from "outrageous" to "deeply troubling."

In April Ross Levinsohn received an anonymous e-mail alleging that Tom Anderson had been operating a pornography website called Team Asian.com. Talk about bad timing. The last thing MySpace needed in the midst of the frenzy about online safety was a story about MySpace's founder and "first friend" being outed as a pornographer.

News Corp. hired an investigator, who confirmed that Anderson had been involved in the website and had received checks from it. There wasn't any evidence linking DeWolfe to the site. When News Corp. president Peter Chernin confronted Anderson, he was nonchalant. Anderson argued that the site was no big deal and that he had not cashed any of the checks.

Levinsohn was horrified; he worried that MySpace's already skittish advertisers would flee and attorney generals would have a field day with the information. Levinsohn suggested moving Anderson to China, where he could stay out of the limelight and oversee MySpace's Asian expansion.

But Murdoch and Chernin didn't agree. The link between TeamAsian and MySpace was tenuous. The domain name TeamAsian.com was not registered in Anderson's name. The only easily available evidence was Anderson's postings on Usenet urging people to visit TeamAsian.com, which didn't prove anything. News Corp. was used to dealing with scandals involving TV and movie stars. Murdoch and Chernin agreed to keep Anderson in his role and to hope for the best.

Their bet paid off. Rumors of Anderson's involvement in pornography appeared on Silicon Valley blogs, but none of the mainstream press picked up the story because it couldn't be proved.

In this environment, News Corp. realized that it had to bring in some big guns to deal with the safety issues on the site. The company announced it was hiring a former federal prosecutor, Hemanshu Nigam, as chief security officer for Fox Interactive. Feffer was given another job, and Aftab from WiredSafety stopped advising the site. In addition, News Corp. announced that it was donating millions of dollars of free airtime on its television channels to public service ads by the National Center for Missing and Exploited Children. The donation won MySpace a powerful ally in Washington, D.C. "We have never had this kind of corporate commitment from a single player in this industry," said Ernie Allen, the center's chief executive.

Nigam set about pulling together a team of MySpace engineers—which he called the "Red Team"—to focus on safety issues. The Red Team had a delicate mandate: Clean up the site just enough to appease regulators and marketers, but not enough to scare away its millions of far less reverent users. Red Team engineer Steve Pearman thought of a possible solution when he and Nigam were attending a conference at Microsoft over the summer. During the session, Pearman pushed a piece of paper over to Nigam with a drawing of a mom as an intermediary between a teen and his or her computer. Nigam immediately understood Pearman's idea: to let parents monitor their kids' MySpace usage.

It was a radical idea that risked upsetting MySpace's teen users. But Pearman and Nigam hoped that they could let parents monitor kids without actually spying. Parents would be able to see only how their children were representing themselves on MySpace in terms of name, age, and location. They would not be able to read their children's e-mail or even see the child's profile page. The idea was to "give parents a tool to force a discussion with their kid," Nigam said.

The Red Team code-named its project Zephyr and put it on the list of items that MySpace developers were working on. Unfortunately, the developers had a long list of urgent items, ranging from combating hackers to upgrading the advertising systems. In the meantime, the criticism of MySpace continued to mount.

By the summer, the News Corp.–owned Fox News Channel had jumped on the bandwagon. Its most popular host, Bill O'Reilly, hosted several programs about the dangers of MySpace. In July, O'Reilly discussed the case of a twenty-eight-year-old elementary school teacher, Pamela Rogers, who had sex with a thirteen-year-old male student and communicated with him, in part, through MySpace.

"We need to shut down the MySpace.coms of the world," said O'Reilly's guest, defense attorney Drew Findling.

"I'm with you there, boy," O'Reilly agreed. "You get that going, and I'm right there with you."

Chapter 21

PEBBLE BEACH

On Monday evening, July 31, 2006, Rupert Murdoch was entertaining the rock star Bono with shots of tequila at the Carmel Mission Inn in Pebble Beach, California. Murdoch was at the famous golf resort to hold one of his trademark executive retreats. He had flown in his top two hundred fifty executives and their spouses from around the world.

Every few years, Murdoch stages one of these gatherings to let his top executives rub shoulders with political bigwigs and great thinkers. The idea is to inspire the News Corp. team with fresh ideas and get them jazzed up about working at News Corp. Of course, Murdoch also enjoys showing off his ability to attract heavyweight speakers.

At the 2006 conference, Murdoch was on top of the world—in large part because of MySpace's success. Despite the concerns about sexual predators, MySpace had more than doubled in size since the News Corp. acquisition, attracting more than fifty-four million visitors in July, compared with twenty-one million visitors at the time the deal closed the previous September. The press was lionizing Murdoch's Internet prowess. Wearing a pin-striped suit, he graced the cover of the July issue of *Wired* magazine—just as Intermix chief executive Richard Rosenblatt had predicted a year earlier. The *Wired* headline blared, "Rupert Murdoch: Teen Idol! News Corp. and the Future of MySpace."

Enthusiastic about News Corp.'s digital future, investors had bid up its stock to nearly $20—up 33 percent from a low of $15 in November—while other media stocks were languishing.

Politically, Murdoch was also making news with his sudden affinity for liberal causes. As founder of the conservative Fox News Channel and publisher of the conservative tabloid the *New York Post,* Murdoch had long been considered a staunch right-winger. But in recent months, he had been drifting left—driven in part by the mood of the country, which had turned against President George W. Bush and the Iraq war. In a particularly controversial move, Murdoch hosted a fund-raising breakfast for Democratic senator Hillary Clinton of New York in July.

The lineup of speakers at Pebble Beach reflected Murdoch's newfound interest in a wide range of political views: British prime minister Tony Blair delivered the opening remarks on Monday morning; Al Gore made his famous presentation about climate change—the documentary film version of which, *An Inconvenient Truth,* would later win an Academy Award; Los Angeles police chief Bill Bratton discussed innovations in policing; former Speaker of the House Newt Gingrich spoke about political change; and Bill Clinton spoke about "inspiring change." The evening's dinner was to be graced with a speech by U2 front man Bono about his efforts to combat injustice and poverty—causes to which Murdoch was newly sympathetic.

Conservatives were aghast as the News Corp. agenda for Pebble Beach leaked out. "The nature of the event . . . confirms our suspicion that Murdoch may be moving left as the 2008 U.S. presidential election approaches, and that he may bring his 'conservative' news properties with him," Cliff Kincaid, a conservative commentator, wrote on his website.

Murdoch was typically unfazed by his critics. Before the speech, Murdoch and his executives mingled, drank tequila, and chatted with the conference speakers. Some News Corp. business was also getting done. During the cocktail hour, Tom Anderson grabbed the legendary Silicon Valley venture capitalist John Doerr, a nerdy-looking guy with a skinny frame and big glasses, and informed him about the status of MySpace's search engine competition.

News Corp. was running an auction to choose a new search engine for MySpace. The site was using Yahoo's search technology and was making a paltry few million dollars a year from the ads that Yahoo placed near the search results. That was a terribly low number given MySpace's fifty-four million monthly users.

Whichever firm won the search rights for MySpace would also win the right to sell advertising alongside the search results. Although MySpace would get the bulk of the advertising revenue generated, it would likely be a lucrative deal for the search engine as well. Locked in a race to become the top search engine, each of the players was willing to pay big fees for guaranteed traffic from a website as popular as MySpace.

MySpace also needed to upgrade its search function from a technology standpoint. It was nearly impossible to find anyone through a MySpace search. A search for "John Smith" returned pages of results of people who mentioned a John or a Smith in their profile, and there didn't seem to be any ranking that put people who listed their names as John Smith ahead of other results. To find people on MySpace, many MySpace users had started to use Google or specialized search engines such as Icerocket—which was designed to search blogs but added a MySpace search function.

Murdoch and Peter Chernin had initially considered buying or building a search engine for MySpace, but by June they realized that wouldn't be feasible. Buying or building would likely overtax MySpace's technology staff and cost millions of dollars in technology and engineers. Instead they borrowed a page from AOL's playbook. A year earlier, AOL had run a competitive auction, pitting rivals Google, Microsoft, and Yahoo against one another to win the right to provide search technology and advertising to AOL's audience. Murdoch hoped that MySpace would be able to run an even more hotly competitive auction.

Ross Levinsohn had chosen Jim Heckman to head the search auction, in part because of his pit-bull personality. Heckman, the founder of Scout.com, was a workaholic fond of sending e-mails at all hours of the night. After News Corp. acquired Scout, Levinsohn tapped Heckman to be the chief strategy officer at Fox Interactive Media. But as he awaited Bono's speech, Heckman worried about the bidding process. The bids had been submitted on Thursday night: Microsoft bid about $450 million, Yahoo bid $750 million, the tiny search engine Ask.com proposed a joint venture, and Google didn't submit anything at all. Yahoo's $750 million was way beyond Heckman's projections. But as a consummate deal maker, he still wanted to try for a bigger number. Heckman wasn't sure he could get a bidding war going among Microsoft, Yahoo, and Ask without Google's deep pockets in the mix.

So Heckman was pleased that Anderson had buttonholed the venture capitalist Doerr. Heckman joined them; he knew that Doerr was a Google board member.

"Google didn't show up with a bid," Heckman said to Doerr.

Doerr was shocked. Not only was he a Google board member, but he was also the unofficial dean of Silicon Valley venture capitalists. Heckman was in luck: Doerr thought Google was passing up a huge opportunity by not participating in the MySpace auction. Doerr's command could sway even the notoriously iconoclastic founders.

Doerr swung into action. He called Google cofounder Larry Page, who was vacationing in the south of France, and urged Google to get into the game.

Bono's speech was, for many attendees, the highlight of the conference. Wearing his trademark pink-tinted wraparound sunglasses, and a black suit with a black T-shirt underneath, Bono stood in front of a podium draped in faded yellow brocade with red accents.

Bono started off with a bit of false humility, shuffling some papers and clearing his throat. "Sorry, I'm a little nervous speaking to crowds of less than fifty thousand," he said. "You've spent the day in serious panels with serious people—this rock star is nervous!" But Bono soon warmed to his theme, flattering Murdoch for his support of Bono's efforts to fight AIDS in Africa and urging News Corp. executives to use their power to do more good.

At one point, Bono read a poem he had written celebrating the Murdoch empire and envisioning a future for the company "in the service of the greater good." The poem began:

> *As the satellites blink*
> *and the presses cough ink*
> *can we see News Corp. through time?*

Bono then called on the audience to help him reach his next goal. "I say we put every child in the world who wants to go to school, in school," he said. "One hundred million, that's the number who want to go but can't. Ten billion dollars—that's how many dollars a year to put them in school . . . If you don't see schools as the front line in the war on terror, the terrorists will. Where others spread hatred, we can spread hope."

Bono finished with an appeal to an even higher authority. "God may be in the mansions on the hill. I sure hope so, because I have one," he said. "But God is definitely in the slums, in the cardboard boxes where the poor play house, in the cries of war. And God is with us if we are with them. Hope all of you will come on like the tide. Thank you."

The audience gave Bono a standing ovation.

After Bono's speech, Doerr made a few more phone calls and then told Heckman that Google was ready to negotiate a deal.

"The number for you to be competitive is seven hundred fifty million dollars," Heckman said.

Doerr agreed to facilitate negotiations. The two rented a hotel suite, arranged a conference call with Google executives, and stayed up all night hammering out an agreement. By six in the morning, they had drafted a one-page document outlining a $750 million deal between MySpace and Google that they planned to present to teams from both companies. Summoned by Doerr, Google cofounder Sergey Brin flew down from Silicon Valley in a helicopter, along with a contingent of executives, including Google's top advertising executive, Tim Armstrong. News Corp.'s team was led by Chernin and included Ross Levinsohn, Heckman, attorney Mike Angus, and MySpace's Chris DeWolfe and Tom Anderson.

Tuesday morning was cold and foggy as the teams from Google and News Corp. gathered in a ground-floor conference room at the Inn at Spanish Bay. The room overlooked the golf fairway, which was shrouded in mist.

The meeting was too large to be a very effective negotiation. But Chernin got his point across: The deal had to be done by Monday because News Corp. wanted to announce the deal when it reported earnings on Tuesday. After the meeting, Chernin took Heckman onto the golf course. He put his hand on Heckman's elbow. "What do you need to get this thing done?" Chernin asked.

Heckman said he needed a focused attorney assigned to the deal, and he needed to be isolated from the rest of News Corp. executives during the discussions. Heckman worried that involving too many players could slow down the focus and momentum of the deal makers. Chernin agreed that it was best to have a small negotiating team, so he designated Heckman to work with Levinsohn, Mike Angus, and Fox's new head of advertising, Michael Barrett.

In order to attend the conference, DeWolfe had left his wife at home awaiting the birth of their first child within days. Now DeWolfe had just been sidelined from the biggest deal in his corporate history.

The tension between MySpace and News Corp. had been coming to a head for months. As it became clear that MySpace was the biggest and most important part of Fox Interactive, DeWolfe and Anderson were increasingly resentful of interference from their corporate overseers. At the same time, the corporate executives at Fox Interactive were increasingly resentful that MySpace wouldn't take any of their suggestions.

The dispute had spilled out in public in a *New York Times* article in April about MySpace's financial prospects. In an interview with the reporter, Levinsohn had suggested that MySpace could charge bands to promote concerts or sell songs on the site. The next day, DeWolfe dismissed the idea during his interview with the same reporter. "Music brings a lot of traffic into MySpace," he said, "and it lets us sell very large sponsorships to those brands that want to reach consumers who are interested in music. We never thought charging bands was a viable business model."

In the same article, Fox Interactive executive Mark Jung was quoted suggesting that MySpace could sell profile pages to small businesses such as car dealerships. DeWolfe dismissed that idea as well: "If it was a really commercial profile—the gas station down the street—no one is going to sign up to be one of their friends," he told the reporter. "There is nothing interesting about it."

Levinsohn and Jung couldn't force their suggestions down DeWolfe's throat. But they did control advertising across all the Fox Interactive properties, including MySpace, and thus they controlled the search engine auction. This deal was their chance to prove the merits of Fox Interactive to the recalcitrant MySpace founders.

Despite Microsoft's low bid of $450 million compared with Yahoo's and Google's $750 million, the search deal was really Microsoft's to lose.

FoxSports already had an advertising relationship with Microsoft. Heck-man had been negotiating a possible search deal with Microsoft since January. During those discussions, Microsoft had thrown out numbers as high as $800 million.

Months earlier, Heckman had given a presentation to Murdoch and Chernin, declaring that the search engine contest gave News Corp. an opportunity to be a kingmaker on the Internet. Google was the leading search engine, while Microsoft and Yahoo were the underdogs.

In that presentation, Heckman argued that awarding the deal to Google could give too much power to an already powerful player. He likened MySpace to a young Luke Sykwalker in *Star Wars,* choosing be-tween the forces of good and evil. "We can go to the dark side with Google," Heckman said, "or we can restore balance to the universe with Microsoft or Yahoo."

For eight months, Heckman had been negotiating closely with Microsoft, but he was disappointed with Microsoft's approach. Micro-soft kept sending over long complicated term sheets filled with complex provisions requiring, for example, MySpace users to fill out registration forms for Microsoft products. MySpace executives were opposed to shar-ing their members' data with Microsoft. News Corp. also worried about the timing of a Microsoft deal; Microsoft was also in the midst of up-grading its search technology, which wouldn't be ready for another year. News Corp. wanted revenues to start rolling in sooner than that.

Still, Heckman needed to nudge Google along to get to the number that Murdoch would accept. Heckman told Google that if it was going to beat Microsoft's offer, it would need to submit a clean bid with fewer clauses, special provisions, and other nonsense. Just a guaranteed mini-mum payment for the advertising revenues expected to be generated by the deal.

By Wednesday morning, the weather had warmed up. Yahoo chair-man Terry Semel was at Pebble Beach for his appearance on a News Corp. panel called "Business and the World: How Companies Are Adapting to a Flattened World."

Since the Google team was ensconced in the hotel's conference room, Chernin borrowed the hotel manager's office for a meeting with Semel. After a brief discussion of the auction, Chernin and Semel walked out to the hotel lobby—and ran smack into Google's Sergey Brin. Semel and Brin chatted briefly, but the message to Google was clear. Semel could be chatting with Chernin for only one reason: to bid on the MySpace auction. Google started scrambling to finalize its bid.

Meanwhile, the News Corp. team had gathered in the tented conference area that had been erected on the tennis courts at Pebble Beach. Across the court, DeWolfe was introducing Nicholas Negroponte to the crowd of News Corp. executives. Negroponte, chairman emeritus of the MIT Media Lab, was spearheading an initiative to distribute cheap laptops to children in the third world, to which News Corp. had pledged $2.5 million.

But Heckman, Levinsohn, Chernin, and Barrett weren't listening to Negroponte or DeWolfe. They were sitting in a tented lounge outside the conference area, going over the latest terms of the Google proposal. It was more than they had ever expected to get. At the beginning of the auction process, Heckman predicted that MySpace could probably get $250 million. Now he had provided it with a $750 million bid from Google.

Even so, the News Corp. team agreed that Heckman should try to stir up the other bidders to see if they could get a bigger number.

Heckman called Microsoft to tell them that their bid had been trumped.

Ask.com, which had hoped that its novel idea of a joint venture would win it some consideration, also dropped out when it heard the numbers being bandied about.

Meanwhile, Yahoo started backing away from its initial $750 million bid and asking for more opportunities to sell MySpace banner ads instead of just search advertising. Yahoo was moving to bolster its market dominance. Although Yahoo lagged behind Google in search advertising, it was the leading seller of so-called display advertising on the Internet. Display ads are graphical banners and squares that make up the bulk of Internet advertising.

Yahoo's proposal included a provision that Yahoo could sell some of MySpace's display advertising. But MySpace wasn't sure it wanted to give Yahoo a piece of that business as well as its search business.

Microsoft came around with another bid, sending over a PowerPoint slide presentation with a generous new offer: $1.12 billion in guaranteed payments over three years. But it still included lots of conditions that MySpace was likely to reject.

Heckman knew this was his only leverage point. He told the Google team that its $750 million bid had been topped. He also told Google that the competing offer was a giant hairball of conditions. "So, if you can keep yours clean, you can still win," Heckman said.

Working together, Heckman and Google's top negotiator, Tim Armstrong, came up with a creative way to reach $900 million: They extended the length of the deal from thirty months to thirty-six months, giving Google more time over which to spread out the payments. The new agreement also gave Google the right to sell advertising on the websites that MySpace was planning to roll out internationally.

"You need to promise me in blood that you'll stop all conversations with any other company if we agree to the nine hundred million," Armstrong told Heckman.

Heckman agreed. They shook hands and toasted the deal with glasses of red wine and hamburgers at the Pebble Beach golf clubhouse.

On Thursday evening Murdoch closed the conference with a rousing speech. He described News Corp. as being at a "great turning point" in its history.

"The first [turning point] came when we went international, expanding outside Australia into Britain in 1969, then into the United States in 1973," he said. "The second turning point saw the transformation of News Corp. from a newspaper business into a true media company . . . with our investment in Twentieth Century Fox studio in 1985 and the launch of the Fox television businesses.

"This turning point will be the most fundamental," Murdoch said. "Today we must transform ourselves from simply a media company into a powerhouse of the digital age . . . The Internet is central to this revolution . . . it is a transforming technology that will have just as great an impact on our civilization as the invention of the wheel, the printing press, steam power, and the combustion engine."

It took a few more days for the Google deal to get finalized. Chernin got the News Corp. board to approve it on Friday. Then Heckman flew home to Seattle with Google executive Tim Armstrong and spent a day huddled in Heckman's former Scout.com office finalizing details.

Finally, on Sunday night, at a charity dinner hosted by a News Corp. executive in Los Angeles, Chernin and Levinsohn were glued to their cell phones as they gave their final approval to the terms.

Sadly, the deal proved to be a breaking point in Heckman's crumbling marriage. His wife, who attended the conference, was unhappy that she hadn't seen him the whole time at Pebble Beach. The retreat was supposed to be a vacation for the two, who had often been apart while Heckman commuted to Los Angeles from their home in Seattle. A month later the two separated.

On Monday, August 7, News Corp. announced the deal after the market closed. Chernin bragged to the press that the Google deal paid for the MySpace acquisition in one fell swoop.

Wall Street was thrilled. In after-hours trading, News Corp. shares finally broke through the $20 mark, an all-time high. Finally News Corp. could prove that its nearly $1.5 billion Internet spending spree had been worthwhile.

"The size of this deal is staggering," said Wall Street analyst Richard Greenfield at Pali Capital. "Twelve months ago, MySpace was generating two and a half to three million dollars a month in advertising revenue. Now you're talking about search alone being worth twenty-five million dollars a month."

That night, Murdoch took his top digital executives to dinner at the Hotel Bel-Air to celebrate. Peter Chernin, Ross Levinsohn, Chris DeWolfe, Tom Anderson, and Chief Financial Officer Dave DeVoe enjoyed a leisurely dinner. But DeWolfe and Anderson, who were left out of the big-time deal making once again, weren't feeling very celebratory.

The Google deal effectively halted another deal DeWolfe and Anderson were working on: an arrangement with eBay that would let MySpace users buy and sell items from one another using eBay's online commerce tools such as PayPal. DeWolfe and Anderson called it "peer commerce" and believed it could be a huge revenue opportunity for MySpace, which could take a cut of the transactions.

But the Google deal, as preliminarily drafted, would prohibit MySpace from working with eBay—and would likely force MySpace to use Google's online payment system, Checkout, which was trying to gain market share from PayPal.

DeWolfe's and Anderson's concerns about eBay, however, had fallen on deaf ears. Chernin, Levinsohn, and others at News Corp. were far too interested in sealing the $900 million deal to quibble about such a minor point with Google. Over dinner, Anderson vented his frustration on another topic: He complained to Murdoch that Chernin hadn't let him hire enough engineers to build new features for the site. Chernin was annoyed that Anderson would undermine him in front of his boss, but he didn't say anything.

DeWolfe and Anderson would spend the next year battling with Google to get the eBay restrictions dropped from the deal. Ultimately Google ended up delaying its initial payments to News Corp. by a few months, and News Corp. ended up extending the arrangement by an additional six months.

In retrospect, Heckman regretted not having included DeWolfe and Anderson in the deal negotiations at Pebble Beach. "If I had it to do all over again, I probably would have involved them more," he said later. "But I was very concerned that having too many cooks in the kitchen would slow the process—and the number was so big, I didn't want to take any risks to that deal."

The negotiations estranged Heckman and DeWolfe, who had attended college together, and further alienated MySpace from Fox Interactive Media. "It was harmful from a relationship standpoint and probably caused MySpace to be more isolated from FIM management," Heckman admitted.

Viacom chairman Sumner Redstone was also seething. His chief rival, Murdoch, had sealed a huge deal with Google and was being acclaimed as an Internet visionary, reshaping the MTV generation. Meanwhile, Viacom's share price had been sinking since the company split into two in January.

The company called Viacom, run by Tom Freston and comprised primarily of MTV and other cable channels, had made a few small Internet investments, but its own Internet initiatives hadn't caught on. The press was starting to ask questions. "Will Viacom Remain a Wallflower?" a *BusinessWeek* headline asked. "Viacom Discovers Kids Don't Want Their MTV Online," the *Wall Street Journal* declared.

Redstone hated to be trumped by his archrival. "No! Not him!"

he yelled at a journalist. "I don't want to lose to him . . . It was a humiliating experience . . . I know Murdoch well. There's no chance of outbidding him! I wanted MySpace before that, before Murdoch got interested."

Redstone pinned the blame on Freston for not buying MySpace. "It sat there for weeks while Tom, in his methodical way, was studying it, having committee meetings, doing due diligence. It went on and on! Tom let it get away!" On September 5, the Monday after Labor Day, about a year after News Corp. completed its acquisition of MySpace, Freston had just finished playing tennis at a friend's house. He got a call from Redstone asking him to come over to his Beverly Hills mansion. When Freston arrived, Redstone fired him.

The media industry was shocked. Freston was a much-admired executive with a twenty-year track record. Now he would be known as the man who got fired for losing MySpace to Murdoch. It was an especially unfair label for Freston, whose efforts to buy MySpace had been thwarted at every turn by the internal politics at Viacom.

Chapter 22

WAR AGAINST WEB 2.0

I n the fall of 2006, so-called Web 2.0 companies in Silicon Valley became the focus of a growing frenzy. Coined in 2004 by technology industry veteran Tim O'Reilly, the term had several meanings. At one level, Web 2.0 was a catchall for a generation of Internet companies: The first generation was embodied by Yahoo, AOL, and Netscape; the second generation, by Google, MySpace, and YouTube. At another level, Web 2.0 described companies that used the Web as a "platform"—meaning that they built technology to run on the Web the way that software companies built programs to run on operating systems such as Microsoft Windows.

Until the fall of 2006, News Corp.'s acquisition of MySpace had been the biggest financial event of the Web 2.0 community. But then the action moved to the center of gravity for technology companies: to Silicon Valley.

San Bruno–based YouTube was rumored to be for sale for more than $1 billion. Palo Alto–based Facebook, a social networking site with just one-quarter the audience of MySpace, had recently turned down an $800 million offer from Yahoo. Even tiny websites had huge valuations: *Business Week* ran a cover story titled "How This Kid Made $60 Million in 18 Months," about the founder of a San Francisco–based news aggregation website, Digg.

For News Corp. the Web 2.0 mania was a double-edged sword: It validated the fact that News Corp. got a great deal on MySpace, but it also made it more expensive for News Corp. to buy more Internet properties. News Corp. president Peter Chernin declared that News Corp. had a solution: It would build its own Web 2.0 businesses.

Speaking at a Merrill Lynch investment conference on September 12, 2006, Chernin issued a warning to companies "driven off the back of MySpace." "Virtually any so-called Web 2.0 applications, whether it's YouTube, whether it's Flickr, whether it's Photobucket . . . Almost every single one of them gets well over 50 percent of their traffic from MySpace, and there's no reason we can't build a parallel business, and not necessarily take them over, but certainly be a real competitor to almost any one of those businesses," Chernin said.

His comments sent shock waves through the Web 2.0 community. This was not how business was done in Silicon Valley. Media conglomerates might be used to controlling all aspects of their content and distribution, but technology companies worked differently. In Silicon Valley, companies strived to build platforms on which other developers could build. Convincing other programmers to write software for your platform was considered a win.

Already hundreds of developers had staked their future on MySpace. The MySpace ecosystem had evolved into a vast and complex array of websites where MySpace users shopped for wallpaper, videos, and slide shows to place on their profile pages. The wide range of options available through third parties was one of the main reasons for MySpace's popularity.

Few of the MySpace ecosystem sites made money, and few of them had any kind of formal relationship with MySpace. In fact, even executives at the biggest sites in the MySpace ecosystem had rarely spoken to anybody at MySpace prior to the News Corp. acquisition. Afterward, however, MySpace had quietly begun flexing its muscles, cracking down on sites that infringed on its terms of service or were using the MySpace name inappropriately. MySpace even quietly launched some products that competed with the biggest members of the ecosystem.

Chernin's comments made the newfound hostility explicit. The influential tech blog TechCrunch declared Chernin's speech to be "both dangerously arrogant and like a real validation of fears that MySpace dependency is too risky for outside developers."

...

The website whose success most irked News Corp. was YouTube. Created in mid-2005, its founders, Chad Hurley and Steve Chen, originally conceived of YouTube as a video version of HotOrNot.com, the website where users ranked photos of one another by attractiveness. Quickly, however, YouTube's easy-to-use site transformed itself into a popular destination for all sorts of homemade videos—particularly among MySpace users.

At the time that YouTube launched, most online video had to be played on clunky video players from RealNetworks, Microsoft, or Apple QuickTime. To watch a video, users had to download the correct video player first (not all videos were compatible with all players). Next the user had to wait for the video to download. Finally, he could play it. Often, one of these steps would malfunction, leading users to be endlessly frustrated with their online video experiences.

YouTube changed the rules of the game by offering videos that employed Flash technology. Flash software was designed in 1996 to help create animation, but by 2003 it had evolved to include the ability to create video. Flash video is not as high resolution as other kinds of Web video, but it provides a much more convenient consumer experience. Although Flash requires users to download a small application that allows their Web browser to run Flash animation, Flash has become so ubiquitous that most Web surfers already have it installed on their computers— even if they don't know it.

When YouTube launched its Flash video site, users could watch videos with a simple click of a button. There was no player to download, no waiting time—just instant gratification. Soon MySpace users were embedding YouTube videos in their pages, driving huge traffic to YouTube's website. YouTube's momentum was such that by October 2005, just a few months after its launch, YouTube raised venture capital financing at a $15 million valuation, despite having absolutely no revenue—since it didn't sell advertising on its site.

As YouTube's popularity soared, Chernin increasingly worried that YouTube would gain a monopoly on distribution of online video, which could harm News Corp.'s ability to negotiate fair prices for distribution of its TV and film video content in the future. Distribution is a big

concern for big media companies like News Corp. Creating content, whether it's movies or television or music, is extremely expensive. To ensure control over how their content is distributed, many media conglomerates have purchased distribution channels. Disney owns ABC, Time Warner owns a cable company, Viacom owns CBS, and News Corp. owns Fox.

The media conglomerates would have liked to purchase similarly powerful distribution channels on the Internet, but the most popular sites were expensive, and it wasn't clear if they could hold their audiences over time. Even so, News Corp. wanted to buy YouTube, but its backers insisted the site was not for sale.

In early 2006 Chernin had launched a two-prong assault on YouTube. First, MySpace released its own version of Flash video in January. It proved extremely popular but didn't surpass YouTube's popularity. Then in the spring, Chernin and Viacom copresident Tom Freston began discussing the idea of building a YouTube competitor that would host their television and film videos. They hoped to get one more studio to join, so that the effort would seem like a one-stop shop for big media content. Disney refused to join, not wanting to dilute its brand. For a while, CBS was interested, then NBC. But by September the talks had fallen apart.

In his Merrill Lynch speech in September 2006, Chernin declared his intent to double down on MySpace's effort to overtake YouTube. "We have one person working on MySpace video, and the numbers I see are we have sixty percent to seventy percent of the traffic on YouTube on MySpace video already," he said. "It is one of the things we're going to invest in the next several months."

The most indispensable part of the MySpace ecosystem, however, was not the glamorous YouTube but the decidedly unglamorous Photobucket. The brainchild of two Colorado engineers, Photobucket was important for one simple reason: MySpace couldn't afford to provide enough storage for all the photos that its users wanted to post on their profile pages.

This problem was not unique to MySpace; it had dogged earlier social networks as well. The reason was twofold: First, and most important, none of the social networks was making money; and, second, what

money they had was thrown into providing servers and databases for their core service. So most services, including MySpace, allowed users to upload only a small number of photos. Photobucket founder Alex Welch first noticed this problem on a small photo website he was running called Picturefuse.com. A cheerful redhead, Welch worked during the day as an engineer at a big telecommunications company in Broomfield, Colorado, while running Picturefuse on the side. In 2003 the company from which he was leasing his computers began calling to complain that Picturefuse was using too much bandwidth. That didn't seem possible to Welch, since his tiny site had only two thousand users. But when he checked his records, he noticed that a lot of the traffic on his website wasn't *his* users but were websites like eBay, LiveJournal, and Xanga. Welch realized that his users were right-clicking on the photos on Picturefuse, picking up the Web address (URL) for the photo, and putting it on their eBay profiles or their blogging pages. As Welch investigated, he noticed that most other photo sites didn't allow their users to do that kind of linking.

Sensing a market need, Welch created Photobucket.com, the sole purpose of which would be to allow people to link photos to other websites. The images on Photobucket were low resolution, not high resolution, like photos that were meant to be printed out. But since the photos were intended only for Web viewing, the quality was perfectly adequate. Social networking users flocked to Photobucket's service. By the time of Chernin's speech in September 2006, a Photobucket analysis showed that more than 60 percent of MySpace pages contained a link to Photobucket.

Photobucket wasn't minting money. Revenues from advertising on its site were less than $30 million, but it had raised venture capital financing at an $85 million valuation—due in large part to the success of MySpace. Chernin's threat seemed like it could seriously damage Photobucket's business.

The most unruly parts of the MySpace ecosystem were the MySpace layout sites. Since 2005, hundreds of flashing, blinking websites had popped up to help MySpace users decorate (or in the lingo of MySpace users, "pimp") their profile pages. Before the layout sites existed,

technology-savvy users wrote simple Web codes into their profile pages to decorate them. If other people liked the way a person had decorated his or her profile, they could just copy the code and put it on their own profile pages.

Eventually a few enterprising MySpace users realized that they could set up their own websites offering the codes for MySpace layouts. The first was Thomas' MySpace Editor, at StrikeFile.com, created in mid-2004 by a high school student, Thomas Zwaagstra, from Huntington Beach, California. During his freshman year in high school, Zwaagstra began changing the layout on his MySpace profile as a way to experiment with the computer programming languages he was teaching himself. Soon his friends were asking for help with their MySpace pages. "This became tedious after a short time," Zwaagstra said, "and eventually I made a single CSS [Cascading Style Sheet] code that could easily be adapted to use different color schemes."

Zwaagstra began posting his Web layout codes online so that his friends could customize profiles without his help. Whenever someone used one of Zwaagstra's layouts, a small link to Zwaagstra's website would appear on that person's MySpace profile. As a result, word of Thomas' MySpace Editor soon spread like a virus through MySpace. Eventually his one-man operation attracted an average of three hundred thousand visitors a day and between $150,000 and $250,000 a year in advertising revenue. Not bad for a high school student working part-time.

Inevitably, others sought to replicate Zwaagstra's success. In mid-2005 Andrew Thompson,[1] a seventeen-year-old from Denver who had just dropped out of high school, decided that he could improve on Zwaagstra's design. "I saw Thomas' Editor, and I thought it could be done a lot better," he said. In August Thompson launched his website, MySpaceSupport.com, with easier-to-use layouts and codes. He attracted a huge audience—as high as one million page views in a single day—and was savvy about placing lots of advertisements on his site. As a result, Thompson struck financial gold. In 2006 MySpaceSupport generated $1.4 million in revenues for a teenager who had been broke, unemployed, and sharing an apartment with two friends. Suddenly Thompson was rich, and his life changed dramatically.

[1] Thompson is in the process of legally changing his last name to Fashion.

"The money was fluke money," Thompson later wrote on his blog. "I didn't do what some of the MySpace flukes did and go buy some $1 million dollar home (no joke) and blow all my money on stupid things. I think I personally did very well with such great amounts of money coming in and not blowing it all on alcohol and drugs (like some MySpace flukes I know did)."

On his blog, Thompson detailed how he spent his "fluke" MySpace money:

Smart Expenses

420k House (80k down)—Personally, I think this was a smart move, although I don't like my house anymore . . . But oh well . . .

32k Nissan Titan (paid off)—I think the truck was probably the best choice I made; because I live in Colorado, it's all I need. ☺

110k Drivable.com investment—Obviously this is a new company I am trying to start, so I think the investment was worth it to me.

20k Perfection Apparel—Clothing, tougher than I thought, but not going to give up on it.

20k Photography—I love photography, so it was worth it to me.

Dumb Expenses

120k BMW M6—Cool. If I made the money I was making back then, I could keep it.

70k BMW 330xi—I should of just stuck with the truck (includes car + mods).

10k Drift Car—Drifting is fun but not worth what I put into it right now.

10k Birthday Parties—Plain ole fucking stupid.

The lure of big money, especially for a simple website that could be run by one person, prompted a kind of MySpace gold rush among layout sites. By the time Chernin made his speech, MySpace layout sites were selling for huge sums to speculators. Even the previous owner of the domain name MySpace.com, Ari Freeman, had turned his website, FreeDiskSpace.com, into one of the more popular layout sites, simply on the basis of its name previously being associated with MySpace. In October 2006 Freeman sold FreeDiskSpace.com for approximately $125,000.

In January 2006 MySpace sent cease and desist letters to some of the layout sites that were using MySpace in their name, claiming they were violating MySpace's trademark. As a result, MySpaceCity.com changed its name to Tower Codes. Thompson of MySpaceSupport.com contacted a friend at Photobucket who helped him get in touch with someone at MySpace to discuss the issue. Thompson added legal disclaimers on his page, and MySpace dropped the issue.

Chernin's speech reactivated the layout community's fears that MySpace would compete with them by launching its own profile editing tools.

The fastest-growing segment of the MySpace ecosystem was a category called widgets. Widgets are small bits of software that can be embedded in a website and provide constantly updated information, usually from another website. Widgets started out as utilities that could bring news or information to your computer. On MySpace and other social networking sites, however, widgets evolved into units of self-expression.

MySpace members use widgets to decorate their profiles with slide shows, music videos, or games and quizzes for their friends to play. They use widgets to count the number of visitors to their site, display maps, or make their text and photos glitter and shimmer.

Like YouTube, the top widget site, Slide, was inspired by the photo-ranking website HotOrNot.com. In early 2005 Max Levchin, the co-founder of PayPal, borrowed some photos from his friend James Hong at HotOrNot to create what he called a "babe ticker"—a scrolling ticker of pictures of good-looking women that bored cubicle dwellers could place on their desktop. In August 2005 Levchin rebranded the ticker as a free downloadable "photo playback" device that users could load with any set of photos. Soon the ticker evolved into a widget that anybody could place on a website to display a slide show of photos. By the time of Chernin's speech, Slide claimed to have millions of daily viewers of its slide shows.

Slide's fiercest competitor, RockYou, was born a few months later out of a conversation between Silicon Valley veteran Lance Tokuda and his volleyball teammate Sandi Sayama at Bennigan's restaurant. It was the fall of 2005, and Sayama was complaining about how difficult it was to make a slide show of photos for her MySpace profile. To build a slide show, she was trying to master a kind of Web markup language called "marquee tags," which were designed for creating text that scrolls across the screen—not for photos.

Tokuda, who has a PhD in computer science, wasn't a MySpace user, but he was intrigued by Sayama's dilemma. So Tokuda and Jia Shen, his colleague at an e-mail security firm, built a little slide show application that could be placed on MySpace. They put it up on a website called RockMySpace.com, and the interest in it was torrential.

In November Tokuda and Shen posted notices of their invention six times in a MySpace user forum. Within thirty days, RockMySpace had acquired sixty thousand users. The traffic to its website was so huge that the server went down on seventeen of the first thirty days. Tom Anderson even sent the founders an e-mail saying, "Hey—saw that lots of my-space people are utilizing your site . . . congrats." By January 2006 Tokuda and Shen had left their jobs and founded the company that is now known as RockYou.

Neither Slide nor RockYou was profitable, largely because MySpace prevented them from running any advertisements inside the widgets. They could run ads on their home pages, but the vast majority of their viewers were on MySpace pages.

Still, MySpace sought to compete with the slide show widget makers. In August 2006 MySpace launched a bare-bones slide show widget of its own. By the time of Chernin's speech, MySpace's efforts had failed to make a dent in Slide and RockYou's business, but his threat seemed to imply a bigger threat looming. To hedge their bets, Slide and RockYou soon began looking to develop partnerships with social networks other than MySpace.

On Monday, October 9, Google announced that it was acquiring YouTube for $1.65 billion in stock. Ross Levinsohn was furious. Levinsohn believed that a YouTube-MySpace combination would be "game over"—allowing News Corp. to completely dominate the Web 2.0 world.

Levinsohn had courted YouTube for months, even as YouTube claimed it was not for sale. In the week just prior to Google's announcement, Levinsohn had felt that he was making significant progress. Levinsohn had presented his vision of a combined MySpace-YouTube to YouTube founders Chad Hurley and Steve Chen. He had visited Michael Moritz, the venture capitalist backing YouTube. The answer was always the same: "We're not for sale."

As Levinsohn heard rumors of the deal over the weekend, he felt tricked. He had his general counsel send a letter to YouTube asking it to give News Corp. a chance to bid—with the implied threat that News Corp. might sue to block the deal. YouTube never responded.

To be sure, it wasn't at all clear that News Corp. would have agreed to pay the $1.65 billion price tag for YouTube or would have been willing to defend the copyright infringement lawsuits that were likely to be filed against a deep-pocketed YouTube owner. But it bothered News Corp. executives to be left out of the bidding for a site that, in their view, MySpace had practically created.

Levinsohn also worried that MySpace would lose its leverage over YouTube. Previously MySpace had shut off YouTube videos on its site due to concerns about pornography. Now MySpace would have to brave Google's wrath if it wanted to shut down YouTube.

Levinsohn's concerns were right on the mark. The tables were indeed turning in the Web 2.0 world; the sites that Chernin claimed were "driven off the back of MySpace" were amassing growing power of their own.

MySpace would soon learn that lesson the hard way.

Chapter 23

NUMBER ONE IN EVERY MARKET

On November 8, 2006, Chris DeWolfe and Tom Anderson stood in their hotel suite overlooking Tokyo Harbor and surveyed the landscape they hoped to conquer.

In Japan, a social networking site called Mixi had already amassed 5.7 million monthly visitors. Founded in February 2004, Mixi was more restrictive than MySpace, requiring users to be invited to join the network, and prohibiting members from customizing their pages. But its clean, fast-loading pages and Japanese sensibility had caught on with the youth in Japan, making the site third only to Yahoo and Google in page views. In September, when Mixi issued shares to the public on the Tokyo Stock Exchange, its stock price doubled on the first day of trading.

MySpace was the underdog in Japan, with just six hundred thousand monthly visitors. DeWolfe and Anderson had been preparing for this day for months. Creating a Japanese language version of the site had been a huge headache; it had consumed MySpace programmers during the previous three months and delayed other necessary projects, including the installation of the Google search engine on MySpace.

Now that they had a test site up and running, DeWolfe and Anderson were determined to make a splash. Rupert Murdoch joined them in Tokyo for a press conference announcing a $10 million joint venture with the Japanese media company SoftBank Corp. to launch a Japanese version of MySpace. A few days later, MySpace hosted a concert by Noel

Gallagher, the guitarist for the rock band Oasis, for six hundred MySpace users at a Tokyo nightclub.

SoftBank chief executive Masayoshi Son bragged that MySpace Japan would differentiate itself from Mixi by not requiring new members to be invited to join. In fact, anyone in Japan could set up a MySpace account even without the SoftBank joint venture. The venture's customized Web site simply allowed MySpace users in Japan to automatically see a Japanese-language version of the site, which highlighted Japanese musicians and local events in Japan. At the same time, Japanese users could still view and communicate with U.S. users. "The idea is to still maintain a global community where they can interact with each other in any language," Anderson said.

If MySpace has a proprietary feature that helps the site compete, it is Anderson himself. Every night he trolls the website to see what features are being used the most and help members navigate the site. Every day Anderson receives about forty thousand e-mails from MySpace members with suggestions, questions, and criticism; he tries to read about two thousand to three thousand of those e-mails each day.

Anderson steps in with gusto to right wrongs and do well by users, even while traveling. While in Japan, for instance, he noticed that News Corp.'s Fox television network had snatched the profile name MySpace.com/Bones to promote a new television show called *Bones*. But a Louisiana rock band named the Bones had already been using the name. The band complained in an e-mail to Anderson.

He immediately fixed the problem and sent off a note to the band: "I heard about what happened with your URL. I gave it back to ya . . . Sorry about that! As we grow in size, sometimes people make decisions I don't know about. This was obviously the wrong decision. The Bones URL is yours once again. :-)"

To many of MySpace's millions of users, Anderson represents the soul of the site. In each international market, MySpace makes sure to set up an Anderson equivalent. In Japan every user's first friend was named "Ozzie." Ozzie would be there to answer questions and be the eyes and ears of the site.

Still, like many Western companies, MySpace faced an uphill battle in

Japan. Within a month of the launch, Ozzie had amassed just 51,470 friends—far fewer new members than Anderson collects in the United States each day.

Ross Levinsohn wasn't invited to the Japanese launch of MySpace. Instead he was speaking at the Web 2.0 Summit, a technology conference in San Francisco, and he was feeling defensive.

Although MySpace was by far the biggest social networking site in the world, rivals were popping up everywhere. And there were worrying signs that MySpace had peaked: In the fall, MySpace's traffic had plateaued at about fifty-six million U.S. visitors a month. Levinsohn told the audience that the site was still growing overseas. "We're still adding globally—I actually just looked at the number—we added over three hundred twenty thousand new profiles yesterday," Levinsohn told the crowd. "Think about it: To make a joke about it, we're adding the size of Buffalo every day."

Levinsohn admitted, however, to being worried about MySpace's future. "It is a fantastic property today that if we don't pay one hundred percent attention to, just like any other business, it's at risk," he said. "It's why I don't sleep. It's why I put on thirty pounds in the last year. It's terrible."

MySpace was coming off of a difficult summer. In the year since it was purchased, News Corp. had poured tens of millions of dollars into MySpace's computer infrastructure. In a single year, MySpace had gone through eight tons of cardboard just unpacking new computer servers. Even so, MySpace was still struggling to keep the site up and running on a consistent basis.

First there was the problem of users getting an "unexpected error" message when a portion of MySpace would unexpectedly shut down. "We were scratching our heads for about a month trying to figure out why our Windows 2003 servers kept shutting themselves off," said Jim Benedetto, MySpace vice president for technology. Finally, after investigating, MySpace realized that Microsoft Windows was mistaking the huge number of people logging on to MySpace at a single time for hackers trying to break into the system. Usually computer systems try to prevent so-called denial of service hack attacks by limiting the number of simultaneous connections. But MySpace simply had so many users that it looked like a hack attack when it wasn't. The problem was solved when MySpace shut off the antihacker feature of Windows.

Then there were the *real* hack attacks. In July MySpace discovered a worm in the Adobe Flash software that changed users' "About Me" section to include a link to a website blaming the United States for the terrorist attacks of September 11, 2001. MySpace responded by shutting down the old version of Adobe Flash software—which powered nearly all the videos, music players, and widgets on MySpace—and urging users to upgrade to the new version of Flash that had just been released.

Anderson notified MySpace members of the forced upgrade in a bulletin: "Latest Update: 05:15PM PST, Monday, July 17th. hey folks—we are moving myspace music players and video players to flash 9.0. flash 9 has security fixes so that people can't mess with you on myspace. if your 'about me' got screwed up this weekend, you could have been safe if you had flash 9 installed."

However, MySpace failed to notify all the widget makers that their widgets were suddenly going to stop working on MySpace, causing a huge uproar in the MySpace ecosystem.

"This is a sloppy move by MySpace," wrote influential blogger Pete Cashmore. "This is the equivalent of eBay suddenly breaking the thousands of third-party tools that plug into it, without even notifying the developers. With companies like Slide, Photobucket, and RockYou investing millions of dollars into the MySpace economy, it's time that MySpace realized it's now a platform."

Two days later, a power outage in Los Angeles took down the entire MySpace website for about twelve hours. Most websites, including MySpace, have backup data centers set up for this kind of emergency. But some of MySpace's crucial data was stored only in Los Angeles—so the backup centers could not independently run the site. MySpace quickly made plans to move copies of that data to its backup sites in other states.

Of course, the fix caused further angst for MySpace users. A week later, MySpace users started complaining that their accounts were being deleted. Even Anderson's profile appeared to be down. Anderson eventually posted an explanation: "hiya—your accounts are not being deleted. we're just moving some databases around to a new data center. we're workin on things right now."

In August MySpace registered its one hundred millionth account—a historic moment. But the one hundred millionth account was broken. Visitors saw this message: "Invalid Friend ID. This user has either cancelled their membership, or their account has been deleted."

In September Murdoch publicly acknowledged that MySpace was struggling to keep up with the one and a half million new users it was signing up each week. "We have about three hundred jobs open at the moment," Murdoch said. "It's not easy to recruit high-quality software engineers at the moment; they are in such demand. We're going as fast as we can."

MySpace was so busy putting out fires that it hadn't released any substantial upgrades for a year. The site was still relying on its outdated blogging feature, its clunky in-house instant messaging system, its slow-to-load video player, its bare-bones e-mail system, and its inadequate photo storage. In the fast-paced world of Internet startups, a year without an upgrade was the equivalent of falling behind.

Levinsohn feared that MySpace was losing ground. But he couldn't convince its executives to take any of his suggestions. "MySpace is a fragile community," Levinsohn warned his boss, Peter Chernin.

Meanwhile, Facebook was on a tear. MySpace was still three times larger than Facebook, with 57.2 million visitors in November compared with Facebook's 16.7 million. But Facebook had narrowed the gap through two innovative moves.

First, in September Facebook had launched a feature called "News Feed," which provided members with updates about their friends' activities on Facebook. For instance, if a Facebook member added new photos to his or her profile page, friends would be notified in a news item on their own profile pages.

This seemingly simple innovation was, in fact, technically quite difficult. For each member, Facebook sorts through about thirty thousand possible updates to choose the sixty that are most likely to be interesting to the Facebook member. Facebook users can also adjust their News Feed settings, for instance, by requesting fewer updates when friends change their photos or by requesting more updates when their friends change e-mail addresses.

To sort through the updates, Facebook built an algorithm that takes into account each user's explicit settings, as well as his behavior—which updates he clicks on and which profiles he visits. "News Feed works so well that it's sometimes easy to forget how sophisticated it is under the covers," said Facebook engineer Justin Rosenstein. "If you have a lot of friends, your Facebook home page is displaying only a tiny fraction of what's going on in your social network. The system that selects the right subset is impressive from both an AI [artificial intelligence] perspective—with a ranking algorithm that uses signals based on user behavior throughout the site—and a systems perspective, efficiently processing 1.2 trillion story candidates every day."

At first News Feed caused a backlash from Facebook users upset about their privacy. But after Facebook released enhanced privacy settings to let users control more of the "news" broadcast about them, the furor subsided, and News Feed became one of the most popular features on Facebook.

A few weeks after News Feed launched, Facebook took another bold step: It opened its service to anyone. Initially Facebook accepted only members with valid e-mail addresses from universities. Then in September 2005, Facebook expanded to high school students. In June 2006 it began allowing members with valid e-mail addresses from corporate and government workplaces. Finally, on September 26, 2006, Facebook opened the floodgates, allowing anyone to join.

The combination of News Feed and the open membership boosted traffic by 26 percent between September and November 2006. At the same time, MySpace's U.S. traffic increased only 3 percent.

Levinsohn believed that MySpace needed professional managers to beef up its technological development. After all, his experienced advertising team had crafted the incredible $900 million advertising deal for MySpace. If they could get their hands on the website, he believed they could improve its features. Over a six-month period, Levinsohn had presented five different management reorganization plans to his boss, Chernin. One plan involved sending Anderson to China to launch the Chinese version of MySpace, and sending DeWolfe around the world to promote the rest of MySpace's international sites. With Anderson and DeWolfe busy evangelizing, Levinsohn hoped to install a seasoned team of executives from IGN and FoxSports to run MySpace on a day-to-day basis. Levinsohn hoped that his team could quickly build or buy features that would bring MySpace up to date and open up the site to outside software developers.

But Chernin turned down Levinsohn's proposed reorganizations. He wanted Anderson and DeWolfe to keep running MySpace, and Levinsohn to focus more on the day-to-day operations of Fox Interactive. Murdoch had promised autonomy to Anderson and DeWolfe; Chernin wasn't in a position to overturn that promise. But Chernin was in a position to police Levinsohn—and in Chernin's view, Levinsohn's performance was disappointing.

Chernin believed that Levinsohn had made little progress pulling together the disparate operations of Fox Interactive. Instead Levinsohn had been busy scouting for acquisitions and flirting with companies like YouTube. Levinsohn also had failed to complete an important task: learning how to get along with Anderson and DeWolfe.

DeWolfe and Levinsohn were constantly clashing. For instance, DeWolfe opposed Levinsohn's decision to install former AOL ad sales executive Michael Barrett as Fox Interactive's chief revenue officer. DeWolfe thought his friend, Colin Digiaro, was doing a fine job running MySpace ad sales and didn't like the fact that Barrett would now be reaching out to the advertising community.

DeWolfe also wanted Levinsohn to redistribute the profit-sharing formula at Fox Interactive. Only about one-third of the profits were allocated to MySpace employees, even though MySpace was by far the biggest part of Fox Interactive. But Levinsohn resisted changing the initial formula.

By November Chernin had decided that something had to be done. The time had come to fire Levinsohn—he just needed to check with Murdoch first. The two were riding in a car in Tokyo during the MySpace launch festivities.

"I'm going to fire Ross," Chernin told Murdoch.

"Fine," Murdoch replied. Murdoch was usually content to let Chernin be the bad guy.

"Keep it quiet," Chernin said. "I want to wait until I'm back."

Murdoch nodded. He had other things on his mind; he was on his way to China to find opportunities for MySpace.

...

Murdoch had huge global ambitions for MySpace. Unlike most American media moguls, who tend to be parochially focused on the U.S. market, he has always focused on a broader landscape. Murdoch wanted MySpace to be a global portal for youth, just as Yahoo and Google had become first stops on the Internet for people all over the world. Over the summer, Murdoch declared that he wanted MySpace to be in about a dozen of the world's biggest markets by the end of the year.

MySpace's global rollout began in June, when it launched a version of its website in Britain. In August it launched in Australia. In September MySpace launched in Germany and France. November was Japan. MySpace missed Murdoch's end-of-the-year deadline for the rest of its ten countries, but made up for it in January, launching Spain, Canada, Mexico, New Zealand, and Italy in a single frenzied month.

In most markets, MySpace faced at least one established competitor. At the time it launched its British version, for instance, MySpace faced a savvy competitor, Bebo, which had 3.9 million visitors compared with MySpace's 5.2 million. But in France, MySpace had not yet caught up with local hit Skyblog.com, with its more than 5 million bloggers. DeWolfe told a reporter: "Our goal is to be number one in every market, but we're not so arrogant as to think we will be number one in every market."

Murdoch was particularly hopeful that MySpace could be the wedge that finally allowed him to break into the Chinese market. He had been trying to tap the Chinese audience for twenty years. To promote his satellite television operations in China, Murdoch had taken several heavily criticized actions to appease the Chinese government over the years. In 1993 Murdoch sold the Beijing newspaper *South China Morning Post,* saying at a news conference that he wanted to avoid having Star TV shut down because of the opinions of some of the newspaper's editors. In 1994 Star TV stopped carrying the British Broadcasting Corporation's international news channel, which had infuriated Beijing with its coverage of the Tiananmen Square protests of 1989. And in 1998 Murdoch's publishing house, HarperCollins, canceled a book that was critical of the Chinese government, by Chris Patten, the last British governor of Hong Kong. Still, in 2005 Murdoch's attempt to break into the prime-time Chinese TV market was derailed by a government crackdown on local and foreign media. "We've rather hit a brick wall in China," he declared. The following year, he scaled back his Chinese holdings further.

After the acquisition of MySpace, Murdoch's enthusiasm for China picked up again. In the summer of 2006, he told an interviewer, "We're going to attempt to get in [to China] through new media, with, say, MySpace and things like that, to get a foothold in there." In the fall, Murdoch sent his wife, Wendi, a native of China, to seek opportunities for MySpace in China with MySpace's DeWolfe and Anderson. "We have to make MySpace a very Chinese site," Murdoch told a group of investors. "I have sent my wife across there because she understands the language."

News that Murdoch's wife—who had not played a role in News Corp.'s management since she married the boss—was on the road with the MySpace founders raised eyebrows among investors and News Corp. executives. For DeWolfe and Anderson, though, their close relationship with the boss's wife made them untouchable. Suddenly, senior News Corp. executives were afraid that saying no to the MySpace founders would be the same as defying Mrs. Murdoch.

Even with Wendi Murdoch on board, cracking the Chinese market would be tough. Other U.S. Internet companies such as Google, Yahoo, and eBay had stumbled on the deep cultural differences between the United States and China.

The Chinese Internet culture flourished in anonymity, where users posted to bulletin boards and blogs without revealing their identity. In general, the Chinese are not very interested in the flashy graphics and personalization that characterize individual MySpace pages in the West. Most individual expression was limited to private communications on the wildly popular QQ instant messaging service. "It is not always about me, and me trying to be cool," said Chinese Internet consultant Sam Flemming. "It's *our* space."

Chinese government regulations also required that MySpace enter China with a local partner. To handle the negotiations, Wendi Murdoch set up an office in the conference room next to DeWolfe's office in Beverly Hills, was given a $100,000 annual salary, and traveled frequently to Beijing. Over nearly a year of negotiations, Wendi Murdoch, who has an MBA from Yale, structured an innovative joint venture: News Corp. would own 51.5 percent of MySpace China, along with two other investors, International Data Group's Chinese venture capital arm, and the investment company of Edward Tian, the former CEO of China Netcom Group Corporation. But rather than run the site as a controlling partner, News Corp. would license the MySpace technology to the joint venture and give the local operators control.

"Our team here will have the sole right to decide on the operating model, the technology platform, as well as the product strategy," said Luo Chuan, the CEO of MySpace China. "That's very unlike the other multinationals you might have seen in the Chinese market."

Eventually Chuan decided that the U.S. model of having one first friend for each MySpace user wouldn't be enough. Chinese users are more comfortable in groups, so MySpace China allows new members to automatically join a group when joining the site. As a result, MySpace China planned to be a bit like Facebook, where users are affiliated with a group—usually a college or a workplace—and cannot enter other groups without an invitation.

While MySpace was expanding overseas, some of its global rivals were arriving at its doorstep. In October one of the most successful social networking sites in the world, Cyworld, developed in South Korea, unveiled its U.S. version to much fanfare.

Founded in 1999 by four graduates of the Korea Advanced Institute of Science and Technology, Cyworld began as a way for friends and families to connect with one another. Unlike MySpace, however, Cyworld users cannot pretend to be someone else. Cyworld requires them to provide the equivalent of a Social Security number proving their identity when they join. In 2003 South Korean's largest wireless carrier, SK Telecom, bought Cyworld for $8.5 million. By 2006 more than one-third of the entire population of South Korea had joined Cyworld.

The sensibility of Cyworld is completely different from MySpace. Cyworld members express themselves through building avatars and 3-D virtual homes called minihompies. There is very little advertising on Cyworld, but its members spend nearly $300,000 a day on virtual items such as wallpaper, "furniture," and background music to decorate their minihompies.

For its foray into the United States, Cyworld set up an office in San Francisco and hired an army of consultants. When it launched, it had cut back on the cutesiness of its minihompies, made its avatars less cherubic, and cut out the field in members' profiles asking for blood type. (Koreans view blood type similarly to a zodiac sign.) However, Cyworld retained much of its wholesome home-decorating approach in the hopes of appealing to teen girls.

Still, it was a risky gamble. Cyworld estimated that at least thirty other social networking sites were launching in the United States around the same time. "Some people might consider this a saturated market," said Cyworld USA CEO Henry Chon. "But we think we're a nice alternative to these other sites."

When Chernin got back to Los Angeles from Japan, he called Ross Levinsohn into his office.

"You're not happy, are you?" Chernin said.

"No, I'm not," Levinsohn agreed.

"This isn't working out, is it?" Chernin said.

"No, it's not," Levinsohn replied.

"We should probably part ways," Chernin said.

"Yes," Levinsohn replied.

In this way, Levinsohn was fired. He was almost relieved to be let go; he knew he had lost the battle for control with DeWolfe and Anderson. Levinsohn's view was that if he couldn't run MySpace effectively, there was no point in staying in the job any longer. He planned to capitalize on his reputation as the guy who bought MySpace by starting a venture capital fund with his friend Jon Miller, recently ousted as chief executive of AOL.

To run Fox Interactive, Chernin chose one of his longtime loyal aides, Peter Levinsohn, an eighteen-year veteran of Fox. Strangely, Peter Levinsohn and Ross Levinsohn were distant cousins who had not met until they crossed paths at News Corp. Peter Levinsohn had limited experience with the Internet; he had been negotiating digital rights for Fox movies and televisions shows. But Chernin believed Peter Levinsohn would be better able to run Fox Interactive Media's sprawling international operations, which had grown to twelve hundred employees located in ten offices worldwide.

"We were entering into a different stage, where it was less about deals," Chernin later told Wall Street analysts about the management shuffle. "This is now about maximizing what we have . . . This, more than any other part of the business, is characterized by 'move forward or die.' I don't ever want to be in a position where MySpace a year from now is the same as MySpace today."

For DeWolfe, the message was clear: MySpace must pick up the pace of innovation. Peter Levinsohn's arrival was a brief respite from his battles with Ross Levinsohn. But it also meant that DeWolfe would be reporting to his fourth boss in three years. First there had been the volatile Brad Greenspan. Second was Richard Rosenblatt, who had sold MySpace out from under DeWolfe. Third was Ross Levinsohn, who had sought to undermine DeWolfe. And now DeWolfe would be working for Peter Levinsohn, who knew nothing about MySpace's business. It wasn't an auspicious beginning.

Chapter 24

BEYOND THE BANNER AD

In November 2006 MySpace dethroned Yahoo as the number one website on the Internet in terms of page views for the month. That meant that although more people visited Yahoo, MySpace's users stuck around longer—which is important to advertisers.

After the Fox Interactive holiday party in the office courtyard, Peter Levinsohn joined the MySpace staff at a nearby bar for a round of kamikaze shots.

It was a heady time for MySpace. In just three short years, Chris DeWolfe and Tom Anderson had built MySpace into a cultural phenomenon and reshaped the media landscape. Their site had propelled Rupert Murdoch to new heights in the media world and caused the downfall of another media mogul, celebrated Viacom veteran Tom Freston.

Most important, MySpace had given teenagers the world over a virtual street corner where they could interact without adult supervision, and express and discover themselves in a creative, liberating way. Sociologist Danah Boyd calls MySpace a "digital public" space that empowers alienated youths to find communities of shared interest that might not be available to them in their hometowns. "Publics are critical to the coming-of-age narrative because they provide the framework for building cultural knowledge," she argues.

Acknowledging the creativity of users who decorated the webpages of sites like MySpace, *Time* magazine declared "You" its Person of the Year for 2006. The magazine stated that 2006 was "a story about community and collaboration on a scale never seen before. It's about the cosmic compendium of knowledge Wikipedia and the million-channel people's network YouTube and the online metropolis MySpace. It's about the many wresting power from the few and helping one another for nothing and how that will not only change the world, but also change the way the world changes."

Rupert Murdoch was also feeling bullish about MySpace—because it was finally making money. In December 2006 Fox Interactive Media posted its first profitable month; the division would have been profitable earlier but for the combined $75 million in compensation that the MySpace founders had negotiated during the sale to News Corp.

By February 2007 Murdoch was predicting that the Fox Interactive division would exceed its goal of $500 million in revenues for the year ending June 2007 and would likely hit $1 billion in revenues for the year ending June 2008—with MySpace accounting for most of the division's success. "MySpace is such a dominant part of FIM that basically they're one [and] the same," Peter Chernin told Wall Street analysts.

The advertising department was the one division of MySpace that News Corp. had completely rebuilt. Despite DeWolfe's objections, Ross Levinsohn had installed former AOL executive Michael Barrett as chief revenue officer of Fox Interactive Media in June 2006, effectively giving Barrett oversight of all the advertising functions of MySpace.

Barrett, well liked on Madison Avenue, had worked in Internet advertising since its early days, when he sold ads for the community website GeoCities. After Ross Levinsohn was fired, Barrett was one of the few senior executives at Fox Interactive who remained in place. IGN chief executive Mark Jung, who had been Levinsohn's chief operating officer, and Scout.com founder Jim Heckman, who had been Fox's chief strategy officer, both left Fox around the same time as Levinsohn.

MySpace's expected $500 million in annual revenues was still a drop in the bucket compared with Web behemoths like Yahoo, which took in revenues of $1.7 billion in just the first three months of 2007. But at least the advertising dollars were finally rolling in. The site's advertising potential was unproven when News Corp. bought MySpace in the fall of

2005. Just one year later, advertisers were starting to see its benefits. After all, MySpace had sheer numbers on its side: In the month of February 2007 alone, MySpace had a U.S. audience of more than sixty-four million people.

In part, MySpace was benefiting from the broader surge in Internet advertising. Between 2002 and 2006, U.S. advertisers had ramped up their spending on the Internet nearly threefold to $16.9 billion, up from $6 billion in 2002.

The Internet still accounted for a small slice of the $150 billion spent on U.S. advertising in 2006, but the increase came largely at the expense of television, newspaper, and magazine budgets. Strangely, the shift did not reflect that people were watching less television, despite constant news reports about the death of that medium. In fact, television viewership continues to rise each year in the United States. The average American household tuned in to television for an astounding eight hours and fourteen minutes per day during the 2005–2006 television season, up 14 percent from seven hours and fifteen minutes per day in the 1995–1996 television season, according to Nielsen Media Research.

But many Americans claim that they are watching less television than ever. Every year since 2000, the University of Southern California's Center for the Digital Future has surveyed more than two thousand people across the United States and found that about one-third of them claim to spend less time watching television since they began using the Internet.

What accounts for this contradiction? The truth is that the media landscape is fragmenting. It used to be that just a few broadcast television networks were the main source of entertainment in the American home. Now hundreds of television channels compete with home movie systems, the Internet, video games, iPods, and a myriad of other media devices. As a result, Americans are still watching a lot of television, but they are often surfing the Internet, reading a magazine, or listening to music at the same time.

Young people, in particular, are becoming adept at multitasking with media; the Kaiser Family Foundation's comprehensive survey of what it calls "Generation M" indicates that media-savvy kids are increasingly using two or more forms of media at once.

In some sense, all the dire warnings about the death of television are true, but slightly off point. Television is not dying, but people's willingness to pay attention to television is increasingly threatened. Nobel Prize–winning economist Herbert Simon summarized the problem best: In 1971 he declared that "a wealth of information creates a poverty of attention."

MySpace appeals to advertisers because the attention attracted by their ads can be measured. When an advertiser builds a MySpace profile for its product, it can measure the success of the profile by the number of friends it attracts and how many comments are posted on its page. This level of interaction with the audience is revolutionary for advertisers. Fox Interactive's Barrett calls the appeal of MySpace the "quantification of engagement"—meaning that advertisers can quantify how engaged users are in their ads.

Until MySpace, most Internet advertisers hoped that Web surfers would click on their banner ads to find out more about their product. But the percentage of people who click on banner ads has been steadily declining on the Internet—down to less than 1 percent in many cases—leaving advertisers with little information about the impact of their ads.

By comparison, MySpace is a giant popularity contest in which the winners are those with the most friends and the most comments on their pages.

Musicians were among the first to realize that adding friends on MySpace was cheaper and more effective than any other type of direct marketing. Soon the practice spread to porn stars and pinup models such as Tila Tequila and ForBiddeN. Slowly, mainstream advertisers started to realize that MySpace might provide an accurate tally of how many people were really paying attention to their marketing messages.

Hollywood was an early adopter of MySpace. In May 2006, Buena Vista Pictures Marketing, a unit of Walt Disney, hosted a two-week contest on MySpace, asking dancers to submit videos for a chance to appear in the credits of Touchstone Pictures' upcoming low-budget movie *Step Up*. Despite the short time frame, Disney received several hundred submissions—far more than it expected—and accumulated more than 120,000 friends on its MySpace profile. "We were curious to see how mobilized youth could be," said Jack Pan, vice president of marketing at Walt Disney Studios Motion Pictures. "It was a little overwhelming."

The winners of the contest appeared in a music video, and many of the dance submissions appeared during the movie end credits as well.

Buena Vista Pictures Marketing also used its MySpace community to spread the word about the movie opening by sending out bulletins to the film's friends and advertising on MySpace's home page. The viral marketing appeared to pay off: *Step Up* took in $20.7 million on its opening weekend, more than doubling industry expectations and opening weekend projections.

During the same summer, News Corp.'s 20th Century Fox movie studio placed an even bigger bet on MySpace for its blockbuster *X-Men III: The Last Stand.* While the film industry, on average, spent only about 2 percent of its budget online at the time, Fox decided to spend 8 percent of its budget online for *X-III,* up from 2 percent for the second installment and 1 percent for the first *X-Men* in 2000. The online budget increase came largely at the expense of radio advertising in the days leading up to opening weekend—and the online bet paid off in spades.

The campaign kicked off on May 7, 2006, when a small item appeared on the comic book fan website, SuperHeroHype.com, noting that a MySpace profile had popped up for *X-Men III.* The news quickly spread among fans of the science fiction comic book series. Within three days, the *X-Men* profile had attracted fifty-three thousand visitors simply through word of mouth. Visitors were lured, in part, by the fact that the profile offered a feature allowing them to expand the number of top "friends" displayed on their profiles to sixteen from eight. The day before the movie opened, MySpace devoted the entire front page of its site to an *X-Men* promotion at an estimated cost of $1 million.

By the time the movie opened, nearly 984,000 MySpacers had put the *X-Men* on their friends list, making it the largest promotion ever on MySpace. Exit polling showed that 15 percent of the under-twenty-five audience for *X-Men III* on opening weekend had heard about the movie on MySpace. *X-Men III* went on to earn $459 million in worldwide ticket sales.

Soon other mainstream advertisers wanted to build profiles for their brands as well. Adidas built a profile to promote its sponsorship of the World Cup soccer tournament; Honda built a profile for its compact sports utility vehicle Element; and Jack in the Box restaurants built a profile for its mascot, Jack.

By the end of the year, a MySpace profile was seen as a great way to break through the information overload of the modern era—a way to win attention in an attention-starved marketing environment.

...

MySpace was ill prepared to handle the surge in demand for custom pro-files in late 2006. Strangely, it didn't even sell customized profiles directly to marketers. Marketers had to buy tens of thousands of dollars' worth of banner advertising on MySpace, which earned them "development credits" toward building a profile. Advertisers then had to submit to MySpace a Photoshop document detailing how they wanted their profile to look. MySpace's developers would then build the customized profile for the advertiser.

Building custom profiles was a slow and laborious process, taking, on average, four weeks to create. Once a profile was completed, if the adver-tiser wanted changes, the profile went back into the developers' queue. Then the profiles would often sit around for two weeks waiting to be loaded onto the site. The process was extremely frustrating for advertis-ers, who are used to creating and controlling their commercials from start to finish.

"Developing and executing a fully integrated campaign on MySpace may be more technologically challenging than anywhere else on the Web," said Ian Schafer, chief executive of Deep Focus, an advertising agency that specializes in building MySpace profiles.

The basic problem was that MySpace hadn't built what is known in the industry as an application programming interface, or API. An API is essentially a guidebook that details how an advertiser or developer can build a feature to run on MySpace without running into technical prob-lems. APIs are common in Silicon Valley: Microsoft offers an API for programmers building software to run on Windows; Sony publishes an API for developers building games for its PlayStation; and Google offers an API for developers who want to integrate Google Maps into their data.

Without an API, advertisers could only build a MySpace profile using the same basic Web codes available to all MySpace users. But advertisers who wanted profiles with whizbang features that would attract lots of visitors had to get in line and wait for MySpace to build such profiles for them. Fox Interactive executive Michael Barrett argued that MySpace should build an API for advertisers. But for MySpace's overburdened de-velopers, that was just one of two dozen urgent items on their task list.

MySpace was a strange environment for advertisers in other ways as

well. In newspapers and magazines and on television and radio, advertisements are usually clearly identifiable. And most Internet sites, such as
Google and Yahoo, take great pains to differentiate advertisements from
the editorial content. But on MySpace, it's a guessing game. The Dream-
Works SKG movie studio's MySpace profile for the fictional character
Ron Burgundy is not labeled as an advertisement. And, in fact, it's hard
to tell the "real" studio-created Ron Burgundy profile from dozens of
fan-created Ron Burgundy profiles on MySpace.

Some celebrities were less than thrilled about the fakes. At one point,
attorneys for the actor Chuck Norris started barraging MySpace with letters complaining about the proliferation of copycat Chuck Norris profiles. Eventually MySpace staffer Jason Feffer arranged for Norris and his
family to take a tour of MySpace's Santa Monica offices. "I explained to
him that all people who had Chuck Norris profiles were his fans," Anderson recalled. Norris dropped his objections.

For fans hoping to connect with a celebrity, however, the proliferation
of fake profiles could be frustrating. Several services sprang up to help
fans distinguish between the real and the fakes. But MySpace was not
very tolerant of independent verification systems. In 2006 celebrity consultant and publicist Bryant McGill started a group on MySpace aimed
at debunking fake celebrities on MySpace, but after his site was featured
in the *Wall Street Journal*, MySpace deleted McGill's group. He re-
created it three times, but each time MySpace deleted it without explanation. Finally, in 2007, McGill moved his celebrity authentication
service to ProVIPs.com. MySpace eventually launched its own directory
of authentic celebrity MySpace pages in January 2008.

Advertisers also have little control over the use of their brand names
on MySpace. Take Coca-Cola, for instance. MySpace.com/coke is a
private profile of a twenty-three-year-old Nevada resident named Nico.
MySpace.com/cocacola is a private profile of an eighteen-year-old girl
named Breanna. But MySpace.com/cherrycoke is a promotion for
Cherry Coca-Cola. MySpace is also home to at least two anti-Coca-
Cola groups—one called Killer Coke and another called Boycott
Coca-Cola.

MySpace also didn't offer another standard feature advertisers often
desire: targeted banner ads.

With MySpace users sharing so much information about themselves on their profiles, it would make sense for MySpace to allow advertisers to display different advertising banners to different user groups—such as women who love fishing, or men who identified themselves as Volkswagen enthusiasts. But MySpace didn't have the technology to provide such targeting.

As a result, most MySpace users viewed the same banner ads over and over—usually flashing, blinking ads promoting screen savers or cursors. These low-cost advertisements were the dregs of Internet advertising; remnant ads placed by third-party networks. Some of the advertisers paid prices as low as 5 cents per thousand viewers, while others didn't pay at all unless someone clicked on their ad.

MySpace was forced to accept these ads because most big-name advertisers preferred to build their own profiles or advertise on the front page. They were still wary of advertising broadly across all the profiles on MySpace.

When Michael Barrett joined Fox Interactive in the summer of 2006, he began a project to "scrape" and collect all the personal data from MySpace users' profiles in order to build an ad targeting system. In February 2007, after protracted negotiations, Fox agreed to pay $100 million to acquire a technology vendor called Strategic Data Corp, which would help MySpace analyze the profile data and display relevant ads.

Barrett hoped that the new technology would allow MySpace to start charging higher prices for its remnant ads. The targeted advertising project was put on a fast track: It launched in the fall of 2007. MySpace found that people who listed cars or autos as a hobby or interest were more than twice as likely to click on a car ad.

MySpace also had no real strategy for capturing advertising dollars from small and medium-sized business advertisers.

MySpace is home to thousands of small businesses—ranging from tattoo parlors to T-shirt outlets—but most do not pay for their profile pages. The site generally tolerates these businesses as long as they don't try to sell stuff too blatantly on their profile pages.

"If it's a pure commerce profile, we have the right to take it down," Barrett explained. "But we don't really exercise it."

The problem was that MySpace didn't have enough people to effectively police small businesses or to solicit ads from them. In late 2006 Barrett set out to build an online automated system that would let small businesses buy banner ads across MySpace through an automated system similar to Google's. Google's automated system had allowed hundreds of thousands of small advertisers to purchase ads on Google and had propelled Google's ad revenue to astronomical heights. Small businesses preferred these automated systems because they could buy ads in small increments—as little as $10. Without an automated system, it was hard to get an advertising sales representative to write such small orders. It would take more than a year for Barrett to get his self-serve advertising system built.

In the meantime, competitors were rushing into the social networking arena, sensing a chance to steal some market share from MySpace. The research firm eMarketer estimated that in calendar year 2006, MySpace generated $180 million in U.S. revenues, while its myriad competitors, including Facebook, Friendster, Bebo, Orkut, MSN Space, Yahoo 360°, and AIM Pages, collectively reaped about $90 million.

Some advertisers had even begun experimenting with creating mini-MySpaces of their own. Coca-Cola added social networking features to its MyCoke.com website. Nike launched a social networking site for soccer fans called Joga.com. Martha Stewart announced plans to add social networking features to her website.

A few such social networking sites became instant hits. Mattel's Barbie Girls, for instance, attracted four million members in less than four months. Although Nike's Joga.com didn't pan out, the NikePlus social networking site has become a popular place for runners to compare workout data. Toyota's social network for hybrid car enthusiasts has attracted more than fifteen thousand members.

However, most of the advertiser-created networks flopped. Wal-Mart shut down its social networking site "the Hub" after just ten weeks. Anheuser-Busch's ambitious attempt to build a video-sharing social network called Bud.TV proved disappointing and was revamped. Soon after Walt Disney built its own social networking features on Disney.com, the company decided to jump-start its efforts by acquiring the popular kid's social networking site Club Penguin.

In April Barrett invited one hundred fifty of the nation's biggest advertisers—from the top ad agencies and the top marketers such as

Coke—to an exclusive gathering at the Beverly Wilshire Hotel for an all-expenses-paid junket to learn about MySpace.

The event was a huge change from MySpace's usual shoestring approach to marketing. Shawn Gold, head of marketing for MySpace, was hired by DeWolfe in 2005 with a goal of turning marketing into a profit center for MySpace. He delivered on his promise with programs such as Secret Shows—a program of free concerts for MySpace members that was designed as marketing for MySpace. It cost MySpace $20,000 a month to host the shows, but Gold sold Chili's restaurants the sponsorship rights to the program for $3 million a year.

Called "Never Ending Friending," Barrett's event was a far cry from MySpace's pay-your-own-way approach of the past. Advertisers were wined and dined with cocktails by the hotel pool and lavish meals. Speakers included social networking researcher Danah Boyd, TV producer Ben Silverman, and Fox Interactive chief security officer Hemanshu Nigam.

Barrett had also prepared a report highlighting the "momentum effect" of building a profile on MySpace. The momentum sets in, Barrett argued, when visitors to the profile tell their friends to visit, or share some digital elements of the profile with their friends.

Even so, MySpace was going to need some serious momentum of its own to hit Murdoch's extremely aggressive goal of $1 billion in revenue by June 2008. It took Google five years to reach $1 billion, and Yahoo, eight years. MySpace was only three and a half years old.

Chapter 25

THE FACEBOOK REVOLUTION

O n May 24, 2007, Facebook founder Mark Zuckerberg bounded onto the stage of the San Francisco Design Center, wearing jeans, a black zip-up fleece sweatshirt, and Adidas sandals, and declared war on MySpace.

"Today, together, we're going to start a movement," the skinny twenty-three-year-old told an audience of eight hundred enthusiastic software developers.

The "movement" was, in fact, the release of Facebook's application programming interface, or API—a guidebook that enabled developers to write programs that would run on Facebook's website. MySpace had no such guidebook, although from the beginning, it had allowed outside developers to build small programs such as slide shows—often referred to as widgets—to run on MySpace pages.

The launch of a guidebook for writing widgets doesn't sound like a big deal, but to software developers, such guidebooks are essential. Without an API, developers can only guess at how their programs will interact with the underlying code on a website. An API provides specific instructions and software code that allows for a smooth interaction between the website and the program running on top of it.

Even more important, Facebook's guidebook provided a clear road map for how widget developers could make money. For the first time, Facebook would begin allowing software developers to sell ads on specifically designed pages within the Facebook environment. By comparison, MySpace prohibited all third parties, including widget makers, from advertising anywhere within MySpace.

As a result, the software developers were incredibly enthusiastic about the opportunity to profit from the social networking boom through Facebook.

"Imagine all the things we're going to be able to build together," Zuckerberg told the crowd.

Together was not a word MySpace often used when referring to software developers. In fact, in its four years of existence, MySpace had spent little to no energy cultivating relationships with the widget makers that helped make its site so popular.

For example, the top widget maker, Slide, which made online slide shows that users could post on their MySpace profiles, had an audience of 117 million in April. As of the summer of 2007, Slide's chief executive, Max Levchin, had met with MySpace executives only once, and that was when he drove down to Los Angeles on his own initiative in 2006. At that meeting, MySpace's Josh Berman told Levchin that the widget companies were "implicit partners" with MySpace, but he declined to finalize any potential revenue-sharing arrangements.

Similarly, the second-largest widget maker, RockYou, which had eighty-two million users in April, also had very little dialogue with MySpace. When RockYou launched its site in November 2005, Tom Anderson sent a congratulatory note to the founders. But since then, RockYou executives had little contact with their counterparts at MySpace. "We've gone to their office multiple times, but there's no formal relationship," RockYou founder Lance Tokuda said in the summer of 2007.

Even Photobucket, which hosted pictures for more than half of MySpace users, and was eventually bought by MySpace, had a limited relationship with MySpace before the purchase. "The most interaction we had with them was on content moderation. We would send them links [to photos] that were violating their terms of service," said Photobucket cofounder and chief executive Alex Welch in May 2007.

Without clear guidelines for the relationship, these MySpace-dependent sites lived in fear of getting shut down by MySpace without notice. In the first few months of 2007, MySpace pulled the plug on several small widget makers that it believed had violated its terms of service—including video players from Revver, webcams from Stickam, Web trackers from Trackzor, the music-buying service of Imeem, and ousted Intermix chief executive Brad Greenspan's video player called vidiLife.

Even Tila Tequila, the model who built her career through MySpace, was not immune to MySpace's shutdowns. In March Tequila posted a music and video player called the Hoooka on her MySpace profile, but Tom Anderson asked her to take it down. Tequila vented her frustration to her 1.7 million MySpace friends:

"The reason why I am so bummed out about Myspace now is because recently they have been cutting down our freedom and taking away our rights slowly," Tequila wrote in a bulletin. "I feel like they've become so corporate and won't even allow me to do fun stuff on my page anymore such as post up cool new widgets from other websites . . . I feel really sad about this."

Privately, Tequila was even more strident. In an e-mail to her manager titled "Fuck MySpace!" she claimed that Anderson was penalizing her as part of a business dispute. "When you guys told Tom that you didn't want to sign the exclusive deal," Tequila wrote, "Tom immediately told me that I am to take down EVERYTHING off my page that was not involving myspace." She claimed that MySpace was also preventing her from changing her top eight friends and had removed her from search results.

MySpace's alleged bullying continued one month later, when MySpace pulled the plug on Photobucket videos, claiming that Photobucket violated the no-advertising rule by offering users a *Spider-Man*-themed frame for slide shows. Photobucket chief executive Alex Welch publicly protested the move, declaring, "We believe this action by MySpace is a retrograde step in the evolution of the Web and an unacceptable attempt to limit the freedom of the very people who are its lifeblood—its users." Still, Photobucket agreed to shut down the *Spider-Man* slide show and to work with MySpace on sponsored slide shows in the future.

In nearly all the cases, MySpace was shutting down websites that violated its prohibition on displaying advertising on MySpace. But MySpace's seemingly arbitrary enforcement actions—often implemented without warning or explanation—created an opportunity for Facebook to present itself as a kinder, gentler partner for the widget sites.

...

Zuckerberg's announcement stirred up a frenzy of excitement about Facebook in Silicon Valley.

Facebook's strategy of locking up the loyalties of the development community was straight out of the Silicon Valley playbook. Technology companies have long realized the importance of tapping the software development community. All the big technology companies, from Microsoft to eBay, hold regular conferences for developers and try to generate excitement. After all, big technology companies recognize that they are not always going to be on the leading edge of innovation. As they get bigger, tech companies can get bogged down trying to build new features and come up with new ideas. That's where young, hungry start-ups can step in and fill the gap.

Often, the coolest new ideas come from the most unlikely places. For instance, one of the first overnight sensations on Facebook was a widget called "Where I've Been," which let people mark all the countries they've visited on a world map. Built by twentysomething freelance programmer Craig Ulliott, the application attracted four hundred thousand users in its first three weeks. "We never thought it would get this big," Ulliott said.

By July 29 developers had built more than two thousand widgets for Facebook. And just two months after the launch of Facebook's API, venture capitalists were lining up to fund new Facebook developers. Two Silicon Valley venture firms, Altura Ventures and Bay Partners, even announced programs exclusively dedicated to funding Facebook developers.

MySpace's biggest developers were among the first to defect to Facebook. For instance, RockYou immediately switched most of its resources toward building widgets for Facebook instead of MySpace. "Each social network is like another girlfriend," RockYou founder Jia Shen said.

Suddenly the leading social networking site in the world was being jilted by Silicon Valley.

All the excitement about new Facebook widgets spurred a surge in traffic to Facebook's website—up 26 percent to 33.7 million unique visitors in August from 26.7 million in May, while MySpace remained fairly stagnant at 68 million visitors during the same period. Even more important, Facebook seemed to be attracting a larger share of the nation's elite. In a landmark essay, social networking researcher Danah Boyd described the class differences between the two sites as follows:

> The Goody Two-shoes, jocks, athletes, or other "good" kids are now going to Facebook. These kids tend to come from families who emphasize education and going to college. They are part of what we'd call hegemonic society. They are primarily white, but not exclusively. They are in honors classes, looking forward to the prom, and live in a world dictated by after school activities.
>
> MySpace is still home for Latino/Hispanic teens, immigrant teens, "burnouts," "alternative kids," "art fags," punks, emos, goths, gangstas, queer kids, and other kids who didn't play into the dominant high school popularity paradigm. These are kids whose parents didn't go to college, who are expected to get a job when they finish high school. These are the teens who plan to go into the military immediately after school. Teens who are really into music or in a band are also on MySpace. MySpace has most of the kids who are socially ostracized at school because they are geeks, freaks, or queers.

By her own admission, Boyd's distinctions were not perfect. MySpace was so large that its audience was composed of members of nearly every demographic segment, and Facebook was also beginning to attract members from beyond its core base of students and alumni of prestigious universities. Even so, Boyd's broad categories helped explain the incredible buzz around Facebook, a site half the size of MySpace. The nation's elite was excited about a social networking service devoted to its own demographic:

"Facebook has emerged as the 'it' service," declared AOL cofounder Steve Case.

"Mark Zuckerberg of Facebook is being touted as the new Steve Jobs, and his company as the next Google," *The Economist* magazine wrote.

Even Rupert Murdoch appeared to be entranced by Facebook and its young founder. In May Murdoch invited Zuckerberg to speak at a News Corp. executive retreat in Monterey, California. "Murdoch sat next to Zuckerberg, and he was clearly enchanted; they stayed head-to-head all through the meal," dinner attendee Jeff Jarvis later wrote on his blog. "Mark left to get back up north, and in a flash, MySpace founder and now Murdochian Chris DeWolfe came dashing over, as if he were jealous of the attention Dad had given that other kid."

A few weeks later, Murdoch gave an even more public indication of his interest in Facebook and displeasure with MySpace. In an interview regarding his takeover bid for the *Wall Street Journal,* Murdoch was asked whether the newspapers were declining because readers were defecting to websites like MySpace.

"I wish they were," Murdoch said. "They're all going to Facebook at the moment."

Facebook soon began copying some of MySpace's best features. After years of requiring profiles to be built by real individuals, Facebook began allowing advertisers and musicians to build profiles as well—a strategy that had been very successful on MySpace.

Facebook also took note of the targeted advertising network being built by MySpace, which let businesses display their banner ads to specific groups of MySpace users, targeted either by geography, demographics, or interests. During the summer, MySpace had been testing the system and found that the targeted ads generated much more interest than the regular ads running on MySpace. Facebook began planning an even more ambitious ad network, which would not only target users by interest but would also notify Facebook users when their friends purchased things online from sites such as eBay. With his typical bravado, Zuckerberg announced that Facebook's approach to advertising would be a sea change for the media industry.

"Once every hundred years, media changes. The last hundred years have been defined by the mass media. The way to advertise was to get into the mass media and push out your content. That was the last hundred years," Zuckerberg told a crowd of advertisers. "In the next hundred years, information won't be just pushed out to people, it will be shared among the millions of connections people have. Advertising will change."

Zuckerberg was widely ridiculed for his arrogant pronouncement. And soon afterward, Facebook users began protesting the idea of having their online purchases displayed on Facebook.

Inevitably, a backlash against Facebook began to take shape. The attorney generals who had been investigating MySpace turned their attention to Facebook. In July Connecticut attorney general Richard Blumenthal lambasted Facebook for hosting the profiles of three convicted sex offenders, and announced that his coalition of attorney generals would more aggressively investigate Facebook.

In September New York attorney general Andrew Cuomo subpoenaed Facebook documents and said he had been conducting an undercover investigation of Facebook's safety policies. Cuomo said that his office had set up several profiles pretending to be teens aged twelve to fourteen, and that those profiles had received sexual solicitations from adult users. Cuomo's office complained about the solicitations to little avail. "Facebook in many instances ignored the complaints and took no action against the reported sexual predators," Cuomo's office said in a press release.

Facebook moved quickly to settle the dispute with Cuomo, agreeing in October to respond to all complaints within twenty-four hours and to be subject to independent monitoring. But the dispute only encouraged the other attorney generals to step up their investigations of Facebook.

"New York's settlement with Facebook is a step forward, but giant strides are needed to make the site safer," Blumenthal said. He demanded that Facebook begin requiring parental permission for users under eighteen and hiding minors' profiles from adults.

The pressure on Facebook gave MySpace some more breathing space on safety. In February MySpace had won an important victory when a Texas court dismissed a lawsuit by the mother of a fourteen-year-old girl who was sexually assaulted by a nineteen-year-old she met on MySpace. The widely publicized lawsuit charged MySpace with negligence and fraud, for failing to take reasonable safety measures to keep young children off its site. But U.S. District Court Judge Sam Sparks declared the plaintiffs' "artful pleading to be disingenuous." Relying on the Communications Decency Act of 1996, which provides Internet providers immunity from liability for third-party content, Sparks wrote, "If anyone had a duty to protect Julie Doe, it was her parents, not MySpace."

Sparks's ruling was not only a win for MySpace but a strong signal to the attorney generals that the legal foundations were shaky for a case against either MySpace or Facebook on the age-verification issue.

Ken Dreifach, former head of the New York attorney general's Internet bureau, declared that in the wake of the Sparks ruling, "the AGs actually face a steep uphill battle in seeking to impose age-verification requirements on these sites."

As a result, MySpace quietly postponed its plans to start offering parental monitoring software—code-named Zephyr—that would allow parents to keep tabs on their kids' MySpace accounts. Zephyr would not let parents read their kids' e-mails but would simply alert them to the location of their child's MySpace account and any changes their child made to his or her age.

MySpace had launched a test version of Zephyr over the summer but hadn't advertised it for fear that teenagers would rebel against being monitored by their parents. Now that the attorney generals were focused on Facebook, MySpace didn't feel the need to risk alienating teens by launching parental monitoring software.

Six months later, MySpace reached a compromise with the attorney generals investigating it, led by Richard Blumenthal. MySpace agreed to study age-verification techniques and to beef up its monitoring of photos and online discussion groups. Those were small concessions; MySpace had essentially emerged unscathed from the nearly two-year investigation.

Chapter 26

MYSPACE 2.0

Chris DeWolfe and Tom Anderson were surprised by the quick turn of events. In January 2007 they had been on top of the world, having surpassed Yahoo as the most popular website in the United States. By summer the world seemed to have turned against them: Every new Facebook announcement was trumpeted breathlessly in the press, while MySpace was increasingly ignored or derided.

Even News Corp.'s announcement that MySpace had turned a profit didn't turn the tide. On August 8 News Corp. announced that in the year ending June 30, 2007, the Fox Interactive Media division had eked out its first profit of $10 million on sales of $550 million. On a conference call with analysts, Rupert Murdoch predicted that the division's sales should exceed $1 billion in the coming year. Even so, one week later, on August 16, News Corp. shares dipped to their lowest point all year, $19.68.

Anderson was inclined to be defensive. "Everyone believes all the b.s. press that says MySpace is done for and Facebook has passed us," he complained to a reporter.

It wasn't a good time for DeWolfe and Anderson to lose their bargaining power. Their employment contracts were set to expire in October, and they were negotiating for lucrative new contracts. Neither one seemed interested in starting a new venture outside of News Corp; Anderson enjoyed being the public face of MySpace, and DeWolfe was happy to have some stability in his job while his marriage was falling apart.[1]

DeWolfe and Anderson had asked for an audacious $50 million over two years, plus a $15 million development fund that Josh Berman would dole out for new technologies. News Corp. counteroffered with $30 million for DeWolfe and Anderson over two years and no development fund.

Facebook's rise highlighted the technological stagnation at MySpace. DeWolfe and Anderson hadn't rolled out any groundbreaking new features since the acquisition. Instead they had pursued a low-risk strategy of launching me-too offerings, such as a video player to compete with YouTube.

MySpace's few attempts to be creative got bogged down. In 2006, for instance, Anderson purchased an online karaoke service called kSolo. But it wasn't until two years later, in 2008, that MySpace managed to integrate the karaoke service into its site. Similarly, it's much-anticipated news aggregator, called MySpace News, was panned by critics when it launched in April 2007. "MySpace News . . . Kinda Sucks," blogged Pete Cashmore, who tracks the social networking space.

"It's difficult to innovate within a corporation," said one MySpace executive defensively. But, in fact, it was the corporate executives at Fox Interactive who had done the most innovating for MySpace, by building a sophisticated targeted advertising system and crafting the lucrative Google deal.

At first MySpace didn't think it needed to compete with Facebook on the widget front. After all, MySpace was the original platform for widgets. By opening itself up to outside developers from the beginning, MySpace had created the market for the widget makers.

MySpace had also conducted focus groups with users who had defected from MySpace to Facebook and found that widgets were not the reason people were leaving. In fact, the defectors said they didn't really like the proliferation of widgets on Facebook—it felt too much like spam. Over the summer, as the internal debates raged, News Corp. presi-

---

[1] DeWolfe's wife filed for divorce on April 3, 2008.

dent Peter Chernin stepped into the breach. He called up DeWolfe and
DeWolfe's boss, Peter Levinsohn, and said, "I need a plan for dealing
with Facebook in two weeks."

It wasn't easy for MySpace executives to admit that they couldn't build
every cool feature on their own. This had been the source of the dispute
between Tom Anderson and former Fox Interactive Media president
Ross Levinsohn. Levinsohn had wanted to acquire companies with innovative features, while Anderson had argued that MySpace could build its
own features.

In May MySpace acquired Photobucket for about $300 million. The
purchase was a tacit admission that MySpace wasn't going to build its
own expanded photo storage, and that some features it should just acquire.

"A mistake we made was trying to do too many things at one time,"
DeWolfe said in July. "We realized we're not going to be able to compete
with thousands of developers.

"We haven't done the greatest job communicating with the development community," he added. "We're trying to rectify that."

In the fall of 2007, MySpace began quietly rolling out its Facebook
counteroffensive. The first step was Fox Interactive Media president
Peter Levinsohn's presentation at a Merrill Lynch conference in September, where he addressed the Facebook challenge head-on.

"I realize every person in this room wants to ask me about Facebook,
and, frankly, I want to talk about Facebook," Levinsohn said. "We've
never really had a direct significant competitor for MySpace . . . But the
truth is, we offer our audience a radically different experience than what
they get on Facebook."

Armed with a series of slides, Levinsohn presented statistics showing
how MySpace continued to trump Facebook: MySpace users visit the site
30 percent more frequently than Facebook users and spend twenty-eight
more minutes on the site per month than Facebook users, he said. For
advertisers, those metrics were very important.

Levinsohn also hinted that MySpace would announce its own API, or
widget maker's guidebook, by the end of the year. After Levinsohn's
speech, News Corp. shares inched up slightly.

Rumors soon started to swirl that MySpace was going to announce
the API at the influential and exclusive Web 2.0 summit in San Francisco
in October.

...

DeWolfe's plan was simple, and straight out of MySpace's usual play-book: Copy a rival's best features. That meant creating an API for widget developers, and creating some of the viral features that Facebook users seemed to love—such as News Feed, which updates users about actions their friends have taken on Facebook.

News Feed was a particularly difficult feature to replicate: Facebook had developed a proprietary algorithm that sorts through all the actions taken by a user's friends and decides which ones to display. These customized feeds had to be calculated individually for each Facebook user—a difficult computing task.

To build such ambitious features, or even slightly less ambitious versions, MySpace needed some technology firepower. Already MySpace had opened an office in Seattle to try to recruit Microsoft developers familiar with MySpace's Microsoft infrastructure. But DeWolfe recognized that MySpace also needed an outpost in Silicon Valley to recruit the top minds of the industry. "All the models and actresses move to L.A., and all the smart tech guys move to Silicon Valley," he said.

However, MySpace wasn't planning to open an office in the heart of Silicon Valley—in one of those featureless office parks in Sunnyvale or Cupertino where engineers often buy lunch from a taco truck that travels between office parking lots. Instead MySpace found a location in San Francisco's equivalent of Santa Monica, the trendy South of Market area, populated with bars, restaurants, and nightclubs, and within walking distance of San Francisco's baseball stadium.

Still, moving to the belly of the beast was a big step for MySpace. It was an admission that despite its dominance, the company still had more to learn. In some ways, it was a more comfortable role for MySpace, which had been at its most innovative when it was a scrappy underdog.

"It's the first time I feel like we have a real competitor," Tom Anderson said. "It's a good thing overall, because if there was any complacency within the company, now there's someone you can look at and say, 'Hey, we've got to be better.' "

Silicon Valley wunderkind Mark Zuckerberg of Facebook still got top bill-ing as the kickoff speaker at the Web 2.0 summit. In front of a standing-room-only hotel ballroom in downtown San Francisco on Wednesday afternoon, October 17, Zuckerberg settled onto a red leather couch. Wearing his usual jeans, hooded sweatshirt, and Adidas sandals, he faced moderator John Battelle, a Silicon Valley author and blogger, and the conference organizer.

The first question was about Facebook's recent fund-raising discussions.

"Don't you think you're kind of selling yourself a little short at fifteen billion dollars?" asked Battelle, referring to rumors that Facebook investors now valued the company at $15 billion.

Zuckerberg smirked. "We'll see," he said. The audience laughed.

Zuckerberg then alluded to the distinction between Facebook and MySpace. "We're not really a media company," he said. "The types of stuff we build and solve are deeply technical problems."

The next day, comScore Media Metrix announced that in September, Facebook had suffered a massive 9 percent drop in traffic, to 30.6 million unique visitors, down from 33.7 million in August. MySpace remained flat at 68 million. But the Facebook craze continued unabated. A week later, Facebook raised $240 million from Microsoft, based on an astounding $15 billion valuation.

Chris DeWolfe and Rupert Murdoch had their turn on the Web 2.0 stage in the evening. During dinner the two chatted onstage with John Battelle. DeWolfe wore a suit with a bright yellow oxford shirt, and Murdoch stuck to his usual dark suit with light blue shirt. Neither one wore a tie.

Sitting cross-legged on the stage's red leather couch and leaning forward toward Murdoch, DeWolfe started by announcing that he had signed a contract to spend another two years at MySpace.

The contract was both a victory and a defeat for DeWolfe. Although he didn't disclose the figure publicly, DeWolfe and Anderson had agreed to News Corp.'s terms: $30 million over two years. It was still more money than most top executives at News Corp. earned, but not as much as DeWolfe and Anderson had hoped for.

DeWolfe then followed up with a vague statement about how MySpace would soon offer an API for widget makers sometime in the next few months. MySpace executives had been hoping to have the API ready to release at the conference but hadn't met the deadline.

Since most people in the audience already knew that MySpace was working on an API, DeWolfe's announcement failed to impress. Even as he was speaking, somebody yelled out from the audience "We read it on TechCrunch [a technology blog] fifteen minutes ago!"

DeWolfe also announced that MySpace had opened its first San Francisco office earlier in the week. The office planned to hire fifty engineers as soon as possible. He said that MySpace would never give up on its Los Angeles roots but had come to acknowledge that there are some things you can get only in Silicon Valley. "There's a certain talent level here where the big technical brains end up," he said. "We think we have the best of both worlds."

Murdoch also took the opportunity onstage to gently trash Facebook and express support for MySpace. When asked about Facebook, he replied, "It's like a utility. We're more media. We're different, and in spite of all the hype, we seem to be growing faster."

When asked about Facebook's $15 billion valuation, Murdoch said, "What that tells you is that News Corp. is totally underpriced" at its market valuation of about $70.5 billion.

After the dinner, Murdoch, DeWolfe, and the rest of the Web 2.0 attendees walked down the street to MySpace's Silicon Valley coming-out party at the San Francisco Museum of Modern Art. MySpace had transformed the building's four-story-high atrium into a sea of white, with white leather tablecloths, round white banquettes, and molded white chairs to complement the soaring white walls. Even the glass doors were covered with white drapes. From a gallery on the second floor, a DJ spun tunes, and projectors streamed colored spotlights and images from MySpace onto the walls. Waiters clad in white circulated with drinks and desserts. Several people tried to steal the glowing orange plastic balls that served as centerpieces on the tables.

The geeky guys from the Web 2.0 conference, with their jeans and soft briefcases, looked out of place amid the well-dressed MySpace executives, their gorgeous dates, and the hipsters invited by MySpace's party cosponsor, the glossy, upscale San Francisco magazine 7 × 7. It was probably one of the only technology parties in Silicon Valley where people actually ended up dancing rather than doing deals.

In all, about three hundred fifty people attended the party, including the rapper MC Hammer and YouTube founder Chad Hurley. For most of the night, Murdoch and DeWolfe were surrounded by throngs of attendees hoping for a chat. (The ever-antisocial Tom Anderson did not appear.) Finally, at 1:23 a.m., the police were called to break up a fight among three partygoers.

MySpace might be coming to Silicon Valley, and it might be releasing something geeky like an API, but it was going to do it on its own terms—with a cooler than cool vibe.

Embracing Silicon Valley was a turning point for MySpace. Acknowledging weakness seemed to make the site stronger. A rapid series of technological developments soon followed:

In November MySpace agreed to join Google's efforts to build a common set of APIs across multiple social networking sites. MySpace's decision was, in part, a recognition that Google could build a better technological platform than MySpace could build in-house. But it was also a smart political move, putting Facebook on the defensive against a coalition of social networking sites and the biggest technology company.

In December MySpace launched "Friend Update"—its version of Facebook's popular News Feed. This was not a shining moment for MySpace: Friend Update was one year later than Facebook's feature and fairly rudimentary. But it was a start, and MySpace began improving it slowly but surely.

In February 2008 MySpace finally launched its API, celebrating the moment with another San Francisco party for developers. Within the first two months, more than seven thousand developers had created more than one thousand new applications for MySpace such as "Truth Box," a virtual box in which friends can send each other anonymous messages, and "Own Your Friends," which allows friends to bid to "own" a friend.

Finally, in May 2008, MySpace got ahead of the development curve by being the first in the industry to offer users an easy way to transfer their MySpace photos, videos, and friends network to other websites. As more and more social networks popped up, consumers had been clamoring for an easy way to bring all their friends from one site to another. Most big sites had resisted the idea, for the obvious reason of not wanting to make it easy for users to defect to other sites. But MySpace, which had always erred on the side of giving its members freedom, decided to risk it.

MySpace's move was greeted with enthusiasm in Silicon Valley. "His-

torically, MySpace has lagged behind Facebook in terms of innovation,"
wrote influential blogger Michael Arrington. "But they definitely 'get it'
this time . . . By acting first, MySpace takes the lead and has a shot at
being the long-term winner."

Murdoch's billion-dollar dream for MySpace, however, didn't pan out.
In May 2008 News Corp. acknowledged that Fox Interactive wouldn't
reach its goal of $1 billion in revenues for the twelve-month period end-
ing in June.

"We will fall short of what were very aggressive initial projections,"
Peter Chernin told investors in a conference call. "But it's worth pointing out that in a tough economy, our shortfall will be slight, roughly only
about ten percent."

The advertising shortfall combined with MySpace's newfound technical prowess gave DeWolfe the ammunition he needed to gain control
of the one portion of MySpace that he didn't oversee: advertising sales.
In April Peter Levinsohn dismantled Fox Interactive's corporate ad
sales unit and gave control of ad sales back to each website. As a result,
Fox Interactive's top ad salesman, Michael Barrett, who pioneered the
targeted advertising system and helped craft the $900 million Google
deal, quit.

"This change recognizes that our individual business units have
evolved to a point where it is clear they are best served by dedicated professionals who live and breathe those products alone," Levinsohn wrote
in a memo to staff.

The announcement meant that DeWolfe was finally off probation
at News Corp. For two and a half years since MySpace was acquired,
DeWolfe held the title of CEO of MySpace without the full responsibilities implied by it. He controlled the website, but did not control the advertising sales—which was the most important part of MySpace from
News Corp.'s perspective.

Now, finally, DeWolfe controlled all aspects of the website. It was a
remarkable moment for a man who had never been in full command of
his creation. At Intermix DeWolfe had struggled to get permission for
MySpace expenditures as small as T-shirt purchases and as large as computer equipment. The moment that he tried to break free and raise
money to take MySpace public, Intermix sold the company out from
under him. Finally, four years after founding the most popular website in
America, DeWolfe had gained control of it.

Chapter 27

DIGITAL IDENTITY

In November 2007 Rupert Murdoch declared that Facebook was just a "Web utility similar to a phone book." By comparison, he said, MySpace has "become so much more than a social network. It connects people, but it's evolved into a place where people are living their lives. A social platform packed with search, video, music, telephony, games."

Indeed, the differences between the two sites were profound. The rival websites had come to embody the two competing visions of digital identity online. MySpace represented the freewheeling spirit of the Web, where anonymity allows people to experiment with their identity and express their views freely. In contrast, Facebook represented a more structured view of online identity, where people authenticate their offline identity in the hopes of creating a community of trust.

Both visions of digital identity have their pros and cons. MySpace began by appealing to the so-called Fakesters, who wanted the freedom of anonymity online. But MySpace's freedoms have also been abused, as sexual predators, cyber-bullies, and others with bad intentions have been able to don the mask of anonymity to ill effect.

Privacy advocates argue that protecting the right to be anonymous is key to protecting our freedom of speech. The U.S. Supreme Court supported that view in a 1995 opinion, *McIntyre v. Ohio Elections Commission*, in which the Court overturned a fine levied on an anonymous pamphleteer.

"Under our Constitution, anonymous pamphleteering is not a pernicious, fraudulent practice, but an honorable tradition of advocacy and of dissent," Justice John Paul Stevens wrote for the majority. "Anonymity is a shield from the tyranny of the majority . . . The right to remain anonymous may be abused when it shields fraudulent conduct. But political speech by its nature will sometimes have unpalatable consequences, and, in general, our society accords greater weight to the value of free speech than to the dangers of its misuse."

However, there are places online where people are willing to trade in their privacy for the privileges of joining a community of trust. On Facebook, for instance, people often disclose their real e-mail addresses and phone numbers, since their profile information is automatically restricted to their approved list of friends. The advantage of this kind of network—based on offline connections—is that it is harder for sexual predators and others with bad intentions to penetrate.

However, communities of trust are not foolproof, either. Facebook has twice abused the trust of its users by unilaterally deciding to share information about its users without adequately informing them of the changes: first, when it started providing updates about changes in users' profiles, and, second, when it began broadcasting users' purchases on other websites to their friends. Both incidents highlight the dangers of putting personal data in the hands of a profit-making business enterprise.

There are no easy solutions to the problems of digital identity. It seems likely that both visions of social networks will evolve online—the anonymous version and the authenticated identity version.

Social networking researcher Danah Boyd says, "Every day we dress ourselves in a set of clothes that convey something about our identity— what we do for a living, how we fit into the socioeconomic class hierarchy, what our interests are, and so on. This is identity production."

On MySpace, members can experiment with different identities, creating multiple profiles representing different parts of their personality. On Facebook, users often amplify their offline identity; rather than lying about their age or their gender, they can still lie about their favorite books and music—pretending to be more intellectual or trendy than they really are. Either way, both sites allow people a new way in which to represent (and misrepresent) themselves to others.

Social science researchers describe the process of sorting through all these representations to find someone's true self, "signaling theory."

"Signalling theory describes the relationship between a signal and the underlying quality it represents," Judith Donath and Danah Boyd wrote in *BT Technology Journal* in 2004. "Most of the qualities we're interested in about other people—Is this person nice? Trustworthy? Can she do this job? Can he be relied on in an emergency? Would she be a good parent?—are not directly observable. Instead we rely on signals, which are more or less reliably correlated with underlying quality."

Social networking sites allow users to factor in a person's friends as part of the signal, which can be a useful tool. "A public display of connections can be viewed as a signal of the reliability of one's identity claims," Donath and Boyd wrote. "In theory, the public display of connections found on networking sites should ensure honest self-presentation because one's connections are linked to one's profile; they have both seen it and, implicitly, sanctioned it."

In some cases, it's important to send clear signals—such as when seeking a spouse. "In this market [for spouses], it is important to signal capacity for commitment," wrote Harvard Business School professor Mikolaj Jan Piskorski in an unpublished paper. By emphasizing connections with people who are not seeking spouses, he wrote, spouse seekers "blunt the signal of market participation."

But for job seekers who don't want their bosses to know they are looking for work, Piskorski argued, signal ambiguity is appropriate. "By pooling themselves with actors who are using online networks to utilize their social capital better, the employed job seekers can be on the market, while claiming that they are not."

In other words, people have different signaling needs at different times in their lives. The challenge for social networks will be to keep up with the evolving needs of their users. Donath and Boyd recommend that social networks should allow for "contextual privacy," so, for instance, "one could have a category of 'work colleagues' who would see only work-related information and not be made aware of the more outrageous connections . . . The ability to make one's network display nuanced and adaptable could be an important piece in making social networking sites more generally useful."

As social networks evolve, it's likely that users will become more sophisticated about demanding control of their personal information. Massachusetts Institute of Technology professor Henry Jenkins writes, "We are increasingly discovering that everything we do online becomes part of our public and permanent record, easily recoverable by anyone who knows how to Google, and that there is no longer any statute of limitations on our youthful indiscretions."

But more than anything, social networks such as MySpace did something incredibly important: They inspired an entire generation to view media as offering a forum not just for passive entertainment but for proactive personal creativity and ongoing self-discovery.

"I think we have replaced MTV," Tom Anderson boasted in an interview. "On MySpace you can pick your own channel and go where you want."

It looks like the future wants to have its own channel.

Epilogue

The executives who were touched by MySpace were changed by it. Most are still actively improving or changing social networking.

Chris DeWolfe and Tom Anderson continue to run MySpace. Anderson remains highly engaged with users, asking them for feedback on new features and posting updates about tweaks to the site. DeWolfe continues running the business side and has put a lot of effort into improving relations with Silicon Valley.

Their efforts at improving MySpace have paid off, so far. MySpace remains the dominant social networking website, with seventy-two million monthly visitors in the United States, as of April 2008. Facebook is just about half the size, with thirty-five million U.S. visitors.

Former Intermix chief executive Brad Greenspan is still suing Intermix for selling MySpace too cheaply. His many lawsuits are wending their way through the court system and have been joined by major class-action attorneys. He also attempted unsuccessfully to bid against Rupert Murdoch for the *Wall Street Journal.* Greenspan runs several websites, including the video networking site LiveVideo.com, which competes with MySpace.

One year after selling Intermix to News Corp., former Intermix chief executive Richard Rosenblatt bought back most of Intermix's websites—including websites such as Grab.com and Casesladder.com—from News Corp. for a rumored price of $18 million. News Corp. kept the Alena wrinkle-cream business.

Rosenblatt used the Intermix assets to help seed his startup, Demand Media, which uses social media tools and "Internet ready" content to grow its vertical network of websites and large partner websites such as as News Corp.'s BSkyB, *USA Today,* and Lance Armstrong's Livestrong Foundation. He has raised $355 million and hopes to file for an initial public offering. Demand Media is headquartered in MySpace's old offices in Santa Monica—and Rosenblatt sits in DeWolfe's old office on the ground floor.

Former Fox Interactive Media president Ross Levinsohn has created a venture fund along with former AOL chief executive Jonathan Miller and the partners of the existing ComVentures fund. The fund, called Velocity Investment Group, has $1.5 billion in assets and is focused on investing in Internet and media companies.

Rupert Murdoch remains focused on the Internet as the future of News Corp. He has called MySpace the "digital centerpiece" of his company and has predicted that MySpace could fetch more than $6 billion if it were sold. "This will be the biggest single mass platform for advertising in the world," he predicts.

Acknowledgments

This book couldn't have been written without my mother. A talented writer and editor, she nurtured every aspect of the book, from the proposal to the epilogue, and was a constant source of encouragement and inspiration to me. I hope that her wonderful fiction will get the acknowledgment it deserves.

I also owe a huge thanks to the sources who supported this project from the beginning: Richard Rosenblatt, Brett Brewer, Brad Greenspan, Jason Feffer, David Carlick, Michael Montgomery, and others who can't be named. Talking to me was risky for many of them because of the pending lawsuits regarding the MySpace sale. I appreciate their trust in me and hope it has been repaid with a fair and accurate account.

I am also grateful to *The Wall Street Journal,* which granted me a year of book leave. I especially benefited from the support of many talented *Journal* colleagues, including Dan Hertzberg, Mike Miller, Alan Murray, Almar Latour, Cathy Panagoulias, Richard Turner, Laurie Hays, Stuart Karle, Jeffrey Trachtenberg, Kevin Delaney, Sarah Ellison, Ellen Byron, Suzanne Vranica, Ethan Smith, and Martin Peers among many others. Special thanks to Bob Levey, formerly of *The Washington Post,* who gave me my start in journalism and remains an insightful reader and friend.

My researcher, Neena Lall, was extremely gracious and meticulous under pressure. *Wall Street Journal* researcher Leslie Norman also unearthed a trove of extremely important documents for me.

This book shared a gestation period with my son, Avinash, who was born four days after I submitted the manuscript. I deeply appreciate his sense of timing and owe special thanks to my incredible midwives, Barbara Sellars and Elisabeth Boyce, who made his entry into the world a pleasant one. My wonderful husband, Vijay, and delightful daughter, Mira, were also extremely forgiving of the demands of my two babies— the book and Avinash. My father was an extremely patient proofreader, and my great-aunt Blanche diligently sent me all the MySpace news she came across. My brother Ilan helped me cross the finish line, valiantly amusing the children while I copyedited the manuscript poolside in India. And my dear friends Motoko Rich, Lisa Tharpe, Tracy Kenny, Anjali Fedson Hack, Jacobia Dahm, Sheryl Spain, Alison Sommers-Sayre, and Lisa Friedman were always there for me.

My agent, Todd Shuster, was a gem, forcing me to be rigorous in my thinking and writing. I couldn't have done it without him. The Random House team—Will Murphy, Courtney Turco, Barbara Fillon, and Avideh Bashirrad—was unbeatable in their optimism and enthusiasm.

Finally, others who generously gave of their time include Joe Flint of the Paley Center for Media, Richard Easton at Skadden Arps, Stephen Kline of Xanga, Richard Kang of MTV Networks, and Michele James of James & Co. Julie Henderson, Andrew Butcher, and Teri Everett of News Corp. were extremely gracious in declining to cooperate.

Notes

CHAPTER 1 STEALING MYSPACE

3 *Richard Rosenblatt's heart was pounding:* Author's interview with Richard Rosenblatt, November 16, 2006.

3 *It was the warm afternoon of July 12, 2005:* "Global Weather Fahrenheit," Associated Press, July 13, 2005.

3 *Rosenblatt had arrived early for his meeting:* Author's interview with Richard Rosenblatt, November 16, 2006.

3 *"At murdochs . . . going in soon.":* E-mail from Richard Rosenblatt to Brett Brewer, July 12, 2005.

3 *Finally an aide came to usher him up:* Author's interview with Richard Rosenblatt, November 16, 2006.

3 *"If you want to sell your company to us":* ibid.

3 *As soon as Rosenblatt stepped into Murdoch's spacious neutral-toned office:* ibid.

4 *Rosenblatt took a seat offered to him:* ibid.

4 *17.7 million visitors:* E-mail from Richard Rosenblatt to Ross Levinsohn, July 12, 2005.

4 *"Mr. Murdoch, MySpace is the perfect media company":* Author's interview with Richard Rosenblatt, November 16, 2006.

4 *"You have built the most incredible global media company":* ibid.

4 *"This deal will not only make you relevant":* ibid.

4 *"I heard you've been asking for twelve dollars a share":* ibid.

4 *Intermix's stock was trading that day at $9.96 a share:* ibid.

4 *"Rich, you've got a reputation":* ibid.

5 *"With all due respect, the company is worth it":* ibid.

5 *"You got it"*: ibid.

5 *"I never go back on my word"*: ibid.

CHAPTER 2 CIRCLE OF FRIENDS

6 *MySpace launched on August 15, 2003:* E-mail from Chris DeWolfe, August 15, 2003.

6 *a blazing hot, overcast Friday afternoon:* "The Weather Elsewhere," Associated Press, August 15, 2003.

6 *When the U.S. invaded Iraq:* Bob Sullivan, "Patriotism? No, Just More Pop-ups," MSNBC.com, May 20, 2006.

6 *"Targeting is not working":* E-mail from Chris DeWolfe to Brad Greenspan, August 15, 2003.

7 *The struggling dot-com survivor:* Intermix Media Inc., form 10-K, filed March 31, 2003.

7 *ResponseBase's e-mail marketing efforts were increasingly:* Author's interview with Duc Chau, June 16, 2007.

7 *ResponseBase's online sales of items:* Author's interview with Brett Brewer, June 16, 2007.

7 *Now eUniverse wanted to shut down ResponseBase:* Author's interview with Brad Greenspan, May 8, 2007.

7 *in just a few months:* Author's interview with Duc Chau, June 16, 2007.

7 *DeWolfe's twenty-five-person Internet division:* Author's interview with Brett Brewer, August 1, 2007.

7 *"We launched MySpace":* E-mail from Chris DeWolfe to Brad Greenspan, August 15, 2003.

9 *In July 2008 Web surfers viewed 41.4 billion pages on MySpace:* Author's interview with Andrew Lipsman, comScore Media Metrix senior manager, September 8, 2008.

9 *Yahoo and Google still attracted more visitors per month:* "Top 20 Websites," Hitwise US, February 2008.

9 *In July 2008 it attracted seventy-five million visitors:* comScore, "ComScore Media Metrix Ranks Top 50 Web Properties for July 2008," comScore press release, August 15, 2008.

10 *Dupré was also an amateur singer:* Mallory Simon, "Dupré's MySpace Page Evolves with Scandal," CNN.com, March 14, 2008.

10 *"I like being around creative people":* Patricia Sellers, "MySpace Cowboys," *Fortune* magazine, September 4, 2006.

10 *Born in December 1965:* ibid.

10 *DeWolfe grew up in Portland, Oregon:* ibid.

10 *He was the younger son of two academics who hoped that he would follow in their footsteps:* ibid.

10 *His father, Fred DeWolfe:* "Portland Historian, Author Frederick DeWolfe Dies," *Oregonian,* December 11, 1997.

10 *His mother, Brigitte, taught German:* Author's interview with a person familiar with the situation.

10 *The DeWolfe family lived in a relatively small house:* ibid.

10 *At Lincoln High School:* Lincoln High Alumni Directory.

10 *DeWolfe was a jock:* Michaela Bancud, "His Space Is Your Space," *Northwest Examiner,* July 2007.

10 *"Beezer":* ibid.

10 *He was president of his junior class:* ibid.

10 *"He was kind of a cool man":* ibid.

11 *"He was a really good basketball player":* ibid.

11 *Andrew Wiederhorn was a close friend of DeWolfe's:* Author's interview with Andrew Wiederhorn, May 1, 2007.

11 *often wearing suits to school:* Author's interview with a person familiar with the situation.

11 *starting a Jet Ski business:* USC Marshall alumni magazine, summer 1998.

11 *Later in life, Wiederhorn spent a year in prison:* USDOL settlement agreement, order No. CRO4-238 BR.

11 *During most of Wiederhorn's incarceration, DeWolfe remained on the board:* Fog Cutter Capital Group Inc., form 8-K, April 28, 2005.

11 *supported its controversial decision to keep paying:* Fog Cutter Capital Group Inc., form DEF 14A, December 8, 2004.

11 *DeWolfe graduated high school in 1984:* Lincoln High Alumni Directory.

11 *moved to Seattle to attend the University of Washington:* University of Washington, Graduate Directory, Degree Validation.

11 *In college he was an enthusiastic member:* Phyllis Bowie, assistant archivist, Beta Theta Pi National Chapter, November 13, 2007.

11 *received a degree in finance in 1988:* Fog Cutter Capital Group Inc., form DEF 14A, October 29, 2004.

11 *"Business school was my opportunity to think":* Patricia Sellers, "MySpace Cowboys," *Fortune,* September 4, 2006.

11 *At USC he fell in love with marketing:* ibid.

11 *In 1997, for a class called "The Impact of Technology on Media and Entertainment":* ibid.

11 *DeWolfe also fell in love with a fellow business school student:* "Verification of Confidential Marriage" between Christopher Thomas DeWolfe and Lorraine Turgeon Hitselberger, on file at the Los Angeles County Recorder's Office. Date of verification: November 29, 2007.

11 *the couple moved into a condominium in Pasadena:* Real estate records.

11 *DeWolfe's childhood friend Wiederhorn hired him:* Author's interview with Andrew Wiederhorn, June 29, 2007.

11 *Back in 1987, when he was just twenty-one, Wiederhorn had founded Wilshire Financial Services Group:* USC Marshall Alumni Magazine, summer 1998.

11 *By the time he was thirty-two:* ibid.

12 *DeWolfe joined the dot-com industry:* Michael Montgomery's interview with Josh Berman, San Diego Venture Group, June 6, 2007.

12 *had been working as an accountant:* ibid.

12 *In 1999 Berman agreed:* ibid.

12 *Founded by two brothers, Brett and Steven O'Brien:* Chris Chandler, "Xdrive Marks the Spot," *Santa Monica Mirror,* August 24, 2000, and author's interview with Brett O'Brien July 17, 2007.

12 *From five o'clock to eight o'clock each morning:* Josh Berman interviewed by Michael Montgomery, the San Diego Venture Group Fifth Annual Venture Summit, June 6, 2007.

12 *XDrive raised a huge amount of money—about $110 million:* Author's interview with Brett O'Brien, July 17, 2007.

12 *ranks swelled to about three hundred people:* Author's interview with Karl Klessig, May 11, 2007.

12 *burned through about $4 million a month:* Author's interview with Brett O'Brien, July 17, 2007.

12 *DeWolfe oversaw more than eighty people:* Author's interview with Karl Klessig, May 11, 2007.

12 *DeWolfe's team developed an e-newsletter called* IntelligentX: Author's interview with Karl Klessig, May 11, 2007.

12 *The offices were in one of Santa Monica's fanciest buildings:* "Xdrive Files Chapter 11," *Los Angeles Business Journal,* July 29, 2002, and author's interview with Karl Klessig, May 11, 2007.

13 *in 2000 after graduating from the University of California, Los Angeles (UCLA) with a master's in film studies:* Patricia Sellers, "MySpace Cowboys," *Fortune,* September 4, 2006.

13 *He was walking through his neighborhood:* Real estate records.

13 *he saw a flyer:* Jeff Howe, "The Hit Factory," *Wired,* issue 13.11, November 2005.

13 *Hoping for some quick cash:* ibid.

13 *he had spent most of his twenties:* Patricia Sellers, "MySpace Cowboys," *Fortune,* September 4, 2006.

13 *"one crazy idea after another":* ibid.

13 *Born on November 8, 1970:* Public records and commercially available data, confirmed by college graduation records and Library of Congress author listing.

13 *grew up in Escondido:* Kenneth Smith, Scoop Stevens, "Viva La Politica, " *San Diego City Beat,* June 2, 2004; "Golden Legend 1986, Footsteps in Time," San

Pasqual High School, Escondido, CA. *Sophomores,* p. 144, Thomas Anderson; real estate records.

13 *By the time he was a young teenager:* Patricia Sellers, "MySpace Cowboys," *Fortune,* September 4, 2006.

13 *Bill Landreth, known as "the Cracker":* Bill Landreth, *Out of the Inner Circle: A Hacker's Guide to Computer Security,* Microsoft Press, 1985.

13 *In 1983 sixteen-year-old Landreth:* ibid.

14 *Apple Computer had just gone public:* "Apple Computer to Sell Public Shares Next Week," *Washington Post,* December 10, 1980.

14 *IBM had just launched a rival personal computer:* "Personal Computer Announced by IBM," IBM (Information Systems Division, Entry Systems Business) press release, August 12, 1981.

14 *Microsoft was racing to build:* Jeremy Reimer, "A History of the GUI," ars technical, May 5, 2005.

14 *The movie* War Games *had just been released:* " 'War Games' Film Cited in Computer Bank Intrusion," *New York Times,* November 6, 1983.

14 *A group of Milwaukee hackers:* "Beware: Hackers at Play," *Newsweek,* September 5, 1983.

14 *He was convicted of wire fraud:* Armando Acuna, "Genius Unplugs, Puts Life on Hold, Famed Computer Whiz, Hacker Spurns Money for Existence on the Street," *Los Angeles Times,* March 19, 1989.

14 *Landreth also won a $25,000 advance to write a book:* Author's interview with Bill Gladstone, October 25, 2007.

14 *"I looked up to him a lot":* Armando Acuna, "Genius Unplugs, Puts Life on Hold, Famed Computer Whiz, Hacker Spurns Money for Existence on the Street," *Los Angeles Times,* March 19, 1989.

14 *In October 1985 Anderson's computer equipment was confiscated:* "For the Record: Hacker's Friend Not Arrested or Convicted," *Los Angeles Times,* December 13, 1986.

14 *"Tom seemed the most normal":* Author's interview with Bill Gladstone, October 25, 2007.

14 *In September 1986 Landreth and Anderson decided:* Tom Gorman, "A Strange Disappearance," *Los Angeles Times,* December 10, 1986.

14 *"He started to write the proposal":* ibid.

15 *But after Landreth's friends found a letter:* ibid.

15 *"We used to joke":* ibid.

15 *Almost a year later:* Armando Acuna, "Genius Unplugs, Puts Life on Hold, Famed Computer Whiz, Hacker Spurns Money for Existence on the Street," *Los Angeles Times,* March 19, 1989.

15 *When Landreth returned:* ibid.

15 *"Before, he was just real smart":* ibid.

15 *Anderson dropped out of high school:* Author's interview with Steve Burnap, October 28, 2007.

15 *Top Hatt:* ibid.

15 *got arrested together:* ibid.

15 *"All of a sudden":* ibid.

15 *Anderson didn't take it seriously:* ibid.

15 *"I'm going to be so rich":* ibid.

15 *"Watching him, it was hard to know how much he believed":* ibid.

16 *"He was convinced":* ibid.

16 *with an advance of about $5,000:* Author's interview with Bill Gladstone, October 25, 2007.

16 *a type of software that:* John McCormick, "Crosstalk MK.4 Caters to the Power Communicator," *Government Computer News,* May 13, 1988.

16 *"Because Tom was so young":* Author's interview with Bill Gladstone, October 25, 2007.

16 Using Crosstalk Mk.4: Tom Anderson, Using Crosstalk Mk.4, Library of Congress online catalog; ISBN 0673880939.

16 *In 1994 he enrolled at the highly competitive University of California at Berkeley:* Degreechk, UC Berkeley graduate confirmation, and author's research.

16 *He double majored in English and rhetoric:* Jeff Howe, "The Hit Factory," *Wired,* issue 13.11, November 2005.

16 *edited a poetry and fiction journal:* Murmurz, "MySpace.com, a Place for Friends," *Forward Motion,* vol. 14, story 1.

16 *wrote video game reviews:* ibid.

16 *for the website GameRevolution.com:* Tom Anderson, "Yellow Flag! Hold Your Position Until the Patch," Game Revolution PC Review Page, December 1997.

16 *sometimes he used the name of a friend, Melissa Loeffler:* Melissa Loeffler, "Help me clean my pots!" Usenet posting in rec.autos.simulators, April 20, 1998, 2:00 a.m.

16 *"I believe it was Nietzsche that said":* Tom Anderson, "The CLAIMS of High Heat . . . Let's break this down (LONG)," Usenet posting in comp .sys.ibm.pc.games.sports, April 26, 1998, 2:00 a.m.

16 *"Tom's quoting Nietzsche":* The Perfect Game, "The CLAIMS of High Heat . . . Let's break this down (LONG)," Usenet posting in comp.sys.ibm.pc.games .sports, April 26, 1998, 2:00 a.m.

16 *Anderson moved to San Francisco:* Jeff Howe, "The Hit Factory," *Wired,* issue 13.11, November 2005.

16 *"I'm currently living in San Francisco":* Tom Everett, "American Rock Singer Seeks Japanese Band," Usenet posting in soc.culture.japan, December 31, 1998, 4:00 a.m.

17 *"Can anyone tell me about Mucha or Panchiao?":* Tom Everett, "Can anyone tell me about Mucha or Panchiao," soc.culture.taiwan Usenet group, January 5, 1999.

17 *"I'm a night person and usually go to bed around 4:00 a.m.":* Tom Everett, "Can anyone tell me about Mucha or Panchiao," soc.culture.taiwan Usenet group, January 6, 1999.

17 *"I'm a little worried about learning to drive":* ibid.

17 *"It costs to use the phone in Taiwan even for local calls?":* Tom Everett, "ISP in Taiwan," soc.culture.taiwan Usenet group, January 10, 1999.

17 *"Here's my problem: I don't own a laptop":* Tom Everett, "Packing a computer for airline," alt.travel Usenet group, January 15, 1999.

17 *But he quickly returned, in the fall of 1999:* Patricia Sellers, "MySpace Cowboys," *Fortune,* September 4, 2006.

17 *"Does anyone know where you can buy/rent Taiwanese films":* Tom Everett, "Hou Hsaio-Hsien," soc.culture.taiwan Usenet group, October 29, 1999.

17 *After graduating from the two-year film program in one year:* Jeff Howe, "The Hit Factory," *Wired,* issue 13.11, November 2005.

17 *In July 2000 he posted:* Tom Everett, "Vietnamese LeAnna Scott porno," rec.arts.movies.erotica Usenet groups, July 17, 2000.

18 *A colleague recalls Anderson describing the site:* Author's interview with a person familiar with the situation.

18 *In August 2000 Anderson posted twice on Usenet's alt.sex.women:* Tom Anderson, "Asian girls," alt.sex.women Usenet groups, August 14, 2000, and August 15, 2000.

18 *News Corp. later found evidence:* Author's interview with a person familiar with the situation.

18 *"I'm quitting":* Peter Chernin's interview with Chris DeWolfe, Paley Media Center, Beverly Hills, California, July 30, 2007.

18 *"Tom was so obviously full of smart ideas":* Jeff Howe, "The Hit Factory," *Wired,* issue 13.11, November 2005.

18 *"You can work from home":* Peter Chernin's interview with Chris DeWolfe, Paley Media Center, Beverly Hills, California, July 30, 2007.

18 *"go figure out how to make money":* Patricia Sellers, "MySpace Cowboys," *Fortune,* September 4, 2006.

18 *When Karl Klessig arrived at XDrive:* Author's interview with Karl Klessig, May 11, 2007.

18 *Klessig had been brought in by XDrive's new chief executive:* ibid.

18 *Very few people had signed up for XDrive's premium:* ibid.

18 *XDrive was trying to reposition itself as a paid storage provider:* ibid.

18 *"It was the largest marketing division":* ibid.

18 *founded three technology companies:* "XDrive Technologies Names High Tech

Industry Veteran Karl Klessig as Executive Vice President; Move Reunites Successful Team of Klessig and CEO Paul Gigg," Business Wire, February 22, 2001.

19 *that were e-mailed to more than 6.5 million:* "EUniverse Purchases IntelligentX," eUniverse press release, June 7, 2001.

19 *"I wish I could understand what you are doing":* Author's interview with Karl Klessig, May 11, 2007.

19 *One year later, still hemorrhaging cash, XDrive filed for bankruptcy:* Samantha Lee, "Xdrive Files Chapter 11," *Los Angeles Business Journal,* July 29, 2002.

19 *By that time, DeWolfe, Berman, and Anderson had started:* ibid.

CHAPTER 3 RISING FROM THE ASHES

20 *By March 2001, the Nasdaq composite index:* Yahoo Finance: March 10, 2000, $5,048; March 9, 2000, $2,052.

20 *thirteen thousand people:* Lisa Girion, "Dot-Com Layoffs Up 23% over December Tally," *Los Angeles Times,* January 30, 2001.

20 *at places like eToys:* Kick Kelsey, "EToys Cuts 70% of Staff, Shuts Two Warehouses," *Newsbytes News Network,* January 4, 2001.

20 *and the Walt Disney Company's Web portal Go.com:* Jesse Hiestand, "Disney's Go.com Shuts Down, 400 Workers Laid Off," *Los Angeles Daily News,* January 30, 2001.

21 *whom the others called the "chief nerd":* Michael Montgomery's interview with Josh Berman, San Diego Venture Group, Fifth Annual Venture Summit, June 6, 2007.

21 *"We've just left XDrive":* Author's interview with Matt Coffin, June 14, 2007.

21 *Coffin saw the dot-com bust as an opportunity:* ibid.

21 *Coffin had just cut a deal:* ibid.

21 *To pay for the lease:* ibid.

21 *Government regulators were investigating aspects of the bankruptcy:* Author's interview with Andrew Wiederhorn, December 31, 2007.

21 *"His business plan was conservative":* Author's interview with Andrew Wiederhorn, May 1, 2007.

21 *$300,000 in DeWolfe's company directly and through an investment vehicle, TTMM L.P.:* ibid.

21 *For their investment, Wiederhorn and TTMM received a gigantic 50 percent stake:* ibid.

22 *During the dot-com bust:* Kim MacPherson, "It Is Rocket Science," *Incisive Interactive Marketing,* November 8, 1999.

22 *There were more than thirty-five different state laws:* Author's interview with Quinn Jalli, chief privacy officer of DaTran Media, July 20, 2007.

22 *a website called MySpace.com:* Author's interview with MySpace.com founder Ari Freeman, April 24, 2007.

22 *7.5 million users:* Bonnie Rothman Morris, "In Web Storage World, No Space at MySpace," *New York Times,* June 7, 2001.

22 *slightly more storage space—300 Mb:* Author's interview with Ari Freeman, April 24, 2007.

22 *MySpace website went dark:* Bonnie Rothman Morris, "In Web Storage World, No Space at MySpace," *New York Times,* June 7, 2001.

22 *DeWolfe bought the domain name:* Author's interview with Ari Freeman, April 24, 2007.

22 *for $5,000:* Michael Eisner's interview with Chris DeWolfe, "Conversations with Michael Eisner," CNBC.

23 *DeWolfe issued a press release announcing the formation of his new company:* "ResponseBase Announces Round of Funding," Business Wire, June 20, 2001.

23 *promised that it would replicate the success of the* IntelligentX *newsletters:* ibid.

23 *"Our mission is to share":* ibid.

23 *One of ResponseBase's first clients:* Author's interview with Matt Coffin, June 14, 2007.

23 *a newsletter called* Cost Cutter: ibid.

23 *The author was Tom Anderson:* ibid.

23 *Within thirty days, ResponseBase had turned a profit:* Michael Montgomery's interview with Josh Berman, San Diego Venture Group, June 6, 2007.

23 *Its clients included some of the remaining dot-coms in Los Angeles:* Harriman Consulting, case study, "ResponseBase Development."

23 *which the ResponseBase founders had copied when they left XDrive:* Author's interview with a person familiar with the situation.

23 *"distilled information delivered directly to your in-box":* Sitereleases.com, October 13, 2002.

23 *"It claims I had registered for something called 'XDrive'":* Michael Cheves, SpamCop-List, July 26, 2001.

23 *"Russ3llr" posted a complaint:* EZboard.com, August 20, 2001.

23 *"It seems like shitty Tom is collecting IP numbers":* Wolfgang Moser, "I couldn't believe it!" Usenet posting on de.admin.net-abuse.mail, August 18, 2001.

24 *One month after the terrorist attacks:* Author's interview with Matt Coffin, June 14, 2007.

24 *They found some space at another dying dot-com:* ibid.

24 *Winebaum was using an entire floor:* ibid.

24 *On October 26 LowerMyBills and ResponseBase moved:* ibid.

24 *The three companies divided the floor:* ibid.

24 *received several bomb threats:* ibid.

24 *Coffin and DeWolfe joked:* ibid.

24 *By February 2002 ResponseBase had expanded:* Author's interview with Gabe Harriman, July 31, 2007.

24 *ResponseBase had noticed that its e-mail advertising clients:* ibid.

24 How to Date Pretty Girls: Author's interview with Gabe Harriman, January 10, 2008.

24 *"If you've always wanted to be taller":* "Make Money Fast Hall of Humiliation" bulletin board, posted February 26, 2003.

25 *Users would pay by credit card:* ibid.

25 *Selling e-books transformed ResponseBase:* Author's interview with Gabe Harriman, July 31, 2007.

25 *The company hired Gabe Harriman:* ibid.

25 *In one month, Harriman built an e-commerce system:* ibid.

25 *ResponseBase attracted 2.3 million visitors to PayMe2Shop.com:* Leslie Walker, "Mass-Appealing, and Sometimes Appalling," *Washington Post,* May 30, 2002.

25 *That same month, nine hundred thousand people visited ResponseBase's Cool OnlineProducts.com:* ibid.

25 *"Ever wonder where your kids or spouse visit":* ibid.

25 *The phone number that was listed as a way to opt out:* Author's interview with a person familiar with the situation.

25 *In October 2001 Anderson even registered:* Mahatma Kane Jeeves, news .admin.net-abuse.sightings, May 11, 2002.

25 *11970 Walnut Lane:* Real estate records.

26 *"See Everything That Happens on Anyone's Computer":* Mahatma Kane Jeeves, news.admin.net-abuse.sightings, May 11, 2002.

26 *In March 2002 Anderson registered the domain name StationsNetwork.com:* Tsu Dho Nimh, "Spammed by Bell South, investor@bellsouth.com informed," Usenet posting in news.admin.net-abuse.email, June 19, 2002.

26 *"Try AOL 1,000 Hours FREE for 45 Days Today!":* MNJazz.com, "Try AOL 1,000 Hours FREE for 45 Days Today!" Usenet posting in news.admin .net-abuse.sightings, May 22, 2002.

26 *"Mortgage Search Certificate Exclusively for You":* Samuel Hooks, "Mortgage Search Certificate Exclusively for You," Usenet posting in news.admin .net-abuse.sightings, May 5, 2002.

26 *"Get Paid to Shop!":* Root, "Get Paid to Shop! Get Paid to Eat Out! (fwd)," Usenet posting on news.admin.net-abuse.sightings, May 18, 2002.

26 *"Special Offers on BellSouth":* Tsu Dho Nimh, "Special Offers on BellSouth(R) FastAccess(R) DSL," Usenet posting in news.admin.net-abuse-sightings, June 19, 2002.

26 *"Attract More Women":* Gary McGath, "Attract more women with my unique reverse approach!" Usenet posting in news.admin.net-abuse.sightings, May 18, 2002.

26 *"How to Hypnotize"*: MNJazz.com, "Jeremy I couldn't believe this worked," Usenet posting in news.admin.net-abuse.sightings, June 17, 2002, 3:29 a.m.

26 *"Get Paid for Your Opinions!"*: "Get Paid for Your Opinions!" Usenet posting in news.admin.net-abuse.sightings, April 21, 2003, 9:56 p.m.

27 *Anderson recruited his college roommate*: Author's interview with a person familiar with the situation and real estate records.

27 *DeWolfe brought over his friend Colin Digiaro*: ibid.

27 *"It was a big issue with them trusting me"*: Author's interview with Jason Feffer, March 6, 2007.

27 *It was a young, hip environment*: Author's interview with a person familiar with the situation.

27 *colleagues often worked late*: ibid.

27 *Anderson and Brinkman shared an apartment*: Author's interview with a person familiar with the situation and real estate records.

27 *Aber Whitcomb and Gabe Harriman, the programmer hired to build the e-commerce system*: Author's interview with Gabe Harriman, July 31, 2007.

27 *He worked around the clock and didn't drink*: Author's interview with Jason Feffer, March 6, 2007.

27 *He was more retro than trendy*: Author's interview with a person familiar with the situation.

27 *he drove a 1984 Jaguar*: Steve Jones's interview with Tom Anderson, "Jonesy's Jukebox," Los Angeles 103.1 FM, November 29, 2005.

27 *He was antisocial*: E-mail from Tom Anderson to corp.everyone@euniverse .com, August 28, 2003.

27 *"If I sent him an e-mail or instant message"*: Author's interview with Jason Feffer, March 6, 2007.

27 *It started on April 1, 2002*: Author's interview with a person familiar with the situation.

27 *One afternoon the young woman told Anderson*: ibid.

27 *Anderson sent an e-mail to the young woman*: ibid.

28 *the two discussed how they could reduce the tension*: ibid.

28 *Anderson asked her to keep their conversation private*: ibid.

28 *"I went to Starbucks"*: ibid.

28 *"I thought I told you not to say anything"*: ibid.

28 *"I didn't"*: ibid.

28 *Outraged by Anderson's scolding*: ibid.

28 *Anderson convinced DeWolfe*: Author's interview with Matt Coffin, June 14, 2007.

28 *DeWolfe sent him off to China*: ibid.

28 *everything from scooters*: Author's interview with Jason Feffer, March 6, 2007.

28 *to spy cameras you could slip in your shoe*: Author's interview with Matt Coffin, June 14, 2007.

28 *"We had a hard time getting him to come back"*: Author's interview with Jason Feffer, March 6, 2007.

29 *ResponseBase's monthly revenues soared:* Author's interview with a person familiar with the situation.

CHAPTER 4 THE TRAILER PARK OF THE INTERNET

30 *"EUniverse was really the trailer park of the Internet"*: Author's interview with Matt Coffin, June 14, 2007.

30 *Twenty-six-year-old Brad Greenspan founded eUniverse in 1999:* Intermix Media, Inc., form 10-K/A, filed July 31, 2000.

30 *grew up in privileged Atherton:* Author's interview with Brad Greenspan, May 17, 2007.

30 *Greenspan now says Brewer does not deserve the title of cofounder:* Author's interview with Brad Greenspan, July 9, 2008.

31 *Greenspan played varsity soccer:* Author's interview with Brad Greenspan, December 3, 2007.

31 *"He would declare war on people"*: Author's interview with a person familiar with the situation.

31 *grew up in Turlock:* Author's interview with Brett Brewer, June 16, 2007.

31 *in fourth grade he bought up:* Charlie Anderson, "Brewer's Pursuit of Net Profits Isn't New," *Kansas City Business Journal,* May 12, 2006.

31 *"My SATS, I got a 1,090"*: Melissa Moniz, "The Story of MySpace," *Midweek,* December 8, 2006.

31 *I would be that guy who would have to study:* ibid.

31 *"Hey, it's Brett and the gang"*: Author's interview with Brett Brewer, March 20, 2007.

31 *After graduating in 1997 Brewer and Greenspan moved:* ibid.

31 *The three all worked:* Author's interview with Brad Greenspan, May 17, 2007.

31 *Brewer began selling and leasing office space:* Author's interview with Brett Brewer, March 20, 2007.

31 *$17,000 a year:* Author's interview with Brett Brewer, August 1, 2007.

31 *And Greenspan set up his own company:* Author's interview with Brad Greenspan, May 17, 2007.

31 *Every day he scoured newspapers:* ibid.

32 *Sometimes he would make $5,000 or $10,000 a pop:* ibid.

32 *Brewer also tried to broker similar deals:* ibid.

32 *Greenspan's mother had agreed to pay his rent:* ibid.

32 *Brewer paid $365 a month:* Author's interview with Brett Brewer, March 20, 2007.

32 *Brewer drove a tiny two-seat Toyota coupe:* ibid.

32 *Greenspan drove a used blue Acura Integra:* ibid.

32 *The three friends would meet at Islands:* ibid.

32 *making nearly $35,000, including commissions:* Author's interview with Brett Brewer, August 1, 2007.

32 *"I wasn't that far from throwing in the towel":* Author's interview with Brett Brewer, March 20, 2007.

32 *He lined up a $45 million financing:* ibid.

32 *The two friends rented office space:* ibid.

33 *"Brett, listen to this":* ibid.

33 *Abrams had cofounded a company, Software Toolworks:* Author's interview with Joe Abrams, October 22, 2007.

33 *sold the company for $462 million:* ibid.

33 *"I'd like to do exactly what you did":* ibid.

33 *"I'd like to take that model":* ibid.

33 *"I had no idea how old he was until I met him":* ibid.

33 *Netscape planned to sell its shares to the public at $28 a share:* Paul Festa, "Netscape: Bowed, but Not Broken," *CNET News,* October 13, 2004.

33 *Greenspan would put in all the money:* Author's interview with Joe Abrams, October 22, 2007.

33 *They decided to name the new company Entertainment Universe:* Author's interview with Brett Brewer and Chris Lipp, April 9, 2007.

34 *Eventually they found Emanuel Gerard, cofounder and chairman at a respected New York firm, Gerard Klauer Mattison:* Intermix Media Inc., form 10K-A, filed July 31, 2000, and Neena Lall's interview with Emanuel Gerard, October 23, 2007.

34 *agreed to put in $250,000:* Intermix Media Inc., form S-1A, filed October 15, 1999.

34 *Greenspan then tapped another relationship:* Author's interview with a person familiar with the situation.

34 *in a $6.6 million fund-raising round:* eUniverse, form S-1A, October 15, 1999.

34 *Working unpaid for the promise of a small stake in eUniverse, he searched for a shell public company:* Author's interview with Brett Brewer, March 20, 2007.

34 *method of going public known as a "reverse merger":* Author's interview with Joe Abrams, October 22, 2007.

34 *it bought CD Universe for $1.9 million in cash and $7.3 million worth of stock:* Intermix Media Inc., form 10K-A, filed July 31, 2000.

34 *eUniverse bought Case's Ladder for stock valued at $7 million:* ibid.

34 *The newly created firm went public on April 14, 1999:* Author's interview with Brett Brewer, November 7, 2007.

34 *Greenspan, then twenty-six, was suddenly chairman:* Intermix Media, Inc., form 10-K/A, filed July 31, 2000.

34 *Brewer, twenty-seven, was vice president of e-commerce:* ibid.

34 *Abrams served in an advisory role:* Author's interview with Joe Abrams, October 22, 2007.

34 *CD Universe was losing $400,000 a month:* Author's interview with Brett Brewer, March 20, 2007.

35 *he and Brewer negotiated to sell CD Universe back to its founder, who had been working for eUniverse, for $1 million:* Intermix Media Inc., form 10K, filed July 16, 2001.

35 *a six-bedroom house that Brewer rented:* Author's interview with Adam Goldenberg, May 3, 2007.

35 *"I have a certain style of research that I can do":* Author's interview with Brad Greenspan, May 17, 2007.

35 *website he had bought called FunOne.com:* Author's interview with Brett Brewer, May 20, 2007.

35 *which paid a finder's fee of as much as $40:* ibid.

35 *By March 31, eUniverse was in dire straits: It had $218,000 in cash and $13.4 million in debt:* Intermix Media Inc., form 10-K, filed March 31, 2001.

35 *"All right, everybody, put on your hard hats":* Author's interview with Brett Brewer, June 16, 2007.

36 *The front door was locked:* ibid.

36 *The Sony executives' eyes widened:* ibid.

36 *It was looking to unwind:* Author's interview with Mark Wachen, June 4, 2007.

36 *fewer than two million subscribers, and expended its reach to nine million subscribers:* ibid.

36 *The day-to-day business was being managed by twenty-year-old Adam Goldenberg:* Author's interview with Adam Goldenberg, May 3, 2007.

36 *It agreed to sell* InfoBeat *to eUniverse for $9.94 million:* Intermix Media Inc., form 10-K, filed July 1, 2002.

36 *invest $5 million cash in eUniverse:* ibid.

36 *In May 2000 eUniverse moved into its first real office space:* Author's interview with Barbara Saunders, August 1, 2007.

37 *So eUniverse decided to diversify:* Author's interview with Joe Varraveto, June 7, 2007.

37 *In the second half of 2001:* Intermix Media Inc., form 10K, filed July 1, 2002.

37 *CupidJunction had attracted 450,000 paying subscribers:* ibid.

37 *the company launched FitnessHeaven.com:* Author's interview with Joe Varraveto, June 7, 2007.

37 *In July eUniverse bought the* IntelligentX *newsletter:* Digital Media Wire, June 7, 2001.

37 *from XDrive for a few hundred thousand dollars:* Author's interview with Brad Greenspan, June 16, 2007.

37 *it made $2 million net income on $10.1 million in revenues:* Intermix Media Inc., form 10Q, filed February 14, 2002.

37 *a well-funded animation website called Icebox.com and an animation site, Romp.com:* Digital Media Wire, February 7, 2001. Tim Swanson, "Romp Stumbles Offline," *Variety,* February 22, 2001.

37 *In early 2002 eUniverse chief financial officer:* Author's interview with Joe Varraveto, June 7, 2007.

38 *"We needed to build a bench of deeper talent":* ibid.

38 *who was in his forties and was one of the oldest executives:* ibid.

38 *When Greenspan got in touch with DeWolfe:* Author's interview with Brad Greenspan, May 17, 2007.

38 *managed more than thirty million e-mail accounts:* Intermix Media Inc., form 10K, filed August 22, 2003.

38 *"Our e-mail marketing group":* Author's interview with Dan Mosher, June 20, 2007.

38 *"We valued the [eUniverse] stock at zero":* Michael Montgomery's interview with Josh Berman, San Diego Venture Group, June 6, 2007.

38 *$3.3 million in cash:* Intermix Media Inc., form 10K, filed August 22, 2003.

CHAPTER 5 STRUGGLING TO SURVIVE

39 *Chris DeWolfe pulled up to the Belmont nightclub:* Author's interviews with Brett Brewer, March 30, 2007, and June 16, 2007.

39 *"Chris, you're just like Hansel from* Zoolander*":* ibid.

39 *its best quarter ever:* Intermix Media Inc., form 10-K, filed August 22, 2003.

40 *an increase in profits of 60 percent:* Intermix Media Inc., form 10Q, filed February 14, 2003.

40 *The increase was due in large part:* ibid.

40 *ResponseBase raked in $2.5 million in sales:* Author's interview with a person familiar with the situation.

40 *In April* BusinessWeek *had profiled eUniverse:* Arlene Weintraub, "eUniverse's Secret for Net Profits," BusinessWeek Online, April 24, 2002.

40 *eUniverse stock had recently traded as high as $7 a share:* Intermix Media Inc., form 10-K, filed August 22, 2003.

40 *eUniverse human resources director Barbara Saunders:* Author's interview with Barbara Saunders, August 1, 2007.

40 *That night, she handed out a record amount—nearly $2,000:* Author's interview with Brett Brewer, June 16, 2007.

40 *At first the separation was mutually agreeable:* Author's interview with a person familiar with the situation.

40 *ResponseBase grumpily succumbed to its new owners' request:* ibid.

41 *"They weren't so nice to us":* Michael Montgomery's interview with Josh Berman, San Diego Venture Group, June 6, 2007.

41 *accrued $1.3 million in its earnout:* Intermix Media Inc., form 10K, filed August 22, 2003.

41 *"We make as much money":* Author's interview with a person familiar with the situation.

41 *"Brad, why hasn't our rent been paid?":* Author's interview with Brad Greenspan, May 17, 2007.

41 *Greenspan hired a consultant:* ibid.

41 *The Federal Trade Commission had launched an antispam effort:* Federal Trade Commission, "FTC Introduces Internet Safety Mascot, 'Dewie the Turtle,' at Privacy2002 Conference," FTC press release, September 26, 2002.

42 *New York attorney general Eliot Spitzer had started prosecuting spammers:* Office of the New York State Attorney General, "State Lawsuit Seeks to End Spam E-mails Sent by Niagara Falls Company," Office of the New York State Attorney General press release, May 28, 2002.

42 *"It was a daily battle":* Author's interview with Dan Mosher, June 20, 2007.

42 *ResponseBase's clients were reducing:* ibid.

42 *getting an influx of returns:* ibid.

42 *$99 kids' electric scooters:* Spam Buster, "Electric Scooter, the Number One Christmas Gift," Google Groups, news.admin.net-abuse.sightings, December 6, 2002.

42 *$24.99 remote-controll rechargeable minicars:* SpamUsNot, "Mini RC Cars, Sold Out in Stores—$24.99," Google Groups, news.admin.net-abuse.sightings, November 26, 2002.

42 *ResponseBase dropped the price of its mini remote-control motorcycle:* 13X Forums, "For the MINI Guys," January 31, 2003.

42 *mini spy cameras for less than $100:* Darren Thrower, "Spycam Better Than the X10," UK Home Automation Archive, February 3, 2003.

42 *falling from $2.5 million in December to $1.8 million in January:* Author's interview with a person familiar with the situation.

42 *to $1.4 million:* ibid.

42 *its $29.99 e-booklet* GetPaid4Opinions.com: RipoffReport.com, Report #47273, February 27, 2003.

42 *"I did this, and it is a scam":* Make Money Fast Hall of Humiliation, March 4, 2003.

42 *paid for but never received a $19.95 e-book:* RipoffReport.com, Report #66941, September 14, 2003.

42 *"The phone number they provide always answers with a recording":* ibid.

42 *ResponseBase experimented with setting up a kiosk on the Santa Monica:* Author's interview with Brett Brewer, June 16, 2007.

42 *Cary A. Jones:* Grace Aquino, "On Your Side: PC Speed-Up Slows Down Reader," *PC World,* February 1, 2003.

43 *"I don't care what your technical ability is":* ibid.

43 *"If you don't like the package for any reason":* ibid.

43 *Most Americans in early 2003:* Anne Kandra, "Fast Cheap Net Access? It's Possible," *PC World,* February 1, 2003.

43 *Only 13 percent of U.S. households were using broadband:* ibid.

44 *On April 9 the U.S. Marines rode into one of Baghdad's central squares:* CNN.com, Wednesday, April 9, 2003.

44 *Brooks said the military had produced two hundred decks:* Nicole Winfield, "Saddam's the Ace in This Notorious Deck of Cards," Associated Press, April 11, 2003.

44 *None of the decks for sale online was the real thing:* Lisa Burgess, "Buyers Beware: The Real Iraq 'Most Wanted' Cards Are Still Awaiting Distribution," *Stars and Stripes,* April 17, 2003.

44 *"Don't be fooled by the many cheap imitations":* Posted on bbs.clutchfans.net, quoting a promotion received for CoolOnlineProducts.com/dodcards, April 17, 2003.

44 *"Where's the quarterly report?":* Author's interview with Brad Greenspan, May 17, 2007.

44 *"There are a few items totaling fifty thousand dollars":* Author's interview with Brad Greenspan, May 17, 2007, and author's interview with Joe Varraveto, December 12, 2007.

44 *"How's it looking?":* Author's interview with Brett Brewer, June 16, 2007.

45 *"I don't know if the numbers are right or wrong":* ibid.

45 *"Stay here," he said. "I'll go call Brad and the other guys":* ibid.

45 *"Wait a second, I just said we had the greatest quarter ever":* Author's interview with Brad Greenspan, May 17, 2007.

45 *The finance team's numbers didn't match:* Author's interview with Joe Varraveto, June 7, 2007.

45 *The company had two e-commerce divisions:* Intermix Media Inc., form 10-K, filed March 31, 2003.

45 *The unit's monthly revenues in May:* Author's interview with a person familiar with the situation.

45 *DeWolfe e-mailed Greenspan about his desire to combine business units:* E-mail from Chris DeWolfe to Brad Greenspan, March 25, 2003.

45 *On May 6 eUniverse announced publicly:* Intermix Media Inc., form 10-K, filed March 31, 2003.

45 *The Nasdaq immediately halted trading on the stock at $3.62 a share:* ibid.

45 *down from a high of $7.30:* ibid.

46 *The Securities and Exchange Commission (SEC) began an investigation:* ibid.

46 *Eight separate shareholder lawsuits were filed:* ibid.

46 *He threw himself into the plans for a new company called GameUniverse:* Author's interview with Brad Greenspan, May 17, 2007.

46 *Brewer started pursuing Ronco Corporation:* ibid.

46 *Bob Sullivan, a reporter for MSNBC.com, was appalled:* Author's interview with Bob Sullivan, May 18, 2007.

46 *"Show your support for our troops":* Bob Sullivan, "Patriotism? No, Just More Pop-ups," MSNBC.com, May 20, 2006.

46 *The software, called KeenValue:* ibid.

47 *"EUniverse is not in the spyware business":* ibid.

47 *Greenspan, always sensitive to press coverage, asked DeWolfe:* E-mail from Brad Greenspan to Chris DeWolfe, May 15, 2003.

47 *"Can we reduce what Keen is keeping/tracking":* ibid.

47 *VantagePoint managing director David Carlick:* Author's interview with David Carlick, May 10, 2007.

47 *"They had traffic":* ibid.

48 *"marketing has always been kind of on the scary edge of ethical":* ibid.

48 *"Every day you have to write a new monologue":* ibid.

48 *After Carlick's visit, Carlick wanted to loan eUniverse $2 million:* ibid.

48 *"I'll be chairman, and we'll find a CEO":* Author's interview with Brad Greenspan, April 12, 2007.

48 *"You should check out these free car sites":* Author's interview with Bob Sullivan, May 18, 2007, and author's interview with Jon Sorenson, July 19, 2007.

48 *Sullivan found that dozens of sites had sprung up:* Bob Sullivan, " 'Free Car' Spam a Growing Problem," MSNBC.com, June 20, 2006.

48 *"These people have created a real headache for us":* ibid.

48 *"Get paid* real money *to drive your car":* Rick Troha, "Get paid real money to drive your car," Google Groups, news.admin.net-abuse.sightings, June 1, 2003.

48 *"Free new cars for the taking!":* Canned Ham, "Free New Cars for the Taking! Ntgnd," Google Groups, news.admin.net-abuse.sightings, September 13, 2002.

49 *"Basically, this fee is to cover our expenses":* Bob Sullivan, " 'Free Car' Spam a Growing Problem," MSNBC.com, June 20, 2006.

49 *its revenues had shrunk:* Author's interview with a person familiar with the situation.

49 *"Instead of going back and forth":* Author's interview with Brett Brewer, January 13, 2008.

49 *"as far away from direct e-commerce marketing":* ibid.

CHAPTER 6 THE FAKESTER REVOLUTION

50 *raised more than $1 million in its second round of financing:* Author's interview with Toni Graham, assistant to Jonathan Abrams, November 16, 2007.

50 *turned down Google's offer to buy it for $30 million:* Gary Rivlin, "Wallflower at the Web Party," *New York Times,* October 15, 2007.

50 *"Friendster is truly a revolution":* E-mail from Chris DeWolfe to Brad Greenspan, September 4, 2003.

50 *Jonathan Abrams, a former programmer:* Lessley Anderson, "Attack of the Smartasses," *SF Weekly,* August 13, 2003.

50 *"With JDate, a guy is almost bound to be twenty pounds heavier":* Alexandra J. Wall, "Jonathan Abrams," *Something Jewish,* February 11, 2003.

51 *shot up to one million members:* Gary Rivlin, "Wallflower at the Web Party," *New York Times,* October 15, 2007.

51 *On the WELL . . . , founded in 1985:* Katie Hafner, "The Epic Saga of the WELL," *Wired,* issue 5.05 May 1997.

51 *On GeoCities, founded in 1994:* Author's interview with David Bohnett, April 12, 2007.

51 *Xanga . . . both founded in 1999:* Federal Trade Commission, "Xanga.com to Pay $1 Million for Violating Children's Online Privacy Protection Rule," FTC press release, September 7, 2006.

51 *and Blogger, both founded in 1999:* Blogger/Trellix, "Trellix Acquires License to Pyra Lab's Blogger Technology," Blogger/Trellix press release, April 16, 2001.

51 *Match.com, founded in 1995:* Match.com, "Match.com Introduces Friends Feature," Match.com press release, December 18, 2003.

51 *Friendster had stumbled onto a corollary called Reed's Law:* David P. Reed, "Digital Strategy: Weapon of Math Destruction," *Context Magazine,* Spring 1999.

52 *In 1996 twenty-eight-year-old New York entrepreneur Andrew Weinreich created SixDegrees.com:* Author's interview with Andrew Weinreich, July 11, 2007.

52 *At the site's New York City launch party:* ibid.

52 *"Today networking is the same":* ibid.

52 *about 3.5 million members at its peak:* ibid.

52 *In 1999 Weinreich sold SixDegrees:* ibid.

52 *In 1999 Portland programmer Brad Fitzpatrick:* SixApart.com, "SixApart History," 2006.

53 *"We were able to see early on":* Author's interview with Andrew Weinreich, July 11, 2007.

54 *"The whole point of Friendster is that you're connected to somebody through mutual friends":* Lessley Anderson, "Attack of the Smartasses," *SF Weekly,* August 13, 2003.

54 *"On the Internet, nobody knows you're a dog":* Peter Steiner cartoon from page 61 of July 5, 1993, issue of the *New Yorker* (vol. 69, no. 20).

55 *Calling themselves the "Borg Collective":* Lessley Anderson, "Attack of the Smart-asses," *SF Weekly,* August 13, 2003.

55 *"Identity is provisional:* apophenia, "The Fakester Manifesto," August 17, 2003.

55 *Anderson was fed up with eUniverse:* Joe Nocera's interview with Tom Anderson, "Sunday with the Magazine" event, May 20, 2007.

55 *Anderson barged into DeWolfe's office:* Jeffe Howe, "The Hit Factory," *Wired,* issue 13.11, November 2005.

55 *"Dude, we've got to talk":* ibid.

55 *"The idea was that if it was a cool thing to do online":* ibid.

56 *"I kind of blew it off":* Peter Chernin's interview with Chris DeWolfe, Paley Media Center, Beverly Hills, California, July 30, 2007.

56 *But the next day, DeWolfe received three friend requests from Friendster:* ibid.

56 *"It seemed like an amazing kind of marketing":* ibid.

56 *But DeWolfe decided to take a chance:* ibid.

56 *"I bet the farm on it":* ibid.

56 *"allowing access to everything":* E-mail from Chris DeWolfe to Brad Greenspan, September 4, 2003.

57 *YoPeeps.com and Comingle.com:* Author's interview with Jason Feffer, April 9, 2007.

57 *"It sounded like kind of a funny name":* Author's interview with Brett Brewer, January 13, 2008.

57 *thought it was an intriguing service:* E-mail from Mike Menta to Brad Greenspan, July 4, 2003.

57 *Greenspan asked an associate to check out if Friendster was interested in selling or partnering:* E-mail from Todd Smith to Brad Greenspan, July 2, 2003.

57 *"Maybe we spin MySpace into GameUniverse":* E-mail from Brad Greenspan to Justin Beckett, September 11, 2003.

57 *Kyle Brinkman managed the creation of MySpace:* Author's interview with Duc Chau, June 16, 2007.

57 *ResponseBase's e-commerce programmer, Gabe Harriman, built the MySpace data-base:* Author's interview with Gabe Harriman, January 10, 2008, and author's interview with Duc Chau, June 16, 2007.

57 *Finally, on August 15, they were ready to launch their bare-bones site:* Author's interview with Duc Chau, June 16, 2007.

57 *features, including horoscopes:* Author's interview with Jason Feffer, March 6, 2007.

57 *and blogging, then called journals:* Author's interview with Duc Chau, June 16, 2007.

57 *"We didn't know what it was going to be about":* Author's interview with Jason Feffer, March 6, 2007.

57 *"When we flipped the switch, everybody raced to sign up for the first account":* Author's interview with Duc Chau, June 16, 2007.

58 *Chief technology officer Aber Whitcomb got the third account:* Author's interview with Jason Feffer, March 6, 2007.

58 *didn't sign up until September 2:* Tom Anderson, http://myspace.com/tom.

58 *"It was me who said, 'Let's do this' ":* Murmurz, "MySpace.com, a place for friends," *Forward Motion,* vol. 14, story 1.

CHAPTER 7 BUILDING MYSPACE

59 *shot up to 25 percent from 15 percent:* John B. Horrigan, "Broadband Adoption at Home in the United States: Growing but Slow," Pew Internet and American Life Project, paper presented to the 33rd Annual Telecommunications Policy Research Conference, September 24, 2005.

59 *Their main uploading activity:* ibid.

59 *the early adopters of broadband were older, affluent men:* Amanda Lenhart, John Horrigan, and Deborah Fallows, "Content Creation Online," Pew Internet and American Life Project, February 29, 2004.

59 *teenage girls were among the first groups:* Amanda Lenhart, Mary Madden, Alexandra Rankin Macgill, and Aaron Smith, "Teens and Social Media," Pew Internet and American Life Project, December 19, 2007.

60 *Duc Chau, quit:* Author's interview with Duc Chau, June 16, 2007.

60 *No one else at the company knew the Perl programming language:* Author's interview with Gabe Harriman, July 31, 2007.

60 *DeWolfe paid Gabe Harriman $2,000:* ibid.

60 *Greenspan also hired a former eUniverse employee, Toan Nguyen:* Author's interview with Toan Nguyen, November 30, 2007.

60 *Harriman and Nguyen made a mistake:* ibid.

60 *"Hey, there's a problem":* Author's interview with Toan Nguyen, June 15, 2007.

60 *Nguyen and Brinkman considered fixing the omission:* David F. Carr, "Inside MySpace," *Baseline Magazine,* January 16, 2007.

61 *"users come first, and this is what they want":* ibid.

61 *By the end of 2004, more than half the nation's teenagers:* Amanda Lenhart and Mary Madden, "Reports: Family, Friends and Community," Pew Internet and American Life Project, November 2, 2005.

61 *"There are senders and receivers, and nothing in between":* Author's interview with Aram Sinnreich, May 14, 2008.

61 *"a much more nuanced world":* ibid.

61 *The majority of teens surveyed in 2004:* Amanda Lenhart and Mary Madden, "Reports: Family, Friends and Community," Pew Internet and American Life Project, November 2, 2005.

61 *"People kept telling us, 'You have to have a closed network' ":* Patricia Sellers, "MySpace Cowboys," *Fortune,* September 4, 2006.

62 *Social networking researcher Danah Boyd surveyed MySpace users:* Danah Boyd, "Friends, Friendsters, and Top 8: Writing Community into Being on Social Network Sites," *First Monday,* vol. 11, no. 12, December 2006.

62 *"In the pre-internet days":* Joel Stein, "You Are Not My Friend," *Time,* October 4, 2007.

63 *"People are competing":* Author's interview with Jeremy Liew, June 27, 2007.

63 *In the beginning, MySpace members didn't have much control over their top eight:* Author's interview with Peter Amiri, March 24, 2008.

63 *The top eight were simply the first eight people:* Danah Boyd, "Friends, Friendsters, and Top 8: Writing Community into Being on Social Network Sites," *First Monday,* vol. 11, no. 12, December 2006.

63 *MySpace was an aggregator:* Author's interview with Peter Amiri, October 24, 2007.

63 *"We would fast and furiously build something":* ibid.

63 *"That was the name of the game":* ibid.

63 *Founded in 2000 by two Silicon Valley graduate students:* Author's interview with James Hong, June 27, 2007.

63 *Borrowing a good idea:* ibid.

64 *In November Xanga sent a letter threatening to sue MySpace:* Settlement Agreement between Xanga.com Inc. and MySpace Inc., April 2005.

64 *MySpace agreed to pay Xanga $40,000:* ibid.

64 *But they were a "miserable failure":* Joe Nocera's interview with Tom Anderson, "Sunday with the Magazine" event, May 20, 2007.

64 *Anderson . . . personally sent e-mails to five hundred of his friends:* ibid.

64 *Brett Brewer, president of eUniverse, sent an e-mail to all two hundred fifty of his employees:* E-mail from Brett Brewer to Chris Lipp, Brad Greenspan, and Adam Goldenberg, August 26, 2003.

64 *"MySpace.com is a fun new way to meet people":* ibid.

64 *"I was getting too many friend requests":* Dixon Christie's interview with Tila Tequila, PunkTV.ca, January 10, 2007.

65 *Tequila, a Vietnamese model whose real last name is Nguyen:* ibid.

65 *"No one was really on there":* Lev Grossman, "Tila Tequila," *Time,* December 16, 2006.

65 *Feeling vindictive, Tequila e-mailed all forty thousand of her Friendster friends:* Tila Tequila, MySpace blog, posted on March 18 2007.

65 *MySpace had its biggest day ever, attracting six thousand new users:* E-mail from Chris DeWolfe to Brad Greenspan, September 26, 2003.

65 *"MySpace huge 2 days":* ibid.

65 *MySpace rose from the thirty thousandth:* Jeff Howe, "The Hit Factory," *Wired,* issue 13.11, November 2005.

65 *Anderson, a baseball fan, flew to San Francisco:* ibid.

66 *"Many new users":* Tom Anderson, MySpace news post [Internet], September 19, 2003. Available: collect.myspace.com/misc/news.html.

66 *By October MySpace had attracted one hundred thousand users:* Jason Calacanis, "Another Day, Another Friendster Knock Off: MySpace Works the 'Free' Angle," SocialSoftware.Weblogsinc.com, October 10, 2003.

66 *"In the future, MySpace may add paid premium services":* ibid.

66 *"Perhaps they're embarrassed":* ibid.

66 *Two of the most difficult tasks:* Professor Mikolaj Jan Piskorski, "Friendster (A)," Harvard Business School case study, February 15, 2007.

66 *Often its servers would slow to a crawl:* ibid.

66 *In October 2003 Friendster obtained $13 million in funding—at an astounding $53 million valuation:* ibid.

67 *Friendster, founded by engineers, wanted to be on the cutting edge of technology:* ibid.

67 *MySpace . . . had no appetite for expensive technology:* David F. Carr, "Inside MySpace.com," *Baseline Magazine,* January 16, 2007; author's interview with Brett Brewer, May 30, 2007.

67 *On September 24 MySpace requested that eUniverse purchase two more Dell servers:* E-mail from Josh Berman to Aber Whitcomb, September 24, 2007.

67 *EUniverse leased the equipment through 0 percent no-cash-down leases:* E-mail from Michael Mincieli to Brad Greenspan, Brett Brewer, and Tom Flahie, September 25, 2003.

67 *"Within a week (or maybe even less time, hard to remember)":* Tom Anderson's MySpace profile, blog post, July 13, 2007.

68 *"I made myself the first friend":* ibid.

68 *his actual birth date, November 8, 1970:* Public records and commercially available data, confirmed by college graduation records and Library of Congress author listing.

68 *Friendster's pages were taking twenty seconds to load:* Patricia Sellers, "MySpace Cowboys," *Fortune,* September 4, 2006.

CHAPTER 8 THE BOARDROOM COUP

69 *eUniverse had $1.9 million in the bank and was losing $300,000 a month:* Author's interview with Brad Greenspan, April 12, 2007.

69 *owed payments that would likely total about $1 million:* ibid.

69 *promised investment of an additional $10 million:* ibid.

69 *In late August eUniverse had finally issued:* Intermix Media Inc., form 10K, filed August 22, 2003.

69 *slashed revenue by $5.9 million and cut net income by $6.1 million:* ibid.

69 *making just $553,000 on sales of $65.7 million:* ibid.

69 *shares had climbed above $2 a share:* ibid.

69 *invest at a valuation of only $1.33 a share:* ibid

70 *Greenspan didn't like the fact that Garrick planned to continue living:* Author's interview with Brad Greenspan, April 12, 2007.

70 *"George isn't an operator":* ibid.

70 *prevented him from raising more than $2.5 million:* Intermix Media Inc., form 10K, filed August 22, 2003.

70 *DeWolfe and his team had been patiently awaiting their earnout:* Author's interview with Brad Greenspan, April 12, 2007.

70 *owed about $500,000 by the end of October:* ibid.

70 *MySpace could get 10 percent of MySpace's after-tax profits for three years:* E-mail from Brad Greenspan to Chris DeWolfe, October 7, 2003.

70 *On October 6 Tom Flahie was appointed chief financial officer:* Intermix Media Inc., form 10Q, filed on November 13, 2003.

70 *"We're not forming one more new entity!":* Author's interview with Brett Brewer, April 9, 2007.

70 *On October 9 VantagePoint sent a letter:* Author's interview with Brad Greenspan, April 12, 2007.

70 *The venture capitalists wanted to extend the deadline to October 17:* ibid.

71 *ThinkEquity was willing to raise $2.5 million at $1.85 a share:* eUniverse, "Board Notes," October 14, 2003.

71 *VantagePoint was offering to invest $8 million at $1.33 a share:* Intermix Media, Inc., form DEF 14A, filed December 30, 2003.

71 *biggest individual shareholder in eUniverse, with a 21.3 percent stake:* ibid.

71 *would provide VantagePoint with the right to block eUniverse:* Intermix Media Inc., form 10-K, filed June 15, 2004.

71 *on his way to the Direct Marketing Association conference in Orlando:* E-mail from Chris DeWolfe to Brad Greenspan, October 12, 2003.

71 *thought his team should get 100 percent of the MySpace assets in return for forgiving the $500,000 owed to ResponseBase:* ibid.

71 *"Although MySpace revenue model is unproven, we are excited about the project":* ibid.

71 *"smaller than the X-10":* abuse_report, "Wireless Video Camera—Smaller than the X-10," Usenet posting in news.admin.net-abuse.sightings, September 6, 2003, 4:10 a.m.

72 *"We have quite a bit planned for XoomDigital":* E-mail from Chris DeWolfe to Brad Greenspan, October 12, 2003.

72 *"tenable solution that could be a win-win for everyone":* ibid.

72 *On October 16 Greenspan presented the idea of his alternative investment:* Author's interview with Brad Greenspan, April 12, 2007.

72 *"Because of the company's cash position":* eUniverse, "Board Notes," October 16, 2003.

72 *On October 17 he proposed a new slate for the coming year:* Author's interview with Brad Greenspan, April 12, 2007.

72 *the* Los Angeles Business Journal *wrote an article pointing out that Moreau had a spotty track record:* RiShawn Biddle, "Facing Restatements, eUniverse Turns to Venture Group Veteran," *Los Angeles Business Journal,* July 7, 2003.

72 *nominated a new slate of directors who he said would "upgrade the quality of the board":* Author's interview with Brad Greenspan, April 12, 2007.

72 *he became irate and threatened to resign:* eUniverse, "Board Notes," October 16, 2003.

72 *David Carlick flew to Los Angeles on Tuesday, October 22:* Author's interview with Brad Greenspan, April 12, 2007.

73 *"We have other financing":* Author's interview with David Carlick, May 10, 2007.

73 *"The people at VantagePoint":* Author's interview with David Carlick, January 9, 2008.

73 *"You can invest on the same terms as the new offering":* Author's interview with Brad Greenspan, April 12, 2007.

73 *"We will consider legal options":* ibid; author's interview with David Carlick, January 9, 2008.

73 *"Get out of my office!":* Author's interview with David Carlick, May 10, 2007.

73 *"I'm not going to do your deal":* Author's interview with Brett Brewer, August 1, 2007.

73 *Carlick walked downstairs:* Author's interview with David Carlick, January 9, 2008.

73 *Moreau did not want to be seen:* ibid.

73 *The two drove off:* Author's interview with David Carlick, May 10, 2007.

73 *Edell . . . had just joined the eUniverse board two weeks earlier:* Author's interview with Jeff Edell, May 4, 2007.

73 *"I pledge to try not to get so hot around the collar":* E-mail from Brad Greenspan to Jeff Edell, October 21, 2003.

74 *"If you change those things in your deal by Monday":* Author's interview with Jeff Edell, May 4, 2007.

74 *That night, Carlick and Brett Brewer had dinner:* Author's interview with Brett Brewer, August 1, 2007.

74 *such violent mood swings were part of Greenspan's character:* Author's interview with David Carlick, January 9, 2007.

74 *Carlick said that VantagePoint would not wire money:* ibid.

74 *Brewer discussed the problem:* Author's interview with Brett Brewer, August 1, 2007.

74 *"At that point, I would have made him best man at my wedding":* Author's interview with Adam Goldenberg, May 3, 2007.

74 *By Friday, October 23, Greenspan had $2.3 million in escrow:* Author's interview with Brad Greenspan, April 12, 2007.

74 *negotiate an improved compensation package for himself with eUniverse board member Dan Mosher:* Author's interview with Dan Mosher, June 20, 2007.

75 *On Monday, October 27, a carefully orchestrated coup at eUniverse was set in motion:* Author's interview with Brad Greenspan, April 12, 2007; eUniverse, "Board Notes," October 27, 2003.

75 *"Wait a minute, Brad. Isn't there something you need to tell us?":* Author's interview with Jeff Edell, May 4, 2007.

75 *Greenspan realized that they must all be in it together:* Author's interview with Brad Greenspan, April 12, 2007.

75 *"You need to send your proposal to the board in the next hour":* Author's interview with Jeff Edell, May 4, 2007.

75 *He needed one of the fund's two directors to sign the eUniverse financing term sheet before he could send it over:* Author's interview with David Carlick, May 10, 2007.

75 *"Look, this thing has been agreed to six ways from Sunday!":* ibid.

76 *"I've just received the proposal from VantagePoint":* Author's interview with Brad Greenspan, April 12, 2007.

76 *He realized it had all been well thought out:* ibid.

76 *"This is fraud":* ibid.

76 *Edell asked another board member, Dan Mosher, to call VantagePoint:* eUniverse, "Board Notes," October 27, 2003.

76 *The $2.5 million that Greenspan wanted to raise from ThinkEquity would only be a "temporary and inadequate solution to the company's liquidity crisis":* ibid.

76 *Greenspan argued that eUniverse was endangering the company:* Author's interview with Brad Greenspan, April 12, 2007.

76 *The board should accept the $2.5 million "to avoid a further drop in share price":* ibid.

76 *"You are trying to become CEO of this company":* ibid.

76 *signed all the documents approving the $2.5 million ThinkEquity financing:* ibid.

76 *Greenspan took his top executives, Brewer, Lipp, Flahie, and Goldenberg:* ibid.

77 *"Tonight he played all the cards":* E-mail from Jeff Edell to independent board members, October 28, 2003.

77 *Josh Berman sent an e-mail to eUniverse's controller:* E-mail from Josh Berman to Michael Mincieli, October 29, 2007.

77 *In the six months ending in September:* Author's interview with a person familiar with the situation.

77 *ResponseBase also had a relatively large staff of thirty-six employees:* Author's interview with a person familiar with the situation.

77 *Flahie suggested that MySpace's assets should be divided into thirds:* Author's interview with Brett Brewer, April 9, 2007.

77 *The next day, Friday, eUniverse finalized the VantagePoint agreement:* Intermix Media Inc., form 10-K, filed June 15, 2004.

77 *The board offered Greenspan a package:* Author's interview with Brad Greenspan, April 12, 2007.

77 *his favorite sushi joint, Tengu:* Author's interview with Brett Brewer, August 1, 2007.

77 *"You lost me millions of dollars of options":* Author's interview with Adam Goldenberg, May 3, 2007.

77 *"Are you fucking joking?":* Author's interview with Brett Brewer, August 1, 2007; author's interview with Adam Goldenberg, November 12, 2007.

78 *To Goldenberg, it was ludicrous for Greenspan to be quibbling:* Author's interview with Adam Goldenberg, November 12, 2007.

78 *"To hell with this":* Author's interview with Brett Brewer, August 1, 2007; author's interview with Adam Goldenberg, November 12, 2007.

78 *"Forget it":* ibid.

78 *alleging that the directors breached their fiduciary duty in accepting the Vantage-Point financing:* Intermix Media Inc., form 10-K, filed June 15, 2004.

78 *Greenspan launched an aggressive proxy contest against eUniverse:* ibid.

78 *Greenspan argued that eUniverse's preferred shareholders:* Brad Greenspan, "Solicitation in Opposition to Management at the 2003 Annual Meeting of Stockholders of eUniverse," 2003.

79 *Brewer argued to investors that their only hope of recouping:* Author's interview with Brett Brewer, April 9, 2007.

79 *"Greenspan wanted to protect his job, not your investment":* Intermix Media Inc., form DEFA 14A, filed January 7, 2004.

CHAPTER 9 THE FIX-IT-LATER PHILOSOPHY

80 *On November 4, 2003, Tom Anderson was exhausted:* Tom Anderson, "PacMan Last Night," Tom's Blog, MySpace.com, November 4, 2003.

80 *"Hey folks. I'm going to Hong Kong":* Tom Anderson, "Leaving for Hong Kong," Tom's Blog, MySpace.com, October 20, 2003.

80 *MySpace put up a game of Pac-Man:* Tom Anderson, "PacMan Last Night," Tom's Blog, MySpace.com, November 4, 2003.

81 *"Starting around 6:00pm last night":* ibid.

81 *"Get it out fast, fix it later":* Aber Whitcomb at Web 2.0 Summit, October 17, 2007.

81 *Peter Amiri, who was hired in October:* Author's interview with Peter Amiri, October 24, 2007.

81 *"When I joined":* ibid.

81 *"We would push it out":* ibid.

81 *After numerous debates:* ibid.

82 *"Fine, send me the code":* ibid.

82 *"Okay, I'll get the developer to build it":* ibid.

82 We just spent forty-five minutes arguing about code: ibid.

82 *"Not sure how long I can keep going":* Tom Anderson, "Ooh I'm tired," Tom's Blog, MySpace.com, October 16, 2003.

82 *"Hey Folks—The site was a little slow":* Tom Anderson, MySpace news, October 10, 2003.

82 *The first party was organized by MySpace member Gary Sato:* Author's interview with Gary Sato, June 25, 2008.

82 *"YES, I will actually be OFFLINE!":* Tom Anderson, MySpace news, November 7, 2003.

82 *which could hold six hundred people:* Tom Anderson, "MySpace Party Aftermath," Tom's Blog, MySpace.com, November 13, 2003.

82 *was packed:* Author's interview with a person familiar with the situation.

82 *"it was all dudes":* Author's interview with a person familiar with the situation.

82 *on December 5 in New York:* Tom Anderson, MySpace news, September 19, 2003.

83 *"I'm going to Miami":* Tom Anderson, "Party in Miami on Monday," Tom's Blog, MySpace.com, January 16, 2004.

83 *"So, Floridians, please discuss amongst yourselves":* ibid.

83 *On New Years Eve 2003:* Bill Jensen, "Hard Core and Bleeding," *Miami New Times,* May 20, 2004.

83 *RJ's roommates came home and found him dead on the floor:* ibid.

83 *it was too late for the police to gather much information:* Author's interview with Jason Feffer, March 6, 2007.

83 *MySpace hadn't captured any information from RJ or Katylynn's pages:* Author's interview with Jason Feffer, January 9, 2007.

83 *the website needed someone who could help police capture information:* ibid.

83 *volunteered to set up a system of storing files and a twenty-four-hour hotline phone number:* ibid.

83 *"Fef.B.I.":* ibid.

84 *Chris DeWolfe and Josh Berman argued that they were owed about $400,000:* Author's interview with Jeff Edell, January 11, 2008.

84 *EUniverse disputed the figure:* Author's interview with Jeff Edell, May 4, 2007.

84 *"We thought we made a great deal":* Author's interview with Jeff Edell, January 11, 2008.

84 *the board was divided:* Michael Montgomery's interview with Josh Berman, San Diego Venture Group, June 6, 2007.

84 *"Can't we do this with little or no capital?":* Author's interview with Andrew Sheehan, June 19, 2007.

84 *EUniverse and MySpace agreed to jointly create a budget:* Author's interview with Jeff Edell, January 11, 2008.

84 *The agreement also gave MySpace a "put" option:* ibid.

84 *"The other divisions got pissed":* Author's interview with Jeff Rajewski, April 19, 2007.

84 *Finally, in January 2004, as MySpace was nearing its millionth member:* MySpace.com timeline.

85 *"We were so proud of taking ten servers":* Author's interview with Peter Amiri, October 24, 2007.

85 *"Prior to that, we were running off of used IBM boxes":* Author's interview with Peter Amiri, October 24, 2007.

85 *DeWolfe and Anderson prowled the Viper Room:* Patricia Sellers, "MySpace Cowboys," *Fortune,* September 4, 2006.

85 *In October 2003 AOL had attracted more than three million listeners to Spears's debut of "Me Against the Music":* "AOL Music: Total Monthly Streams," *Billboard,* December 20, 2003, and "New Britney Spears Single Is America Online's 100th First Listen," Business Wire, October 2, 2003.

85 *DeWolfe and Anderson recruited more than five thousand acts:* PR Newswire, "Indie Bands and Their Fans Flock to MySpace.com," March 18, 2004.

85 *"MySpace is fast becoming what mp3.com should have been":* ibid.

85 *MySpace hired Gabe Harriman:* Author's interview with Gabe Harriman, July 31, 2007.

86 *Harriman worked on the player for three months:* ibid.

86 *"They left me hanging out to dry":* ibid.

86 *MySpace terminated Harriman's status as the first MySpace account:* Author's interview with Duc Chau, June 16, 2007.

86 *Finally, in July:* Author's interview with Gabe Harriman, July 31, 2007.

86 *One of the early bands on MySpace:* "The online phenomenon continues," Billionaire Boys Club Journal, December 11, 2003.

86 *"Friendster is so two months ago":* Leigh Nelson, "Out of Our Box," Billionaire Boys Club Journal, April 13, 2004.

86 *In April Anderson invited the Billionaire Boys Club:* ibid.

86 *"We hung around after the show":* ibid.

86 *"We danced all night":* ibid.

87 *Anderson met someone:* Tom Anderson, "San Francisco Launch Party," Tom's Blog, MySpace.com, May 17, 2004.

87 *Skillet, whose roommate was Michael Vincent:* Author's interview with Michael Vincent, May 9, 2007.

87 *"shooting booty":* ibid.

87 *Vincent would waive his usual $500 fee:* ibid.

87 *"I'm like a mini Hugh Hefner":* ibid.

87 *In June 2004 they embarked on a seventeen-city tour:* ibid.

88 *"We helped create a cool buzz":* ibid.

88 *the site had to start using image review software:* Author's interview with Peter Amiri, October 24, 2007.

88 *"ninety-nine percent of the time you could get a nude image":* ibid.

88 *Rumors were flying:* ibid.

88 *So in April, MySpace developed:* ibid.

88 *But in April Friendster fired:* Professor Mikolaj Jan Piskorski, "Friendster (A)," Harvard Business School case study, February 15, 2007.

88 *"If we had five thousand sign-ups":* Author's interview with Peter Amiri, October 24, 2007.

89 *Sign-ups initially plummeted from ten thousand a day:* ibid.

89 *By July MySpace visitors were viewing more than twice as many:* "MySpace Build or Sell?" MySpace Board Meeting Notes, August 31, 2004.

CHAPTER 10 OPERATION SHOW TIME

90 *Brett Brewer was exhausted:* Author's interview with Brett Brewer, March 30, 2007.

90 *I just can't do this alone anymore:* ibid.

90 *His mind turned to his neighbor:* ibid.

90 *"I just wanted his positive energy":* ibid.

90 *Rosenblatt, then thirty-four:* Author's interview with Richard Rosenblatt, January 7, 2007.

90 *He made his first million:* Author's interview with Richard Rosenblatt, April 2, 2007.

91 *While selling ads for a weekly newspaper:* ibid.

91 *In its peak year, the business earned about $1 million:* ibid.

91 *Rosenblatt went straight to law school at the University of Southern California:* ibid.

91 *By his final year, he was spending more time on the pay phone:* ibid.

91 *Rosenblatt was intrigued by what his father was telling him:* ibid.

91 *In 1994 Rosenblatt's father quit his job:* ibid.

91 *which iMall acquired for $160,000 in stock:* iMall, Inc., form 10QSB, filed on May 20, 1997.

91 *stock opened at $18 and within a few months had soared as high as $112:* iMall, Inc., form SB-2, filed June 30, 1998.

92 *By 1997, however, iMall shares had sunk to $9:* ibid.

92 *"Operation Show Time":* Federal Trade Commission, "Operation Show Time Targets Seminars Selling Fraudulent Business Opportunities," FTC press release, May 5, 1998.

92 *Government regulators were concerned:* Federal Trade Commission, "Complaint for Injunction and Other Equitable Relief, iMall Inc.," legal filing, 1998.

92 *Rosenblatt quickly shut down the seminar business:* iMall Inc., form 8-K, filed September 23, 1998.

92 *In 1999 iMall agreed to pay a $750,000 fine:* ibid.

92 *sell iMall for $425 million:* iMall Inc., form 8-K, filed July 12 1999.

92 *market valuation of $35 billion:* ibid.

92 *the deal was worth only $347 million:* At Home Corporation, form 10-Q, filed October 31, 1999.

92 *Rosenblatt's 16.3 percent stake:* iMall Inc., form DEFS 14A, filed January 12, 1999.

92 *he celebrated by buying himself a Ferrari:* Paul Ollinger's interview with Richard Rosenblatt, "Richard Rosenblatt: How I Sold MySpace," Dog & Pony, Bnet video, 2007.

93 *Commonwealth Associates, which had backed iMall:* Author's interview with Mel Tang, April 10, 2007.

93 *Founded in 1999:* ibid.

93 *agreeing to pay $89 million over four years:* Tamara Straus, "The Demise of Krkoop.com: A Riches to Rags Internet Story," *AlterNet,* April 1, 2000.

93 *with two hundred employees:* Author's interview with Mel Tang, April 10, 2007.

93 *Rosenblatt and Commonwealth raised $27 million:* ibid.

93 *In December 2001 Drkoop.com filed for bankruptcy protection:* Tamara Straus, "The Demise of Krkoop.com: A Riches to Rags Internet Story," *AlterNet,* April 1, 2000.

93 *"It hit me hard":* Author's interview with Richard Rosenblatt, March 8, 2007.

93 *"Ohmigod, this would be so fun":* Author's interview with Brett Brewer, April 9, 2007.

93 *Brewer, perennially hot, kept the thermostat in his office at 63 degrees:* Author's interview with Brett Brewer, January 13, 2008.

94 *"I went back and looked at iMall, and it never had any profits":* Author's interview with Brett Brewer, April 9, 2007.

94 *IMall incurred nearly $20 million in losses:* iMall Inc., form SB2, filed June 30, 1998.

94 *"I don't disagree with you":* Author's interview with Brett Brewer, April 9, 2007.

94 *Rosenblatt's fate was still unresolved when, on January 29:* Author's interview with David Carlick, May 10, 2007.

94 *Greenspan issued his fifteenth letter to shareholders:* Intermix Media Inc., form DFAN 14A, filed January 28, 2004.

94 *"Brett Brewer was not responsible":* ibid.

94 *"Chris Lipp is the lawyer who remained silent":* ibid.

94 *"Don't be fooled by Mr. Greenspan's empty rhetoric":* Intermix Media Inc., form DEFA 14A, filed January 26, 2004.

94 *"Ask yourself, how are Mr. Greenspan's threats in your best interest?":* ibid.

94 *garnered about 18.4 million votes:* Intermix Media Inc., form 10-K, filed June 15, 2004.

95 *During the one-hour phone conversation:* Author's interview with David Carlick, May 10, 2007.

95 *"I fell in love with the guy"*: ibid.

95 *To assure themselves, the board made Rosenblatt take the Myers-Briggs psychological test:* Author's interview with Richard Rosenblatt, January 7, 2007.

95 *Rosenblatt's test showed:* ibid.

95 *When Rosenblatt arrived at the company:* "eUniverse Restructures Operations, Announces Name Change and Provides Fiscal Year 2005 Outlook," by PR Newswire, May 24, 2004.

95 *had been posting losses of about $3 million a quarter:* Intermix Media Inc., form 10-K, filed June 15, 2004.

95 *"Hey, we've put up this site called MySpace.com":* Author's interview with Richard Rosenblatt, November 16, 2006.

95 *"You have my one hundred percent support":* ibid.

CHAPTER 11 ARE WE MISSING THE NEXT GOOGLE?

96 *In March 2004 MySpace claimed to have surpassed:* MySpace press release, "MySpace.com's Market Leadership in Social Networking Category," PR Newswire, March 1, 2004.

96 *"By allowing our users to dictate the features":* MySpace press release, "MySpace.com's Market Leadership in Social Networking Category," PR Newswire, March 1, 2004.

96 *The release obscured the fact:* Nielsen/NetRatings Net View, U.S., Home and Work, January '03 to June '07 Monthly Trend of Various Sites.

96 *with more than one million monthly unique visitors:* "MySpace Build or Sell?" MySpace Board Meeting Notes, August 31, 2004.

96 *with its 756,000 monthly visitors:* ibid.

96 *revenues were paltry—just $135,000 for the month of March:* Author's interview with a person familiar with the situation.

96 *Rosenblatt estimated that MySpace had lost $319,000:* Author's interview with a person familiar with the situation.

97 *for the minuscule price of less than 20 cents per thousand viewers:* Author's interview with a person familiar with the situation.

97 *During his state-of-the-company address to the eUniverse board on April 22, 2004:* Author's interview with a person familiar with the situation.

97 *a new social networking site called Grab.com:* Author's interview with Richard Rosenblatt, May 16, 2008.

97 *Rosenblatt began spending one-third of his time:* ibid.

97 *But MySpace viewed Grab.com as competition:* Author's interview with a person familiar with the situation.

97 *MySpace's ascent caught the eye of David Siminoff:* Author's interview with David Siminoff, October 23, 2007.

97 *Siminoff and the newly installed MatchNet chief executive:* ibid.

98 *Siminoff and Chris DeWolfe met:* ibid.

98 *"You're a suit who is a wannabe rocker":* ibid.

98 *"MySpace is not a direct marketing company":* ibid.

98 *Siminoff was impressed with DeWolfe:* ibid.

98 *Still, MatchNet founder Shapira was enthusiastic:* ibid.

98 *Under the terms of the agreement:* Asset Acquisition Agreement, MySpace Ventures LLC and eUniverse Inc., December 17, 2003.

98 *"ensured the business forever":* Author's interview with Brett Brewer, July 18, 2007.

98 *In the year ending March 31, 2004:* Intermix Media Inc., form 10-K, filed June 15, 2004.

98 *had generated $7 million:* ibid.

99 *also added $1.2 million to eUniverse's losses:* ibid.

99 *In March eUniverse's shares were trading at $2.75:* ibid.

99 *Rosenblatt decided to rename the company Intermix Media:* Author's interview with David Carlick, January 9, 2008.

99 *Hydroderm alone brought in $6.9 million:* ibid. (Form 10-K states that "Revenues from the sale of Dream Shape and Hydroderm products were approximately 15 percent and 24 percent respectively of fiscal year 2004 product marketing segment revenues." And "product marketing segment producing $29.1 million in revenues in fiscal year 2004.")

99 *But the free trial wasn't free:* Los Angeles Better Business Bureau, "Hydroderm, LLC, Company Report," July 11, 2001.

99 *Internet message boards were full of complaints:* Hydroderm "Better than Botox" SCAM, postings on Scam.com, and postings on EssentialDaySpa.com.

99 *After investigating the complaints:* Los Angeles Better Business Bureau, "Hydroderm, LLC, Company Report," July 11, 2001.

99 *Alena's diet pill was also under fire:* "Warning Letter for Weight Loss Products 'Dream Shape,' " FDA letter, March 26, 2004.

99 *"We have reviewed these claims":* ibid.

99 *Intermix sent some clinical substantiation:* Author's interview with Adam Goldenberg, November 12, 2007.

100 *Rosenblatt then reorganized the remaining Intermix divisions:* eUniverse, "eUniverse Restructures Operations, Announces Name Change and Provides Fiscal Year 2005 Outlook," press release, May 24, 2004.

100 *Rosenblatt also sold several unprofitable businesses:* Intermix Media Inc., form 10-K, filed June 15, 2004.

100 *Skill games were legal:* Author's interview with Justin Beckett, May 2, 2007.

100 *Intermix bought his former company:* Intermix Media Inc., form 10-K, filed June 29, 2005.

100 *"We exchanged our ownership in Superdudes for Intermix":* Author's interview with Gerald Cramer, March 26, 2007.

100 *Rosenblatt defended:* Author's interview with Richard Rosenblatt, June 24, 2008.

100 *"It allowed us":* ibid.

100 *"It was bad deal":* Author's interview with Dan Mosher, June 20, 2007.

101 *Intermix board member Andrew Sheehan felt out of place:* Author's interview with Andrew Sheehan, June 19, 2007.

101 *"Hello, Mr. Sheehan":* ibid.

101 *"How did you know who I was?":* ibid.

101 *"Have you heard of MySpace?":* ibid.

101 *"Are you kidding?":* ibid.

101 *Fall Out Boy had just joined MySpace:* Fall Out Boy MySpace profile.

101 *My Chemical Romance, joined MySpace in May:* My Chemical Romance MySpace profile.

101 Three Cheers for Sweet Revenge *hit number one: Billboard,* "Top heatseekers," Information Access Company, June 26, 2004.

101 *"We've got to blow up the MatchNet deal":* Author's interview with Andrew Sheehan, December 17, 2007.

102 *Todd Tappin walked into the Ivy:* Author's interview with Brett Brewer, July 18, 2007.

102 *"I think we can still do the forty million dollars, but it will be primarily all stock":* ibid.

102 *MatchNet . . . it had discovered that its cash reserves were plummeting:* MatchNet, form S-1, filed August 4, 2004.

102 *By the end of the evening, they had convinced themselves:* Author's interview with Brett Brewer, July 18, 2007.

102 *A few weeks later, Tappin quit MatchNet:* Gilbert Alorie, "MatchNet Cancels Offering," *CNET news,* August 13, 2004.

102 *Siminoff's first thought was Geoff Yang:* Author's interview with David Siminoff, October 23, 2007.

102 *Siminoff called up Yang:* Author's interview with Geoff Yang, August 20, 2007.

102 *"Are you guys interested . . . ?":* ibid.

102 *"We're really not":* ibid.

102 *"These guys really need some help":* ibid.

103 *Rosenblatt still wasn't sure:* Author's interview with Dan Mosher, June 20, 2007.

103 *"Do we sell MySpace?":* ibid.

103 *MySpace had 3.3 million members:* ibid.

103 *MySpace lost $600,000:* ibid.

103 *Rosenblatt estimated that it would cost:* ibid.

103 *Intermix could sell MySpace for $50 million:* ibid.

103 *Chris DeWolfe and Josh Berman presented the board with statistics:* ibid.

103 *MySpace employed thirty people:* ibid.

103 *"There are fifteen to twenty features":* ibid.

104 *Rosenblatt pointed out that MySpace was worthwhile:* Author's interview with Richard Rosenblatt, January 3, 2008.

104 *the board hedged its bets:* Author's interview with Dan Mosher, June 20, 2007.

104 *agreeing to spend $350,000 on the new site, Grab.com, and $200,000 on MySpace:* ibid.

104 *thus trimming MySpace's staff to fifteen:* ibid.

104 *Geoff Yang wasn't impressed:* Author's interview with Geoff Yang, August 20, 2007.

104 *"Tell me what you want to be when you grow up":* ibid.

104 Wow: ibid.

104 This guy has espoused a vision: ibid.

105 *In late October Rosenblatt was in his hotel room:* Author's interview with Richard Rosenblatt, July 30, 2007.

105 *"Let's use the MySpace technology":* ibid.

105 *Kagle flew down to Los Angeles:* Author's interview with Andrew Sheehan, June 19, 2007.

105 *wanted to increase the time users spent on Friendster:* Mikolaj Jan Piskorski and Carin-Isabel Knoop, "Friendster A," Harvard Business School case study 9-707-409, revised February 15, 2007.

105 *DeWolfe wasn't impressed:* Author's interview with Richard Rosenblatt, July 30, 2007.

105 *For Rosenblatt, the sticking point was the structure:* Author's interview with Richard Rosenblatt, January 3, 2008.

106 *Friendster was proposing to spin the combined companies:* ibid.

106 *dip below 50 percent:* ibid.

106 *By October MySpace had rocketed to reach 3.4 million visitors:* "Log on, Link up; Social Networking Sites Try to Find New Ways to Keep Users Interested," Verne Kopytoff, *San Francisco Chronicle,* December 13, 2004.

106 *Friendster was stagnant at about 945,000 monthly visitors:* ibid.

106 *"The backers of Friendster would never take less than fifty percent":* Author's interview with David Carlick, January 9, 2008.

106 *By December Yang was ready:* Author's interview with Geoff Yang, August 20, 2007.

106 *In the summer of 2004, the movie studio:* Jennifer Saranow, "Advertisers Seek Friends on Social-Network Sites," Wall Street Journal Online, September 3, 2004.

106 *"It was a no-brainer":* ibid.

106 *In December 2004 Procter & Gamble:* Kevin Kelleher, "A Site Stickier Than a Barroom Floor," *Business 2.0 Magazine,* June 1, 2005.

107 *"We wondered":* ibid.

107 *Satisfied, Yang began negotiating:* Author's interview with Geoff Yang, August 20, 2007.

107 *with its market valuation of about $430 million:* Stephen Baker, "Where the Real Internet Money Is Made," *BusinessWeek,* December. 27, 2004; iVillage, form 10-K, filed March 16, 2005.

107 *Yang thought that would be a home run:* Author's interview with Geoff Yang, August 20, 2007.

107 *He was frustrated with the constraints of working within Intermix:* ibid.

107 *Rosenblatt had hoped that MySpace would be a team player:* Author's interview with Andrew Sheehan, June 19, 2007.

107 *"I want to be independent":* ibid.

107 *"To get full value for MySpace":* Author's interview with Richard Rosenblatt, January 3, 2008.

107 *Rosenblatt would agree to a split-up only if Intermix could benefit:* ibid.

CHAPTER 12 TSUNAMI

108 *his 10,000-square-foot Federal-style beachfront mansion:* Author's interview with a person familiar with the situation; Christina S. N. Lewis, "Rupert Murdoch to Offer Home on Long Island," Real Estate Journal, Wall Street Journal Online, June 18, 2007.

108 *Murdoch, then seventy-three, was not very tech savvy:* Author's interview with a person familiar with the situation.

108 *He asked Robert Thomson:* Author's interview with a person familiar with the situation.

108 *"In a booming economy":* Author's interview with a person familiar with the situation.

108 *"That was a wakeup call":* Author's interview with a person familiar with the situation.

109 *So Murdoch called up one of his employees with Internet experience:* Author's interview with a person familiar with the situation.

109 *the thirty-one-year-old had run several Internet properties in Australia:* Author's interview with a person familiar with the situation.

109 *It was July 1998. Murdoch had gathered his top executives:* Author's interview with a person familiar with the situation.

109 *Murdoch had been married to Anna for thirty years:* William Shawcross, *Murdoch,* Simon & Schuster, 1992.

109 *Anna wasn't just a wife, she was a member of the board:* Author's interview with a person familiar with the situation.

109 *She had an office and an assistant. And most of News Corp.'s top executives knew her personally:* Author's interview with a person familiar with the situation.

109 *At the time, Murdoch was in his late sixties:* Author's interview with a person familiar with the situation.

109 *He started spending time with:* Martin Peers, Julia Angwin, and John Lippman, "Strained Relations: At News Corp.," *Wall Street Journal,* August 1, 2005.

110 *When Murdoch was apologizing:* Author's interview with a News Corp executive familiar with the story.

110 *One year later, the two were married:* Martin Peers, Julia Angwin, and John Lippman, "Strained Relations: At News Corp.," *Wall Street Journal,* August 1, 2005.

110 *He was sixty-eight, she was thirty—younger than his daughter, Elisabeth:* Sally Singer, "A Woman of the World," *Vogue,* March 2008.

110 *At home he turned in his London diet:* Author's interview with a person familiar with the situation.

110 *On his honeymoon in Tuscany:* Caroline Daniel, James Harding, and Ashling O'Connor, "News Corporation the Internet Retreat," *Financial Times,* January 16, 2001.

110 *Yahoo's market value:* Frank Rose, "Rupert Discovers the Internet," *Wired,* issue 8.03, March 2000.

110 *He summoned some of his top executives:* Caroline Daniel, James Harding, and Ashling O'Connor, "News Corporation the Internet Retreat," *Financial Times,* January 16, 2001.

110 *Five years later:* Julia Angwin and Andy Pasztor, "Weaker Reception: Satellite TV Growth Is Losing Altitude as Cable Takes Off—Fewer Viewers Choose Dishes as Earthbound Rivals Offer Phone and Internet Service—Talk of an Industry Merger," *Wall Street Journal,* August 5, 2006.

111 *Murdoch flew to Los Angeles:* Spencer Reiss, "His Space," *Wired* magazine, issue 14.07, July 2006.

111 *Levinsohn joined News Corp. in 2000:* ibid.

111 *Levinsohn, forty-one, was stunned:* ibid.

111 *"Should I buy AskJeeves.com . . . ?":* Author's interview with a person familiar with the situation.

111 *"it would be a bad idea":* Author's interview with a person familiar with the situation.

111 *One month later, Levinsohn stood on the stage:* Author's interview with Michael Wolf, April 25, 2007.

112 *So he turned to McKinsey's top media consultant, Michael Wolf:* ibid.

112 *Orchestrating a companywide strategy was unusual at News Corp.:* ibid.

112 *Well funded by its partnership with Microsoft:* ibid.

112 *"Rupert really wanted to run it himself":* Author's interview with a person familiar with the situation.

112 *in a groundbreaking speech:* Rupert Murdoch, transcript of speech to American Society of Newspaper Editors, April 13, 2005.

113 *"In the face of this revolution":* ibid.

113 *"We've sat by and watched"*: ibid.

113 *"I do not underestimate the tests before us"*: ibid.

113 *"It is a monumental, once-in-a-generation opportunity"*: ibid.

113 *The next day, McKinsey submitted:* McKinsey and Co,. "News Corporation: Developing the Strategy to Win Online," April 14, 2005.

113 *MySpace was mentioned on pages 24 and 25:* ibid.

113 *MySpace was mentioned as a possible "small acquisition"*: ibid.

113 *"Rupert was very clear that existing content would not carry the day"*: Author's interview with Michael Wolf, April 25, 2007.

113 *"When you looked at Yahoo"*: ibid.

114 *"It's great, it's terrific"*: Author's interview with a person familiar with the situation.

114 *The next morning, Levinsohn presented:* Ross Levinsohn, "Interactive Strategy Presentation," May 4, 2005.

114 *"You can't do that!"*: Om Malik, "Sly Fox," *Business 2.0 Magazine,* June 28, 2006.

114 *"Of course we can"*: ibid.

114 *By June he'd compiled his list:* Author's interview with a person familiar with the situation.

114 *Levinsohn presented his list:* Author's interview with a person familiar with the situation.

114 *"Why don't we buy all three . . . ?"*: Author's interview with a person familiar with the situation.

114 *"Can we do that?"*: Author's interview with a person familiar with the situation.

114 *"Sure"*: Author's interview with a person familiar with the situation.

CHAPTER 13 INDEPENDENCE

115 *"Chris, I want to make sure"*: Author's interview with a person familiar with the situation.

115 *"I don't think we can do that"*: Author's interview with a person familiar with the situation.

115 *Rosenblatt wanted the Intermix logo on MySpace's T-shirts:* Author's interview with a person familiar with the situation.

115 *Rosenblatt wanted the Intermix logo on MySpace business cards:* Author's interview with a person familiar with the situation.

115 *But DeWolfe's request:* Author's interview with Andrew Sheehan, June 19, 2007.

115 *He went to Intermix board member Andrew Sheehan:* ibid.

116 *"That was the tipping point"*: ibid.

116 *On November 2, 2004, MySpace signed up its 5 millionth account:* "MySpace corporate timeline," MySpace public relations.

116 *up from just 1 million on February 15:* ibid.

116 *had increased to 3.5 million visitors:* "Intermix Collects $4M for MySpace," Paul Bonanos, TheDeal.com, December 9, 2004.

116 *from just 550,000 monthly visitors:* Author's interview with Dan Mosher, June 20, 2007.

116 *MySpace finally turned a profit:* MySpace board minutes, April 5, 2005.

116 *"I would say MySpace is actually more effective than our real website":* Jason Moon Wilkins, "The Pink Spiders," *Tennessean,* November 11, 2004.

116 *A typical request from MySpace:* Author's interview with Peter Amiri, October 24, 2007.

116 *"By the time we got the request up the ladder":* ibid.

116 *"the site was dying":* ibid.

116 *Every few months, DeWolfe and Josh Berman:* Author's interview with Brett Brewer, November 7, 2007.

117 *25 percent of MySpace to Redpoint for $11.5 million:* Intermix Media Inc., form 10-K, filing for the period ending March 31, 2005.

117 *MySpace was guaranteed a fixed price of $125 million:* ibid.

118 *an unusual agreement that allowed MySpace to block Intermix:* ibid.

118 *Geoff Yang of Redpoint was reluctant:* Author's interview with Geoff Yang, August 20, 2007.

118 *"I didn't want to risk losing the deal":* ibid.

118 *DeWolfe had a nice big office:* Author's visit to office, June 15, 2007.

119 *some employees started storing:* Author's interview with Jason Feffer, March 6, 2007.

119 *The staff began frequenting the happy hours:* ibid.

119 *"People would come in the next morning":* ibid.

119 *Back in July 2004, when MySpace was a small site:* Author's interview with Dan Mosher, June 20, 2007.

119 *"It's growing like a hockey stick":* Author's interview with a person familiar with the situation.

119 *In August 2004, Viacom copresidents:* Author's interview with a person familiar with the situation.

119 *MTV had largely ignored the Internet ever since 2000:* Joseph Gallican, "MTVI Faces the Music; Fired 25% of Staff, Cans Plans for IPO," *Business,* September 28, 2000.

119 *At the Viacom show-and-tell confab, Hirschhorn presented MTV's acquisition wish list:* Author's interview with a person familiar with the situation.

119 *"Go for it":* Author's interview with a person familiar with the situation.

120 *"Listen, we love what you're doing":* Author's interview with a person familiar with the situation.

120 *The MTV executives loved the vibe:* Author's interview with a person familiar with the situation.

120 *MySpace was growing so fast:* Author's interview with a person familiar with the situation.

120 *The Digital Millennium Copyright Act:* Wendy N. Davis, "Downloading a File of Copyright Woes," *ABA Journal,* March 1, 2007.

120 *One of Geoff Yang's partners:* Author's interview with Geoff Yang, August 20, 2007.

120 *"I don't even know":* ibid.

120 *traffic was increasing by about 6 percent a week:* "Users Rediscover the Buzz of Social Networking," press release by Hitwise, February 24, 2005.

120 *twelfth most visited website in the United States:* ibid.

120 *In his twenty years:* Author's interview with Geoff Yang, August 20, 2007.

121 *"Let's go buy it for five or ten million dollars":* ibid.

121 *Zuckerberg, then twenty:* Ellen McGirt, "Hacker. Dropout. CEO," *Fast Company,* issue 115, May 2007.

121 *Facebook was attracting more than one million:* ibid.

121 *growing at an even faster rate:* "Users Rediscover the Buzz of Social Networking," press release by Hitwise, February 24 2005.

121 *a social graph:* "Book Value—Face Value," *The Economist,* July 21, 2007.

121 *Zuckerberg wanted $75 million:* Author's interview with Geoff Yang, August 20, 2007.

121 *"We went on our merry way":* ibid.

122 *On February 11, 2005, MySpace won partial independence:* Intermix Media Inc., form 10-K, filing for the period ending March 31, 2005.

122 *Under the agreement:* "Intermix Completes Previously Announced Investment in MySpace Inc. by Redpoint Ventures," press release, PR Newswire, February 15, 2005.

122 *Redpoint would own 25 percent:* Intermix Media Inc., form 10-K, filing for the period ending March 31, 2005.

122 *also reluctantly agreed to invest $4 million:* Author's interview with Geoff Yang, August 20, 2007.

122 *"We looked at it as an entrance fee":* ibid.

122 *"We were a Los Angeles company":* Joe Nocera's interview with Chris DeWolfe, *New York Times* "Sunday with the Magazine" event, May 20, 2007.

122 *MySpace had amassed three million accounts:* David F. Carr, "Inside MySpace .com," *Baseline Magazine,* January 16, 2007.

122 *"scale up" or "scale out":* ibid.

122 *David Carlick called his friend:* Author's interview with Peter Adams, September 12, 2007.

122 *Adams recommended:* ibid.

123 *"It was really tough medicine":* ibid.

123 *several computers that each stored data for one million:* David F. Carr, "Inside MySpace.com," *Baseline Magazine,* January 16, 2007.

123 *the seventh database:* ibid.

123 *"That became a full-time job for about two people":* ibid.

123 *MySpace was also struggling:* Author's interview with Peter Amiri, October 24, 2007.

123 *"Our servers were melting":* ibid.

123 *So MySpace developed what it called the "four on, four off":* ibid.

123 *transitioning from ColdFusion:* David F. Carr, "Inside MySpace.com," *Baseline Magazine,* January 16, 2007.

123 *Andrew Sheehan, who had joined MySpace's fledgling board, helped MySpace:* Author's interview with Andrew Sheehan, June 19, 2007.

123 *"We were going one hundred miles per hour":* Author's interview with Geoff Yang, August 20, 2007.

123 *Yang thought he had found the perfect candidate:* ibid.

124 *Sullivan . . . got a panicked call:* Author's interview with Bob Sullivan, May 18, 2007.

124 *Sullivan had never heard of MySpace:* Author's interview with Parry Aftab, August 31, 2007.

124 *"Have you heard of MySpace?":* ibid.

124 *"Nobody goes there":* ibid.

124 *6.8 million:* "Behaviors of the Blogosphere: Understanding the Scale, Composition and Activities of Weblog Audiences," comScore Media Metrix, August 2005.

124 *9.6 million:* ibid.

124 *Aftab told Sullivan she didn't think:* Bob Sullivan, "Kids, Blogs and Too Much Information," MSNBC.com, April 29, 2005.

124 *"There are underage kids":* ibid.

124 *"They are engaging in highly provocative conversations":* ibid.

125 *Aftab called MySpace's general counsel:* Author's interview with Parry Aftab, August 31, 2007.

125 *"We want to make sure everybody is safe":* Author's interview with Parry Aftab, December 26, 2007.

125 *Since then, the FTC has taken action:* Federal Trade Commission, "Xanga.com to Pay $1 Million for Violating Children's Online Privacy Protection Rule," Federal Trade Commission press release, September 7, 2006.

125 *Studies show that kids who engage in risky behaviors online:* Michele L. Ybarra, Kimberly J. Mitchell, David Finkelhor, and Janis Wolak, "Internet Prevention Message: Targeting the Right Online Behaviors," *Arch Pediatric and Adolescent Medicine,* vol. 161, February 2007.

125 *New York attorney general Eliot Spitzer forced Yahoo to shut down chat rooms:* Office of the Attorney General, "Agreement Removes and Bars Predators' Chatrooms," Office of the New York State Attorney General press release, October 12, 2005.

126 *One of Aftab's first recommendations was for MySpace to lower:* Author's interview with Parry Aftab, August 31, 2007.

126 *One year earlier, MySpace safety czar Jason Feffer:* Author's interview with Jason Feffer, March 6, 2007.

126 *"Anytime a teen puts their own photo":* Brendan McKenna, "High School Bans Blogging," *Rutland Herald,* March 29, 2005.

126 *13.5 million monthly visitors:* Steve Rosenbush, "Why MySpace Is the Hot Place; This 20-Month-Old Social-Networking Site Has Left Pioneer Friendster Way Behind. Now It's Looking to Cash In on Its Ever-Growing Cachet," *BusinessWeek,* May 31, 2005.

126 *comScore Media Metrix's closely watched list of the top fifty:* "Online Consumers Catch Spring Fever in April," press release by comScore Media Metrix, May 18, 2005.

126 *revenues totaled $1.69 million:* MySpace, "March budget v. actual," presented in May 4, 2005, board meeting.

126 *MySpace projected that within a year:* ibid.

127 *"something akin to the hottest bar in town":* Steve Rosenbush, "Why MySpace Is the Hot Place; This 20-Month-Old Social-Networking Site Has Left Pioneer Friendster Way Behind. Now It's Looking to Cash In on Its Ever-Growing Cachet," *BusinessWeek,* May 31, 2005.

127 *We're crushing it:* ibid.

CHAPTER 14 THE KING OF SPYWARE

128 *In the fall of 2004, New York attorney general Eliot Spitzer:* Author's interview with Ken Dreifach, May 16, 2007.

128 *Earlier in the year, Utah passed the nation's first antispyware law:* Anita Ramasastry, "Can Utah's New Anti-Spyware Law Work?" CNN.com International, June 3, 2004.

128 *In 1999 he was the first state attorney general:* Author's interview with Ken Dreifach, May 16, 2007.

128 *With about fifteen people:* ibid.

128 *the first high-profile spam cases:* Julia Angwin, "Elusive Spammer Sends EarthLink on Long Chase," *Wall Street Journal,* May 7, 2003.

128 *winning more than $3.5 billion in settlements:* Brooke A. Masters, *Spoiling for a Fight: The Rise of Eliot Spitzer,* Times Books, 2006, p. 2.

128 *Ken Dreifach, the chief of the New York attorney general's Internet bureau:* Author's interview with Ken Dreifach, May 16, 2007.

129 *"had both cleaned up their act":* ibid.

129 *christened the space "the Lab":* ibid.

129 *"It was painstaking work":* ibid.

129 *Brookman found his target: Intermix:* ibid.

129 *even defending ResponseBase's cursor spyware:* ibid.

129 *a screen saver called "Hot Jalapeno Dance:"* "The People of the State of New York by Eliot Spitzer Against Intermix Media," filed in Supreme Court of the State of New York, April 18, 2005.

130 *Brookman suspected that Intermix:* Author's interview with a person familiar with the situation.

130 *"there's considerable incentive":* Author's interview with Ken Dreifach, May 16, 2007.

130 *So on December 3 Brookman sent a letter:* References in letter to Justin Brookman from Manatt, Phelps & Phillips LLP, December 23, 2004.

130 *When Spitzer's request arrived:* Author's interview with a person familiar with the situation.

130 *On December 23 Goldstein's associate sent Brookman:* references in letter to Justin Brookman from Manatt, Phelps & Phillips LLP, December 23, 2004.

130 *At the same time, Intermix sent all of its download partners:* references in letter to Justin Brookman from Manatt, Phelps & Phillips LLP, February 16, 2005.

131 *Intermix also turned over to Spitzer's office boxes:* Office of the New York Attorney General, "Review of Documents Obtained Under the New York State Freedom of Information Law #07180," October 2, 2007.

131 *"Operation Super Trojan":* E-mail from Brad Greenspan to Adam Goldenberg and Brett Brewer. Subject: Operation Super Trojan, October 31, 2002, 8:35 p.m.

131 *"Goal: get deeply integrated":* ibid.

131 *In February Intermix squeaked out its third consecutive profitable quarter:* Q2 2005 Intermix Media Inc., Earnings Conference Call transcript, Fair Disclosure Wire, February 7, 2005.

131 *$12.4 million in the quarter:* "Q3 2005 Intermix Media Inc., Earnings Conference Call," Fair Disclosure Wire, February 7, 2005.

131 *"Alena utilizes a technology-driven marketing solution":* ibid.

132 *a quarterly net income of $38,000:* ibid.

132 *The correspondence between Spitzer's office and Intermix:* Author's interview with Ken Dreifach, May 16, 2007.

132 *Intermix was quietly pressuring one of its download partners:* "The People of the State of New York by Eliot Spitzer Against Intermix Media," filed in Supreme Court of the State of New York, April 18, 2005.

132 *Acez had earned $173,810:* ibid.

132 *Sambrook told Intermix that he wanted to terminate the relationship:* ibid.

132 *"I just hate for you to give up all the revenue":* ibid.

132 *"I just don't see how anyone did anything wrong":* ibid.

132 *The final straw came in mid-March:* Author's interview with a person familiar with the situation.

132 *"This is bizarre":* Author's interview with Ken Dreifach, May 16, 2007.

132 *"Let's draft the papers":* ibid.

132 *On April 5 he mailed:* Certified letter from Justin Brookman to Manatt, Phelps & Phillips LLP, April 5, 2005.

133 *Rosenblatt and Lipp called Ken Dreifach:* Author's interview with Ken Dreifach, May 16, 2007.

133 *"It was a little too late":* ibid.

133 *Late on Tuesday night, April 12:* Intermix Media, "Intermix Media Expects to Report Record Fiscal Year 2005 Fourth Quarter Revenue and Provides a Forecast for Fiscal Year 2006," Intermix Media Inc. press release, April 12, 2005.

133 *The company's stock price plunged from $8 to $4 per share:* Intermix Media Inc., form 10-K, filed June 29, 2005.

133 *"Eliot Spitzer is turning up the heat":* Spencer Ante, "Spitzer's Spreading Spyware Net," *BusinessWeek,* May 5, 2005.

133 *The penny-stock blog:* CitronResearch, "Stocklemon Reports on Intermix Media (MIX) Part 3," Citron Reports, June 15, 2005.

133 *AOL's Advertising.com subsidiary pulled its ads:* Author's interview with Brett Brewer, January 13, 2008.

133 *DeWolfe was incensed:* Author's interview with Geoff Yang, August 21, 2007.

133 *He called AOL:* Author's interview with Brett Brewer, September 18, 2007.

133 *Still, DeWolfe estimated that MySpace lost:* E-mail from Chris DeWolfe to Geoff Yang, Andy Sheehan, and Richard Rosenblatt, May 17, 2005.

133 *"To me, the obvious thing":* Author's interview with a person familiar with the situation.

134 *Hirschhorn had no authority:* Author's interview with a person familiar with the situation.

134 *Rosenblatt decided his only option:* Author's interview with Richard Rosenblatt, March 8, 2007.

134 *Rosenblatt knew it was important to settle with regulators:* ibid.

134 *Two days later, on April 14, Intermix celebrated:* Author's interview with Brett Brewer, August 3, 2007.

134 *"Spitzer has offered to settle the case":* ibid.

134 *Rosenblatt and Brewer were shocked:* Author's interview with Richard Rosenblatt, July 30, 2007.

134 *Intermix's global profits from downloads:* Office of the New York State Attorney General, "Consent and Stipulation in the Case of *the People of the State of New York vs Intermix, Inc.,*" September 2005.

134 *"Are you sitting down?":* Author's interview with Richard Rosenblatt, July 30, 2007.

134 *"No, I'm driving":* ibid.

134 *"Well, you better pull over":* ibid.

135 *"Eliot Spitzer wants fifty million dollars":* ibid.

135 *Spitzer had read the Internet division's case:* Author's interview with a person familiar with the situation.

135 *Intermix had only about $7.5 million in cash:* Author's interview with Richard Rosenblatt, September 24, 2007.

135 *He started to think:* Author's interview with Richard Rosenblatt, July 30, 2007.

135 *On April 29, one day after Spitzer filed his lawsuit:* Intermix Media Inc., form DEFM14A, filed August 25, 2005.

135 *Rosenblatt met with Los Angeles investment banker Michael Montgomery:* Author's interview with Richard Rosenblatt, July 30, 2007.

135 *Montgomery advised Rosenblatt:* Author's interview with Michael Montgomery, May 5, 2007.

135 *Rosenblatt met several times:* Author's interview with Richard Rosenblatt, September 24, 2007.

135 *It was a prescient decision:* Martin Williams, "Livedoor's Horie, Other Executives Indicted," IDG News Service, February 14, 2006.

135 *AOL was trying to become a portal:* Author's interview with a person familiar with the situation.

136 *"Mix majority ownership of MySpace":* MySpace board meeting minutes, May 4, 2005.

136 *had shut off MySpace's ad revenues to the tune of $500,000:* ibid.

136 *"Some reporters are mentioning MySpace":* ibid.

136 *"Mix will realize a higher return on their investment":* ibid.

136 *many of them were ResponseBase insertion orders:* Office of the New York Attorney General, "Review of Documents Obtained Under the New York State Freedom of Information Law #07180," October 2, 2007.

137 *"So, are you here to learn about MySpace . . . ?":* Author's interview with Richard Rosenblatt, January 3, 2008.

137 *"Well, let me tell you why you ought to be here":* Author's interview with Shawn Colo, December 11, 2007.

137 He could easily have spent fifteen minutes: ibid.

137 *"I don't think this makes sense":* ibid.

137 *No one wanted to pay more than $4:* Author's interview with Richard Rosenblatt, July 30, 2007.

137 *shares had just sunk to a low of $3.20:* Intermix Media Inc., form DEFM14A, filed August 25, 2005.

138 *On May 17, the day after Rosenblatt's speech:* E-mail from Chris DeWolfe to Geoff Yang, Andy Sheehan, and Rich Rosenblatt, May 17, 2005.

138 *In the e-mail, DeWolfe claimed:* ibid.

138 *As you all know:* E-mail from Richard Rosenblatt to Chris DeWolfe, Geoff Yang, Andy Sheehan, and Chris Lipp, May 18, 2005.

138 *"You are going to put our company out of business":* Author's interview with Richard Rosenblatt, July 30, 2007.

138 *Rosenblatt offered to give Spitzer all the money:* ibid.

138 *Intermix agreed to pay $7.5 million over three years:* Intermix Media Inc., schedule 14A, 2005.

139 *October Brad Greenspan agreed to pay:* Office of the New York State Attorney General, "Internet Exec Held Accountable for Adware, Spyware," Office of the New York State Attorney General press release, October 20, 2005.

139 *Greenspan also donated $50,000 to the antispyware efforts at the Center for Democracy and Technology:* Center for Democracy and Technology, "Brad Greenspan Grants $50,000 to CDT to Fund Anti-spyware Efforts," CDT press release, June 28, 2005.

CHAPTER 15 SCHMUCK INSURANCE

140 *from 5.8 million unique visitors:* "Intermix Announces Record Third Quarter Revenues Company Increases Revenue Forecast for Fiscal Year 2005," PR Newswire, February 7, 2005.

140 *to 11.3 million:* Gary Rivlin, "Skeptics Take Another Look at Social Sites," *New York Times,* May 9, 2005.

140 *attracting 15.6 million unique visitors:* " 'The Force' Draws Millions to Online Movie Ticket Merchants in May comScore Media Metrix Rankings Reflect Impact of Latest *Star Wars* Release, Mother's Day and Other Spring Events," PR Newswire, June 16, 2005.

140 *About.com with its twenty-two million monthly visitors:* "Times Company to Buy About.com for $410 Million," *New York Times,* February 17, 2005.

140 *sold to the* New York Times: Seth Sutel, "NY Times Buys About.com for $410 million," *USA Today,* February 18, 2005.

140 *for $410 million in cash:* "Times Company to Buy About.com for $410 Million," *New York Times,* February 17, 2005.

140 *Shopping.com with twenty-two million monthly visitors:* James Niccolai, "EBay Buys Shopping.com for $620 Million," Industry Standard, June 2, 2005.

140 *sold to eBay:* AFX News Limited, "Ebay snaps up Shopping.com for $620 million-UPDATE 2, Forbes.com, June, 1, 2005.

140 *for $620 million in cash:* James Niccolai, "EBay buys Shopping.com for $620 Million," The Industry Standard, June 2, 2005.

140 *Shopzilla, with fourteen million monthly visitors:* "E. W. Scripps Buys Shopzilla for $525M," socialTECH.com: news, June 7, 2005.

140 *sold to E.W. Scripps:* Louise Story, "E.W. Scripps to Buy Shopzilla," *New York Times,* June 7, 2005.

140 *for $525 million in cash:* "E. W. Scripps Buys Shopzilla for $525M," socialTECH.com: news, June 7, 2005.

140 *In February, when MySpace obtained financing:* Intermix Media Inc., form 10-K, filed June 29, 2005.

141 *Under the terms of the option agreement:* ibid.

141 *Time Warner chief executive Richard Parsons employed:* Tom Lowry, "Dick Parsons on the 'Urge to Merge,' " *BusinessWeek,* December 22, 2003.

141 *"I like to call it schmuck insurance":* ibid.

141 *But the MySpace option was to expire in February:* Intermix Media Inc., form 10-K, filed June 29, 2005.

141 *And Intermix could not exercise its option:* ibid.

141 *On June 9 banker Michael Montgomery presented:* Intermix Media Inc., form DEFM14A, filed August 25, 2005.

141 *Montgomery calculated that MySpace would have to sell:* Author's interview with Michael Montgomery, October 15, 2007.

142 *Two things could prevent Intermix:* ibid.

142 *"There's no way we can talk to Viacom":* ibid.

142 *"The sale has to be very carefully done":* ibid.

142 *Legally, in fact, he would be breaching his fiduciary duty:* Author's interview with Richard Rosenblatt, July 14, 2008.

142 *In 1986 the Delaware Chancery Court handed down a landmark opinion: Revlon v. MacAndrews & Forbes Holdings Inc.,* 506 A.2d 173 (Del. March 13, 1986).

142 *Montgomery determined that he could satisfy:* Author's interview with Michael Montgomery, October 15, 2007.

142 *Under Delaware corporate law, the directors of a majority shareholder:* Martin Sikora, "Delaware Court Sends a Message to Controlling Shareholders: Ruling in the Digex Case Warns About Treatment of Minority Owners in Takeover Offers," *Mergers and Acquisitions: The Dealmakers Journal,* April 1, 2001.

143 *Montgomery's view was that other bidders:* Author's interview with Michael Montgomery, October 15, 2007.

143 *"I wanted a binding offer that put the company in play":* ibid.

143 *Montgomery already had in mind the idea of a buyer for Intermix:* ibid.

143 *Google had gone public the previous year:* Google Investor Relations, "When was Google's initial public offering and at what price?" Google Investor FAQ.

143 *and by July 2005 it was trading at around $280 per share:* Google Finance. Historical Stock Quotes, Google.

143 *Josh Berman, MySpace's chief operating officer:* Author's interview with Richard Rosenblatt, October 31, 2007.

143 *Montgomery set up a matchmaking meeting:* Author's interview with Michael Montgomery, October 15, 2007.

144 *On June 23 Montgomery and Rosenblatt:* Intermix Media Inc., form DEFM14A, filed August 25, 2005.

144 *"We'd consider working with Fox":* Author's interview with a person familiar with the situation.

144   *"we should just acquire you guys"*: Author's interview with a person familiar with the situation.

144   *"Name ur next kid rich"*: E-mail from Richard Rosenblatt to Andrew Sheehan, June 23, 2005.

144   *At the five o'clock MySpace board meeting on June 30:* E-mail from Richard Rosenblatt to Ross Levinsohn and Mike Lang, June 30, 2005. "June 30, 2005 From: Richard Rosenblatt To: Ross Levinsohn, Mike Lang CC: Montgomery, Chris Lipp Ross and Mike—Coincidentally my 5pm MySpace board meeting centered around the Intermix option and management's request for us to forgo that option and all focus on building Myspace into a public multi-billion dollar company. They believe that the option restricts their hiring of a world-class CTO and CFO. Obviously, we did not agree to the relinquishment of our options and Josh (COO) suggested that they simply call Viacom and Yahoo and ask them to send their offers. I told them to do whatever they needed to do and we understand the situation. I then spoke at length with Chris DeWolfe and we decided that Chris, myself, Mike and Ross should meet next Wednesday at Montgomery's office for a couple hours to see if we all have the same vision (essential for both myself and Chris) and see if we can structure a deal that suits everyone. Chris very much appreciated that both Intermix and Fox wanted to meet with him and discuss his role and his team's corp instead of just exercising the option. I also made him aware that we all needed to be open to ideas because we *could* simply sell Intermix to some media company and management would end up with an illiquid of 47% of a major subsidiary which is the worse case scenario. Chris and I continue to be on the same page and our conversation was very constructive and positive. In fact, I am quite relieved and this should make us all determine if there is a deal or not much quicker—and if we can not form a deal our strategy discussions will help us partner in the future. Can you both check if Wednesday can work for both of you. Thanks, RR"

144   *"They believe that the option restricts their hiring"*: ibid.

144   *Josh Berman, always the hotheaded one:* Author's interview with a person familiar with the situation.

144   *"Do whatever you need to do"*: E-mail from Richard Rosenblatt to Ross Levinsohn and Mike Lang, June 30, 2005.

144   *"I also made him aware that we all needed to be open"*: ibid.

145   *"Chris very much appreciated"*: ibid.

145   *"Chris and I continue to be on the same page"*: ibid.

145   *"My kids are bringing friends, so I will be working"*: E-mail from Richard Rosenblatt to Andrew Sheehan, July 1, 2005.

145   *It was Thomas Weisel:* Author's interview with Richard Rosenblatt, April 2, 2007.

145   *Weisel's friend Michael Dolan had just been appointed:* Author's interview with Thomas Weisel and Blake Warner, November 15, 2007.

145 *"Viacom realizes Intermix controls MySpace":* ibid.

145 *"Great, I'd love to meet Viacom":* ibid.

145 *My advise [sic], ignore him:* E-mail from Michael Montgomery to Richard Rosenblatt, July 2, 2005.

145 *"The Game is on!":* E-mail from Richard Rosenblatt to Ross Levinsohn, July 10, 2005.

CHAPTER 16 THE GAME IS ON

146 *On Tuesday July 5, 2005:* Christopher Smith, "Sun Valley Airport to Give Moguls' Jets Priority," Associated Press Newswires, July 1, 2005.

146 *Other attendees of the exclusive conference:* Tim Arango, "Media Bigs Are Cleared for Landing in Sun Valley," *New York Post,* July 6, 2005; Tim Arango, "Big Wigs On Guard—Security Concern at Moguls' Confab," *New York Post,* July 8, 2005.

146 *the conversation turned to the same topics:* "Media Moguls Gather for Annual Sun Valley Conference," *Dow Jones International News,* July 3, 2005.

146 *"The age of the conglomerate is over":* "Viacom's Redstone Says Conglomerate Model Broken," Reuters News, July 8, 2005.

146 *as the guests wandered into the ski lodge for a seven o'clock breakfast:* Author's interview with a person familiar with the situation.

146 *Sony chief executive Howard Stringer:* Joshua Chaffin, "Companies International: Moguls Seek Solace in Sun Valley," *Financial Times,* July 11, 2005.

146 *Murdoch, whose older children, James and Liz:* Author's interview with a person familiar with the situation.

147 *"We want to buy three Internet companies":* Author's interview with a person familiar with the situation.

147 *"Great, go do it":* Author's interview with a person familiar with the situation.

147 *"We've only got a forty-eight- to seventy-two-hour head start":* Author's interview with a person familiar with the conversation.

147 *"I have always wanted to be number one":* Clayton Hirst, "The Lowdown— 'Mr. Viacom' Says—Bring on Rupert Murdoch," *Independent on Sunday,* July 15, 2001.

148 *During the summer of 2005, the two men were reacting very differently:* ibid.

148 *The problem was that Redstone:* ibid.

148 *His two deputies, Tom Freston of MTV and Leslie Moonves of CBS:* ibid.

148 *Rosenblatt was making the same presentation to Viacom:* E-mail from Richard Rosenblatt to Michael Montgomery, July 7, 2005.

148 *Montgomery believed that it would be difficult to negotiate with Viacom:* Author's interview with Michael Montgomery, October 15, 2007.

149 *"You need to dance with them":* E-mail from Michael Montgomery to Richard Rosenblatt, July 6, 2005.

149   *"I love Ross":* E-mail from Richard Rosenblatt to Michael Montgomery, July 7, 2005.

149   *MTV had nine executives present:* E-mail from Richard Rosenblatt to Michael Montgomery, July 7, 2005.

149   *Joseph Ianniello, who had just been appointed:* "Joseph Ianniello Named Senior Vice President and Treasurer of Viacom," PR Newswire, July 29, 2007.

149   *"We typically use bigger firms":* Author's interview with Thomas Weisel and Blake Warner, November 15, 2007.

149   *Bankers typically charge between 0.5 percent and 1 percent:* ibid.

149   *With Intermix shares trading at about $8:* Intermix Media Inc., form 10-K, filed June 29, 2005.

149   *"We're not in the business just for the marketing benefits":* Author's interview with Thomas Weisel and Blake Warner, November 15, 2007.

149   *"We gave them a golden opportunity to get in on the ground":* ibid.

149   *The MTV executives were shocked:* ibid.

150   *Viacom then scrambled to line up:* ibid.

150   *"Hey, Rich, let us represent you":* ibid.

150   *"Aren't you retained by Viacom?":* Author's interview with Richard Rosenblatt, October 31, 2007.

150   *"No, I would rather be retained by you":* ibid.

150   *it would be nice to have the added credibility:* ibid.

150   *"Not sure it makes sense to have the two banks":* E-mail from Andrew Sheehan to Richard Rosenblatt, July 8, 2005.

150   *Intermix's two sets of bankers began quarreling:* Author's interview with Michael Montgomery, October 15, 2007; author's interview with Thomas Weisel and Blake Warner, November 15, 2007.

150   *"The last thing I wanted was another banker":* Author's interview with Michael Montgomery, October 15, 2007.

150   *"It was very tricky game theory":* ibid.

150   *Weisel Partners team was shocked to learn that News Corp. had information:* Author's interview with Thomas Weisel and Blake Warner, November 15, 2007.

151   *"It would have required somebody with very unique and in-depth knowledge":* ibid.

151   *he only trusted "you and Richard":* E-mail from Mike Lang to Michael Montgomery, July 14, 2005.

151   *On the Tuesday after the Fourth of July weekend:* E-mail from Richard Rosenblatt to Andrew Sheehan, July 1, 2005.

151   *Montgomery's banking team:* Author's interview with Michael Montgomery, October 15, 2007.

151   *James Min estimated that in the year ending December 31, 2005:* E-mail from James Min to Sherman Atkinson, July 6, 2005.

151   *"discuss the best approach to Chris DeWolfe the following morning":* E-mail from Richard Rosenblatt to Andrew Sheehan, July 1, 2005.

151 *"Obviously this meeting is":* E-mail from Richard Rosenblatt to Mike Lang and Ross Levinsohn, July 1, 2005.

152 *"We're thinking of doing":* Author's interview with Richard Rosenblatt, September 24, 2007.

152 *Levinsohn and DeWolfe met at ten o'clock:* E-mail from Richard Rosenblatt to Andrew Sheehan, July 1, 2005.

152 *The meeting was meant to be a high-level discussion:* Author's interview with Michael Montgomery, October 15, 2007.

152 *DeWolfe sat quietly:* ibid.

152 *"If you really want to do this":* ibid.

152 *"You know, I've been thinking":* ibid.

152 *"Don't think of us as a big, stodgy media company":* Patricia Sellers, "MySpace Cowboys," *Fortune,* September 4, 2006.

153 *"Ross is fired up":* E-mail from Richard Rosenblatt to Michael Montgomery, July 6, 2005.

153 *"DeWolfe is in":* ibid.

153 *"All, On our last board meeting":* E-mail from Richard Rosenblatt to Brett Brewer, David Carlick, and Dan Mosher, July 6, 2005.

153 *On Friday, July 8:* Author's interview with Andrew Left, owner of Stock lemon.com, September 19, 2007.

153 *"Stocklemon believes that Intermix Media":* "Stocklemon Reports on Intermix Media Part II," Stocklemon.com, June 13, 2005.

153 *Left attributed his reversal:* Author's interview with Andrew Left, owner of Stocklemon.com, September 19, 2007.

153 *"One day I woke up, and there were fourteen or fifteen stories":* ibid.

154 *"We are sweetening our 'lemon' assessment":* "A Tale of Two Companies," Stock lemon.com, July 8, 2005.

154 *Within two days:* Historical Intermix stock quotes from Sungard.com.

154 *Intermix shares had soared to nearly $10, up from about $8:* Intermix Media Inc., form PREM14A, filed August 12, 2005.

154 *Ross Levinsohn was furious:* Author's interview with a person familiar with the situation.

154 *Intermix's market value had shot up to nearly $441 million from about $350 million:* ibid. Based on 44,112,135 common shares outstanding.

154 *his goal of selling Intermix for $12 per share:* Author's interview with Richard Rosenblatt, April 12, 2007.

154 *Rupert Murdoch and Peter Chernin arrived:* E-mail from Ross Levinsohn to Richard Rosenblatt, July 10, 2005.

154 *Murdoch . . . was undaunted by Intermix's increased stock price:* Author's interview with a person familiar with the situation.

154 *Chernin was mulling tactics:* Author's interview with a person familiar with the situation.

154 *Chernin also believed that Geoff Yang:* Author's interview with a person familiar with the situation.

155 *"Left u a voicemail":* E-mail from Richard Rosenblatt to Ross Levinsohn, July 12, 2005.

155 *Von [sic] just called w lots of luv:* E-mail from Richard Rosenblatt to Sherman Atkinson, July 12, 2005.

155 *Too funny:* E-mail from Sherman Atkinson to Richard Rosenblatt, July 12, 2005.

155 *Murdoch issued what is known in the industry as an "exploding offer":* Author's interview with Richard Rosenblatt, April 2, 2007.

CHAPTER 17 PROJECT IVORY

156 *On Thursday, July 14, 2005:* E-mail from Richard Rosenblatt to Ross Levinsohn, July 14, 2007.

156 *"Things are moving really fast":* Author's interview with Richard Rosenblatt, December 16, 2006.

156 *"We're going to do a deal by Sunday":* ibid.

156 *Freston, a seasoned business executive:* Author's interview with Richard Rosenblatt, October 30, 2007.

156 *Freston had approved Viacom to bid:* Author's interview with a person familiar with the situation.

157 *"If it's moving that quickly":* Author's interview with Richard Rosenblatt, November 15, 2006.

157 *"No one believed it except me and Murdoch":* Author's interview with Richard Rosenblatt, October 30, 2007.

157 *"The one big issue":* E-mail from Mike Lang to Michael Montgomery, July 14, 2005.

157 *under the terms of the MySpace option:* Author's interview with Andrew Sheehan, June 19, 2007; Intermix Media Inc., form 10-K, filed June 29, 2005.

157 *News Corp. declined to send over a faxed preliminary offer:* Author's interview with Richard Rosenblatt, January 3, 2008.

157 *"All Viacom had to do":* ibid.

157 *"We are holding hands":* E-mail from Richard Rosenblatt to Ross Levinsohn, July 10, 2005.

158 *23.4 percent of the Intermix shareholder votes:* Intermix Media Inc., form DEFM14A, filed August 25, 2005.

158 *Sheehan flew down:* Author's interview with Andrew Sheehan, June 19, 2007.

158 *"Chernin is a huge player":* E-mail from Richard Rosenblatt to Andrew Sheehan, July 14, 2005.

158 *"What kind of deal . . . ?":* E-mail from Andrew Sheehan to Richard Rosenblatt, July 14, 2005.

158 *Sheehan suggested to Chernin that Rosenblatt would do a great job:* Author's interview with Andrew Sheehan, December 17, 2007.

158 *News Corp. was worried:* Author's interview with a person familiar with the situation.

158 *Sheehan couldn't give away:* Author's interview with Andrew Sheehan, June 19, 2007

158 *"Am I meeting . . . ?":* E-mail from Ross Levinsohn to Richard Rosenblatt, July 13, 2005.

158 *"Yes. Chris will land in a couple of hrs.":* E-mail from Richard Rosenblatt to Ross Levinsohn, July 13, 2005.

158 *it wasn't until Friday morning:* Author's interview with Richard Rosenblatt, March 8, 2007.

159 *"I want to get you involved":* ibid.

159 *DeWolfe took the news:* ibid

159 *"You need to work out your deal":* ibid.

159 *Rosenblatt was specifically not invited:* Author's interview with a person familiar with the situation.

159 *"We're not going to tell you":* Patricia Sellers, "MySpace Cowboys," *Fortune,* September 4, 2006.

159 *"We'll be a better owner":* Author's interview with a person familiar with the situation.

159 *the reason Intermix was being sold for $580 million:* "News Corporation to acquire Intermix Media Inc.," News Corporation press release, July 18, 2005.

159 *Instead Murdoch and Chernin did a little dance:* Author's interview with a person familiar with the situation.

159 *DeWolfe wanted $40 million after taxes:* Author's interview with a person familiar with the situation.

160 *DeWolfe was rewarded:* Author's interview with a person familiar with the situation.

160 *On Saturday morning, Viacom's deal-making executives:* Author's interview with Thomas Weisel and Blake Warner, November 15, 2007.

160 *"Do not tell him anything":* E-mail from Andrew Sheehan to Maria Giron-Holmes, July 15, 2005.

160 *"We are coming in with a bid":* E-mail from Judy McGrath to Richard Rosenblatt, July 15, 2005.

160 *News Corp. announced the formation:* "News Corporation to Acquire Intermix Media Inc.," News Corporation press release, July 18, 2005.

160 *"This is the first step toward creating":* ibid.

161 *The idea was that Levinsohn:* Julia Angwin, "News Corp. Unites TV Web Activities Under One Unit," *Wall Street Journal,* July 18, 2005.

161 *"I hope this doesn't tip":* E-mail from Richard Rosenblatt to Ross Levinsohn, July 15, 2007.

161 *At four o'clock:* Author's interview with Richard Rosenblatt, November 15, 2006.

161 *Intermix's entire executive team:* Author's interview with Brett Brewer, August 1, 2007.

161 *The bankers from Thomas Weisel Partners did not show up:* Author's interview with Thomas Weisel and Blake Warner, November 15, 2007.

161 *"We were trying to maintain the theatrics":* ibid.

161 *"We want you in our offices":* ibid.

161 *"They tried to trap us into a conference room":* ibid.

162 *Brett Brewer and Rosenblatt shared:* Author's interview with Brett Brewer, May 1, 2007.

162 *Sheehan, the VantagePoint venture capitalist, got so exhausted:* Author's interview with Andrew Sheehan, June 19, 2007.

162 *At one point, Fox negotiator Mike Lang told a joke:* Author's interview with a person familiar with the situation.

162 *"Who the fuck are you?":* Author's interview with Brett Brewer, May 1, 2007.

162 *On Saturday afternoon Rosenblatt stormed out:* ibid.

162 *"Ross, I'm done":* Author's interview with Richard Rosenblatt, July 30, 2007.

162 *In fact, Rosenblatt eventually caved in:* Intermix Media, Inc., form DEFM14A, filed August 25, 2005.

163 *We are not offering the sale of MySpace alone:* Author's interview with Thomas Weisel and Blake Warner, November 15, 2007.

163 *Intermix's banker Bob Kitts:* ibid.

163 *"Viacom has a board meeting over the next few days":* Author's interview with Stuart Epstein, May 19, 2008.

163 *Accounts of the rest of this conversation differ:* Author's interview with Thomas Weisel and Blake Warner, November 15, 2007, and Stuart Epstein, May 19, 2008.

163 *Epstein relayed the message:* Author's interview with Stuart Epstein, May 19, 2008.

163 *"Intermix seems to be moving the goalposts":* ibid.

163 *Collectively, Epstein, Bakish, and Fricklas decided to stick to their original plan:* ibid.

164 *Finally Epstein called Kitts back:* Author's interview with Thomas Weisel and Blake Warner, November 15, 2007.

164 *"We were completely shocked":* Author's interview with Richard Rosenblatt, October 31, 2007.

164 *Intermix insisted on a relatively small $25 million breakup fee:* Intermix Media Inc., form DEFM14A, filed August 25, 2005.

164 *David Carlick, wearing a T-shirt and pants:* Author's interview with David Carlick, January 9, 2008.

164 *"An Irishman walks past a bar":* Author's interview with David Carlick, May 10, 2007.

164 *The board also unanimously approved:* Intermix Media Inc., form DEFM14A, filed August 25, 2005.

164 *Rosenblatt's employment agreement required:* Intermix Media Inc., form 10-K, filed June 15, 2004.

165 *Geoff Yang of Redpoint was lying in his bed:* Author's interview with Geoff Yang, August 21, 2007.

165 *"I cursed":* ibid.

165 *"You've got to be kidding":* ibid.

165 *"This came together really quickly":* ibid.

165 *Although Chernin and others believed that Yang was out of town:* Author's interview with a person familiar with the situation.

165 *Early Monday morning:* Author's interview with a person familiar with the situation.

166 *Hirschhorn was speechless:* ibid.

166 *News Corp. announced:* "News Corporation to Acquire Intermix Media Inc.," News Corporation press release, July 18, 2005.

166 *News Corp. had agreed to "loan" Intermix:* Intermix Media Inc., form DEFM14A, filed August 25, 2005.

166 *suddenly worth nearly $48 million:* ibid.

166 *Two days later, the dispirited MTV team appeared:* Author's interview with a person familiar with the situation.

166 *"There's still room to bid":* Author's interview with a person familiar with the situation.

166 *"What took so long?":* Author's interview with a person familiar with the situation.

166 *adding that she supported a counterbid:* Author's interview with a person familiar with the situation.

166 *"There's no harm in losing":* Author's interview with a person familiar with the situation.

167 *"Rupert is not afraid of overpaying":* Bryan Burrough, "Sleeping with the Fishes," *Vanity Fair,* December 2006.

167 *Longtime Viacom board member Philippe Dauman:* ibid.

167 *"Last year's MySpace was Friendster":* Julia Angwin, "Media Firms Dig into War Chests for Latest Assault on the Internet," *Wall Street Journal,* September 28, 2005.

167 *"I want to thank you and Peter for moving so quickly":* E-mail from Richard Rosenblatt to Rupert Murdoch, July 22, 2005, 2:19 p.m.

167 *"I remember telling you that this transaction":* ibid.

167 *Later in the fall, after the News Corp. deal:* Author's interview with Brett Brewer, October 15, 2007.

167 *The MySpace executives were not invited:* Author's interview with Thomas Weisel and Blake Warner, November 15, 2007.

167 *"They weren't our client":* Author's interview with Thomas Weisel and Blake Warner, November 15, 2007.

167 *The couples were greeted by limousines:* ibid.

167 *"Thanks for your effort with Intermix":* Author's interview with Brett Brewer, January 3, 2008.

168 *On Saturday night the entire Intermix board:* ibid.

168 *"Everybody had written us off for dead":* Author's interview with Richard Rosenblatt, October 31, 2007.

168 *"Now we've created the biggest media company":* ibid.

CHAPTER 18 HOLDING A TIGER BY THE TAIL

169 *Rupert Murdoch's right-hand man:* Author's interview with a person familiar with the situation.

169 *on the verge of closing a $550 million deal:* Author's interview with a person familiar with the situation.

169 *"We've got forty-eight hours":* Author's interview with a person familiar with the situation.

169 *Chernin's short list of Internet acquisitions:* Author's interview with a person familiar with the situation.

169 *"I think IGN is going to get away":* Author's interview with a person familiar with the situation.

169 *amassed about fifty million unique visitors per month:* "News Corp. to Acquire IGN Entertainment Inc.," News Corporation press release, September 8, 2005.

169 *Viacom was at about forty million:* Julia Angwin, "Media Firms Dig into War Chests for Latest Assault on the Internet," *Wall Street Journal,* September 28, 2005.

169 *IGN's twenty-eight million monthly:* "News Corp. to Acquire IGN Entertainment Inc.," News Corporation press release, September 8, 2005.

169 *"We have a choice":* Author's interview with a person familiar with the situation.

170 *"Go get it":* Author's interview with a person familiar with the situation.

170 *That morning, IGN's venture capital backer:* Author's interview with a person familiar with the situation.

170 *"I have a bird in the hand":* Author's interview with a person familiar with the situation.

170 *"That's more than we think we can do":* Author's interview with a person familiar with the situation.

170 *"That's the deal":* Author's interview with a person familiar with the situation.

170 *"Okay, we'll do it":* Author's interview with a person familiar with the situation.

170 *with sales of just $42.9 million and losses of $14.2 million:* IGN Inc., form S-1, filed July 13, 2005.

170 *Viacom copresident Tom Freston personally apologized:* Author's interview with a person familiar with the situation.

170 *In August News Corp.'s Internet unit had agreed to acquire Scout.com:* News Corporation, form 10-K, filed September 1, 2005.

170 *In August Murdoch's chief financial officer told investors:* "NWS Q4 2005 The News Corporation Limited Earnings Conference Call," Thomson Street Events, August 10, 2005.

170 *"I don't want to be held":* Anthony Noto's interview with Rupert Murdoch at Goldman Sachs Communicopia, September 21, 2005.

170 *On September 8, three days after announcing the acquisition:* Author's interview with a person familiar with the retreat.

171 *The goal of the retreat:* Author's interview with a person familiar with the retreat.

171 *The heads of Scout.com and IGN quickly recognized:* Fox Interactive Media, "Fox Interactive Media (FIM) Makes Key Management Appointments," FIM press release, March 7, 2006.

171 *His idea was to build a feature called "Grab This":* Author's interview with Brett Brewer, October 15, 2007.

171 *News Corp. launched a website with essentially the same concept:* Hulu.com, About Us.

171 *tried to lobby MySpace founders:* Author's interview with a person familiar with the situation.

171 *"Look, you're part of a bigger company":* Author's interview with a person familiar with the situation.

171 *"We just want to be left alone":* Author's interview with a person familiar with the situation.

172 *Many rank-and-file Intermix employees were angry with Richard Rosenblatt:* Author's interview with Barbara Saunders, August 1, 2007.

172 *It didn't help that IGN negotiated:* Author's interview with a person familiar with the situation.

172 *"Everyone thinks I sold them out":* E-mail from Richard Rosenblatt to James R. Quandt, July 20, 2005.

172 *Murdoch came up with the idea after:* Author's interview with a person familiar with the situation.

172 *Whitman and Schmidt told Murdoch:* Author's interview with a person familiar with the situation.

172 *Collectively they got only one-third of the shares:* Author's interview with a person familiar with the situation.

173 *It was rumored that News Corp. was looking to sell:* Author's interview with a person familiar with the situation.

173 *Although Intermix was helping to add blogs:* Author's interview with Brett Brewer, October 15, 2007.

173 *the Intermix employees felt neglected:* Author's interview with a person familiar with the situation.

173 *At a Goldman Sachs conference on September 21:* Anthony Noto's interview with Rupert Murdoch at Goldman Sachs Communicopia, September 21, 2005.

173 *"The other day we launched a film":* ibid.

173 *"Are you in favor of this NewsCorp. deal?":* E-mail from Brad Greenspan to Chris DeWolfe, July 18, 2005.

173 *on its first day of trading as a public company:* Author's interview with Brad Greenspan, October 14, 2007.

173 *"I always wanted her to see a return on that":* ibid.

174 *"If I find people to buy it and keep it public":* Author's interview with Brad Greenspan, December 15, 2007.

174 *DeWolfe and Berman seemed interested:* ibid.

174 *On September 23, he sent a letter:* Intermix Media Inc., form 8-K, filed September 26, 2005.

174 *Greenspan pitched his offer:* "Major Intermix Investor Offers Stockholders $13.50 per Share for Intermix Shares and Ongoing Equity Interest in MySpace.com," Business Wire, September 23, 2005.

174 *But the MySpace founders never signed on:* Author's interview with Brad Greenspan, December 15, 2007.

174 *Even Geoff Yang:* Author's interview with Geoff Yang, August 21, 2007.

174 *Intermix's board of directors rejected:* "Intermix Board Reaffirms Recommendation of Pending Acquisition by News Corporation; Rejects Unsolicited Acquisition Proposal by Brad Greenspan," Business Wire, September 26, 2005.

174 *"We found the proposal to be speculative":* Intermix Media Inc., form DEFA14A, filed September 26, 2005.

174 *In October News Corp. began negotiating:* Andy Fixmer, "Leases Hit the Highs of Dot-com Days," *Los Angeles Business Journal,* October 3, 2005.

174 *Anderson and DeWolfe were horrified:* Patricia Sellers, "MySpace Cowboys," *Fortune,* September 4, 2006.

175 *News Corp. had originally been negotiating:* Andy Fixmer, "Leases Hit the Highs of Dot-com Days," *Los Angeles Business Journal,* October 3, 2005.

175 *Anderson told Chernin, over drinks at a Santa Monica hotel:* Patricia Sellers, "MySpace Cowboys," *Fortune,* September 4, 2006.

175 *some of the more unruly MySpace programmers threw balled-up wet paper towels:* Author's interview with a person familiar with the situation.

175 *"We've gotten a dose of reality":* Patricia Sellers, "MySpace Cowboys," *Fortune,* September 4, 2006.

175 *After three months of attracting about twenty-one million visitors per month:* "Star-Struck Observers Drawn to Space Shuttle Launch Online, Reports comScore Media Metrix, July Traffic to Nasa.gov Rises 60 Percent to Four Million Visitors," PR Newswire, August 17, 2005; "Selected Social Networking Sites, August 2005 to July 2007," comScore Media Metrix.

175 *the site suddenly lured twenty-four million visitors:* "Selected Social Networking Sites, August 2005 to July 2007," comScore Media Metrix.

175 *For the first time, MySpace surpassed:* "MySpace Passes eBay, AOL and Google as Third Most Page Viewed Site Online; With More Than 37 Million Members, MySpace Is One of the Top Three Sites on the Internet with Yahoo and MSN," Business Wire, November 18, 2005.

175 *One of the first large-scale malicious hack attacks:* Author's interview with Gabe Harriman, July 31, 2007.

176 *A MySpace member had placed:* ibid.

176 *MySpace lost half:* ibid.

176 *In October and November 2004:* "New York Teen Pleads Guilty to Making Extortion Threats Against Internet Company," U.S. Department of Justice's Computer Crime Intellectual Property Section press release, March 22, 2005.

176 *threatened to show others how to "open a Pandora's box":* ibid.

176 *MySpace executive Jason Feffer, with the assistance of a high-tech-crime:* Jay Rey, "Teenager Pleads Guilty in Bid to Extort L.A. Web Company," *Buffalo News,* March 24, 2005; author's interview with Jason Feffer, April 4, 2008.

176 *Greco eventually pled guilty:* "New York Teen Pleads Guilty to Making Extortion Threats Against Internet Company," U.S. Department of Justice's Computer Crime Intellectual Property Section press release, March 22, 2005.

176 *At midnight on October 4, 2005:* Eric Lai, "Teen Uses Worm to Boost Popularity," *Computerworld,* October 26, 2005.

176 *"It didn't take a rocket or computer scientist":* ibid.

177 *Kamkar eventually pled guilty:* Dan Kaplan, "MySpace Superworm Creator Sentenced to Probation, Community Service," *Secure Computing,* February 1, 2007.

177 *"holding a tiger by the tail":* Author's interview with a person familiar with the situation.

177 *Facebook was a much smaller website:* "Selected Social Networking Sites, August 2005 to July 2007," comScore Media Metrix.

177 *increased photo capacity:* Ellen McGirt, "Hacker. Dropout. CEO." *Fast Company,* issue 115, May 2007.

177 *"How you holding up . . . ?":* Author's interview with a person familiar with the conversation.

177 *"We're fine:* Author's interview with a person familiar with the situation.

177 *"That's the difference:* Author's interview with a person familiar with the situation.

177 *Facebook . . . had underestimated:* Ellen McGirt, "Hacker. Dropout. CEO." *Fast Company,* issue 115, May 2007.

177 *"It was over one hundred ten":* ibid.

178 *Yahoo was interested in buying a stake in Facebook at $750 million:* Kevin J. Delaney, Rebecca Buckman, and Rob Guth, "Social Whirl: Facebook, Riding a Web Trend Flirts with a Big-Money Deal—As Big Companies Pursue Net-

working Sites, Start-up Is in Talks with Yahoo—Youthful Audience Is Fickle," *Wall Street Journal,* September 21, 2006.

178 *Chernin assigned his longtime friend:* Author's interview with a person familiar with the situation.

178 *"Rich, it doesn't make sense for you":* Author's interview with Richard Rosenblatt, March 8, 2007.

178 *"Am I getting fired?":* ibid.

178 *"No":* ibid.

179 *News Corp shares had fallen 8.5 percent:* Yahoo Finance, Historical Prices for NWS.

179 *"Where's the portal?":* Ross Levinsohn, "Fox Interactive Media, UBS 33rd Annual Global Media Conference," December 6, 2005.

179 *"Why have 1 portal":* ibid.

179 *"How do you know MySpace is not a fad?":* ibid.

179 *"If we keep pacing":* Jill Goldsmith, "Web Fuels Fox Fanfare; Sales Soar Due to Aggressive Acquisitions, Stellar Growth," *Daily Variety,* December 6, 2005.

CHAPTER 19 A FINE LINE BETWEEN RISQUÉ AND DIRTY

180 She's going really fast: Author's interview with Jason Feffer, May 4, 2007.

180 *"Stop":* ibid.

181 *"She has clothing on":* ibid.

181 *"send that picture to this guy":* ibid.

181 *"Page Three" girls:* William Shawcross, *Murdoch,* Simon & Schuster, 1992.

181 *"There's a fine line between risqué and dirty":* Author's interview with a person familiar with Murdoch's views.

181 *$2 million a month:* Julia Angwin, "MySpace Draws Ads by Offering 'Safe' Content," *Wall Street Journal,* June 21, 2006.

181 *AOL was making $109 million a month:* Time Warner Inc., form 10-Q, filed November 1, 2006.

181 *Google was making an astounding $520 million a month:* "Google Announces Third Quarter 2006 Results," Google press release, October 19, 2006.

181 *Feffer's group didn't scan all pictures before they were uploaded:* Author's interview with Jason Feffer, January 9, 2008.

181 *"I wouldn't be caught dead":* Erik Sass, "Major Marketers Avoid MySpace," MediaPost.com, March 21, 2006.

182 *"Why is it that he is so preoccupied . . . ?":* John Plunkett, "Sorrell Accuses Murdoch of Panic Buying," *Media Guardian,* October 27, 2005.

182 *Amerisave Mortgage, for instance:* Julia Angwin, "Web Ads Appear on Racy Sites Despite Checks," *Wall Street Journal,* April 4, 2006.

182 *"It's really alarming":* ibid.

182 *Verizon Communications and Starwood Hotels & Resorts Worldwide:* Julia Angwin, "On the Offensive—A Problem for Hot Web Outfits: Keeping Pages Free from Porn, to Help MySpace Sell Ads, Photo Site Hires Checkers and Tests Software Filters—Mistaking Apple Pie for Nudes," *Wall Street Journal,* May 16, 2006.

182 *Weight Watchers International pulled its ads:* Tom Tapp, "Pornstar Promotion Predicament Leads to MySpace Advertiser Revolt," Hollywood WireTap.com, May 24, 2006.

182 *T-Mobile pulled its ads:* ibid.

182 *"We didn't honestly know":* ibid.

182 *On October 29, Christine "ForBiddeN" Dolce:* James Verini, "Will Success Spoil MySpace," *Vanity Fair,* March 1, 2006.

183 *A Southern California makeup artist who joined:* Xeni Jardin, "Inside For-BiddeN City: MySpace Queen Playboy Debut, BB Q&A," boingboing.net, September 8, 2006.

183 *In November 2004, having amassed about two thousand friends:* Author's interview with Keith Ruby, January 2, 2008.

183 *had amassed more than seven hundred thousand friends:* ibid.

183 "Knock You Out": ibid.

184 *"They're really sticky on allowing you to make money":* Joseph Menn, "MySpace Could Lift Ban on Commerce," *Los Angeles Times,* August 27, 2007.

184 *MySpace's rules prevented Dolce from capturing thousands:* Author's interview with Keith Ruby, January 2, 2007.

184 *She knew she couldn't promote a cologne called Pherlure:* Joseph Menn, "MySpace Could Lift Ban on Commerce," *Los Angeles Times,* August 27, 2007.

184 *"There's a million hot naked chicks":* Lev Grossman, "Tila Tequila," *Time,* December 16, 2006.

184 *"is more than a porn star":* Saul Hansell, "For MySpace, Making Friends Was Easy. Big Profit Is Tougher," *New York Times,* April 23, 2006.

184 *"She is an author and a celebrity":* ibid.

184 *"If we had a site that was 'My Name Is So-and-So, and This Is My Porn Site' ":* ibid.

184 *Male porn star Christian:* Neena Lall's interview with Christian, August 3, 2007.

185 *"a .com to the end of my name. Hint hint!":* Joseph Menn, "MySpace Could Lift Ban on Commerce," *Los Angeles Times,* August 27, 2007.

185 *Dana DeArmond, for instance:* Neena Lall's interview with Dana DeArmond, August 15, 2007.

185 *For the first three years of her career:* ibid.

185 *"MySpace can make you famous":* ibid.

185 *"Before* [MySpace], *agents relied on people":* Neena Lall's interview with Christian, August 3, 2007.

186 *The rules were simple but hard to automate with computers:* Julia Angwin, "On the Offensive—A Problem for Hot Web Outfits: Keeping Pages Free from Porn, to Help MySpace Sell Ads, Photo Site Hires Checkers and Tests Software Filters—Mistaking Apple Pie for Nudes," *Wall Street Journal,* May 16, 2006.

186 *A field of science called "computer vision":* ibid.

186 *So MySpace began testing:* Author's interview with a person familiar with the situation.

186 *In December MySpace began:* Julia Angwin, "On the Offensive—A Problem for Hot Web Outfits: Keeping Pages Free from Porn, to Help MySpace Sell Ads, Photo Site Hires Checkers and Tests Software Filters—Mistaking Apple Pie for Nudes," *Wall Street Journal,* May 16, 2006.

186 *Levinsohn thought it was risky to rely:* Author's interview with a person familiar with the situation.

187 *MySpace shut down the links to YouTube:* Julia Angwin, "The Advertising Report: News Corp. Executive Pitches New Pathways for Online Ads," *Wall Street Journal,* January 25, 2006.

187 *"There wasn't a way to catch people posting explicit clips":* ibid.

187 *YouTube was just six months old and displaying three million videos per day:* "YouTube Opens Internet Video to the Masses," Market Wire, December 15, 2005.

187 *Bloggers railed against MySpace's unilateral move:* Nicholas Wapshott, "Get Out of MySpace, Bloggers Rage at Murdoch," *Independent,* January 8, 2006.

187 *"This is soooo like Fox":* ibid.

187 *When YouTube was shut down, DeWolfe was in Europe:* Author's interview with Jason Feffer, March 6, 2007.

187 *"We said when we bought MySpace":* Julia Angwin, "The Advertising Report: News Corp. Executive Pitches New Pathways for Online Ads," *Wall Street Journal,* January 25, 2006.

187 *MySpace had been selling ads for about 17 cents per thousand viewers:* MySpace Inc. internal document, May 3, 2005.

188 *Levinsohn decreed that MySpace had to stop:* Author's interview with a person familiar with the situation.

188 *Levinsohn directed MySpace to start building more "safe areas":* Julia Angwin, "MySpace Draws Ads by Offering 'Safe' Content," *Wall Street Journal,* June 21, 2006.

188 *"A key condition":* ibid.

188 *MySpace's ad tracking system was crude:* Author's interview with a person familiar with the situation.

188 *IGN was using a sophisticated Oracle database:* Author's interview with a person familiar with the situation.

188 *Ad sales executives at the Fox News Channel:* Author's interview with a person familiar with the situation.

188 *After taking control of Fox News:* Author's interview with a person familiar with the situation.

188 *Fox News executives were upset:* Author's interview with a person familiar with the situation.

189 *"Fine, you can have it back":* Author's interview with a person familiar with the situation.

189 *In January Fox Interactive quietly shed:* Julia Angwin, "After Riding High with Fox News, Murdoch Aide Has Harder Slog," *Wall Street Journal,* October 3, 2006.

189 *In the New York offices, News Corp. built a wall:* Author's interview with a person familiar with the situation.

189 *had fallen 15 percent to $15 per share:* Yahoo Finance, historical prices for News Corporation (NWS).

189 *"It pains us":* Devin Leonard, "A Lonelyhearts Parade, Investors Have Fallen Out of Love with the Entertainment Conglomerates. What Will It Take to Win Them Back?" *Fortune,* December 26, 2005.

189 *On Sunday, January 22, 2006:* John Aizlewood, "How Did This Band of Unknowns Come to Make the Fastest-selling Debut Album Ever?" *Evening Standard,* January 27, 2006.

189 *The group had been quietly building:* ibid.

190 *In February, an eleven-minute online movie:* "Online Parody 'MySpace: The Movie' Helps Launch Amateur's Career," Associated Press, February 27, 2006.

190 *more than six million viewings:* ibid.

CHAPTER 20 "A PLACE FOR FIENDS"

191 *Connecticut attorney general Richard Blumenthal was outraged:* Author's interview with Richard Blumenthal, April 27, 2007.

191 *In February 2006 police in Middletown:* Cara Rubinsky, "Police Investigate Whether Assaults Sparked by MySpace.com," Associated Press, February 2, 2006.

191 *In January police in Bristol:* Alaine Griffin, "Website Called Risk for Teens," *Hartford Courant,* February 3, 2006.

191 *in September police:* "PWPD Arrest in Internet Abuse," *Port Washington News,* October 7, 2005.

191 *He was more familiar with Facebook:* Author's interview with Richard Blumenthal, April 27, 2007.

191 *"Gee, that's pretty cool":* ibid.

191 *"If you were lucky":* ibid.

192 *On February 2 he issued a press release:* "Attorney General Investigating MySpace .com for Allowing Minors Easy Access to Pornography, Inappropriate Material," Connecticut Attorney General's Office press release, February 2, 2007.

192 *"This site is a parent's worst nightmare":* ibid.

192 *Since 2004, the evening newsmagazine:* Peter Johnson, " 'Dateline' Roots Out Predators; Men Seeking for Sex via Internet," *USA Today,* February 15, 2006.

192 *pulled the highest ratings:* "NBC Schedules 'Dateline NBC' on Pedophiles," Associated Press, April 25, 2006.

192 *In that episode:* "Profile: To Catch a Predator III: Online predators come to home rigged with hidden cameras and face Chris Hansen, then are arrested as they're leaving," NBC News: *Dateline NBC,* February 3, 2006.

193 *"Do you check out the MySpace sites . . . ?":* ibid.

193 *"I just—whatever's in a chat room":* ibid.

193 NBC Nightly News *anchorman Brian Williams:* "Profile: Popular websites for teenagers can be hunting ground for sexual predators," *NBC News: Nightly News,* February 3, 2006.

193 *NBC's* Today *show interviewed:* "Police Probe Alleged MySpace-linked Sex Crimes," Associated Press, February 3, 2006.

193 *The* CBS Evening News *reported: CBS Evening News,* "MySpace: Your Kids' Danger?" CBSnews.com, February 6, 2006.

193 *Rita Cosby:* Rita Cosby, "Caught in the Dangers of Web," MSNBC.com, February 6, 2006.

193 *"moral panic":* Danah Boyd, "Friendster Lost Steam. Is MySpace Just a Fad?" Apophenia Blog, March 21 2006.

193 *"Welcome to a generational divide":* ibid.

193 *sexual crimes against children had been declining:* David Finkelhor and Lisa Jones, "Why Have Child Maltreatment and Child Victimization Declined?" *Journal of Social Issues,* vol. 62, no. 4, 2006, pp. 685–716.

193 *Between 1992 and 2006:* David Finkelhor and Lisa Jones, "Updated Trends in Child Maltreatment, 2006," Crimes Against Children Research Center, University of New Hampshire.

194 *During 1999 and 2000, 1 of 5:* David Finkelhor, Kimberly Mitchell, and Janis Wolak, *Online Victimization: What Youth Tells Us, Medical, Legal, and Social Science Aspects of Child Sexual Exploitation: A Comprehensive Review of Pornography, Prostitution, and Internet Crimes,* vol. 1, pp. 437–467, GW Medical Publishing, Inc., 2005.

194 *By 2005 only 1 out of 7:* Janis Wolak, Kimberly Mitchell, and David Finkelhor, "Online Victimization of Youth: Five Years Later," National Center for Missing & Exploited Children Bulletin—#07-06-025. Alexandria, VA, 2006.

194 *most of the victims are over the age of thirteen:* "Just the Facts About Online Youth Victimization," testimony by David Finkelhor, director of the Crimes Against Children Research Center, at the Congressional Internet Caucus Advisory Committee, May 3, 2007.

194 *Only 5 percent:* ibid.

194 *The day after the Connecticut attorney general's announcement:* Author's interview with Richard Blumenthal, April 27, 2007.

194 *Over the weekend, Chris DeWolfe cut his shaggy, long blond hair:* Author's interview with Jason Feffer, March 6, 2007.

194 *"We don't need to see it; we're aware of the issues":* Author's interview with Richard Blumenthal, April 27, 2007.

194 *DeWolfe outlined all the steps:* ibid.

195 *"We want MySpace to be the most open":* ibid.

195 *"We're on a much shorter time frame":* ibid.

195 *a category that MySpace users had requested:* Author's interview with Jason Feffer, April 4, 2008.

195 *"MySpace is not responsible for many of these images":* Author's interview with Richard Blumenthal, April 27, 2007.

195 *The attorney general suggested raising the age limit:* ibid.

195 *DeWolfe and the News Corp. team demurred:* ibid.

195 *"It might be like some neighborhood playgrounds":* ibid.

195 *His colleagues joked that he looked older:* Author's interview with Jason Feffer, March 6, 2007.

195 *On February 23 Stephan M. Letavec:* "Two Out-of-State Men Arrested, Charged, with Using Internet to Engage in Sex with Minors," press release from U.S. Department of Justice's U.S. Attorney's Office for Connecticut, March 2, 2006.

195 *When the two began communicating:* Gary Libow, "Arrests Made in Sex Cases FBI: Young Girls Were Solicited on MySpace.com," *Hartford Courant,* March 3, 2006.

196 *During that time:* ibid.

196 *On August 13:* ibid.

196 *The two had sex:* "Pennsylvania Man Sentenced to 10 Years in Prison for Using Internet to Engage in Sex with Connecticut Minor," press release from U.S. Attorney's Office District of Connecticut, April 9, 2007.

196 *Letavec eventually pled guilty:* ibid.

196 *One day later:* "Two Out-of-State Men Arrested, Charged, with Using Internet to Engage in Sex with Minors," press release from U.S. Department of Justice's U.S. Attorney's Office for Connecticut, March 2, 2006.

196 *Szeto pled guilty:* John Christoffersen, "Man Who Used MySpace to Meet Underage Girl Sentenced to 14 Years," Associated Press, March 6, 2007.

196 *On February 25 two teenage girls:* Susan Abrams, "Have You Seen These Runaways? Two Teenage Girls Linked to Website," *Los Angeles Daily News,* February 25, 2006.

196 *Detectives said that the two:* Susan Abrams, "Detectives Locate Two Missing Teenagers," *Los Angeles Daily News,* March 1, 2006.

196 *Jason Feffer argued that the site should highlight positive cases:* Author's interview with Jason Feffer, April 4, 2008.

196 *After a month of silence . . . DeWolfe gave an interview:* Matt Apuzzo, "DeWolfe: MySpace.com Safe Despite Reports," Associated Press, March 6, 2006.

196 *"This isn't a MySpace issue":* ibid.

196 *"If you go to the mall":* ibid.

197 *Behind the scenes, Jason Feffer's Fef.B.I. division:* Author's interview with a person familiar with the situation.

197 *aided twenty-four hundred police investigations:* Matt Apuzzo, "DeWolfe: MySpace.com Safe Despite Reports," Associated Press, March 6, 2006.

197 *Aftab wrote a guide for law enforcement officers:* Author's interview with Parry Aftab, August 31, 2007.

197 *"They were astounded at how law enforcement friendly":* ibid.

197 *In early 2005 Feffer's team:* Author's interview with a person familiar with the situation.

198 *"I am going crazy":* posting on ConsumerAffairs.com on March 17, 2007.

198 *"No one could respond to all the requests":* Author's interview with Parry Aftab, August 31, 2007.

198 *One day Kornbluth discovered:* "Not My Space" by Josh Kornbluth, posted on "The Josh Kornbluth Show" blog on June 5, 2006.

198 *"I checked":* ibid.

198 *"the stupidest thing I've ever heard of":* Author's interview with Parry Aftab, August 31, 2007.

198 *"Once News Corp. took it over":* ibid.

199 *MySpace once accidentally deleted:* Author's interview with a person familiar with the situation.

199 *Meanwhile, MySpace quietly attempted:* Author's interview with Richard Blumenthal, April 27, 2007.

199 *But on March 30 Ross Levinsohn:* David Goetzl, "MySpace Censors Content to Lure Marketers," MediaPost.com, March 31, 2006.

199 *Tom Anderson was livid:* Author's interview with a person familiar with the situation.

199 *MySpace's concessions hadn't helped:* Author's interview with Richard Blumenthal, April 27, 2007.

199 *In April, Ross Levinsohn received an anonymous e-mail:* Author's interview with people familiar with the situation.

200 *News Corp. hired an investigator, who confirmed:* Author's interview with a person familiar with the situation.

200 *When News Corp. president Peter Chernin:* Author's interview with a person familiar with the situation.

200 *Levinsohn was horrified:* Author's interview with a person familiar with the situation.

200 *But Murdoch and Chernin didn't agree:* Author's interview with a person familiar with the situation.

200 *The company announced:* Emily Steel and Julia Angwin, "MySpace Receives More Pressure to Limit Children's Access to the Site," *Wall Street Journal,* June 23, 2006.

200 *"We have never had this kind of corporate commitment":* Julia Angwin, "News Corp. Sets Online Safety Ads," *Wall Street Journal,* April 10, 2006.

201 *Red Team engineer Steve Pearman:* Author's interview with a person familiar with the situation.

201 *But Pearman and Nigam hoped:* Author's interview with a person familiar with the situation.

201 *"give parents a tool to force a discussion":* Julia Angwin, "MySpace Moves to Give Parents More Information," *Wall Street Journal,* January 17, 2007.

201 *The Red Team code-named its project Zephyr:* Author's interview with a person familiar with the situation.

201 *Its most popular host, Bill O'Reilly: Fox News: The O'Reilly Factor,* transcript, July 13, 2006.

201 *Pamela Rogers, who had sex with a thirteen-year-old male student and communicated with him, in part, through MySpace:* Associated Press, "MySpace Page Puts Teacher Back in Jail," MSNBC.com, April 12, 2006.

201 *"We need to shut down the MySpace.coms of the world": Fox News: The O'Reilly Factor,* transcript, July 13, 2006.

201 *"I'm with you there, boy":* ibid.

CHAPTER 21 PEBBLE BEACH

202 *On Monday evening, July 31, 2006, Rupert Murdoch:* Author's interview with a person familiar with the situation.

202 *He had flown in his top 250 executives:* Author's interview with a person familiar with the situation.

202 *attracting more than fifty-four million visitors in July, compared with twenty-one million:* "Selected Social Networking Sites," comScore Media Metrix, August 2005–July 2007.

202 *"Rupert Murdoch: Teen Idol!":* Spencer Reiss, "His Space," *Wired,* issue 14.07, July 2006.

202 *to nearly $20—up 33 percent from a low of $15:* Yahoo Finance, Historical Prices for NWS.

203 *Politically, Murdoch was also making news:* John Cassidy, "Murdoch's Game," *New Yorker,* October 16, 2006.

203 *The lineup of speakers at Pebble Beach reflected:* ibid.

203 *"The nature of the event . . .":* ibid.

203 *informed him about the status:* Author's interview with a person familiar with the situation.

203 *making a paltry few million dollars a year:* Author's interview with a person familiar with the situation.

203 *fifty-four million monthly users:* "Selected Social Networking Sites," comScore Media Metrix, August 2005–July 2007.

204 *Murdoch and Peter Chernin had initially considered buying or building:* Author's interview with a person familiar with the situation.

204 *but by June they realized that wouldn't be feasible:* Author's interview with a person familiar with the situation.

204 *A year earlier, AOL had run a competitive auction:* Julia Angwin, Kevin J. Delaney, and Robert A. Guth, "Online Relationships: Google Zooms Past Microsoft to Near an Ad Deal with AOL," *Wall Street Journal,* December 17, 2005.

204 *Murdoch hoped that MySpace would be able to run:* Author's interview with a person familiar with the situation.

204 *Heckman, the founder of Scout.com:* John Cook, "Venture Capital: Rivals.com Founder Now Leads Charge as Competitor," *Seattle Post-Intelligencer,* July 1, 2005.

204 *Microsoft bid about $450 million:* Author's interview with a person familiar with the situation.

204 *Yahoo bid $750 million:* Author's interview with a person familiar with the situation.

205 *"Google didn't show up":* Author's interview with a person familiar with the situation.

205 *Doerr was shocked:* Author's interview with a person familiar with the situation.

205 *Doerr swung into action:* Author's interview with a person familiar with the situation.

205 *"Sorry, I'm a little nervous":* Author's interview with a person familiar with the situation.

205 *"You've spent the day":* Author's interview with a person familiar with the situation.

205 *"As the satellites blink":* Author's interview with a person familiar with the situation.

205 *"I say we put every child in the world":* Author's interview with a person familiar with the situation.

206 *"God may be in the mansions":* Author's interview with a person familiar with the situation.

206 *"The number for you to be competitive is seven hundred fifty million dollars":* Author's interview with a person familiar with the situation.

206 *Sergey Brin flew down from Silicon Valley in a helicopter:* Author's interview with a person familiar with the situation.

206 *Tuesday morning was cold and foggy:* Author's interview with a person familiar with the situation.

206 *"What do you need to get this thing done?":* Author's interview with a person familiar with the situation.

206 *Heckman said he needed:* Author's interview with a person familiar with the situation.

206 *Chernin agreed that it was best:* Author's interview with a person familiar with the situation.

207 *DeWolfe had left his wife at home:* Author's interview with a person familiar with the situation.

207 *The dispute had spilled out in public:* Saul Hansell, "For MySpace, Making Friends Was Easy. Big Profit Is Tough," *New York Times,* April 23, 2006.

207 *"Music brings a lot of traffic into MySpace":* ibid.

207 *"If it was a really commercial profile":* ibid.

208 *Microsoft had thrown out numbers as high as $800 million:* Author's interview with a person familiar with the situation.

208 *In that presentation, Heckman argued:* Author's interview with a person familiar with the situation.

208 *"We can go to the dark side with Google":* Author's interview with a person familiar with the situation.

208 *For eight months, Heckman had been negotiating:* Author's interview with a person familiar with the situation.

208 *Microsoft kept sending over long, complicated term sheets:* Author's interview with a person familiar with the situation.

208 *News Corp. also worried about the timing:* Author's interview with a person familiar with the situation.

208 *By Wednesday morning, the weather had warmed up:* Author's interview with a person familiar with the situation.

208 *Yahoo chairman Terry Semel was at Pebble Beach:* Agenda for News Corp. retreat.

208 *Chernin borrowed the hotel manager's office:* Author's interview with a person familiar with the situation.

209 *to which News Corp. had pledged $2.5 million:* Jim Finkle and Kenneth Li, "News Corp. Pledged $2.5 Million to DJ Watchdog Group," Reuters, August 2, 2007.

209 *They were sitting in a tented lounge:* Author's interview with a person familiar with the situation.

209 *Heckman predicted that MySpace could probably get $250 million:* Author's interview with a person familiar with the situation.

209 *he had provided it with a $750 million:* Author's interview with a person familiar with the situation.

209 *Heckman called Microsoft:* Author's interview with a person familiar with the situation.

209 *with a generous new offer: $1.12 billion:* Author's interview with a person familiar with the situation.

210 *if you can keep yours clean:* Author's interview with a person familiar with the situation.

210 *Working together, Heckman and Google's top negotiator:* Author's interview with a person familiar with the situation.

210 *"You need to promise me in blood":* Author's interview with a person familiar with the situation.

210 *"The first [turning point] came when we went international":* Author's interview with a person familiar with the situation.

210 *Chernin got the News Corp. board to approve it:* Author's interview with a person familiar with the situation.

210 *Then Heckman flew home to Seattle:* Author's interview with a person familiar with the situation.

210 *spent a day huddled in Heckman's former Scout.com office:* John Cook, "Venture Capital: UW Grad Wheels, Deals for Fox Firm," *Seattle Post-Intelligencer,* August 25, 2006.

211 *at a charity dinner hosted by a News Corp. executive:* Author's interview with a person familiar with the situation.

211 *Sadly, the deal proved to be a breaking point:* Author's interview with a person familiar with the situation.

211 *On Monday, August 7, News Corp. announced:* Julia Angwin and Kevin J. Delaney, "Google Lands MySpace Search-Advertising Pact," *Wall Street Journal,* August 8, 2006.

211 *News Corp. shares finally broke through the $20 mark:* Yahoo Finance, Historical Prices for NWS.

211 *"The size of this deal is staggering":* Julia Angwin and Kevin J. Delaney, "Google Lands MySpace Search-Advertising Pact," *Wall Street Journal,* August 8, 2006.

211 *That night, Murdoch took his top digital executives:* Author's interview with a person familiar with the situation.

211 *DeWolfe and Anderson called it "peer commerce":* Julia Angwin and Kevin J. Delaney, "MySpace's Pact with Google Hits a Snag," *Wall Street Journal,* February 7, 2007.

211 *But the Google deal, as preliminarily drafted:* Author's interview with a person familiar with the situation.

211 *had fallen on deaf ears:* Author's interview with a person familiar with the situation.

212 *Over dinner, Anderson vented his frustration:* Author's interview with a person familiar with the situation.

212 *Ultimately Google ended up delaying its initial payments:* Author's interview with a person familiar with the situation.

212 *and News Corp. ended up extending the arrangement:* Author's interview with a person familiar with the situation.

212 *"If I had to do it all over again":* Author's interview with Jim Heckman, January 23, 2008.

212 *"But I was very concerned":* ibid.

212 *"It was harmful from a relationship standpoint":* ibid.

212 *Viacom chairman Sumner Redstone was also seething:* Author's interview with a person familiar with the situation.

212 *"Will Viacom Remain a Wallflower?":* Steve Rosenbush and Mark Scott, "Will Viacom Remain a Wallflower?" *BusinessWeek,* August 11, 2006.

212 *"Viacom Discovers Kids Don't Want Their MTV Online":* Matthew Karnitschnig, "Viacom Discovers Kids Don't Want Their MTV Online," *Wall Street Journal,* August 29, 2006.

212 *"No! Not him!":* Bryan Burrough, "Sleeping with the Fishes," *Vanity Fair,* December 2006.

213 *Redstone pinned the blame:* ibid.

213 *"It sat there for weeks":* ibid.

213 *When Freston arrived, Redstone fired him:* ibid.

CHAPTER 22 WAR AGAINST WEB 2.0

214 *Coined in 2004 by technology industry veteran Tim O'Reilly:* Tim O'Reilly, "What Is Web 2.0," O'Reilly, September 30, 2005.

214 *San Bruno–based YouTube was rumored to be for sale:* Author's interview with a person familiar with the situation; Greg Sandoval, "YouTube Could Be a Steal at $1 Billion, *CNET news,* August 24, 2006.

214 *with just one-quarter the audience of MySpace:* "Selected Social Networking Sites," comScore Media Metrix, August 2005–July 2007.

214 *turned down an $800 million offer:* Kevin J. Delaney, Rebecca Buckman, and Robert Guth, "Social Whirl: Facebook, Riding a Web Trend, Flirts with Big Money Deal—as Big Companies Pursue Networking Sites, Start-up Is in Talks with Yahoo," *Wall Street Journal,* September 21, 2006.

214 *"How This Kid Made $60 Million in 18 Months":* Sarah Lacy and Jessi Hempel, "Valley Boys, Digg.com's Kevin Rose Leads a New Brat Pack of Young Entrepreneurs," *BusinessWeek,* August 14, 2006.

215 *"driven off the back of MySpace":* Peter Chernin, "Q&A Session with News Corp. at the Merrill Lynch Media & Entertainment Conference," transcript by Voxant Fair Disclosure Wire, September 12, 2006.

215 *"both dangerously arrogant and like a real validation":* Marshal Kirkpatrick, "MySpace: We Don't Need Web 2.0," TechCrunch, September 12, 2006.

216 *its founders, Chad Hurley and Steve Chen:* John Cloud, "The Gurus of YouTube," *Time,* December 16, 2006.

216 *YouTube changed the rules of the game:* Tom Green, "The Rise of Flash Video, Part I," *Digital Web,* October 9, 2006.

216 *Flash software was designed in 1996:* ibid.

216 *YouTube raised venture capital financing at a $15 million valuation:* Om Malik, "YouTube Gets Sequoia's Cash?" GigaOm.com, October 7, 2006.

216 *As YouTube's popularity soared, Chernin increasingly worried:* Author's interview with a person familiar with the situation.

217 *News Corp. wanted to buy YouTube:* Author's interview with a person familiar with the situation.

217 *First, MySpace released its own version:* Louis Hau and Rachel Rosmarin, "MySpace Takes on YouTube," *Forbes,* October 3, 2006.

217 *Then in the spring, Chernin and Viacom:* Author's interview with a person familiar with the situation.

217 *"We have one person working on MySpace video":* Peter Chernin, "Q&A Session with News Corp. at the Merrill Lynch Media & Entertainment Conference," transcript by Voxant Fair Disclosure Wire, September 12, 2006.

217 *Alex Welch first noticed this problem:* Author's interview with Alex Welch, May 24, 2007.

218 *Sensing a market need:* ibid.

218 *more than 60 percent of MySpace pages:* Author's interview with Alex Welch, December 27, 2007.

218 *Revenues from advertising on its site were less than $30 million:* Author's interview with Alex Welch, May 24, 2007.

218 *at an $85 million valuation:* ibid.

219 *Thomas' MySpace Editor, at StrikeFile.com:* Author's interview with Thomas Zwaagstra, August 11, 2007.

219 *"This became tedious after a short time":* ibid.

219 *his one-man operation attracted an average:* ibid.

219 *"I saw Thomas' Editor":* Author's interview with Andrew Thompson, October 12, 2007.

219 *MySpaceSupport generated $1.4 million:* ibid.

220 *"The money was fluke money":* Andrew Thompson, blog posting on http://www.ecaandrew.com, May 22, 2007.

220 *"Smart Expenses":* ibid.

220 *Ari Freeman, had turned his website:* Author's interview with Tony Norella, May 23, 2007.

220 *Freeman sold FreeDiskSpace.com:* ibid.

221 *In January 2006 MySpace sent out cease and desist letters:* Loren Baker, "MySpace Issues Cease and Desist to MySpace Domain Sites," *Search Engine Journal,* January 12, 2006.

221 *As a result, MySpaceCity.com changed its name to Tower Codes:* ibid.

221 *Thompson added legal disclaimers on his page:* Author's interview with Andrew Thompson, October 12, 2007.

221 *Widgets started out as utilities:* Author's interview with Jeremy Liew, July 25, 2007.

221 *the top widget site, Slide:* Author's interview with Max Levchin, June 18, 2007.

221 *It was the fall of 2005, and Sayama was complaining:* Author's interview with Lance Tokuda and Jia Shen, June 18, 2007.

222 *had acquired sixty thousand users:* ibid.

222 *server went down on seventeen of the first thirty days:* ibid.

222 *"Hey—saw that lots of myspace people are utilizing your site":* Author's interview with Lance Tokuda, December 29, 2007.

222 *By January 2006 Tokuda and Shen had both left their jobs:* Author's interview with Lance Tokuda and Jia Shen, June 18, 2007.

222 *On Monday, October 9, Google announced:* "Google to Acquire YouTube for $1.65 Billion in Stock," Google press release, October 9, 2006.

222 *Ross Levinsohn was furious:* Author's interview with a person familiar with the situation.

222 *"We're not for sale":* Julia Angwin, "Google Looks to Boost Ads with YouTube," *Wall Street Journal,* October 10, 2006.

223 *the $1.65 billion price tag:* ibid.

223 *Levinsohn also worried that MySpace would lose its leverage:* ibid.

CHAPTER 23 NUMBER ONE IN EVERY MARKET

224 *On November 8, 2006, Chris DeWolfe and Tom Anderson:* Author's interview with a person familiar with the situation.

224 *In Japan, a social networking site called Mixi:* Julia Angwin and Jay Alabaster, "MySpace Adds a Friend in Japan—Networking Site Enters Asia as News Corp. and Softbank Set Venture for Local Version," *Wall Street Journal,* November 8, 2006.

224 *Founded in February 2004:* Pete Cashmore, "Mixi, Japan's Biggest Social Network," Mashable.com, July 8, 2006.

224 *site third only to Yahoo and Google:* Pete Cashmore, "Mixi 'Japanese MySpace' Heads for IPO," Mashable.com, September 11, 2006.

224 *its stock price doubled:* Pete Cashmore, "Mixi Founder Becomes a Billionaire," Mashable.com, September 14, 2006.

224 *the underdog in Japan, with just six hundred thousand monthly visitors:* Julia Angwin and Jay Alabaster, "MySpace Adds a Friend in Japan—Networking Site Enters Asia as News Corp. and Softbank Set Venture for Local Version," *Wall Street Journal,* November 8, 2006.

224 *announcing a $10 million joint venture:* ibid.

224 *MySpace hosted a concert by Noel Gallagher:* Simon Bartz, "Noel Gallagher Plays MySpace Japan Show," *Japan Times,* November 17, 2006.

225 *SoftBank chief executive Masayoshi Son:* Julia Angwin and Jay Alabaster, "MySpace Adds a Friend in Japan—Networking Site Enters Asia as News Corp. and Softbank Set Venture for Local Version," *Wall Street Journal,* November 8, 2006.

225 *"The idea is to still maintain":* ibid.

225 *Every day Anderson receives about forty thousand e-mails:* Patricia Sellers, "MySpace Cowboys," *Fortune,* September 4, 2006.

225 *While in Japan, for instance, he noticed:* "Band Loses, Regains MySpace URL," FMBQ.com, November 7, 2006.

225 *"I heard about what happened with your URL":* ibid.

226 *Ozzie had amassed just 51,470 friends:* Jessi Hempel, "Japan's Friend No. 1," *BusinessWeek,* December 4, 2006.

226 *fifty-six million U.S. visitors a month:* "Selected Social Networking Sites," comScore Media Metrix, August 2005–July 2007.

226 *"We're still adding globally":* John Battelle's interview with Ross Levinsohn at Web 2.0 Summit, O'Reilly Network transcript, November 7, 2006.

226 *"It is a fantastic property today":* ibid.

226 *"It's why I don't sleep":* ibid.

226 *News Corp. had poured tens of millions of dollars:* ibid.

226 *In a single year, MySpace had gone through eight tons:* Jo Maitland, "MySpace Tackles Extraordinary Data Storage Requirements," SearchStorage.com, November 29, 2006.

226 *"We were scratching our heads":* David F. Carr, "Inside MySpace.com," *Baseline Magazine,* January 16, 2007.

226 *MySpace realized that Microsoft Windows:* ibid.

227 *In July MySpace discovered a worm:* Brian Krebs, "MySpace Attacked by Flash Worm," TheWashingtonPost.com, July 18, 2006.

227 *"Latest Update":* ibid.

227 *However, MySpace failed to notify all the widget makers:* Pete Cashmore, "MySpace Update Threatens YouTube, RockYou and Hundreds More?" Mashable.com, July 21, 2006.

227 *"This is a sloppy move":* ibid.

227 *Two days later, a power outage:* David F. Carr, "Inside MySpace.com," *Baseline Magazine,* January 16, 2007.

227 *A week later, MySpace users started complaining:* Pete Cashmore, "MySpace Screws Up Again: Accounts Being Deleted?" Mashable.com, July 28, 2006.

227 *"hiya—your accounts are not being deleted":* ibid.

227 *In August MySpace registered its one hundred millionth account:* Pete Cashmore, "MySpace Hits 100 Million Accounts," Mashable.com, August 9, 2006.

228 *"Invalid Friend ID":* ibid.

228 *"We have about three hundred jobs":* Rupert Murdoch's speech, Goldman Sachs Communicopia XIV Conference in New York, September 19, 2006.

228 *"MySpace is a fragile community":* Author's interview with a person familiar with the situation.

228 *with 57.2 million visitors in November:* "Selected Social Networking Sites," comScore Media Metrix, August 2005–July 2007.

228 *compared with Facebook's 16.7 million:* ibid.

228 *Facebook sorts through about thirty thousand possible updates:* "Facebook's News-

feed Knows What You Did Last Summer," Facebook Trending Blog, October 29,

229 *"News Feed works so well that it's sometimes easy to forget how sophisticated it is"*: "Insider Perspectives: Ex-Googler Justin Rosenstein on Making the Jump to Facebook," Inside Facebook Blog, July 9, 2007.

229 *boosted traffic by 26 percent between September and November 2006*: "Selected Social Networking Sites," comScore Media Metrix, August 2005–July 2007.

229 *At the same time, MySpace's U.S. traffic increased only 3 percent*: ibid.

229 *Levinsohn believed that MySpace needed professional managers*: Author's interview with a person familiar with the situation.

229 *Over a six-month period, Levinsohn had presented five different management reorganization plans*: Author's interview with a person familiar with the situation.

230 *But Chernin turned down*: Author's interview with a person familiar with the situation.

230 *Chernin believed that Levinsohn had made little progress*: Author's interview with a person familiar with the situation.

230 *DeWolfe opposed Levinsohn's decision*: Author's interview with a person familiar with the situation.

230 *DeWolfe also wanted Levinsohn to redistribute*: Author's interview with a person familiar with the situation.

230 *"I'm going to fire Ross"*: Author's interview with a person familiar with the situation.

230 *"Fine"*: Author's interview with a person familiar with the situation.

230 *"Keep it quiet"*: Author's interview with a person familiar with the situation.

231 *Over the summer, Murdoch declared*: "NWS Q4 2006 News Corporation Earnings Conference Call," Thomson Street Events, August 8, 2006.

231 *MySpace's global rollout began in June*: MySpace timeline, MySpace.com.

231 *Bebo, which had 3.9 million visitors compared with Myspace's 5.2 million*: comScore, "Leading User-Generated Content Sites See Expotential Growth in UK Visitors During Past Year," comScore press release, September 11, 2006.

231 *But in France*: Pete Cashmore, "Skyblog and Skyrock—The French MySpace," Mashable.com, August 9, 2006.

231 *"Our goal is to be number one in every market"*: Robert Levine, "MySpace Aims for a Global Audience, and Finds Some Stiff Competition," *New York Times,* November 7, 2006.

231 *To promote his satellite television*: Steve Stecklow, Aaron O. Patrick, Martin Peers, and Andrew Higgins, "Calling the Shots: In Murdoch's Career, A Hand on the News—His Aggressive Style Can Blur Boundaries; 'Buck Stops with Me,' " *Wall Street Journal,* June 5, 2007.

231 *In 1993, Murdoch sold*: ibid.

231 *In 1994 Star TV*: ibid.

231 *in 1998 Murdoch's publishing house:* ibid.

231 *"We've rather hit a brick wall":* "Managing Major Media Companies in an Era of Globalization," panel discussion with President Clinton, Rupert Murdoch, Richard Parsons, and Howard Stringer, at the Clinton Global Initiative in New York, September 16, 2005.

232 *"We're going to attempt":* "An hour with the CEO of News Corporation," *Charlie Rose,* PBS, July 20, 2006.

232 *"We have to make MySpace a very Chinese site":* Rupert Murdoch speaking at the Goldman Sachs Communicopia XIV Conference in New York, September 19, 2006.

232 *The Chinese Internet culture:* Geoffrey A. Fowler and Jason Dean, "In China, MySpace May Need to Be 'OurSpace'—News Corp. Seeks to Forge Partnership with Locals to Break into Huge Market," *Wall Street Journal,* February 2, 2007.

232 *"It is not always about":* ibid.

232 *Wendi Murdoch set up an office:* Author's interview with several people familiar with the situation.

232 *$100,000 annual salary:* News Corp., form DEF 14A, filed August 23, 2007.

232 *who has an MBA from Yale:* John Lippman, "Meet Wendi Deng: The Boss's Wife Has Influence at News Corp.," *Wall Street Journal,* November 1, 2000.

232 *structured an innovative joint venture:* Jason Dean, "MySpace China, Under Local Control, Enters the Fray," *Wall Street Journal,* April 27, 2007.

232 *51.5 percent:* News Corp., Form DEF 14A, filed August 23, 2007.

232 *News Corp. would license:* Jason Dean, "MySpace China, Under Local Control, Enters the Fray," *Wall Street Journal,* April 27, 2007.

232 *Our team here:* ibid.

233 *Eventually Chuan decided:* ibid.

233 *MySpace China planned to be a bit like Facebook:* Author's interview with a person familiar with the situation.

233 *In October one of the most successful social networking sites:* Erick Schonfeld, "Cyworld Attacks!" *Business 2.0 Magazine,* October 2, 2006.

233 *Founded in 1999:* ibid.

233 *Cyworld requires them:* ibid.

233 *SK Telecom, bought Cyworld for $8.5 million:* ibid.

233 *More than one-third:* ibid.

233 *There is very little advertising:* ibid.

233 *made its avatars less cherubic:* Elizabeth Woyke, "The Korean Upstart in MySpace's Face," *BusinessWeek,* November 13, 2006.

234 *Koreans view blood type similarly to a zodiac sign:* Erick Schonfeld, "Cyworld Attacks!" *Business 2.0 Magazine,* October 2, 2006.

234 *"Some people might consider":* Elizabeth Woyke, "The Korean Upstart in MySpace's Face" *BusinessWeek,* November 13, 2006.

234 *"You're not happy, are you?":* Author's interview with a person familiar with the situation.

234 *"No, I'm not":* Author's interview with a person familiar with the situation.

234 *"This isn't working out, is it?":* Author's interview with a person familiar with the situation.

234 *"We should probably part ways":* Author's interview with a person familiar with the situation.

234 *"Yes":* Author's interview with a person familiar with the situation.

234 *He was almost relieved:* Author's interview with a person familiar with the situation.

234 *He planned to capitalize on his reputation:* Kevin J. Delaney and Julia Angwin, "Big Media Veterans to Start Internet Investment Firm," *Wall Street Journal,* September 1, 2007.

234 *Peter Levinsohn and Ross Levinsohn were distant cousins:* ibid.

234 *Peter Levinsohn had limited experience with the Internet:* "News Corporation Appoints Peter Levinsohn President of Fox Interactive Media," News Corp. press release, November 16, 2006.

234 *twelve hundred employees located in ten offices:* Author's interview with a person familiar with the situation.

234 *"We were entering into a different stage, where it was less about deals":* Peter Chernin's speech, UBS Global Media & Communications Conference, December 6, 2006.

CHAPTER 24 BEYOND THE BANNER AD

236 *In November 2006 MySpace dethroned Yahoo:* "MySpace Tops Yahoo in Web Traffic for First Time," Associated Press, December 13, 2006.

236 *Peter Levinsohn joined the MySpace staff:* Author's interview with a person familiar with the situation.

236 *a "digital public" space:* Danah Boyd, "Identity Production in a Networked Culture: Why Youth Heart MySpace," American Association for the Advancement of Science, St. Louis, Missouri, February 19, 2006.

236 *"Publics are critical to the coming-of-age narrative":* ibid.

237 *"a story about community and collaboration":* Lev Grossman, "Time's Person of the Year: You," *Time,* December 13, 2006.

237 *In December 2006 Fox Interactive Media posted its first profitable month:* Thompson Street Events, "News Corp. Q2 2007 Earnings Conference Call," February 7, 2007.

237 *By February 2007 Murdoch was predicting:* Mike Shields, "Murdoch: Digital Revenue Is on the Rise," *Mediaweek,* February 8, 2007.

237 *"MySpace is such a dominant part of FIM":* Thompson Street Events, "News Corp. Q2 2007 Earnings Conference Call," February 7, 2007.

237 *Despite DeWolfe's objections, Ross Levinsohn had installed:* Author's interview with a person familiar with the situation.

237 *revenues of $1.7 billion in just the first three months of 2007:* "Yahoo! Reports First Quarter 2007 Financial Results," Yahoo press release, April 17, 2007.

238 *more than sixty-four million:* "Selected Social Networking Sites," comScore Media Metrix, August 2005–July 2007.

238 *$16.9 billion:* "IAB Internet Advertising Revenue Report, 2006 Full Year Results," Interactive Advertising Bureau, May 2007.

238 *The Internet still accounted for a small slice of the $150 billion:* "TNS Media Intelligence Reports U.S. Advertising Expenditures Increased 4.1 Percent in 2006," TNS Media Intelligence, March 13, 2007.

238 *The average American household tuned in:* "Nielsen Media Research Reports Television's Popularity Is Still Growing," Nielsen Media Research press release, September 21, 2006.

238 *the University of Southern California's Center for the Digital Future:* UCLA Center for Communications Policy, "The UCLA Internet Report: Surveying the Digital Future," 2000, 2002, 2003.

238 *Young people, in particular, are becoming adept at multitasking with media:* "Generation M: Media in the Lives of 8 to 18 Year Olds," Kaiser Family Foundation Study, March 2005.

239 *"a wealth of information creates a poverty of attention":* Philip Meyer, "Public Good Is Served When We Know What 'Ain't So,' Too," *USA Today,* March 15, 2006.

239 *"quantification of engagement":* Author's interview with a person familiar with the situation.

239 *acumulated more than 120,000 friends:* Author's interview with Jack Pan, January 3, 2008.

239 *"We were curious to see how mobilized youth could be":* Author's interview with Jack Pan, September 19, 2007.

240 Step Up *took in $20.7 million:* ibid.

240 *more than doubling industry expectations:* ibid.

240 *While the film industry, on average, spent only:* Author's interview with a person familiar with the situation.

240 *Fox decided to spend 8 percent:* Author's interview with a person familiar with the situation.

240 *up from 2 percent:* Author's interview with a person familiar with the situation.

240 *and 1 percent for the first* X-Men: Author's interview with a person familiar with the situation.

240 *on May 7, 2006:* Julia Angwin, "News Corp. Wields Power for X-Men—For Third Film in Franchise, Media Concern Mutates into a Promotional Machine," *Wall Street Journal,* May 26, 2006.

240 *attracted fifty-three thousand visitors:* Author's interview with a person familiar with the situation.

240 *at an estimated cost of $1 million:* Author's interview with Ian Schafer, May 14, 2007.

240 *nearly 984,000 MySpacers:* Julia Angwin, "News Corp. Wields Power for X-Men—For Third Film in Franchise, Media Concern Mutates into a Promotional Machine," *Wall Street Journal,* May 26, 2006.

240 *Exit polling showed:* Julia Angwin, "MySpace Draws Ads by Offering 'Safe' Content," *Wall Street Journal,* June 21, 2006.

240 *$459 million:* "X-Men III: Total Worldwide Box Office Gross" by BoxOffice-Mojo.com.

241 *taking, on average, four weeks:* Author's interview with a person familiar with the situation.

241 *"Developing and executing a fully integrated campaign":* Author's interview with Ian Schafer, January 11, 2008.

241 *Michael Barrett argued that MySpace should build an API:* Author's interview with a person familiar with the situation.

242 *attorneys for the actor Chuck Norris:* Joe Nocera's interview with Tom Anderson, *New York Times,* May 20, 2007.

242 *"I explained to him":* ibid.

242 *Bryant McGill started a group:* Author's interview with Bryant McGill on September 5, 2007.

243 *Some of the advertisers paid prices as low as 5 cents:* Author's interview with a person familiar with the situation.

243 *he began a project to "scrape":* Author's interview with a person familiar with the situation.

243 *agreed to pay $100 million for a technology vendor:* Author's interview with a person familiar with the situation.

243 *It launched in the fall of 2007:* ibid.

243 *"If it's a pure commerce profile":* Theresa Howard, "MySpace Is Crowded; Amanda Beard Is a 'GoDaddy Girl,' " *USA Today,* October 8, 2007.

243 *In late 2006 Barrett set out to build an online automated system:* "MySpace Announces 'Self Serve by MySpace,' Advertising Platform," MySpace press release, November 5, 2007.

244 *The research firm eMarketer estimated that in calendar year 2006:* Debra Aho Williamson, "Social Network Marketing: Carving Out Some MySpace," eMarkerter, August 2006.

244 *Coca-Cola added social networking:* Theresa Howard, "Seeking Teens, Marketers Take Risks by Emulating MySpace," *USA Today,* May 22, 2006.

244 *Nike launched:* ibid.

244 *Martha Stewart announced plans:* Mike Shields, "Martha Stewart to Offer Social Networking App," Mediaweek.com, May 24, 2006.

244 *Mattel's Barbie Girls, for instance, attracted four million members:* Brian Morrisey, "Why Some Brands Seem Anti-Social," *Adweek,* August 27, 2007.

244 *the NikePlus social networking site:* ibid.

244 *more than fifteen thousand members:* Statistic from Toyota.com/HSD website.

244 *Wal-Mart shut down:* Pete Cashmore, "Wal-Mart's MySpace Clone Dead on Arrival," Mashable.com, October 3, 2006.

244 *Anheuser-Busch's ambitious attempt:* Brian Morrisey, "Why Some Brands Seem Anti-Social," *Adweek,* August 27, 2007.

244 *Soon after Walt Disney built:* Merissa Marr and Peter Sanders, "Disney Buys Kids' Social-Network Site," *Wall Street Journal,* August 2, 2007.

244 *In April Barrett invited one hundred fifty of the nation's biggest advertisers:* Author's interview with Ian Schafer, May 14, 2007.

245 *Shawn Gold, head of marketing for MySpace, was hired:* Author's interview with Shawn Gold, November 30, 2007.

245 *It cost MySpace $20,000 a month:* ibid.

245 *$3 million a year:* ibid.

245 *Called "Never Ending Friending":* "Never Ending Friending," TNS, TRU, and Marketing Evolution, commissioned by MySpace, Isobar, and Carat, April 12, 2007.

245 *a report highlighting the "momentum effect":* ibid.

245 *It took Google five years to reach $1 billion:* Peter Chernin, News Corp. Earnings conference call, May 7, 2008.

CHAPTER 25 THE FACEBOOK REVOLUTION

246 *On May 24, 2007, Facebook founder Mark Zuckerberg:* Mark Zuckerberg, "f8 Keynote," Facebook Developers Resources. Available: http://developers .facebook.com/videos.php.

246 *"Today, together, we're going to start a movement":* ibid.

246 *The "movement" was, in fact, the release:* ibid.

246 *For the first time, Facebook would begin allowing software developers:* ibid.

247 *MySpace prohibited all third parties, including widget makers:* MySpace terms of service.

247 *"Imagine all the things we're going to be able":* Mark Zuckerberg, "f8 Keynote," Facebook Developers Resources. Available: http://developers.facebook.com /videos.php.

247 *had an audience of 117 million in April:* " 'ComScore Widget Metrix' Service Launched to Track Widget Usage Across the Web," comScore press release, June 13, 2007.

247 *Slide's chief executive, Max Levchin, had met with MySpace executives only once:* Author's interview with Max Levchin, June 18, 2007.

247 *At that meeting, MySpace's Josh Berman told Levchin:* ibid.

247 *which had eighty-two million users in April:* " 'ComScore Widget Metrix' Service Launched to Track Widget Usage Across the Web," comScore press release, June 13, 2007.

247 *When RockYou launched its site in November 2005:* Author's interview with Lance Tokuda and Jia Shen, June 18, 2007.

247 *"We've gone to their office multiple times":* ibid.

247 *"The most interaction we had with them":* Author's interview with Alex Welch, May 24, 2007.

248 *MySpace pulled the plug on several small widget makers:* Pete Cashmore, "MySpace Blocking Stickam," Mashable.com, October 2, 2006.

248 *Web trackers from Trackzor:* Pete Cashmore, "MySpace Blocks MySpace Tracker (Updated)," Mashable.com, January 9, 2007.

248 *the music-buying service of Imeem:* Brad Stone, "MySpace Restrictions Upset Some Users," *New York Times,* March 20, 2007.

248 *In March Tequila posted a music and video player called the Hoooka:* ibid.

248 *"The reason why I am so bummed out about Myspace":* ibid.

248 *"Fuck MySpace!":* E-mail from Tila Tequila to Simon Renshaw, Gayle Boulware, and Ron Gillyard, March 18, 2007

248 *"When you guys told Tom that you didn't want to sign the exclusive deal":* ibid.

248 *claiming that Photobucket violated the no-advertising rule by offering users a* Spider-Man-*themed frame for slide shows:* Author's interview with a person familiar with the situation.

248 *We believe this action by MySpace is a retrograde step:* Michael Arrington, "Photobucket Videos Blocked on MySpace," TechCrunch, April 10, 2007.

249 *Built by twentysomething freelance programmer:* Justin Smith, "I Have 250,000 Users, Now What?" Inside Facebook, June 21, 2007.

249 *By July 29 developers had built more than two thousand widgets:* Tim O'Reilly and the O'Reilly Radar Team with Niall Kennedy and Dave McClure, "The Facebook Application Platform," An O'Reilly Radar Report, October 2007.

249 *Altura Ventures:* "Who Wants to be a Facebook Millionaire?" Manchester Digital, October 25, 2007.

249 *Bay Partners:* "Bay Partners Accelerates Development of Applications for Facebook Platform," Bay Partners press release, July 11, 2007.

249 *RockYou immediately switched most of its resources:* Author's interview with Lance Tokuda and Jia Shen, June 18, 2007.

249 *"Each social network is like another girlfriend":* ibid.

249 *up 26 percent to 33.7 million:* "ComScore Media Metrix Releases Top 50 Web Rankings for August," comScore Media Metrix press release, September 18, 2007.

249 *from 26.7 million in May:* "Selected Social Networking Sites, Trend: August 2005–July 2007," comScore Media Metrix, July 2007.

249 *MySpace remained fairly stagnant at 68 million:* ibid.

250 *"The Goody Two-shoes, jocks, athletes, or other 'good' kids":* Danah Boyd, "Viewing American Class Divisions Through Facebook and MySpace," Danah.org, June 24, 2007.

250 *"MySpace is still home for Latino/Hispanic teens":* ibid.

250 *"Facebook has emerged":* Steven Levy, "Facebook Grows Up: Can It Stay Relevant?" *Newsweek,* August 20–27, 2007.

250 *"Mark Zuckerberg of Facebook is being touted":* "Book Value–Face Value," *The Economist,* July 21, 2007.

250 *In May Murdoch invited Zuckerberg to speak:* Jeff Jarvis, "My Dinner with Rupert," *Buzz Machine,* May 6, 2007.

250 *"Murdoch sat next to Zuckerberg":* ibid.

250 *"Mark left to get back up north":* ibid.

251 *"I wish they were":* Steve Stecklow and Martin Peers, "Murdoch's Role as Proprietor, Journalist, and Plans for Dow Jones," *Wall Street Journal,* June 6, 2007.

251 *Facebook began allowing:* "Facebook Unveils Facebook Ads," Facebook press release, November 6, 2007.

251 *the targeted advertising network being built:* "Conference Call Transcript, News Corporation at Merrill Lynch Media Fall Preview," September 18, 2007, Thomson Financial.

251 *"Once every hundred years":* Erick Shonfeld, "Liveblogging Facebook Advertising Announcement (Social Ads + Beacon + Insight)," TechCrunch, November 6, 2007.

251 *In July Connecticut attorney general Richard Blumenthal:* Brad Stone, "New Scrutiny for Facebook over Predators," *New York Times,* July 30, 2007.

252 *In September New York attorney general Andrew Cuomo:* "Cuomo Subpoenas Facebook over Use Safety," Office of the New York Attorney General press release, September 24, 2007.

252 *"Facebook in many instances ignored the complaints":* ibid.

252 *Facebook moved quickly to settle:* "Attorney General and Facebook Announce New Model to Protect Children Online," Office of the New York Attorney General press release, October 16, 2007.

252 *"New York's settlement with Facebook":* "Attorney General Urges Facebook to Take Stronger Steps to Protect Kids," Connecticut Attorney General's Office press release, October 16, 2007.

252 *He demanded that Facebook begin requiring parental permission:* ibid.

252 *a Texas court dismissed a lawsuit by the mother of a fourteen-year-old girl:* Jane Doe and Julie Doe v. MySpace Inc., and News Corp., United States District Court, Western District of Texas, Austin Division, Case No.: A-06-CA-983-SS.

252 *"artful pleading to be disingenuous":* ibid.

252 *"If anyone had a duty to protect Julie Doe, it was her parents, not MySpace":* ibid.

252 *"the AGs actually face a steep uphill battle":* Ken Dreifach, "Communications Decency Act, WhoseSpace.com: Social Networking Websites and the Constitution," Electronic Commerce & Law Report Banner, vol. 12, no. 13, p. 281, March 28, 2007.

252 *MySpace quietly postponed:* Author's interview with a person familiar with the situation.

253 *Zephyr would not let parents read their kids' e-mails:* Julia Angwin, "MySpace Moves to Give Parents More Information," *Wall Street Journal,* January 17, 2007.

253 *MySpace had launched a test version:* Author's interview with a person familiar with the situation.

253 *Six months later, MySpace reached a compromise:* "Attorneys General of 49 States, DC Announce Agreement with MySpace Regarding Social Networking Safety," State of Connecticut Attorney General's Office press release, January 14, 2008.

CHAPTER 26 MYSPACE 2.0

254 *DeWolfe and Tom Anderson were surprised:* Author's interview with a person familiar with the situation.

254 *On August 8 News Corp. announced:* "Conference News Corporation F4Q07 Earnings Call Transcript," August 8, 2007, Thomson Financial.

254 *On a conference call with analysts:* ibid.

254 *dipped to their lowest point all year, $19.68:* Yahoo Finance, Historical Prices for NWS.

254 *"Everyone believes all the b.s.":* David Kirkpatrick, "As Facebook Takes Off, MySpace Strikes Back," *Fortune,* September 19, 2007.

254 *Their employment contracts were set to expire:* Author's interview with a person familiar with the situation.

255 *while his marriage was falling apart:* Superior Court of California, County of Los Angeles, Family Law Case: Petition—Marriage. Case Number BD483342, April 3, 2008.

255 *an audacious $50 million over two years:* Author's interview with a person familiar with the situation.

255 *plus a $15 million development fund:* Author's interview with a person familiar with the situation.

255 *News Corp. counteroffered with $30 million:* Author's interview with a person familiar with the situation.

255 *Anderson purchased an online karaoke service called kSolo:* Patricia Sellers, "MySpace Cowboys," *Fortune,* September 4, 2006.

255 *But it wasn't until two years later, in 2008:* Kristen Nicole, "Will You Use MySpace Karaoke?" Mashable.com, April 28, 2008.

255 *"MySpace News . . . Kinda Sucks":* Pete Cashmore, "MySpace News . . . Kinda Sucks," Mashable.com, April 19, 2007.

255 *"It's difficult to innovate within a corporation":* Author's interview with a person familiar with the situation.

255 *MySpace had also conducted focus groups with users:* Author's interview with a person familiar with the situation.

256 *Peter Chernin stepped into the breach:* Author's interview with a person familiar with the situation.

256 *"I need a plan for dealing with Facebook in two weeks":* ibid.

256 *In May MySpace acquired Photobucket:* Author's interview with Alex Welch, May 24, 2007.

256 *"A mistake we made was trying to do too many things":* Peter Chernin's interview with Chris DeWolfe, Paley Media Center, Beverly Hills, California, July 30, 2007.

256 *"We haven't done the greatest job":* ibid.

256 *"I realize every person in this room":* "Conference Call Transcript, News Corporation at Merrill Lynch Media Fall Preview," September 18, 2007, Thomson Financial.

256 *Levinsohn presented statistics:* ibid.

256 *Levinsohn also hinted:* ibid.

256 *After Levinsohn's speech:* Yahoo Finance, Historical Prices for NWS.

257 *"All the models and actresses move to L.A.":* Peter Chernin's interview with Chris DeWolfe, Paley Media Center, Beverly Hills, California, July 30, 2007.

257 *"It's the first time I feel like we have a real competitor":* David Kirkpatrick, "As Facebook Takes Off, MySpace Strikes Back," *Fortune,* September 19, 2007.

258 *on Wednesday afternoon, October 17:* John Batelle's interview with Mark Zuckerberg, Web 2.0 Conference, San Francisco, California, October 17, 2007.

258 *"Don't you think you're kind of selling yourself a little short":* ibid.

258 *We'll see:* ibid.

258 *to 30.6 million unique visitors:* "ComScore Media Metrix Releases Top 50 Web Rankings for August," comScore Media Metrix press release, September 18, 2007.

258 *down from 33.7 million in August:* ibid.

258 *MySpace remained flat at 68 million:* ibid.

258 *A week later, Facebook raised $240 million:* Brad Stone, "Microsoft to Pay $240 Million for Stake in Facebook," *New York Times,* October 25, 2007.

258 *During dinner the two chatted onstage:* John Battelle's interview with Chris DeWolfe and Rupert Murdoch, Web 2.0 Conference, San Francisco, California, October 17, 2007.

258 *DeWolfe started by announcing:* ibid.

258 *DeWolfe and Anderson had agreed to News Corp's terms:* Author's interview with a person familiar with the situation.

258 *DeWolfe then followed up with a vague statement:* John Battelle's interview with Chris DeWolfe and Rupert Murdoch, Web 2.0 Conference, San Francisco, California, October 17, 2007.

259 *"We read it on TechCrunch":* ibid.

259 *DeWolfe also announced:* ibid.

259 *"There's a certain talent level":* ibid.

259 *"It's like a utility":* ibid.

259 *"What that tells you is that News Corp. is totally underpriced":* ibid.

259 *at its market valuation of about $70.5 billion:* Yahoo Finance, Historical prices for NWS, and News Corp., form 10-K, filed August 23, 2007.

259 *to MySpace's Silicon Valley coming-out party:* Author's attendance, San Francisco, California, October 17, 2007.

259 *The geeky guys from the Web 2.0 conference:* ibid.

259 *In all, about three hundred fifty people attended:* ibid.

260 *at 1:23 a.m., the police were called:* Megan McCarthy, "Geeks Gone Wild: Cops Called to Break Up a Fight at the MySpace Party," ValleyWag, October 18, 2007.

260 *In November MySpace agreed to join Google's efforts:* "MySpace and Google Join Forces to Launch Open Platform for Social Application Development," Google press release, November 1, 2007.

260 *In December MySpace launched "Friend Update":* Adam Ostrow, "MySpace Friend Updates Arrive. Is Anyone Still Using MySpace?" Mashable.com, November 29, 2007.

260 *Within the first two months, more than seven thousand developers had created:* Peter Chernin, News Corp. conference call, May 8, 2008.

260 *MySpace got ahead of the development curve:* Michael Arrington, "MySpace Embraces DataPortability, Partners with Ebay and Twitter," TechCrunch, May 8, 2008.

260 *"Historically, MySpace has lagged":* ibid.

261 *"We will fall short":* Peter Chernin, News Corp. conference call, May 8, 2008.

261 *"But it's worth pointing out":* ibid.

261 *As a result, Fox Interactive's top ad salesman, Michael Barrett . . . quit:* Author's interview with a person familiar with the situation.

261 *"This change recognizes that our individual business units have evolved":* Rafat Ali, "Fox Interactive Media Restructuring: Memo from Peter Levinsohn: Optimizing Monetization," paidContent.org, April 3, 2008.

CHAPTER 27 DIGITAL IDENTITY

262 *"Web utility similar to a phone book":* Rupert Murdoch, 2008 News Corporation Earnings conference call, November 7, 2007.

262 *"become so much more than a social network":* ibid.

262 *The U.S. Supreme Court supported that view: McIntyre v. Ohio Elections Commission* (93-986), 514 U.S. 334 (1995).

263 *"Under our constitution":* ibid.

263 *"Every day we dress ourselves in a set of clothes":* Danah Boyd, "Identity Produc-

tion in a Networked Culture: Why Youth Heart MySpace," American Association for the Advancement of Science, St. Louis, Missouri, February 19, 2006.

264 *"Signaling theory describes the relationship between a signal":* Judith Donath and Danah Boyd, "Public Displays of Connection," *BT Technology Journal,* vol. 22, no. 4, pp. 71–82, October 2004.

264 *"A public display of connections":* ibid.

264 *"In this market [for spouses]":* Mikolaj Jan Piskorski, "I am not on the market, I am here with Friends: Using on-line social networks to find a job or spouse," January 15, 2007. Available: http://www.people.hbs.edu/mpiskorski/papers /FA-Platforms.pdf.

264 *"By pooling themselves with actors":* ibid.

264 *"contextual privacy":* Judith Donath and Danah Boyd, "Public Displays of Connection," *BT Technology Journal,* vol. 22, no. 4, pp. 71–82, October 2004.

265 *"We are increasingly discovering that everything we do":* Sarah Wright's interview by e-mail with Henry Jenkins, "Discussions: MySpace and the Deleting Online Predators Act," posted by Sarah Wright of the MIT News on May 30, 2006.

265 *"I think we have replaced MTV":* Frank Hornig's interview with Tom Anderson and Chris DeWolfe for *Der Spiegel,* "We Have Replaced MTV," January 15, 2007.

EPILOGUE

267 *with seventy-two million monthly visitors in the United States:* "ComScore Media Metrix Releases Top 50 Web Rankings for March," comScore Media Metrix press release, April 14, 2008.

267 *with thirty-five million U.S. visitors:* ibid.

267 *Brad Greenspan is still suing Intermix:* Updated information about Brad Greenspan available at http://www.freemyspace.com.

267 *Rosenblatt bought back most of Intermix's websites:* Author's interview with a person familiar with the situation.

267 *for a rumored price of $18 million:* ibid.

267 *the next generation of social media:* Author's interview with Richard Rosenblatt, January 3, 2008.

268 *He has raised $355 million:* Erika Brown, "The Mixologist," *Forbes,* September 26, 2007.

268 *Ross Levinsohn has created a venture fund:* Robert A. Guth, "AOL, Fox Executives Join Venture," *Wall Street Journal,* December 17, 2007.

268 *$1.5 billion in assets:* ibid.

268 *He has called MySpace the "digital centerpiece":* Staci D. Kramer, "Murdoch: News Corp. Could Get 6 Billion for MySpace Now," paid content: UK, November 14, 2006.

268 *"This will be the biggest single mass platform":* ibid.

Index

About the Author

JULIA ANGWIN is an award-winning journalist at *The Wall Street Journal,* where she is a columnist and senior technology editor at WSJ.com.

About the Type

This book was set in Garamond no. 3, a variation of the classic Garamond typeface originally designed by the Parisian type cutter Claude Garamond (1480–1561).

Claude Garamond's distinguished romans and italics first appeared in *Opera Ciceronis* in 1543–44. The Garamond types are clear, open, and elegant.